EDUCATION IN THE SCHOOL OF DREAMS

JENNIFER LYNN PETERSON

EDUCATION IN THE SCHOOL OF DREAMS

Travelogues and Early Nonfiction Film

DUKE UNIVERSITY PRESS | DURHAM AND LONDON | 2013

Printed in the United States of America on acid-free paper ∞
Designed by Heather Hensley
Typeset in Arno Pro by Tseng Information Systems, Inc.
Library of Congress Cataloging-in-Publication Data
Peterson, Jennifer Lynn
Education in the school of dreams : travelogues and
early nonfiction film / Jennifer Lynn Peterson.
p. cm
Includes bibliographical references and index.
ISBN 978-0-8223-5441-3 (cloth : alk. paper)
ISBN 978-0-8223-5453-6 (pbk. : alk. paper)
1. Travelogues (Motion pictures) — United States — History
and criticism. 2. Nonfiction films — United States —
History and criticism. I. Title.
PN1995.9.T73P48 2013
070.1′8 — dc23   2013005286

Duke University Press gratefully acknowledges the support of
the Kayden Research Grants at the University of Colorado Boulder,
which provided funds toward the publication of this book.

FOR CHRISTOPHER

CONTENTS

PREFACE

One of the most famous scenes of cinematic travel takes place in Max Ophüls's melodrama *Letter from an Unknown Woman* (1948). The film is set in Vienna in the early twentieth century, and in the scene, the film's young female protagonist, Lisa, is out on her first and only evening with the famous pianist Stefan Brand, who takes her to an amusement park modeled after the real Wurstelprater in Vienna's Wiener Prater park. Lisa is played by Joan Fontaine, then one of the most important stars at Universal Pictures, and Stefan is played by Louis Jourdan, a French actor newly arrived in Hollywood who was being groomed as a European leading man in the manner of Charles Boyer. The two characters sit in a stationary train car while a painted landscape panorama passes by the window (fig. P.1). As Lisa speaks of her father, a crudely painted landscape of Venice scrolls past, followed by Switzerland: "When my father was alive, we traveled a lot. We went nearly everywhere. We had wonderful times." Stefan, the more experienced of the two, leans in, saying, "Perhaps we've been to some of the same places." As Lisa continues to speak about visiting Rio de Janeiro, we realize from her facetious tone of voice that her travels resemble the painted backdrop passing by: they are imaginary. She soon 'fesses up: "Well, there weren't any trips. Do you mind? You see, my father had a friend in a travel bureau. My father worked across the street. He was an assistant superintendent of municipal waterworks, and he used to bring folders home with him with pictures on them. We had stacks of them. And in the evening, he would put on his traveling coat. That's what he called it. Of course, I was very young."

In this story of Lisa's childhood love for her dead father, imaginary travel serves as a playful escape from the dreariness of everyday life. In the present tense of the scene between Lisa and Stefan, the imaginary travel of the train

FIGURE P.1 Frame enlargement, *Letter from an Unknown Woman* (Max Ophüls, 1948).

car serves as a setting for love and desire—both the narration of Lisa's love for her father and the enactment of her desire for Stefan. As the moving panorama of Switzerland comes to an end, the camera holds on a shot outside the closed train compartment door for several seconds, discreetly evoking the erotic encounter taking place inside, until Stefan emerges to pay the ticket taker for another ride. "Where haven't we been?" he asks the old woman in the booth. "We have no more countries left," she replies. "Then we'll begin all over again," he proclaims, handing the woman a coin. "We'll revisit the scenes of our youth."

The film makes much of the mechanical apparatus and workers powering the moving panorama: the ticket taker, the old man pedaling a rickety bicycle that powers the panorama, the raising and lowering of new landscape backdrops—all are documented with relish by Ophüls's renowned fluid camera. Yet to Lisa within the train compartment, these mechanics appear uninteresting. She resides in the realm of make-believe travel and fantasy love (later giving birth to Stefan's child without telling him about it), fully aware of the mythical status of her experience but stubbornly clinging nonetheless to the fantasy that fuels her most powerful emotions.

FIGURE P.2 Frame enlargement, *Under Basque Skies* (Eclipse, 1913). Courtesy EYE Film Institute Netherlands.

The scene enacts the fantasy dimension of cinematic travel in several ways at once. Not only are two kinds of imaginary travel represented in the scene—that from Lisa's childhood and that of the moving panorama train ride—but the film itself provides a form of imaginary travel for the spectator. *Letter* shows us turn-of-the-century Vienna (represented on a Universal Studios soundstage) from the vantage point of postwar Hollywood, thus inviting the film's spectators to enjoy a kind of time travel along with cinema's intrinsic quality of spatial travel. All of these dimensions are clear, but the specificity of the scene has more insight to offer. For Lisa, imaginary travel (and fantasy love) are more powerful, more moving than actual travel (and an actual relationship). What matters in this melodrama is emotional, not physical, movement. Yet travel—physical, material, geographic travel—provides a means of accessing that emotional movement: travel becomes a metaphor for desire.

Now consider a nonfiction travel film, made roughly around the time in which *Letter*'s story is set: *Sous le ciel Basque* (*Under Basque Skies*), made by the French film company Eclipse in 1913 (fig. P.2). On the surface, nothing could be more different. *Under Basque Skies* is a nonfiction film; it features no stars or even any professional actors. It does not tell a story; instead, it presents a series of disjunctive views of the Basque region of France and

Spain: fishermen, a few towns, a bridge, a train, and a few moving cityscape shots of San Sebastian, which was already a popular resort town in the opening years of the twentieth century. It is a short film, running approximately five minutes. And it is a film from the silent era, which means that when it was originally shown, it would have featured live sound accompaniment (music, or perhaps a lecture) that has not been preserved.

Everyone involved in the production of *Under Basque Skies* is anonymous, from the director and the cameraman to the people depicted in the film. In contrast, *Letter* is a famous masterwork by a revered auteur, Max Ophüls. An impressive list of renowned Hollywood studio personnel worked on *Letter*: John Houseman (producer), Howard Koch (screenplay), Franz Planer (camera), Alexander Golitzen (art director), Travis Banton (costumes). The production of *Letter* has been well documented, and we know that Ophüls himself was responsible for the mock train-ride scene: "Out of his own memories of Vienna came ideas for new scenes such as the one in which the lovers appear to be traveling together in a train compartment, gazing out the window at the exotic, foreign scenery which turns out later to be merely a rotating backdrop in one of the amusement concessions in Vienna's Prada [Prater]."[1] *Letter* is regularly shown in film classes and public screening series and occupies an important place in film history.[2] *Basque*, on the other hand, has been available only in film archives until very recently and remains mostly unseen by the general viewing public. (The Library of Congress lately made its print available for online viewing and downloading, which opens the film to a theoretically vast audience — although it still lacks the renown that would lead viewers to seek it out.[3]) In sum, *Letter* is a well-known text in the film history canon, while *Basque* is an anonymous film.

Both *Letter* and *Basque* are concerned with representing travel, and each provides significant insights about the phenomenon of voyaging in film. On the simplest level, both films provide the spectator with a perceptual experience of motionless travel, and each provides a commentary of sorts on travel as a phenomenon. More important, both films construct travel as a kind of setting for desire, but they do so in different ways. Based only on the two frame enlargements provided here (see figs. P.1 and P.2), one can see that *Basque* captures a melancholy sensibility that seems to emanate from the scenery itself (emphasized further by the distance between the two adult figures who survey the landscape), whereas the melancholy pathos of *Letter* is conveyed not by the clearly artificial landscapes (which create a rather jovial mood) but by the film's story and the actors' performances.

Yet despite the differences between the representational strategies of fiction and nonfiction (not to mention the thirty-five years of changing film style that lie between them), I believe that both of these films have the potential to move and affect the spectator, perhaps even in related ways. In part this is due to the common ground shared by fiction and nonfiction, which both use the "reality effect" of real locations and real bodies to activate the cinematic experience for the viewer. More simply, these films both mobilize the cinema's complex dynamic of identification and fantasy, a dynamic that film studies has made so many attempts to analyze. But this book is not a psychoanalytic account of cinema and desire. Rather, it is a mostly historical account that takes a marginal genre and makes it central. My claim is that at this juncture, *Under Basque Skies* can reveal new insights that *Letter from an Unknown Woman* cannot. It tells us about the difference of early cinema, when, for a moment, "educational" film genres seemed to represent a commercial opportunity for the film industry. It reveals the utopian dimension of early cinema, when virtual voyaging via moving pictures was championed as a democratic form of travel and cosmopolitanism for the masses. In addition, films such as *Basque* openly display the so-called Progressive Era's imperialist ideology, propagating all-too-familiar hierarchies of center and periphery, as well as the stereotypical notions of cultural and racial difference that ruled the day. Finally, I argue that early travelogue films presented audiences with the opportunity to experience a kind of poetic reverie, delivering flashes of wonder and perhaps even the potential temporarily to overcome the strictures of modern life.

Certainly, travel is a huge topic that films have engaged in multiple and complex ways. Film history is filled with scenes of travel, many of which, like the scene in *Letter*, are familiar to scholars, students, and fans of cinema. I am not saying that *Letter* (a film I love) has nothing left to reveal. But unlike such narrative feature films, which have been analyzed frequently, travelogue films such as *Under Basque Skies* have only recently become a subject of film scholarship, even though travelogues have been a staple genre throughout film history. A great many fiction films thematize the subject of travel: *King Kong* (Merian C. Cooper and Ernest B. Schoedsack, 1933), *Lost Horizon* (Frank Capra, 1937), *Mr. Hulot's Holiday* (Jacques Tati, 1953), *Badlands* (Terrence Malick, 1973), *El Norte* (Gregory Nava, 1983), and *After Hours* (Martin Scorsese, 1985), to name just a few. No doubt, the reader will easily come up with many more examples, for the journey is one of the most common narrative themes, as the very genre of road movies attests. This book, however, is concerned with a largely unexplored and relatively anonymous genre of film: the travelogue. The vision of travel presented in *Basque* is no less important than that presented in *Letter*; it is just different. Travelogues provide an unparalleled opportunity to focus on key questions of aesthetics, ideology, and commerce in early cinema. Furthermore, the history of travelogues underscores the fact that in early cinema, films were just one of many significant texts in a complex media landscape. As Rick Altman explains, "Early moving pictures were in many cases like theatrical props," simply one part of a live performance that also involved lecturing and slides, and they were often screened not in moving picture theaters but in town halls, public auditoriums, and other "nontheatrical" spaces.[4] Of course, intertextual complexity still defines the film experience today but in a very different way as the Internet, promotional media, and fan discourse continue to shape a film's meaning just as much as the text itself.

I preface this book by contrasting *Letter from an Unknown Woman* with *Under Basque Skies* to make a point about some of our most basic assumptions of what constitutes cinema. Even today, some forty years after cinema studies began to be accepted as an academic discipline, the popular idea of cinema is still dominated by narrative, feature-length films with characters, stars, and directors. As Jeffrey Ruoff has put it, "Our general histories of motion pictures continue to privilege a distinct minority of feature fiction films, particularly Hollywood movies, and, at best, some documentary and avant-garde alternatives."[5] This default point of view leads many to overlook a wide array of other, equally important kinds of film: educational films, short films, home movies, sponsored films, films that were commercially unsuccessful. A couple of decades ago, most scholarly film books focused on canonical texts such as *Letter*. But in recent years, cinema studies has been transformed by a new attention to film history that has broadened the discipline's focus to include other kinds of cinema beyond well-known, narrative, feature-length films.[6] Thankfully, it is now much less possible to write an account of film history that completely ignores the diversity of that history, which includes early cinema, oppositional cinema, and marginal cinematic practices. Still, there is a strong tide of popular opinion that continues to pull film fans and beginning film students toward the obvious (narrative, feature-length films), fostering a lack of interest or even scorn for what are seen as the side roads of film history. It is time for this narrow focus to broaden, not just within the academy, but also in journalistic and popular discourse. So while this is a scholarly book of film history that aims to address specialists in early cinema,

I also hope that it will be of interest to more casual readers who might find the issues it raises to be pertinent beyond the domain of early film history.

This book, then, defies the two most popular dimensions of film studies: authorship (great directors) and what has been called the "masterpiece tradition" (great films).[7] Although authorship and the masterpiece tradition have been subject to critique for some time now, it is surprising how much they continue to drive much of the field of film studies, evident in any quick survey of courses offered and books published. Most film students and scholars will gladly recite lists of their most beloved films—indeed, one of the pleasures of cinephilia is watching such personal lists evolve over time. However, I would wager that very few travelogues make it onto such lists. Even though they have always been a presence on film screens, travelogues are not typically the kinds of films that inspire warm feelings and fan appreciation. Certain exceptions exist—*Sans Soleil* (Chris Marker, 1983) is a perennial travelogue favorite for a certain kind of film viewer—but this is, once again, a feature-length film made by a famous director. In contrast, the travelogue films I analyze in this book are noncanonical and largely unknown today outside a small community of early cinema specialists. Rather than forcing the issue of the travelogue's importance by artificially inflating its dominance in film history, I acknowledge the travelogue's marginality and explore the alternative space it inhabits. Rather than viewing its marginality as a reflection of the travel film's unimportance, I believe this minor quality is one aspect that renders it significant. I echo Altman's exhortation that film historiography must "consider unsuccessful experiments and short-lived practices."[8] Rather than a procession of great directors and ever greater films, early cinema is characterized by instability and experimentation. Travelogues were not exactly "unsuccessful" (nor were they short-lived); rather, they have consistently maintained a presence, if marginal, within the film industry. To a degree that may seem surprising to us today, these nonfiction, non-narrative subjects were a major part of commercial film shows in the years before the rise of the feature film and the hegemony of "classical" cinema.

In addition to these issues of genre and canon, another set of questions motivates this book: What are the ideologies propagated by early nonfiction film, and how might they have functioned within the complexity of their historical moment? Travelogues are known for being boring and obvious—so much so that they repeatedly have been parodied. However, alongside my exploration of the travelogue's formulaic aspects, this study aims to rehabilitate their enigmatic and unexpected components. Travel films allow us to ask new questions, such as: How can an "educational" genre, one that Charles Musser has called a "cinema of reassurance," contain any elements of wonder or surprise?[9] How does a formulaic genre transcend its prosaic form? What desires and ideologies were mobilized by early travel films, and how might they have been read against the grain by early film spectators?

Early travelogues are filled with some of the most memorable and surprising images in early film history. Even today, a century after they were produced, these films have the power to send the viewer into a daydreaming state of mind. Yet I am not interested in fetishizing these films as precious documents of the forgotten past. Like a series of postcards come alive, these films are filled with clichéd images—sunsets, flowers, smiling women and children—that are fascinating for their very obviousness. This book aims to unpack this arsenal of clichés to discover a wider range of uses to which they might have been put. These films propagated colonialist ideologies, and they simultaneously had a magical ability to captivate their audiences—in fact, the two effects are directly related. Intended to be educational, these films capture much more than their producers realized, from moments of remarkable beauty to moments of unveiled racism. These are films that have not yet learned to disguise the gawking, objectifying nature of their gaze. They present the early twentieth century as a fascinating, diverse world— but a world in which nothing lies beyond the conquering eye of the motion picture camera.

Finally, while this is a historical project it is worth emphasizing that I view these films with an eye that has been influenced by surrealism, experimental filmmaking, and other oppositional artistic practices. In particular, the surrealists strove to confront and view culture in unintended ways, recognizing a transformative potential in even the most prosaic images. My view of early travelogues has been inspired by films such as Luis Buñuel's masterly *Las Hurdes* (1932), which revels in exposing the ideologies of mainstream documentary film practice. In fact, I would venture to speculate that Buñuel, too, might have found a film like *Basque* more interesting than a film like *Letter*, both of which trade in bourgeois notions of travel, but the first of which opens itself up more obviously to critical use. Buñuel was interested in discourses of cruelty, sacrifice, and obscenity, elements that travelogue films try to repress, though they do not always succeed.[10] As Dudley Andrew has written, "The shock of the very first scene of [Buñuel's] first film, the notorious eye slashing of *Un Chien Andalou* (1928), deliberately turns the fat stomachs of the bourgeoisie and cuts the threads that make up the delicate web of their precious subjectivity."[11] Surrealism, which Walter Benjamin described as a methodology of "profane illumination," is a useful interpretive context for travelogue films, whose imperial gaze can be turned inside out through a process of reading against the grain.[12] While your average early cinema spectator was certainly no Buñuel, it is my contention that travelogues and other early nonfiction genres, in revealing their ideologies, formulas, and aesthetic traditions so explicitly, created at least the potential for a mass critical reading practice.

The surrealists were among the first to realize that art can be found not only in the artwork itself but also in the viewer's point of view.[13] Around the time the films in this book were first being shown, the surrealist writer André Breton liked to drop into movie theaters in the middle of a program and leave as soon as the films became boring or began to make too much sense, moving to the cinema a few doors down for another dose of the same. Of this deliberately scattered film-viewing practice, Breton wrote: "I have never known anything so *magnetizing*: it goes without saying that more often than not we left our seats without even knowing the title of the film, which was of no importance to us, anyway. . . . The important thing is that one came out 'charged' for a few days. . . . I think what we valued most in it . . . was its *power to disorient*."[14] This practice of discovering a kind of "involuntary surrealism" has been greatly inspiring to me. As James Clifford has explained, "André Breton often insisted that surrealism was not a body of doctrines or a definable idea but an activity."[15] While this book is certainly not a "surrealist" account of travelogue films, I want to make plain that much of what I find intriguing in these films was not intended by their makers or exhibitors—and perhaps was not perceived by many viewers at the time. Although this is a historical account of the travelogue genre, then, at the same time I view these films against their grain and outside their historical moment (as all histories must necessarily do) in ways that could not have been foreseen.

ACKNOWLEDGMENTS

This book has taken a long time to complete, and I am indebted to a great many people for the various kinds of support they have provided along the way.

At the University of Chicago, Miriam Hansen's advice and encouragement were instrumental to my earliest conceptualization of this research. Miriam was more than just a mentor; her formidable critical presence, combined with her unique sense of humor and affection, were deeply inspirational. One of my greatest regrets about this book's overdue completion is that she is no longer here to see it in print. I was doubly fortunate, however, also to work with Tom Gunning, whose careful readings greatly sharpened my critical skills. Tom's continued support and friendship have meant the world to me. I am grateful to Jim Lastra and Bill Brown, who were early readers of this project, and W. J. T. Mitchell and Yuri Tsivian for guidance and support. Jay Williams taught me the useful skill of copy editing while keeping a sense of humor when I worked as an editorial assistant at *Critical Inquiry*. Members of the University of Chicago's Mass Culture Workshop provided feedback on this project in its earliest stages. Elisabeth Ceppi, Sabine Haenni, and Jacqueline Stewart patiently read numerous early chapter drafts and provided valuable suggestions. Paula Amad, Kaveh Askari, Sam Baker, Dan Morgan, Charles Tepperman, Pam Wojcik, Paul Young, and Josh Yumibe have generously exchanged research and helped shape my critical thinking over the years. Special thanks to Oliver Gaycken, whose own work on early science films reflects our shared fascination with early nonfiction.

When I began this project, what is now the EYE Film Institute Netherlands was then the Nederlands Filmmuseum. My thanks to Daan Hertogs and Mark-Paul Meyer for enabling my research; I am also grateful to Peter Delpeut for his influential early appreciation of silent-era nonfiction. I would like to particularly thank Nico de Klerk, who not only provided translations for all of the Dutch intertitles on the release prints I watched at the Filmmuseum but also has shared and encouraged my fascination with early nonfiction film for many years. Giovanna Fossati, who is now head curator at EYE, has provided valuable friendship and support since we met that first summer when we were both doing research in Amsterdam. Also in the Netherlands, Ivo Blom kindly discussed his work on the Desmet Collection with me, and Nanna Verhoeff has been a source of friendship and inspiration.

My research on this project has been made possible by staff at various other archives, including the Motion Picture, Broadcast, and Recorded Sound Division of the Library of Congress (thanks to Madeline Matz); the George Eastman House in Rochester, New York (thanks in particular to Ed Stratmann); the National Archive of the British Film Institute (BFI) in London (thanks to Elaine Burrows and Bryony Dixon, who provided generous help); the Center for Visual Music in Los Angeles (thanks to Cindy Keefer); the University of California, Los Angeles, Film and Television Archive; and the Frederick Starr Papers at the University of Chicago's Regenstein Library. The Margaret Herrick Library of the Academy of Motion Picture Arts and Sciences holds special importance for me, not only because it provided valuable research material for this book, and not only because I worked there as an oral historian for nearly three years after finishing graduate school, but because of the people I met there, several of whom provided direct support for this project. Barbara Hall helped with Special Collections; Doug Johnson read an early version and later helped with the research on *Letter from an Unknown Woman*; Anne Coco and Russ Butner provided assistance with several of the posters reproduced here.

Don Crafton, Scott Curtis, Dennis Doros, Jane Gaines, Alison Griffiths, Devin Orgeron, Marsha Orgeron, Dan Streible, and Greg Waller have all offered support and shared insights at various conferences, screenings, and festivals over the years. Annette Melville and Scott Simmon were kind enough to invite me to participate as a commentator for several travelogues on the DVD box set *Treasures 5: The West*; they then shared frame enlargements to use in this book. I thank Joseph Eckhardt for providing me with a copy of *The Thames from Oxford to Richmond* (1911), part of an Eclipse split reel he was fortunate to purchase; the frame enlargement on the cover of this book is taken from this lovely film. Thanks also to Malcolm Cook for help in trying to identify the animators whose work was featured in some early travelogues.

I am grateful to Alison Trope and Priya Jaikumar in Los Angeles for exchanging writing and ideas. Elinor Nissley and Alex MacInnis provided lodging and schooled me on the nesting habits of Fauvette birds (which unlocked the meaning of one of the posters reproduced here). Jennifer Doyle has been a model of committed scholarship, and her friendship has helped buoy me through the various ups and downs of the academic profession.

This book was largely completed while I was teaching in the Film Studies Program at the University of Colorado, Boulder. Melinda Barlow's support and friendship there have been invaluable; she first helped me acclimate to the institution and later shared her expertise on the subject of "wonder." Jim Palmer has been a stalwart advocate of my research and a model of engaged teaching and scholarship. Ernesto Acevedo-Muñoz has helped me navigate the channels of bureaucracy with good humor. Phil Solomon has inspired me with his rapturous films and his finely honed sense of taste. Jeanne Liotta's fierce spirit and dazzling films continue to energize me. Christina Battle has been an exacting filmmaker and a comrade in arms. Valuable research assistance on this book was provided by Kimberly Pierce and Emily Shurtz. Thanks also to Shira Segal. Jacob Barreras has tracked down hard-to-find resources with unflagging good nature. Tim Riggs was a great help in preparing the digital images for this book.

Numerous other friends and colleagues in Colorado have helped shape this project. Elissa Auther, Clark Farmer, and Gillian Silverman all read various chapters and provided helpful feedback. Julie Carr and Patrick Greaney have provided wisdom and encouragement. Adam Lerner generously invited me to curate an exhibition of early nonfiction films at the Belmar Lab and embraced my idea for a non-synchronous three-channel video installation accompanied by non-synchronous sound. Experiencing this book project in a more creative form — and watching a diverse group of museumgoers respond to these century-old films — was hugely gratifying.

A grant from the Graduate Committee on the Arts and Humanities at the University of Colorado provided valuable funding for research travel to the BFI. I am also grateful to the Dean's Fund for Excellence at the University of Colorado for multiple grants that enabled me to present this research at conferences. The inclusion of color plates in the book was enabled by a Kayden Research Grant from the University of Colorado. In graduate school, my dissertation research was supported by a Mellon Foundation Summer Research Grant, which provided funding for my first trip to the Nederlands Filmmuseum. A Mellon Foundation Dissertation-Year Fellowship at the University of Chicago provided funding for much-needed writing time. I am also grateful to Cinema and Media Studies at the University of Chicago for awarding me two travel grants and to the Department of English at the University of Chicago for awarding me two Marcia Tillotson Travel Grants.

At Duke University Press, I owe Ken Wissoker special thanks for his patience and unflagging support over the many years it has taken me to complete this book. If he was frustrated with my delays, he never showed it. I deeply appreciate the careful and thorough feedback provided by the several anonymous readers, which saved me from multiple errors and made this book much stronger than it would have been otherwise. Leigh Barnwell was extremely helpful in the final stages of bringing this book to press.

My parents, Larry and Carol Peterson, have encouraged me to follow my own path for as long as I can remember. Their love and steadfast support created the conditions of possibility for me, a first-generation college student, to envision myself capable of producing a book such as this. My family's own complex relationship to migration and place has undoubtedly shaped the critical analysis of travel representations in this book. My mother immigrated to the United States from cockney London as a young teenager, while my father is descended on his mother's side from the Spanish Mexican founders of the California town in which I grew up. Between these two very different family histories, I learned at a young age the power of place as both geography and mythology. My brother, Jeff, and I processed our family's sense of displacement through our mutual appreciation of the View-Master. (A 3D stereoscopic toy that was popular in the 1950s–1970s, the View-Master has a history that traces back to the New York World's Fair of 1939.) In fact, I would locate the germ of my interest in travel representations in those little 3D views of Paris or Fiji (or Charlie Brown) that we glimpsed in the View-Master as children, which represented a fascinating world of places that were somehow always inaccessible. Thanks to Jeff for sharing this with me and, in later years, for helpful computer hardware support.

Ewan Malcolm Fenton appeared on the scene just as I was returning to this book after a hiatus of a few years. Ewan's arrival has reshaped my experience of cinema in surprising ways, and he has made everything else in life more worthwhile. Finally, my greatest debt of gratitude, which cannot be adequately expressed here, goes to Christopher Fenton. Without his support, generous spirit, and sense of adventure, none of this would have been possible. This book is dedicated to him, with love.

An earlier version of parts of this manuscript, especially chapter 2, appeared as "Travelogues and Early Nonfiction Film: Education in the School of Dreams," *American Cinema's Transitional Era*, ed. Charlie Keil and Shelley Stamp (Berkeley: University of California Press, 2004), 191–213. An earlier version of chapter 7 was published as "'The Nation's First Playground': Travel Films and the American West, 1895–1920," *Virtual Voyages: Cinema and Travel*, ed. Jeffrey Ruoff (Durham: Duke University Press, 2006), 79–98. Parts of chapters 3 and 6 appear in "'The Knowledge Which Comes in Pictures': Educational Films and Early Cinema Audiences," *A Companion to Early Cinema*, ed. André Gaudreault, Nicolas Dulac, and Santiago Hidalgo (Malden, Mass.: Wiley-Blackwell, 2012), 277–97.

THE DREAMWORLD
OF CINEMATIC TRAVEL

In October 1911, an anonymous editorial in the trade journal *Motography* asserted the popularity of travelogue films: "Of all forms of motion pictures, scenics are the most popular and will always be so." This is true, the writer explained, because "in all the broad field of motion pictures— dramatic, comic, educational—none are so pleasing to all of us, or bring out the best that is in us, as the perfect reproductions of beautiful scenery. The human craving for scenery is unquestionably the strongest of any purely aesthetic demand of our natures." While it may be surprising today, this sort of claim about the popularity of travelogues (also known as "scenic" films) was in fact commonplace in the early 1910s. Such breathless declarations of the travelogue's dominance were eventually proven incorrect, but for a brief moment in early film history, travel films and other "nonfiction" subjects such as science films, nature films, and industrial films were touted by some as the future of the film industry. Even more striking about the editorial is its attempt to put forth an aesthetic theory, given that aesthetics were not a common concern of the early film trade press:

> Among those who have not thought much about it, there is prevalent a misunderstanding of the function of the scenic picture. It is popularly classified as educational; yet scenery is fundamentally and primarily merely entertaining. That is, it appeals first to our emotional side. We respond to beautiful scenery, whether real or pictured, much as we respond

to beautiful music. It is educational, first because anything that is beautiful and appeals to the better emotions is educational; and second because it gives us a knowledge of the harmony of construction of this beautiful old world of ours. But the educational function is purely secondary. A scenic motion picture is really only a pleasure-giving device. Perhaps if that were better understood, exhibitors would feel less reluctance to show scenic subjects. It is that dry word *educational* that is objectionable.[1]

As the writer indicates, by 1911 scenics were often classified as "educational," an umbrella term for all manner of subjects we would now label "nonfiction." Educational films were an important part of the motion-picture industry's attempt to legitimate itself as a respectable form of entertainment in the early 1910s. But the editorialist is also on to something in arguing, against the tide of the era, that scenics can fulfill a non-educational function. Many questions are raised but left unanswered: How exactly do scenic films give pleasure? What "aesthetic demand" do the films meet? Moreover, the editorialist's conflation of entertainment, aesthetics, and emotion is intriguing, for these are quite different categories. Such imprecision is to be expected—after all, this is not a philosophy tract but a trade paper editorial. Yet the basic idea that travelogues are primarily an aesthetic experience rather than an educational one anticipates the argument of this book. I argue that travelogues exemplify a particular kind of turn-of-the-century attraction that we might call "instructive entertainment," a form of attraction that packaged didactic intentions as an aesthetic commodity. Even though they used observational techniques of photographic realism that would seem to lend them to educational purposes—and, indeed, even though travelogues were overwhelmingly marketed as educational subjects—in fact their representational strategies focused primarily on creating a pleasing, marketable experience for the viewer. In this way, early travelogue films combine the concerns of pragmatism, romanticism, and commercialism.

This book focuses on travel films exhibited in commercial U.S. theaters during early cinema's transitional era, roughly the years 1907 to 1915, when films first began to be shown in dedicated movie houses and cinema emerged as a distinct form of media with its own set of practices. One of the most recognizable genres on cinema screens around the world throughout the silent era, travelogues played an important role in defining popular images of global landscapes. Inextricably linked to discourses of empire, they powerfully shaped early twentieth-century attitudes about race and geography. Connected also to emergent practices of modern tourism, travelogues were regularly celebrated as a form of virtual travel experience for those who could not otherwise afford to travel. As an entirely unique commodity in the early twentieth century—one that provided a new kind of experience, traveling in the cinema—travelogue films provide much of historical and critical interest to explore. In picturing the world that *does* exist, early travel films created a world that *does not* exist: an idealized geography that functioned as a parallel universe on the cinema screen.

Travel films have been present throughout film history. It is well known that many of the earliest actualities were "travel" subjects: the film programs projected by Louis and Auguste Lumière in 1896 included titles such as *Leaving Jerusalem by Railway, Niagara Falls,* and *Hyde Park, London.* The Lumière brothers' films are perhaps the most famous examples, but many of the earliest film companies participated in the manufacturing of "foreign views," as they were first called, featuring street scenes (Paris, Madrid, Moscow, Jerusalem, Tokyo), views of famous natural landmarks (Yosemite, Niagara Falls), or scenes of traditional cultures and everyday life around the world. As Charles Musser has stated, "It was undoubtedly scenes of foreign lands that provided the [Lumière] cinématographe with its chief attraction for American audiences."[2] It is less frequently acknowledged, however, that nonfiction continued to be a major presence on movie screens throughout the nickelodeon period and into the silent feature film era.

Travel subjects began to take shape as a film genre with specific formal and stylistic conventions around 1907. During the 1907–15 period, and particularly in the years 1910–13, travelogues occupied an important position in the burgeoning film industry. At this time, travelogues were shown alongside short comedies and melodramas as part of the "variety format" of the nickelodeon theater, which also typically included live music, stereopticon slides, and audience sing-alongs. During these years, some reformers and entrepreneurs argued that travel films represented cinema's future as a respectable cultural force and a profitable business. While these assertions ultimately proved incorrect, they provide important insight into the developing film industry and the broader cultural values it negotiated in the 1910s.

Travelogues persisted in commercial movie theaters throughout the silent era and into the sound era; one of the best-known travelogue series is James A. FitzPatrick's Traveltalks, produced and distributed by Metro-Goldwyn-Mayer from 1930 through 1954. Travel films continue to thrive today on Imax screens (such as *African Adventure: Safari in the Okavango* from 2007 and *Grand Canyon Adventure: River at Risk* from 2008), television (with the Travel Channel and the Discovery Channel devoting much of their air time to such subjects), and on the Internet (of course, YouTube is full of travel videos).[3] While these later travelogue incarnations involve tendencies that are distinct from its early cinema form, the travelogue has proven remarkably steadfast across more than a century of media history, which suggests that persistent cultural needs are being met by the genre.

Returning to the early cinema context, the *Motography* editorialist's idea of scenic films as a kind of aesthetic education connects to the title of this book: education in the school of dreams. At the time the article was written, travelogues were being marketed as educational films, and reformers who otherwise looked down on the new medium of cinema as a form of cheap amusement began to celebrate travel films and other "educational" genres for their ability to uplift their viewers. Whether or not they were "the most popular," as the writer claimed, travelogues were the subject of a major promotional push during the years covered by this book. While I trace the travelogue's trajectory as an "educational" genre, I also explore how travelogues were not necessarily consumed for their educational merits. Instead of taking the reformers' rhetoric as a description of truth, I argue that travelogues were just as likely to be experienced as a dreamlike reverie involving notions of exoticism and the picturesque. Although they were celebrated for their ability to serve as surrogate travel, I analyze travelogues as a unique experience in their own right: a multimedia sensory interlude in which spectators sat immobile in a darkened theater surrounded by strangers, their eyes and minds mobilized by images of geographical and cultural difference.

It is the travelogue's singular distinction to call attention to the act of looking, perhaps more than any other film genre of the early or "classical" cinema periods. Watching a travelogue film, the viewer becomes a disembodied eye floating through a foreign landscape. The people in these films stare back at the camera, returning the spectator's gaze. These films stoked viewers' fantasies and fears of difference with simulated trips to exotic lands and ultimately created a new vision of a globe filled with wondrous yet manageable people and places. As we shall see, these exotic views were actually quite generic, drawing from older traditions of picturesque travel representation in popular media such as postcards, illustrated magazines, and stereopticon lectures. The films also drew on dominant notions of racial and cultural hierarchy, presenting all forms of difference within a grid of preexisting formulas. It is my contention, however, that despite these quite obvious traditions and formulas—indeed, because of the very obviousness of these traditions and formulas—early travelogue films contained a great deal of oppositional potential.

From its inception, cinema was viewed as a quintessentially "modern" phenomenon. Travelogue films, in capturing landscapes and people in movement, updated older forms such as the photograph, the stereograph, and the magic lantern lecture for the new century. The years I discuss in this book, after the dawn of the twentieth century but before the First World War, represent a particular moment in the history of modernity. The so-called Edwardian Era, or the Progressive Era in the United States, was a moment of rapid transformation (industrialization, urbanization, immigration, new technologies, new cultural forms) that yet held fast to many nineteenth-century values and sensibilities. While the word "modern" contains an age-old paradox in that it seems to indicate "nothing more than the shifting proportions of writers old and new," in fact, as Hans Robert Jauss has argued, this particular era of historical modernity represents the emergence of a new consciousness, or self-consciousness: a "modernity that ultimately only ever distinguishes itself from itself."[4]

In literary and film studies, modernity is often defined experientially as a distinct sensory environment created by new technologies of space and time, such as the railroad and the cinema, and new forms of commodification, such as mass-reproduced images, shopping malls, and tourism. The modernity thesis (so called by those who oppose it) has been the subject of much debate in film studies, and I do not want to rehash those debates here, especially since others such as Ben Singer have done such a thorough job of summarizing them.[5] I do want to underscore an obvious point, however: Not all conceptions of "modernity" are the same, nor do they need to be. For the purposes of materialist historiography, the sensibilities of an era are determined from the ground up—that is, through an analysis of texts and contexts—rather than imposed from the outside. Travel films are "modern" because many of their key features—their technologized view of landscape, their mechanical reproduction of movement, their compulsion to represent all corners of the globe on film—were not possible before the onset of cinema in the 1890s. Likewise, travel films constitute an important (and overlooked) step on the road to the formation of cinema's new mass audience, or what Miriam Hansen has analyzed as the cinema's public sphere: "the commodity form of reception."[6]

One of the primary goals of this book is to argue that travelogues are less monolithic and less politically retrograde than they might appear. Even in the press discourse of the day, we can find at least two competing views of cinema's social significance: Early cinema in general was criticized by reformers as a form of "cheap amusement," but travelogues and other educational genres were singled out as "high-class" subjects. Alongside this contradictory reformist rhetoric is another more theoretical tradition to which we might turn for a critique of travel films as ideological products in the context of modern mass culture. My invocation of dreams in this book's title is meant to resonate with Walter Benjamin's analysis of mass culture as a "dreamworld."[7] In his landmark *Arcades Project*, Benjamin identifies mass culture as a primary source of modernity's alienation effects and political dissolution. His crucial intervention, against the pessimistic critical tide of the era, was to argue that the road to surmounting the decline of experience in modernity can be found only by moving through mass culture. As Susan Buck-Morss explains, Benjamin's "theory is unique in its approach to modern society, because it takes mass culture seriously not merely as the source of the phantasmagoria of false consciousness, but as the source of collective energy to overcome it."[8] For Benjamin, the critic's task was to describe what he called the dreamworld of mass culture and, more important, to dissipate its mythic powers. For Benjamin, the path to overcoming this disenchantment was precisely through the agent of disenchantment: mass culture.

My analysis follows Benjamin's model by looking for the tools for demythification that can be found within mass culture itself, under certain conditions and for certain viewers. I analyze travelogues as a contradictory genre that poses as a form of knowledge but actually functions as a form of mythification. Moreover, my analysis reveals a film genre so fraught with contradiction and ambivalence that it contains many moments of rupture and opportunities for resistance. Although the idea of movies as a "dreamworld" is a cliché that Hollywood had already exploited to its fullest by the 1920s, travelogue films literalize this metaphor of dreaming. As much as they document places, travel films can also be seen as documenting mythologies about those places. Analyzing these myths entails not prolonging the dream but debunking its fictions in the spirit of awakening from the dream.

As a form of landscape representation, travelogues engage questions of territory, nationalism, and political power. Indeed, W. J. T. Mitchell echoes Benjamin with his remark that "landscape might be seen more profitably as something like the 'dreamwork of imperialism.'"[9] This dreamwork—and, by extension, these films—are not seamless purveyors of imperial ideology, however, but fractured images containing multiple meanings. Travelogues are deeply imbricated in the power dynamics of empire, but while they enact an imperial gaze, they also display the contradictions of that gaze. The dream metaphor is useful for signaling the deeply ambivalent nature of the fantasy landscapes conjured up by travelogues: Some dreams become nightmares, after all, and the dreamer does not always triumph in her dreams. This book does not provide a Freudian or psychoanalytic account of travelogues. Rather, I take a historical approach to the travel film genre, mounting a critique of the travelogue's mythologizing power but also paying attention to how it contains within itself the seeds of its own undoing. The act of critical analysis, or reading against the grain, then, is akin to an act of awakening.[10]

Modes of Travel in Modernity

One of modernity's primary characteristics is an increase in mobility of all sorts — the mobility of people (travel, migration, socioeconomic mobility) and of things (commercial goods, images, customs, cultural values). Travelogues are the cinematic corollary of all this new mobility, both reflecting and enacting the modern world's compulsion to find new images and experiences. As an experience of technological modernity, travelogues contributed to a changing human perception of the world: What had been seen before through an inert series of still images now became a moving panorama of consumable places and people.

Who moves and who doesn't? Where do they go, and why do they go there? Travelogue films can help us think through some of these crucial questions of modernity. Travelogues traffic in images of the globe, enabling a trade in place-images to accompany the trade in material goods. As Kristin Whissel has argued, traffic is a central metaphor for modernity, signifying not only the circulation of goods but also "the vehicles, bodies, and disembodied communications that move, in one form or another, through the landscape," and eventually "the various technologies — such as the railway, steamship, telephone and telegraph — that precipitated the annihilation of space and time and gave rise to new forms of 'panoramic perception.'"[11] The travelogue is a technological mode of representation that takes the concept of movement as its very subject.

The early twentieth century was characterized by an unprecedented level of movement, not only of goods but also of people. In the visual culture of travel that emerged out of this climate, a popular taste for foreign views emerged. Travelogue films found a niche in the mass culture of the era (along with stereoscopes, postcards, and illustrated magazines) by catering to this desire to see foreign places and foreign cultures. The new visual culture of travel enabled people to envision the world as a series of consumable places. This sense of consumption is crucial: the various new forms of mass reproduction created a sense that places were now endlessly representable commodities. Indeed, given that the early twentieth century is also the high-water mark of imperial power, this era should also be seen as marking a new kind of visual imperialism, achieved through travel practices and the visualization of travel. As John Mackenzie writes, "The British and other empires were not only empires of war, of economic exploitation, of settlement and of cultural diffusion. They were also increasingly empires of travel."[12]

Travelogue films enact the era's fascination with mobility not just by representing the experience of travel but also by enacting the ideologies of travel. Mary Louise Pratt's notion of contact zones can be usefully adapted to fit the travelogue experience. For Pratt, contact zones are "social spaces where disparate cultures meet, clash, and grapple with each other, often in highly asymmetrical relations of domination and subordination."[13] As films, travelogues function not as true contact zones but as virtual contact zones; thus, any clashing and grappling that the viewer might have experienced was undertaken in the safe zone of the movie theater. Nonetheless, what is so striking about these films is how they capture the awkwardness of the encounter between filmmakers and their subjects. More than a representation of a people or a place, it is this *encounter* that travelogues reenact for the viewer. This is not an actual contact zone but a represented one. The viewer witnesses not only a foreign culture or landscape but the "relations of domination and subordination" that are inscribed by the act of filming that foreign culture or landscape.

As films that are "about" travel—even though they are more frequently about places, not journeys—travelogues are often said to embody a "tourist viewpoint."[14] But while the films' connection with tourism is important, the majority of their viewers were not actual tourists. While leisure travel was accessible to more people than ever before at the turn of the twentieth century, it was still not the common experience it became after the Second World War. International travel in this period still implied high-society leisure, luxurious trains, and ocean liners. Undoubtedly, some travelogue spectators were actual tourists, but more important, the travelogue's association with tourism served to lend cultural prestige to the genre. Therefore, it is more precise to state that travelogues confer a tourist point of view on their spectators, whether or not those spectators were actually tourists. As such, the films were regularly advertised as "high-class" subjects. My analysis teases out the implications of this "high-class" veneer, arguing that while travelogues may have been associated with elite tastes, as products of mass culture they were accessible to diverse audiences. Even though travel films were often figured as a kind of compensatory travel, making tourism available to those who could not otherwise command the power of the tourist gaze, I argue that early travel films constitute an experience in their own right. This is not an experience of travel but an experience of sitting in a darkened movie theater. Travel films use a specific set of cinematic techniques—framing, editing, movement—that tend to call attention to the act of looking. So while the spectator stared at these images on the screen, more often than not, the anonymous people filmed by travelogue cameras stared directly back at the audience. This returned gaze is one way in which travelogues undermine the security conferred by their formulas, and can be opened up to resistant viewings.

Outside the movie theater, too, the experience of actual mobility in the early twentieth century was hardly "exclusive." Although some upper-middle-class travelers undertook international travel in this era, the majority of people crossing international borders were migrants rather than tourists. Migration within Europe for economic reasons was already commonplace as early as the seventeenth century and into the eighteenth; as one historian says of that period, "Stability was a privilege in this world." With industrialization and the population surge of the nineteenth century, migration increased, and "regional migration systems became overlaid with international systems."[15] Migration fed the unprecedented urbanization then taking place in Europe: "Where there had been only 23 cities with populations of more than 100,000 in 1800, 125 stood a century later."[16] The period before the onset of the First World War was one of tremendous population movement, and most of that was economic or political migration.

Caren Kaplan has posed the question, "Why, if the modern experience of forced or voluntary movement has been widespread and diverse, [do] the metaphors and symbols used to represent displacement refer to individualized, often elite, circumstances?"[17] This certainly holds true for travelogues and other popular forms of travel representation, which evoke touristic experiences with regularity but rarely mention other kinds of travel experience. The early cinema period coincides with a peak era of immigration to the United States in the early twentieth century. But despite the fact that many early cinema spectators were themselves migrants, migrancy was infrequently depicted in early cinema, although it was a major concern of reformers and educators.

Why were representations of migration suppressed in this period, when so many people were actually migrating? One probable reason has to do with issues of class and cultural distinction. My analysis is indebted to the work of Pierre Bourdieu, whose influential book *Distinction* traces the ways in which "art and cultural consumption are predisposed, consciously and deliberately or not, to fulfil a social function of legitimating differences."[18] Leisure travel is one such form of cultural consumption that serves efforts to shore up distinction. Travel was one way for affluent citizens to display their wealth in the early twentieth century, while recent migration was often a mark of one's lower-class status. Perhaps the emergence of a film genre devoted to tourist imagery in an age of migration is symptomatic of the larger aspirations of upward mobility that characterize the Progressive Era.

As recent scholarship on tourism has established, one of the constitutive points of tension in tourism is that between the tourist and the traveler. Tourism, as one means of conspicuous consumption, has long been a way for the middle and upper classes to distinguish themselves from each other and from those who are less economically endowed. The origin point of modern tourism, the European Grand Tour, emerged in the seventeenth century as a sort of finishing school for the patrician (male) citizens of Great Britain. From the beginning, efforts were made to distinguish the "proper" form of travel from the "improper." By the early 1800s, "tourist" had emerged as a term with negative connotations, useful for distinguishing the more salutary practices of the "traveler," who was thought to have more integrity. This new word made it easier to distinguish between the "authentic" practices of the traveler and the shallow or falsifying practices signified by the "tourist." As Jonathan Culler writes, "The tourist, it seems, is the lowest of the low. . . . Animal imagery seems their inevitable lot: they are said to move in droves, herds, swarms, or flocks."[19] Although popular culture—and even some twentieth-century critics such as Paul Fussell—continues to assert the opposition between tourists and travelers, scholars of tourism such as Culler and James Buzard, who follow on the heels of Dean MacCannell's influential study *The Tourist*, interpret these practices as two parts of a dialectic: "The formation of modern tourism *and* the impulse to denigrate tourists [is] a single complex phenomenon."[20] In this context, the travelogue's irrefutable status as virtual tourism rather than actual travel means that it can never achieve the prestige of a "real" travel experience. Another way to put it is that no matter how "high class" they might have seemed, travelogues always remained motion pictures and carried with them the cultural baggage of cinema's reputation at the time.

Largely because of the construction of the railroads, travel for recreation became more common by the mid-nineteenth century—so much so that in 1850, the *Times* of London wrote, "Thirty years ago not one countryman in one hundred had seen the metropolis. There is now scarcely one in the same number who has not spent a day there."[21] This increase in tourism was also spurred by a wave of World's Fair exhibitions in the second half of the century, beginning with London's Great Exhibition of 1851 in the famous Crystal Palace. According to one estimate, nearly one-fifth of the British population attended the Great Exhibition (still a minority, we should note), and "this massive movement of people marked the beginning of a revolution in leisure."[22] Thomas Cook organized a series of affordable excursions to the Great Exhibition and, building on this and other successes, soon began marketing European package tours to middle-class and working-class British citizens. With the increase in leisure travel came an increase in attempts to distinguish between different kinds of travelers, and the term "Cook's Tour" came to be synonymous with the idea of mass (and thereby debased) tourism.[23]

Today tourism is recognized as the world's largest industry, and tourism has become a subject of academic interest.[24] A massive amount of data and analysis is now available on tourism from a variety of perspectives (geography, anthropology, sociology, economics). Historians do not seem to be able to agree, however, on when the era of mass leisure travel actually began. Some locate it in the Cook's Tour era of the mid-nineteenth century with the advent of the railroad; others locate it in the early twentieth century with the rise of car culture. And some argue that the post–Second World War era was the beginning of truly mass tourism as airplane travel became commonplace.[25] It is clear that the history of tourism is one of increasing access, as more and more middle- and working-class citizens acquired the means to become tourists; moreover, this history is directly tied to changing modes of transport.

While the scope of mass tourism has only continued to broaden since the nineteenth century, the scope of migration has followed a different path. In terms of migration to the United States, before the recent spike in immigration that has occurred since 2000, migration's peak era was the so-called new immigration period of the late nineteenth century and early twentieth. Between 1900 and 1920, almost 14.5 million people, many from Eastern Europe and Southern Europe, entered the country; this influx peaked in 1907 with 1.3 million immigrants, according to the U.S. Census Bureau.[26] Migration fell off with the beginning of the "Great War" in 1914 and began to increase again after the end of the Second World War.

Migration takes many forms and has always been an important part of human history. But representations of migrant experience—including economic migration, forced migration, or migration to escape persecution—have not proven as marketable as representations of tourist experience. When considering travelogue films, we should keep in mind the displacements of migration that are masked by their tourist gaze. When those who were themselves migrants viewed a travelogue film, perhaps of their home country, the film might have served as a compensation for migrancy, enabling the viewer to reconnect with the homeland. But it might have just as well served to underscore the viewer's sense of loss at his or her displacement. All of these social changes are an important context for the travelogue film of the early twentieth century, but aesthetic traditions present another crucial framework for understanding the genre.

Cinema and Landscape: The Major and the Minor

Popular place-images such as travelogues fostered a new way to see the world as representable through techniques of rational observation, a world filled with locations that could be pictured, landscapes made for consumption. Travelogue films were particularly significant because they modernized the landscape by rendering it in motion and by breaking it into fragments through editing. We might begin, then, by thinking of travelogues as a quintessentially modern kind of space: a mechanized landscape. Approaching the films from the perspective of landscape allows us to locate and analyze their position of cultural marginality.

Landscape is a well-established topic in art history and geography, but it has only just begun to be addressed in film studies. In considering a visual medium that traffics so heavily in images of place and space, cinema studies' inattention to landscape is confounding. Perhaps the lack of interest stems from landscape's traditionally marginal status in the history of art, and most certainly it has resulted from a privileging of narrative in cinema studies, given that narratives tend to dominate the landscapes in which they are staged. In fact, the small body of scholarly work on cinematic landscapes thus far has focused on experimental film, since this is the realm in which landscape has received the most extensive interrogation by filmmakers. Scott MacDonald's *The Garden in the Machine* is one of the few volumes to present a sustained analysis of cinematic landscape, focusing on experimental film.[27] Martin Lefebvre's more recent edited collection *Landscape in Film* has provided several useful concepts and textual readings, with which I will engage momentarily.[28] But there is much more to explore: Landscape in film remains an open field.

As a genre of painting, landscape rose to its highest prominence in the nineteenth century; before this, landscape was considered a lower-order subject. During the Renaissance, the European art academies ranked types of paintings by their significance, with landscape following genre painting, portraiture, and history painting in hierarchical importance. The only genre of painting that landscape outranked, in fact, was the still life, according to institutions such as the Academy of Art in Rome, the Academy of Art in Florence, and the Académie des Beaux-Arts in Paris. This hierarchy began to change in the nineteenth century, as British painters such as John Constable and J. M. W. Turner forged a new kind of romantic landscape. For the Romantics, painting was no longer merely a matter of artistic practice but a reflection of the inner moral and religious disposition of the artist. At the same time, a new impetus for realistic documentation in landscape paintings was inspired by the ascendance of rational observation, exemplified by painters such as Thomas Cole and Albert Bierstadt.[29] Certainly, the history of landscape painting is well known, and I am not going to rehearse it here.[30] The point I want to make is that landscape was originally a marginalized genre, but in the nineteenth century it became central. Landscape continued to gather significance in the modern world, and in mass culture it followed a path to increasing commodification and mechanization. Landscape became an essential component of illustrated magazines, chromolithographs, photographs, and stereographs, all of which came to constitute a visual culture of travel in the nineteenth century. This emphasis on landscape continued into the new motion picture medium at the turn of the century.

Landscape's marginalization operated not only in the hierarchy of painting genres but also in a hierarchy that existed within the *content* of landscape paintings themselves. Malcolm Andrews has pointed out that the *narrative element* in landscape paintings "used to be termed the 'Argument' of the picture, that is, its principal theme or subject." In turn, landscape was considered *parergon*, or "by-work . . . the accessory element."[31] During the Renaissance, a landscape painting's narrative Argument and parergon were seen as oppositional, but with the rise of landscape painting in the nineteenth century, what was once a mere accessory element became centrally important. Or, as Lefebvre puts it, "In this sense, the birth of landscape should really be understood as the birth of a way of seeing, the birth of a gaze (that of the painter, the collector, or the critic) by which what was once in the margin has now come to take its place at the centre."[32]

Lefebvre is one of the few scholars to attempt a theory of cinematic landscape, which he establishes by distinguishing between what he calls "landscape as setting" and "landscape as landscape." He writes, "In mainstream cinema, natural or exterior spaces tend to function as setting rather than landscape in the vast majority of cases."[33] In contrast, landscape that is significant for itself — or "autonomous landscape," as Lefebvre calls it — appears infrequently in mainstream narrative cinema.[34] Travelogue films, however, unlike narrative cinema, are often composed of nothing but autonomous landscapes. These films demand a different kind of spectator than narrative films. In fact, Lefebvre's analysis emphasizes the role of the spectator's gaze in viewing cinematic landscapes, pointing out that the spectator of narrative cinema "can pull setting from out of the margin."[35] Early travelogue films cultivate attentive spectators, viewers who must fill in the blanks, so to speak, posing and answering questions that the explanatory intertitles do not adequately address. Landscape's marginality — and its cultivation of an attentive spectator — has important implications for travelogue films.

Starting from landscape's status as a marginal form of representation, I argue that travelogue films fit into a category that we might call "minor cinema," after Gilles Deleuze's concept of "minor literature." The label of minor cinema has been hitherto applied to so-called Third Cinema, to describe the oppositional filmmaking practices of filmmakers such as Ousmane Sembène and Tran Anh Hung.[36] Fernando Solanas and Octavio Getino's influential manifesto "Towards a Third Cinema" called for a politically militant and formally experimental cinema.[37] Film scholars have demonstrated this manifesto's affinity with Deleuze's concept, both of which can be said to express an attitude of "life-experimentation — the creation and exhibition of local difference."[38] In applying the label of minor cinema to travel films, however, a contradiction immediately arises, for Third Cinema is resolutely anticolonial, while travel films tend to support colonialist ideology. Moreover, Third Cinema is avowedly political, while travelogues are only unconsciously political. How, then, can travel films be understood as a form of minor cinema? And what do we gain by this categorization?

If cinema constitutes its own kind of language (as some have argued since the 1910s), then certainly it speaks in both a major and a minor key.[39] Deleuze's essay on minor literature, written with Félix Guattari, is concerned with describing a kind of language that speaks against the major or master language. For Deleuze and Guattari, Franz Kafka's writing is the paradigm. This minor literature has three characteristics: first, "deterritorialized language," by which they mean language that speaks in an oppositional position against the dominant language and is thus "appropriate for strange and minor uses"; second, a political dimension in which the "cramped space" of the minor "forces each individual intrigue to connect immediately to politics"; and third, a collective character: "precisely because talent isn't abundant in a minor literature, there are no possibilities for an individuated enunciation that would belong to this or that 'master' and that could be separated from a collective enunciation."[40]

Travelogues resonate with all three of these characteristics. First, they occupied an oppositional position vis-à-vis story films in the transitional era, and although they were not necessarily intended for "strange and minor uses," this book demonstrates that they could certainly serve such purposes. Second, travelogues are saturated with political significance, unabashedly displaying their colonial ideologies and their belief in progress through industrialization and modernization. As Tom Gunning has argued, early cinema exhibits "a sort of naiveté in which elements that later became camouflaged are frankly displayed."[41] Travel films provide us with a series of object lessons in how to analyze ideology when it is not carefully sublimated. Travelogues also resonate with Deleuze and Guattari's third quality, for in the anonymous nature of their production, travelogues speak to us as precisely this kind of "collective enunciation" of attitudes about travel from the early twentieth century. In early cinema, directors' names were not made public, so this anonymity is both conceptually and historically accurate. While a few travelogue filmmakers are certainly known to film historians today (e.g., Lumière cameramen Félix Mesguich and Alexandre Promio and Burton Holmes's cameraman Oscar B. Depue), in this book I am less interested in tracking down unknown directors (although this is certainly an important task) than I am in unpacking the rhetoric of travelogues as a genre — or, in a larger sense, as a kind of institution.

So travelogues are a form of minor cinema in the dictionary sense in that they have always been a marginal kind of film (along with industrial films, home movies, and a host of other kinds of film that lie outside the mainstream of film production and exhibition, sometimes labeled "ephemeral film").[42] And travelogues are a form of minor cinema in the Deleuzian sense in that they are collective, political, and they contain oppositional potential, even though this was not their intended stance.[43] I believe that travelogues can be understood as a form of minor cinema because they have the ability to undermine what they show, and to a greater degree than other kinds of cinema. To understand travelogues as a form of minor cinema, we must read them against their grain, unearthing the potentially disruptive and oppositional power they contained. Travelogues are not oppositional in the way that avant-garde cinema is, but they do use a formal strategy that is distinctly different from that of fiction films of the same era. In sum, travelogues are not intentionally minoritarian, but they had the potential for minoritarian effects. For Deleuze, it is only from within a minor discourse that real change can be articulated: "There is nothing that is major or revolutionary except the minor."[44] In this context, it is worth remarking that travel films were virtually the only place in which people of color were represented — rather than parodied by fictional stereotype — in early film. While these displays of difference certainly follow colonialist conventions, they also frequently exceed the boundaries of such conventions. Elsewhere, Deleuze and Guattari explain that even seemingly blocked realms are filled with "lines of flight" (or new potentialities, escape from existing conditions): "Territorialities, then, are shot through with lines of flight testifying to the presence within them of movements of deterritorialization and reterritorialization."[45] The question raised by travelogues would seem to be: To what extent are movements of deterritorialization actually opened up in these films that would seem to be precisely about territorialization? They certainly do not constitute what Deleuze calls an "absolute line of flight," or a purely revolutionary discourse. Rather, they contain avenues of escape; moments that puncture the apparent placidity of existing conditions.[46] Travel films allow us to document and catalogue moments of domination and resistance in early cinema. What we gain by seeing travelogues as a form of minor cinema, then, is a larger political resonance for our task of cataloguing these moments of rupture. We also gain a sense of the travelogue's significance as a distinctly modern, potentially unsettling experience for its spectators.

The Travelogue Formula

To a greater degree than many film genres, travelogues follow rigid conventions. I address the question of early film genre (Did genres exist? What forms did they take? How can we identify them?) in the chapters that follow. For now, I will only make a note about methodology. To analyze travel films as a genre, I have undertaken a serial analysis of a large body of films and related texts. This is the approach endorsed by Vinzenz Hediger and Patrick Vonderau in their recent edited volume on the related genre of industrial films, and, indeed, this is arguably the only approach possible when analyzing film genre.[47] While my research for this project involved visiting a number of different film archives, the primary corpus of this book is the group of nonfiction films in the Desmet Collection at the EYE Film Institute Netherlands. This remarkable collection was named to the UNESCO Memory of the World Register in 2011.[48] Jean Desmet was a Dutch importer of films from around the world, and unlike most figures from the early film era, he saved everything: film prints, programs, posters, and so on.[49] Desmet kept film prints from production companies around the world—among them Pathé, Gaumont, Eclipse, Éclair, Ambrosio, Itala, Nordisk, Vitascope, Edison, Kalem, and Lubin—and his collection provides an unparalleled view of the early film industry from an international perspective. Indeed, cinema was more international before the First World War than after, and the phenomenon of travelogues makes this internationalism quite literal.[50] After analyzing hundreds of early travel films, certain patterns of style and rhetoric clearly emerge. In fact, the patterns emerge after watching just a few; what changes is the location being documented in each film rather than the travelogues' semantic or syntactic elements.

The basic formula for the travelogue of the nickelodeon era is a series of single, discrete exterior shots of landscapes and people, each preceded by a brief explanatory intertitle. This alternation between landscapes and portraits is a key dualism of the genre. The stand-alone quality of the shots is another of the genre's most notable formal elements. Most shots have been joined together in a manner that preserves the integrity of each shot rather than, for example, making connections between shots via continuous space or matching on action. Travelogues are not usually organized with any clear sense of progression toward or away from a subject. Rather, shots are typically arranged as a series of scenes that meander without a sense of progression. This discontinuous editing principle creates a sense that the shots form a *collection* rather than a unified whole.

While they are entirely formulaic, the travelogue's organizational principles appear unsystematic or even haphazard. For all of the stereotypical images they display, their images seem scattered, the editing arbitrary: Why assemble this series of shots in this particular order? Locations chosen seem almost random at times: Why film this street rather than that? Why show this man rather than that one? Why shoemakers rather than basket makers? Despite this apparent lack of order, a logic becomes clear when one dispenses with familiar notions of structure derived from fiction film, such as continuity editing. In fact, the same set of formal devices can be found in almost every travelogue film: an overwhelming dominance of extreme long shots, movement in just about every shot, editing that shapes the film into a collection of views. At the same time, travel films contain an element that exceeds these conventions, and that element is the contingency of the real world. The chaos of the real, it seems, is managed by the rigid formulas of the genre. Travelogues certainly do not lack a system, but theirs is a system that makes order out of contingency.

So what precisely did viewers see when watching these films? Early travelogues tend to follow a narrow list of subject matter, such as picturesque natural landscapes, exotic foreign cultures, modern street scenes, parks, flowers, sunsets, water (oceans, lakes, rivers, fountains), smiling women and children, locals in traditional dress, traditional crafts. In fact, this variety of subject matter is presented in the form of two of the most classic image types: landscape and figure. Some films focus on just one of these categories: *L'Orne* (Gaumont, 1912) is composed solely of picturesque landscape shots; *Indian and Ceylonese Types* (Éclair, 1913) features only shots of local inhabitants. Most films, however, alternate between landscapes and figures. *Glacier National Park* (Pathé, 1917), for example, begins with a series of landscape shots and concludes with portraits of local types.[51] "Industrial" films such as *Making Getas in Japan* (Pathé, 1911), which focuses solely on the craft of making shoes, have a slightly different iconography based on production rather than landscape or figure, but many such films bear a strong resemblance to travelogues, so I include them in my analysis.

Travelogues typically conclude with an emblematic shot that serves to epitomize the place being documented, similar to a dramatic tableau.[52] This connects to the early cinema tradition of closing a fiction film with a tableau shot, such as the tableau of Abraham Lincoln at the end of Edwin S.

Porter's *Uncle Tom's Cabin* (1903). The concluding sunset shot is a familiar travelogue cliché; these are typically extreme long shots of a picturesque landscape (a body of water, a city skyline) taken as the sun sets. Such shots participate in the familiar "end of the day" travel narrative convention, which can be found in both nineteenth-century travel literature and the travel lectures of figures such as Burton Holmes. This concluding sunset shot can be found in a variety of films made by different film companies, including *Seeing Los Angeles* (Imp, 1912), *Santa Lucia* (Ambrosio, ca. 1910), and *Under Basque Skies* (Eclipse, 1913). However, the use of this ending convention does not mean that the rest of these films participate in a "day-in-the-life" structure, for other than this concluding shot, none of the films just mentioned follows a temporal trajectory. Rather, the sunset ending shot sums up a film with an emblematic sense of "something picturesque."

Another closure convention of early travelogues is the tableau shot of a smiling child or a smiling woman. The interchangeability of women and children in this concluding slot echoes the familiar rhetorical conflation of these two categories: not "women and children first," but women and children last. The child-at-the-end shot sums up a film with a sense of "something cute," while the woman-at-the-end shot sums up a film with a beckoning "something beautiful." Versions of this ending can be found in *The Touaregs in Their Own Country* (Pathé, 1908), which features a smiling woman and a child, and in *Parks in Japan* (production company unknown, ca. 1915), which concludes with three such shots: one of a smiling woman and two of a pair of cute children holding balloons.

Such tableaux might sound merely kitschy, but their actual effect is much more ambiguous. In the concluding shot of *The Oasis of El-Kantara* (Éclair, 1913), for example, we see two children embracing (tinted blue) who giggle at the cameraman, who obviously is giving them directions from off-screen (see plate 1). They are clearly meant to function as "something cute," but the indexical force of seeing real children—not still but moving and responding moment by moment to the cameraman in front of them—has the effect of creating empathy for them as real people being forced into the service of cliché. Even if the girls are not clearly offering resistance to the camera, what remains is a documentation of the awkwardness of their encounter with the cameraman. The camera's presence is not effaced but highlighted.

These sorts of clichéd images appear often in other forms of represented travel before the emergence of cinema, such as illustrated lectures, postcards, and stereographs. But travelogue films added several crucial new aspects to the itinerary of travel imagery. In addition to portraits (of people, costumes, things) and landscape panoramas (urban, rural, or wild), "tracking" shots (taken from a moving vehicle) are extremely common in travelogue films. While portrait shots are usually stationary, landscape panoramas and tracking shots are all about movement. Portraits were common in travel lecture slides, but no other medium could capture the movement of a panning landscape shot or a shot taken from a moving vehicle. What remains the same is the regime of stereotypical images that cinema co-opted from previous forms of represented travel. Entirely novel, however, are the effects of movement and fragmentation enabled by cinema.

Because I aim to analyze the travelogue broadly as a film genre and as a new form of picturing the world, this book does not restrict its scope to travelogues about particular places (with the exception of chapter 7, a case study of travelogues set in the American West). Instead, this book examines travelogues set in locations worldwide. I have attempted to focus the study, however, by analyzing film exhibition and spectatorship in the United States. To this end, with only a few exceptions, I analyze films that I have positively identified as having been exhibited in the United States. One of the pitfalls of such a global scope is a temptation to lapse into overly broad generalizations; to avoid this, I have worked to draw my conclusions out of close analyses of specific films. I have tried to avoid the limitations of formalism by grounding my close analyses in historical and social context. It is my hope that the global scope of this book results in broad explanatory power, but some universalizing is the unavoidable outcome of this methodological approach. In fact, the travelogue genre is so wide ranging and varied that one can often find exceptions to the systems I map out here. Nonetheless, I believe that this most formulaic of genres will benefit at this juncture from attention to its basic structures and myths.

In chapter 1 I analyze the travel film's nineteenth-century precursors in other media such as stereographs, illustrated lectures, and World's Fairs, with a focus on the travel lecture tradition personified by Burton Holmes. The chapter concludes with a section contrasting the strong authorial presence in Holmes's lectures with the lack of authorial presence in travelogue films. In chapter 2 I explore the place of nonfiction in the early film industry, suggesting the ways that early nonfiction films challenge accepted periodizations of early cinema. I briefly outline the production, distribution, and exhibition of travelogues and discuss early film genre at some length, for in this era, nonfiction genres vastly outnumbered fiction genres. In chapter 3 I explore nonfiction film's role in the campaign to "uplift" the cinema from its reputation as a form of cheap amusement into a respected form of "clean" entertainment. In fact, for a brief moment, some early film businessmen such as George Kleine and Thomas Edison felt that travel films and other "educational" subjects represented the commercial future of the industry. Kleine's efforts ultimately failed, but his attempt to commercialize educational films is a crucial part of the story of early cinema.

In chapter 4 I turn to the aesthetics of the travelogue, with a particular emphasis on questions of editing and movement. I also consider how locations of internal empire, along with colonial locations, were represented in film. Chapter 5 is devoted to an analysis of the picturesque in travelogue films, demonstrating that what began as an aesthetic concept of the eighteenth century had become little more than an advertising term by the twentieth century. By definition, the picturesque refers to a generalized sense of something aesthetically compelling, or "like a picture," but as I point out, in travel films this dynamic has the effect of masking social and political realities with a veneer of clichéd beauty. In chapter 6 I address questions of spectatorship and speculate about the travelogue as an experience. I argue that one appeal of the travelogue may have been to offer a place apart for contemplating other visions of dwelling in the world, a quiet space for fantasy and reverie. I take seriously the travelogue's ability to broaden audiences' horizons and pique audiences' sense of wonder, even though this was brought about through the use of imperial imagery. Chapter 7 is a case study of travelogues of the American West. In focusing for the most part on national parks, early travel films attempted to present a vision of the western United States as timeless and pristine, connecting the nation to an ancient, "prehistoric" past. However, the presence of tourists in so many of these films contradicts this fantasy of a timeless paradise, for tourists render these landscapes modern. Finally, in the epilogue, I gesture toward the travelogue's legacy beyond the early cinema period in theatrical feature films, nontheatrical classroom cinema, and the avant-garde film. I pay particular attention to one avant-garde reworking of the travelogue from the end of the silent era, Oskar Fischinger's *Walking from Munich to Berlin* (1927). As that film suggests, just as they can close off the imagination with formulas and clichés, travelogues have the ability to open up lines of flight for the spectator.

CHAPTER 1

VARIETIES OF TRAVEL EXPERIENCE
Burton Holmes and the Travelogue Tradition

Travel accounts have been produced for millennia, but the travelogue is a multi-media form that emerged at the dawn of the twentieth century. The *Oxford English Dictionary* defines a travelogue as "an (illustrated) lecture about places and experiences encountered in the course of travel; hence a film, broadcast, book, etc., about travel; a travel documentary."[1] The term is usually considered a neologism by the travel lecturer Burton Holmes. The film historian X. Theodore Barber writes, for example, "In 1904 Holmes coined the term 'travelogue' to refer to his show, thereby giving it a greater air of novelty."[2] I have not found corroborating evidence that Holmes coined the term, however, and in fact Charles Musser has located a usage of the word by someone other than Holmes as early as 1899.[3] Regardless of the word's true origin, Holmes did claim to be its originator, and he was certainly the one who popularized it with his renowned illustrated lecture series that toured the United States from the 1890s through the 1950s.

Illustrated travel lectures were hugely popular in the late nineteenth century and early twentieth. In these presentations, live lecturers described foreign lands before a paying audience, accompanying their talks with magic lantern slides. These public speakers, almost always men, were usually celebrity travelers or scholars, which gave them the requisite aura of cultural authority to perform as experts.[4] Lecturers typically took credit for the photographic images that accompanied their talks, even if they had not taken the slides themselves (lantern slides were manufactured and sold by a number of firms).[5] John L. Stoddard, Alexander Black, Lyman Howe, and Dwight L. Elmendorf are some of the other prominent American travel lecturers, but Holmes was the most famous of his contemporaries; in his heyday, he was a well-known media figure.

Because the word "travelogue" was first associated with the phenomenon of the illustrated travel lecture, it is directly connected to the visual medium of photography and associated with public exhibition contexts. In 1897, Holmes became one of the first travel lecturers to incorporate motion pictures into his presentations. What was new about the Holmesian travelogue model and what sets travelogues apart from prior travel accounts is their expanded multimedia hybridity: not just photographic slides and a lecture but now also moving pictures. Even with the broadening of the term "travelogue" later in the twentieth century to include travel literature — and sometimes even travel literature without accompanying photographs — it is clear that hybridity is central to the conceit. (Bruce Chatwin's books, which are often called travelogues, were published without photographs, for example, although he was in fact an avid photographer.)

The travelogue film's most immediate predecessor, and the entertainment form to which it bears the closest resemblance, is the illustrated travel lecture. But there are important differences of voice between travel lectures and travel films. Recent scholarship on travel literature has argued that travel writing tends to be more about the narrating subject than the places through which the narrator travels.[6] In literary travel accounts, the One Who Travels is usually also the Author. Similarly, illustrated travel lectures were marketed largely on the appeal of the lecturer rather than the subject matter he or she presented. Audiences went to see a lecture by John Stoddard or Burton Holmes, not a lecture about Morocco, for example. Travel lectures not only documented other places and other people, they also documented the self — and not so much a "real" self as the lecturer's constructed public persona.

Unlike travel lectures, however, travelogue films exhibited in commercial moving picture theaters typically lacked a first-person narrator. In early cinema, the director was not yet an important category; when any credit was given in this era, it was the name of the production company. Before the sound era, travelogue films narrated in an omniscient voice. This changed with the introduction of synchronized sound, when figures like James A. Fitzpatrick and Lowell Thomas narrated travelogue films for the major studios such as Metro-Goldwyn-Mayer (MGM) and Fox. Holmes was also a pioneer in this area, producing a commercial travelogue film series for Paramount in

1916—although, of course, the series lacked sync sound and thus the specificity of Holmes's speaking voice. But in the early cinema period, travelogue films invoked a generalized, disembodied subject rather than exploring any individual subjectivity (that of Holmes or some other narrating author). The "speaker" in silent-era travelogue films is not a specific person but a kind of ghostly amalgam of the (unseen) cameraman, the production company, and official (or commercial) Western culture at large.

While much of this book will dispense with questions of authorship in favor of examining the travelogue film as an industrial phenomenon (and because directors are unknown for most of these films), in this chapter I analyze an author figure in order to contrast travelogue films with travel lectures. Burton Holmes, as the celebrity "father figure" most identified with travelogues, provides a useful starting point for analyzing the travelogue's particular mode of spectator address, and for investigating the tensions and contradictions at the heart of the turn-of-the-century imperial ideology that fueled these representations of travel. As Jeanette Roan has argued, Holmes's lectures differed from those of his predecessors (such as Stoddard) in that he strove to create for his audiences the illusion of actually traveling: "Holmes invited his audience to feel . . . for themselves through what would be known today as . . . perceptual point-of-view shot[s]." As Roan suggests, Holmes offered himself either as a first-person surrogate for the spectator's perception of travel or as a broader "figure of identification for his audience."[7] I would add to this observation that Holmes also might have functioned as a figure of resistance for some spectators.

In this chapter I analyze the tradition of the illustrated travel lecture in the context of the larger visual culture of travel in the late nineteenth century. My aim is to trace the influence of a figure such as Holmes, who had a strong authorial presence, on the commercial travelogue film of the 1900s and 1910s, which depicted places without an authorial voice, so to speak. The suffix "-logue" usually refers to a speaking subject, as in "monologue." To understand the travelogue film, it is important to understand its origin in the live lecture tradition. Lacking a live narrator or a narrating figure within the film, early travelogue films make room for the spectator's own subjectivity, opening up space for the audience to interact with the film in personal or unexpected ways. Ultimately, I argue, the absence of the authorial figure in early commercial travelogue films enabled the viewing subject to become a stronger participant with the film as a text, encouraging open-ended interpretations, projections, and spectator fantasies.

The Visual Culture of Travel

If travel is about encountering difference, then a variety of media have long been marketing this experience to consumers who do not actually travel. By the end of the nineteenth century, travel had found its way into just about every popular representational form. Against a backdrop of economic and social upheaval, imperial expansion, and growing consumerism, a multitude of popular media contributed to a veritable craze for travel imagery. Before the emergence of cinema in the 1890s, images of travel and foreign lands had been hugely popular in illustrated magazines such as *Harper's* and *The Century*, as well as in photographs, stereographs, chromolithographs, and a variety of other media. The travel film, like much early cinema, poached from preexisting media for its own content and structure. As Tom Gunning has put it, "Cinema did not immediately appear with a defined essence as a medium, but rather, displayed an amazing promiscuity (if not polymorphic perversity) in both its models and uses."[8] Travelogue films quickly became an important part of this broad network of travel representations, drawing on the conventions and tropes established by previous forms of media. Like these other kinds of travel representation, travel films shaped a new sense of what could be pictured in the modern world. Unlike these other representations, however, travelogue films added the crucial element of *movement* to travel imagery. The films also addressed the spectator in ways that differed from these non-cinematic forms, resulting in an experience of virtual travel that was entirely singular in the era.

A survey of all of the different nineteenth-century travel media would easily overflow into another book, so I restrict myself to making just a few points about represented travel in this era. First of all, it is important to note that travel is one of the common threads running through virtually all nineteenth-century (pre-cinema) visual culture. In fact, one would be hard pressed to think of an entertainment form from this period that did *not* take up travel as subject matter. Second, the spaces in which these travel media were consumed can be divided into public and private spheres, with different effects on spectatorship for each category. Travel literature, illustrated magazines, stereographs, and postcards were consumed in the private domain of the home, while travel lectures, panoramas, dioramas, zoos, museums, World's Fair exhibitions, and fairgrounds were public experiences.

Given the ubiquity of interest in exoticism at the time, the differences between media are more numerous than the similarities. World's Fair displays are an important precursor to the travelogue film, but even in this one kind of venue, a variety of different attractions were available. World's Fair exhibitions featured installation and performance-oriented travel displays such as dioramas, panoramas, and native villages that could be experienced only by a live, on-site audience. For example, Emmanuelle Toulet has described how the Universal Exposition in Paris of 1900 offered both "traditional" displays, such as "the Panorama of the Congo, the Panorama of Madagascar, [or] the Diorama of the Sahara," which featured painted canvases that did not move, and the "animated" or "moving" panorama, with a painted canvas that "was not only mobile, but formed part of a full mise-en-scène which sought to create a complete change of environment."[9] The variety of displays here is astonishing, and many of these attractions share similarities with the cinema. The movement of the panorama, as opposed to the stationary diorama, for example, anticipates the movement of cinema. But at the same time, each entertainment form provided something the others did not. As Alison Griffiths has emphasized, World's Fairs "often provided opportunities for direct spectator contact with native peoples appearing in the exhibits (an experience that also relates to the reciprocal fascination of the indigenous peoples with Westerners), unlike the cinema audience's always-mediated and temporally dissociated experience of the Other."[10] In other words, live displays provided direct contact that was precluded by cinema.

World's Fair displays also straddled the boundaries of fiction and nonfiction with their combination of real bodies presented in staged environments with painted backdrops that emphasized the fairground nature of the display. In the early cinema period, the boundary between fiction and nonfiction was defined differently from how it is defined today. Finally, as Mark Sandberg has pointed out, for visitors to exhibitions and museums, "Spectators' impressions of their own mobility still depended . . . insistently on the actual mobility and assembly of objects and bodies in the physical world. . . . A photograph could bring the Alps to the viewer without moving mountains, so to speak, but a museum display had to do just that to be true to its object."[11] Material travel displays required the movement of actual bodies and objects, while travel lectures and cinematic travel displays provided a very different experience of mobility. Not only does the spectator not move in the cinema, but the material on display has not moved, either; instead, what has moved is the apparatus (camera, film print, photographer). In each instance, the goal is to *move* the spectator emotionally and intellectually, but the effects of these different stagings are quite variable.

Another constitutive tension in the nineteenth-century visual culture of travel, which was later picked up by travel films, is the opposition between the "scientific" displays of World's Fairs and museums versus the more explicitly amusement-oriented pastimes of the fairground. This tension between education and entertainment also created a contrast between representations that emphasized the spectacular aspects of foreignness and representations that emphasized the realism and everyday life of the foreign. I am certainly not the first to point out this tension between the exotic and the everyday in travel displays, which has been analyzed by Barbara Stafford, Vanessa Schwartz, and others.[12] In an article about the "ethnographic" exhibitions of non-Western people by the German showman Carl Hagenbeck, Eric Ames argues that "the ethnographic exhibition inadvertently counteracted its very premise that exotic peoples are inherently spectacular.... Live display de-exoticized the other, rendering it familiar and comprehensible, without destroying the lure of the exotic."[13] What is significant here is the historical specificity of this tension in the late nineteenth century and how it changed in the early film period of the 1900s and 1910s. The cinema's addition of represented movement and spatial fragmentation to this tension created new forms of abstraction in this tradition of instructive entertainment. As we shall see, some travel films embody a detached "scientific" curiosity while others are more sensationalizing, but often the same film hits both registers. Travel films, like earlier forms of instructive entertainment, challenge the division between science and sensation.

What is striking about these various travel representations is how they tend to invoke a sense of wonder and awe. World's Fairs and illustrated magazines certainly could have emphasized other aspects, such as the economic and social conditions of the locales being documented, but nineteenth-century travel entertainments overwhelmingly favored the depiction of a particular kind of world: a world not in turmoil but filled with astonishing sights. Picking up on the distinction between tourists and immigrants that I began to develop in the introduction, we might say that travel imagery of the late nineteenth century constructs a tourist vision of the world at the expense of a migrant vision of the world, and in so doing offers a new image of the globe as an endless series of commodified landscapes.

Travel lectures, illustrated magazine articles, and stereographs make this tourist experience quite literal by narrating the travel route that was taken as locations are described and photographs are presented. Many stereographs, for example, contain text on the back of the card that describes the image

FIGURE 1.1 "The Second Pyramid (Khefren) — showing part of original covering — and desert, from Great Pyramid." Stereograph. Underwood and Underwood, 1902. Author's collection.

from a generic and omniscient but still ideologically grounded point of view. A classic image of Egyptian pyramids from a 1902 stereograph by Underwood and Underwood (fig. 1.1), for example, features a narration on the back that describes a travel route: "We have crossed over to the west bank of the Nile at Cairo and come some five miles [southwest] out into the edge of the vast Libyan desert. To get this broad view out over the sand-waves, drifting under the wind, we have slowly, toilsomely climbed up the gigantic slope of the Great Pyramid; now here we are on the summit." In this narrative, the viewer is invited to participate with the nameless traveler describing the journey (by using an ambiguous "we," the narrator implicitly includes the reader: "*We* have crossed . . ."), even though that speaking traveler is not pictured in the photograph that is arguably the point of the entire exercise.

We might push this analysis further, however, to point out an alternative significance for the image. Within the conventions of travel photography (and landscape painting), the two men in the lower left of the frame serve as anonymous lead-in figures. They appear to be tour guides, although the written narration on the back of the card does not mention them. It is possible for a viewer to identify not with the written narration of the traveler — with its air of entitlement and awe — but with the visual image of the tour guides, which captures the viewer's visual attention in a more ambivalent way. That is to say, while Caren Kaplan's point about the "individualized, often elite, circumstances" of travel representations certainly applies here — the primary address of this stereoscope card allies the viewer with the "elite circumstances" of the tourist—alternative possibilities exist for identification with the figures or even identification with the camera that has captured this landscape.[14] These alternative possibilities for identification are not available in the written text. It is important to acknowledge that *both* kinds of identification—with the elite tourist's point of view and with the anonymous "native" figures—are available in this photographic image.

Scholarship on Travel Representations

Travelogues traffic in difference, and postcolonial studies has provided powerful models for critiquing how the Western world has constructed its Others. The founding work in this scholarly tradition, Edward Said's *Orientalism*, was crucial for explaining how Western traditions of representation work to propagate stereotypes, reinscribe dominant power relations, and denigrate the "Orient" (all territories outside the Western world). Said uses a theatrical metaphor that proves apt for a discussion of travelogues: "The idea of representation is a theatrical one: the Orient is the stage on which the whole East is confined. On this stage will appear figures whose role it is to represent the larger whole from which they emanate. The Orient then seems to be, not an unlimited extension beyond the familiar European world, but rather a closed field, a theatrical stage affixed to Europe."[15] This is a good starting place for thinking about early travelogue films, for as much as they depict real images of real places, in many ways they tell us more about the filmmakers who made them—and the system of presumptions that enabled them—than they do about the places and people they represent. We might do well to think of travelogues as *theatricalizations* of the world, for that concept encourages us to focus on the travelogue's fictionalizing strategies. Following from this insight, a next step is to examine how various locations are theatricalized differently, as I will do in later chapters. But first I outline some of the ways recent scholarship has analyzed travel representations to clarify how my analysis fits into and departs from these scholarly traditions.

In the past two decades, literary studies has focused a great deal of productive attention on travel writing. Since the 1992 publication of Mary Louise Pratt's influential *Imperial Eyes*, scholars have been analyzing the specific ways travel literature has engaged with the imperial project of describing the world—a project that necessarily (although not always consciously) serves the interests of those doing the writing. To date, however, there has been very little analysis of travel in the discipline of cinema studies. Early travelogue films, as a form of nonfiction shown in commercial movie houses, functioned similarly to travel literature in that the films were an influential source of knowledge about the world for the mass audiences who saw them. As travel writing "*produced* 'the rest of the world' for European readerships," travel films produced the rest of the world for cinemagoers across the globe.[16] Travel films functioned differently from travel writing, however, in that they produced this knowledge in the public space of the movie theater (or in nontheatrical venues such as lecture halls, churches, and schools), and they produced this knowledge for both literate and illiterate people. They also reached audiences around the world rather than just Euro-American audiences. The public experience of watching travelogue films is quite different from the private experience of reading a travel narrative, and the demographics of these audiences are also different.

In doing the important work of identifying imperial ideologies in travel representations, scholarly writing has tended to overlook the important way in which these ideologies also contradict themselves, leaving openings for resistance. Fatimah Tobing Rony's groundbreaking 1996 book *The Third Eye*, for example, offers a powerful critique of popular ethnography in cinema, but it offers little analysis of the potentially subversive elements of this mode of representation. Rony writes that "within the context of imperialism and entrepreneurial prospecting, panoramic views condition viewers to see other lands precisely as places to be explored and inhabited by Europeans."[17] This analysis continues the direction forged by Said's *Orientalism*, pointing out the reductive binaries of imperial logic and arguing that the "knowledge" produced by these films is a form of dominating power. Rony does argue that ethnography in early cinema had a double-edged quality, for if "savage" racial others represented a threatening degenerative past that had to be kept at arm's length, they also represented a certain authentic purity, symbolizing humankind in a prelapsarian stage. "The Ethnographic was both biological threat and example of authentic humanity: both aspects would be essential to cinema's form of visualizing anthropology."[18] However, it is important to note that the quasi-scientific motion studies of the anthropologist Félix-Louis Regnault, made in the 1890s, are quite different from theatrical travelogues made by commercial film companies in the 1910s, which are yet again very different from the exploitation feature films made by Martin and Osa Johnson in the 1920s, all of which Rony discusses. In fact, travelogues were hardly the only films to represent exoticism at this time: In this era obsessed with difference, all kinds of films and other media were saturated with images of the seemingly bizarre, the colorful, and the foreign. Rony's analysis fixes all these films into a monolithic imperial system, giving the impression that what E. Ann Kaplan has similarly called "the imperial gaze" is the same in all films and the same for all locations depicted.[19] More precise attention to film history and the contradictions within the films themselves can help us unpack some of the specific uses to which these films were put, and can reveal some of the different kinds of imperial discourse — and resistances to imperial power — we can find in them. Indeed, I argue that it was the very diversity of travel representations that contributed to their effectiveness in carrying imperial ideologies, but at the same time, that diversity — different travel media, different kind of films, different exhibition spaces, different depictions of imperial ideology — is what may have enabled audiences to view the films in unintended and surprising ways.

Alison Griffiths's 2002 book *Wondrous Difference* also deals with ethnography and early cinema, but Griffiths spends more time examining the "ambivalence at the heart of visual representations of cultural Otherness."[20] She pays careful attention to questions of history and audience, arguing that "ethnographic authority itself needs to be understood historically" and that "the same ethnographic footage may have meant quite different things to different audiences."[21] Catherine Russell's approach to early ethnography lies perhaps closest to my own, for, as she argues in her 1999 book *Experimental Ethnography*, "seen from a postcolonial, postmodern perspective, [the ethnographic element of early cinema] can be read differently, as a return of the colonial repressed. . . . As a form of experimental ethnography, early cinema offers a model of textual 'openness' in which meaning is not closed down."[22] Indeed, thanks to the ground covered by Rony, Griffiths, and Russell, I have chosen not to focus this book on the tradition of popular ethnography found in early travelogues. Instead, I concentrate on questions of landscape, aesthetics, and educational discourse. Like Griffiths, I also find the return of the gaze in early cinema to be a significant moment of rupture and potential resistance. Unlike this tradition of scholarship, however, I address not only the representation of "faraway" colonial peoples and lands, but also the representation of "nearby" locales: the country and the city of the United States and Europe. How does the sense of documentary entitlement change when the subject matter is more familiar?

Christopher Pinney has discussed the critical tendency to impose reductive ideological readings on photographic images, and his argument is relevant to cinema studies. Following Carlo Ginzburg, he writes, "Much recent writing that seeks to historically contextualize photography's emergence during a period of colonial expansion has drawn on crucial insights from Edward Said and Michel Foucault and has tended to construct photographic imagery and practice as immovably within a 'truth' that simplistically reflects a set of cultural and political dispositions held by the makers of those images. . . . Such debates tend to invoke formal readings of images that are then made to do the work of a preexisting political hypothesis."[23] In other words, what has become for many today a reflexive critical move — to point out the power hierarchy in photographic and cinematic representations — too often becomes a mere inscription of the critic's own (contemporary) hypothesis rather than a nuanced analysis of power in a historically distant time. This observation does not invalidate the crucial political interventions made in the tradition of Said and Foucault but, rather, it demands that our analyses remain sensitive to the complexities of historical and geographical power dynamics.

Pinney's work exemplifies a different critical direction that focuses on the complexity of colonial discourses by recasting Orientalism not as a monolithic discourse but a complex and contradictory series of forces. One strain of antiessentialist critique today thus strives to oppose not only reductive views of race and culture, but also an essentialist view of Orientalism itself, which oversimplifies its power and thus deflates our ability to oppose it. Borrowing from a psychoanalytic framework, Homi Bhabha has written of the powerful "ambivalence" that structures colonial representations: "It is the force of ambivalence that gives the colonial stereotype its currency." For Bhabha, ambivalence is "that 'otherness' which is at once an object of desire and derision."[24] This notion of ambivalence is crucial to understanding the appeal early travelogues had in the early twentieth century. These films did not simply denigrate the otherness they depicted, and they certainly did not reject the power structure in favor of celebrating difference in a manner that today's sensibilities would find compelling. Instead, the films enact a delicate dance between desiring difference and fearing it. Any adequate analysis of travelogues must account for the complexities of this dynamic. Simply denouncing the films as bad objects (they are racist, they are colonialist) does not give us insight into what viewers found so compelling in the genre. As Bhabha and others have persuasively argued, colonial discourse functioned precisely through this ambivalence. Ali Behdad writes that "Orientalism . . . depends for its economy on a 'principle of discontinuity.' . . . Difference, ambivalence, and heterogeneity . . . are fundamental attributes of orientalist representations, and they allow the possibility of multiplicity and dispersion of statements."[25] Travelogues function precisely in this way: Early cinema multiplied statements about places all around the world and dispersed those statements in turn to places all around the world. I believe that travelogues are best understood through this diversity and ambiguity: Each little five-minute film builds its own system, foiling attempts to conflate the genre into a coherent expression of a single ideology.

The discipline of geography offers useful insights for an analysis of travel and film. While this book makes no claim to a geographical methodology, certain geographical approaches—such as thinking power spatially and grappling with the constant fluidity and mutability of space—are enormously useful when considering representations of travel. Geographers—or some of them, anyway—begin with the understanding that "there has always been spatial (or regional) inequality," as Doreen Massey puts it.[26] This is a crucial insight for travelogue films, which, when viewed through the lens of geography, can be seen as defining a spatial hierarchy through their accumulation of place-images. David Sibley's notion of "geographies of exclusion," for example, is useful for thinking about how "inside" and "outside" are constructed spatially. He explains how minorities and various Others are located "elsewhere," which "might be some spatial periphery, like the edge of the world or the edge of the city."[27] That is to say, what Said calls the logic of Orientalism—and what Sibley calls the logic of exclusion—functions not only through discourse but via spatial mapping. This means that stereotype and exclusion can function just as well nearby as far away. It also means that the very act of mapping, of defining a terrain, is an exercise in power.

Massey and other geographers argue that places should not be essentialized but understood as a fluid and porous construction. "They are not so much bounded areas as open and porous networks of social relations."[28] Travelogues, with their seemingly timeless presentation of unchanging places, with their display of people without names who stand as "typical" examples of local populations, certainly work hard to essentialize places. But all this work is only temporarily effective as new representations come in to overlay the old ones. "What is to be the dominant image of any place will be a matter of contestation and will change over time," Massey explains. Travel films were one of the most significant articulations of the meaning of place in the early twentieth century, but some elements of their mapping became outdated quickly, while other elements remained relevant for many decades. Territories changed hands—many colonial lands documented in early travel films became independent a few decades later—and yet much place iconography remained the same. For example, Japan was already defined by geishas and cherry blossoms in the early twentieth century, and a residue of that stereotype remains in imagery of Japan even today. (Of course, today we have irony, but that subject lies outside the scope of this project.) Travelogues attempt to assert an authenticity of place, to fix places in time and space. Geography, in contrast, argues that "there is, in that sense of a timeless truth of an area, built on somehow internally contained character traits, no authenticity of place."[29] Working with the dynamism of place and space changing over time, this insight from geography can be useful for film studies as it contends with questions of location shooting and cinematic space.

Looking, Seeing, and Telling: Holmes and the Illustrated Travel Lecture

"To travel is to possess the world." This was Burton Holmes's well-known motto; he regularly inscribed these words alongside his autograph over the course of his sixty-year career. Some critics have lately taken Holmes to task for this acquisitive, imperialistic motto, but such a sentiment is hardly surprising coming from a wealthy white American man at the peak of the colonial era. The turn of the twentieth century witnessed the culmination of European and U.S. imperialism, an era that Eric Hobsbawm has dubbed "The Age of Empire."[30] Holmes's motto sums up the comfortable privilege of a speaker whose home lies in the colonizing power centers of the world. What interests me more than Holmes's predictable ideological perspective is the influence his particular worldview had on shaping the attitudes of his many audiences, readers, and admirers, not all of whom shared his social privileges. Holmes's travel lectures were known for their popularity among upper-class and middle-class audiences. But surely not everyone in his audience was a wealthy white male, and his vision of travel certainly enabled some less wealthy, non-white, female, and perhaps immigrant audience members to envision themselves in positions of power.

Evidence of Holmes's audiences is hard to come by, however, and lacking that, we can only speculate about audience responses by analyzing his texts. Holmes's particular travel philosophy is well worth unraveling. Equally significant for this book is the influence Homes had on the commercial travelogue films that flourished in early cinema. The travel lecture tradition is the most direct model for travelogue films, which borrow heavily from its rhetoric and pictorial conventions. Yet as I have already suggested, travelogue films lack the strong authorial presence figures such as Holmes gave to their lectures, and this lack of a narrator is a cornerstone of my argument. In the absence of an embodied speaking subject, travelogue films, as shown in commercial nickelodeon theaters, enabled their audiences to envision themselves as the traveler. Thus, commercial travelogue films are a much more open-ended experience than travel lectures; moreover, this open-endedness created space for the rupturing of imperial ideologies, creating potential for resistance to hegemonic power structures. Finally, travelogue films shown in commercial movie houses were patronized by more diverse audiences than Holmes's lectures, and this broader demographic reach, I argue, also created more opportunity to read travel imagery against the grain.

Burton Holmes was born into a wealthy family in Chicago in 1870. His grandfather had become rich in the hotel business and had always loved to travel. Holmes writes in his autobiography with characteristic floridity, "The Gypsy spirit animated Stiles Burton, my grandfather."[31] Holmes's father, a banker, was a less romantic figure but still financially successful. By all accounts, Holmes's love of travel came from his maternal grandparents: His first trip abroad took place with his grandmother and mother when he was sixteen. He had been given a camera three years earlier and was an avid photography enthusiast in his teens, when he became an active member of the Chicago Camera Club. Holmes and his family were "faithful attendants" at the travel lectures of John L. Stoddard, and as a youth Holmes developed a desire to produce travel photography.[32] But even before he wanted to become a travel lecturer, he wanted to be a magician. Holmes was first inspired by Jean Eugène Robert-Houdin and Alexander Herrmann (Herrmann the Great), and his own practice in magic has been credited with giving him a "sense of stagecraft and the value of illusion."[33] This interest in magic puts Holmes in resonance with other early cinema pioneers such as Georges Méliès, and it is worth underscoring that even this figure invested in so-called nonfiction film practice had one foot in the realm of the fantastic. Although he did not perform magic tricks during his lectures, Holmes performed card tricks and sleight-of-hand tricks while traveling as a way to ingratiate himself in foreign lands.[34]

Unlike his peers, many of whom attended Yale, Holmes opted to skip college—or, rather, he convinced his family that travel was a fitting substitute for higher education. After a few trips abroad (twice to Europe, once to Mexico, and once to Japan) and a visit to the World's Columbian Exposition in 1893, Holmes decided to try his hand at travel lecturing. "The Fair had so intensified my love for things foreign, exotic, far-away and unfamiliar that

I resolved," he wrote, "to try to find a way to keep on going places, seeing things, indulging my *wanderlust*."[35] Holmes was fond of the term "wanderlust." The word is of German origin, a combination of *wandern* (to wander or to hike) and *lust* (desire).[36] So explicit a reference to lust might seem surprising for a figure such as Holmes, who personifies buttoned-up bourgeois respectability. Yet his use of the term indicates his affinity for poetic (or purple) turns of phrase. It hardly seems a stretch to interpret "wanderlust" as a term signaling the sublimation of sexual desire in Holmes's lectures, displacing libido into the genteel practice of world travel.

Significantly, Holmes's first public lecture series, on Japan, was a combination of his own lantern slides and text that was borrowed from other sources, as he freely admitted:

> I pilfered my material from right and left, from guide books, histories and notably from unfamiliar writings on Japan by Pierre Loti which, unlike *"Mme. Chrysantheme"* had not been translated and therefore not widely read in the English-speaking world. Enough of my own material was included to salve my conscience and confuse any critic who might check up on my translated plagiarisms. For sixty years I have vainly awaited a critical blast. Even though my text later appeared in print in the 15-volume edition of the Travelogues (of which 40,000 sets were sold), no critic and happily no publisher has thundered at me, "We know where you got that stuff!"[37]

Some of this admission is characteristic Holmesian false modesty (belied by the parenthetical bragging about his book sales), but nonetheless it is notable that the so-called inventor of travelogues was himself borrowing from other texts and traditions. Just as early cinema is an intermedia phenomenon, the illustrated travel lecture was derived from preexisting media. This intermedial borrowing may account for the particularly high level of stereotype and cliché one encounters in travel representations. Certainly, most, if not all, new media incorporate previous traditions, but I argue that travel representations are particularly beholden to them. The history of travel representations amply demonstrates the difficulty of shaking off clichés when one engages in the business of documenting places.

Holmes performed this first public travel lecture series, including "Japan — The Country" and "Japan — The Cities," before Chicago audiences in 1893. His charisma and well-bred manner made the lectures a success — as, no doubt, did the fact that many of the 2,000 invitations he sent went to names culled from his mother's visiting list. It is likely that the presence of his mother's social circle led Holmes to describe his first audience as "large, fashionable, and feminine."[38] At his first lecture, Holmes began a long collaboration with the projectionist Oscar Depue, who went on to shoot his moving pictures. After earning the large sum of $700 for these first two lectures in Chicago, Holmes began touring other Midwestern and Eastern cities and establishing his reputation as a travel lecturer. When Stoddard retired from the lecturing field in 1897, Holmes picked up much of his audience, and his career was secured. Holmes continued lecturing every season until the 1950s. According to one estimate, his "lecture dates filled in thirty-two successive seasons would number many thousand. The audiences would run far into the millions."[39]

Holmes eventually became involved with virtually every form of modern media. As already mentioned, during the 1897–98 lecture season, he added motion pictures to his presentations. At first, Holmes and Depue considered films "a fifteen- or twenty-minute added attraction" at the end of the lecture, and the films shown initially were unrelated to the lecture topics. Soon, however, films became a central feature incorporated within the lectures.[40] In addition to giving live presentations, he published his lectures in a multivolume book series and later produced travelogue films for Paramount and MGM. Holmes continued to use different forms of media throughout his career, including not only lantern slide lectures, stereographs, books, and motion pictures but also, eventually, radio and television. For all of his love of exotic and ancient cultures, Holmes was a thoroughly modern man who embraced emergent technology. In addition to being an early adopter of film, Holmes was well aware of the growing visual education movement and was eager to ally himself with its rhetoric. In his introduction to a volume accompanying a set of Keystone stereo views published in 1926, Holmes explains, "As one who for more than a third of a century has been engaged with purveying 'looks' and 'seeings' of foreign lands by foreign proxy, and in adding to those 'looks' and 'seeings' just enough of 'tellings' to round out their meanings, I am naturally an enthusiastic champion of visual education."[41] The common thread that runs through Holmes's presence in these different forms of media is precisely this looking, seeing, and telling.

In the 1910s, Holmes expanded his use of motion pictures beyond the lecture hall and into the mainstream movie theater. Beginning in 1916, he produced Burton Holmes Travelogues, a successful film series released by Paramount Pictures. While most of the films are not currently available for study, several posters have been collected by the Academy of Motion Picture Arts and Sciences' Margaret Herrick Library, two of which are reproduced in this volume (plates 2–3). Both films were released in 1917, and both posters feature Holmes's recognizable profile, which was a trademark of sorts for him. The poster for *Colorful Ceylon* depicts three women harvesting tea, providing a point of identification for tea-drinking Europeans and North Americans who might otherwise not know much about the region. The poster for *Norway*, in contrast, does not hint at any "ethnographic" subject matter; instead, it highlights scenic beauty, featuring an inset image of a Norwegian fjord at the bottom right of the image. In both cases, the posters play up well-known aspects of the regions depicted, promising a familiar vision and yet hinting that more will come in the film. Holmes's series apparently was quite successful. The motion picture trade press quoted an exhibitor in charge of the Garfield Theater in Chicago (in a "middle class neighborhood," we are told), who wrote about Holmes's films in 1917: "Good program bracers are these single-reel scenics. We have patrons who come to see them alone."[42]

For many years, Holmes's films were thought to be lost, but in 2004 almost five hundred reels were discovered in storage in Pasadena, California. The films were donated to the George Eastman House, which is currently undertaking their preservation.[43] In the meantime, Holmes's published lectures, which reveal a wealth of information about his lecture style and his philosophy of travel, are readily available. These lectures were first published as a ten-volume set in 1901, and they were expanded and republished several times in later editions. Hugely popular, Holmes's published lectures can be found in most public and university libraries today (and as a public domain publication, the complete set is also available for downloading from the Internet Archive).[44] Holmes's work spans the public/private divide: His spoken lectures were delivered in public, but his published *Lectures* were consumed privately by individual readers.

While pre-cinema travel lectures are important precursors to the scenic film, they also stand *parallel* to the travelogue's history in commercial motion picture theaters. That is to say, Holmes may have been one of the first lecturers to use motion pictures in 1897, but from that point on, travel lectures and travel films in theaters followed a separate, if overlapping, course of history. At least at first, films were not the primary focus or draw for Holmes's audiences. This basically sums up film's status in the 1890s, when it functioned as a novelty or an added attraction wherever it appeared, whether in vaudeville theaters, at music halls, or at fairgrounds. By about 1908, how-

FIGURE 1.2 Flyer advertising Burton Holmes's 1908–1909 lecture season.
Courtesy Burton Holmes Archive.

ever, when the cinema was finding its footing as an institution separate from
these other entertainments, the travelogue came into its own as an important film genre and a mainstay of the educational film movement. At this
time, Holmes continued to use films in his lectures as he had for over a decade, as one of many important components of his multimedia presentations. A flyer advertising Holmes's 1908–1909 lecture season (fig. 1.2), for
example, appeared just as the campaign to promote travel and educational
films as a commercially viable and culturally respectable component of nickelodeon shows was gathering steam in the motion picture trade press. By

this time, lectures and nickelodeon theaters were following separate trajectories, but the same films could be shown in each kind of venue.

Holmes's important role as a producer and promoter of travel films in the silent era—indeed, as the figure who personified the travelogue experience—has only just begun to receive attention from film historians. It is likely that the dearth of prior scholarly interest is due to the lack of availability of his films, but I suspect that it is also due to his role as a figure operating largely in the nontheatrical realm of the lecture circuit (at least before his contract with Paramount began in 1916), which historically has received less attention than theatrical cinema. Charles Musser's groundbreaking book on Lyman Howe was an important step in understanding the significance of live lectures for early cinema history.[45] In the past decade, there have been several new analyses of turn-of-the-century lecturers. Kaveh Askari has analyzed the "detective lectures" of Alexander Black, arguing that Black's lectures, which combined still and moving images, involved pictorial "traditions of genre painting and the tableau."[46] Giuliana Bruno has analyzed the work of Esther Lyons, a rare female travel lecturer in the "fraternity" of male lecturers, focusing her analysis on the unique way Lyons represented herself to her audience: "as an explorer who sits still, in front of a mirror."[47]

Holmes himself has been the subject of two relatively recent scholarly analyses. Rick Altman has discussed Holmes's public lecture debut, "Through Europe with a Kodak," which he delivered in 1890 at the Chicago Camera Club and which was later published as "Through Europe with a Camera" in the seventh volume of *Lectures*. Altman's detailed analysis focuses on the interplay between image and narration in Holmes's lecture. He concludes, "What should matter in a travelogue, it would seem, is whether or not an image corresponds to reality. Yet what actually matters here is whether or not an image fits into a recognizable narrative—and narrational—pattern."[48] Rather than focusing on one lecture, Jeanette Roan more broadly analyzes Holmes's lectures on Japan and other Asian locations. Like Altman, Roan works to unpack the familiar tension between realism and fantasy in travel representations. In analyzing Holmes's Japan lecture, with its stereotypical focus on the geisha girl, Roan argues that because "Japan . . . has been imagined through the centuries by generations of travelers" as an exotic fantasyland typified by the image of the geisha, Holmes's lecture could use that myth as a supplement to his "realistic" images. Not only can "the verisimilitude of cinema . . . be used toward fantastic ends, but also . . . the belief in the reality of film lends to film the very capacity to shape the 'real' itself."[49] In other words, Holmes's lectures, like the travel films that were modeled after them and that soon began to accompany them, create a kind of feedback loop in which the fantasy informs the real, which in turn naturalizes the myth, which is built of both parts.

Holmes's travel lectures, in both live and published forms, remained popular for decades—even as late as the 1950s (he did not retire until 1952 and died six years later). After Holmes's retirement, other lecturers continued in his footsteps, and the tradition continues even today, as Jeffrey Ruoff has shown.[50] As the self-anointed "father" of the travelogue, Holmes is well positioned to speak for the larger meaning of represented travel. It is no exaggeration to say that Holmes defined the practice of travelogues for the early twentieth century. In his autobiography, which opens with an invocation of his motto, "To travel is to possess the world," Holmes argues that the metaphorical "possession" enabled by travel is not a material ownership but one of images and memories. "There is no implication of selfishness in the kind of possession of which I speak. Whoever possesses the world through travel takes naught from any man. . . . The wealth is there for all to share." Rather than gaining materially, the traveler becomes "rich in vivid mental pictures of places worth going to, of people worth knowing, of things that are world-famous," he explains. Most important, if one documents this travel in pictures, words, and film, as Holmes did, "You may invite all men and women to travel with you in imagination."[51] Although he tried to deny it, Holmes's words frequently reveal a desire for ownership; in case one has doubts, he titled his autobiography, published in 1951, *The World Is Mine*. This is a reference to Alexandre Dumas's *The Count of Monte Cristo* (1844), whose hero Dantes utters the words when he escapes from fourteen years of wrongful imprisonment. As Holmes clearly understood, the words also serve as an apt expression of his era's worldview.

What we might call Holmes's philosophy of travel, as expressed here and throughout his lectures, epitomizes a particular set of Western liberal-humanist beliefs current at the beginning of the twentieth century: that experience is valuable in itself; that striving for experience is to be commended; and that unabashed material accumulation can be crass. This last point runs counter to Thorstein Veblen's idea of "conspicuous consumption" and allies Holmes's philosophy instead with the antimodernism of Henry David Thoreau, John Ruskin, and the Arts and Crafts Movement.[52] Holmes believed his travelogues made travel democratically available to all and claimed that he kept in mind "the average man and woman" in his lectures, talking neither up nor down to his audiences.[53] And yet Holmes's antimodern tendencies were manifested not in any articulation of a counter-ideology but simply in the guise of an appreciation for the "exotic," which could take the form of anything different. Holmes was no philosopher, as he was the first to admit. He was, rather, a seeker of experiences, and more than anything, he was a popularizer.

In his day, Holmes's travel philosophy was considered progressive; he appeared to be someone who respected difference and who sought to convey "the fundamental humanities . . . common to mankind in every land."[54] Yet to readers today, his rhetoric is most notable for its imperialist ideology. Roan emphasizes, "In these turn-of-the-century lectures, [Holmes] offered his audiences a leisurely reflection on the rationale for imperial expansion, the benefits of territorial possession, and the pleasures of colonial power."[55] While this statement is certainly correct, I argue, in addition, that our understanding of Holmes's travel philosophy must be placed within its context. He was not unusual in this outlook; rather, Holmes was articulating a mainstream idea of the age. Moreover, rather than casting imperial discourse as a monolith, I argue for the importance of locating moments where this imperial ideology ruptures.

Holmes in "Moki Land"

Holmes's voluminous lecture output merits close attention. Although he traveled to and lectured about dozens of locations around the world, I focus here on the lecture titled "Moki Land," which provides a good example of his treatment of one part of the United States as a space of internal empire. Holmes first presented "Moki Land" during the 1899–1900 lecture season, and it was one of his earliest presentations to incorporate motion pictures. In the lecture, Holmes describes the landscape of northeastern Arizona, which had already been designated the Hopi Indian Reservation in 1898–99 when he took the two trips on which his narrative was based. Like most travelogues, Holmes's narrative provides a potpourri of historical trivia, descriptions, and experiences set in what he describes as a distant and unchanging land. And like most travelogues, real-life experience is brought into accord with myth and stereotype. One idea in particular — the opposition between primitive culture and modernity — serves as a conceptual motor driving Holmes's narrative. However, this primitive/modern opposition, so important to travel representations of all sorts, does not simply involve a dismissal of the primitive by the modern. Instead, Holmes's attempt to draw a line between the primitive and the modern ends up contradicting itself. "Moki Land" is not unique—we can locate moments of contradiction and ambivalence in all of Holmes's lectures—but I choose it for its emphasis on difference within the U.S. context.

In his opening sentence, Holmes claims: "Moki Land in Arizona is the home of the strangest of our fellow-countrymen. Moki Land is unique; it is a changeless corner in our land of perpetual change."[56] Holmes's first move is to place the Hopi outside of history and outside of modernity. He equates them with the timeless antiquity of the landscape, a land now appropriated by the forces of U.S. imperialism: "*our* land." Holmes never speaks in the first person, preferring instead the royal "we." He continues: "Moki Land offers us a fascinating picture of primitive America—a picture that will soon fade in the growing light of our civilization. Let us draw aside the protecting curtain of distance and look upon this unique picture before it is too late."[57] Civilization is here rendered an unstoppable territorializing force, echoing the nineteenth-century notion of Manifest Destiny. Employing the teleological concept of "progress" that so dominated the era, Holmes uses the popular trope of the "vanishing Indian" to render his subject outmoded and nostalgic.[58]

Clearly, the opening of the lecture indicates that the Hopi are about to be fixed in a rigid classification system defined by a familiar set of hierarchies: primitive/modern, savage/civilized, fragile/robust, and so forth. Indeed, Holmes's narrative proceeds to disavow Hopi culture as backward or even meaningless—for example, he describes Hopi religious ceremonies as "various rites, the meaning of which is now almost forgotten," filled with "the meaningless songs of the ancients."[59] Yet these disavowals are contradictory, for if the Hopi and their culture are meaningless, why have he and his traveling party visited them, and why should the lecture audience or reader be compelled to learn about them? One partial answer is given about halfway through the lecture, when Holmes begins to describe the Snake Dance that he and his party have come to witness. This is a multi-day ceremony in which tribal members pray for rain, to which Holmes devotes more than thirty pages of text and photographs, although in these pages—and, indeed, throughout the lecture—he maintains a tone of breezy generalization. He begins by calling the rituals "long and tedious," explaining that while some American ethnologists have studied them, "the minute details recorded by the scientists do not interest the casual visitor, intent on the broad picturesqueness of the public ceremony."[60] This statement is significant, for it divulges one of the travelogue's primary representational styles: the picturesque. With this claim, Holmes admits that his interest is general rather than scientific and associates his lecture not with education but with entertainment. Hopi culture might appear "meaningless" to Holmes, but it is entertaining.

Holmes builds up the "entertaining" aspect of Hopi life by stressing difference at every turn. Through the counterpoint between his imagery and his rhetoric, he is able to present images that seem exotic and different but in such a way that this difference is rendered unthreatening, as in a photograph of young girls—their hair made up in the distinctive Hopi squash blossom whorls that indicate their unmarried status—captioned with the words "Hopi Hopefuls" (fig. 1.3). And although he makes many dismissive statements about Hopi spirituality, such as those quoted earlier, at several points Holmes manages to flip that dismissal around by rendering the Hopi fascinating and mysterious, as when he states, "It is an incontrovertible fact that Hopi prayers are usually far more efficacious in bringing rains than are the prayers of the average country clergymen."[61] After the conclusion of the Snake Dance, Holmes describes a "downpour [that] fell only upon the Moki mesas and upon the Moki fields. We were then several miles away, en route to the railway; no rain fell where we stood, halting in silent wonder at the spectacle."[62] Of course, these gestures of dismissal and wonder are just the opposing poles of the same imperial ideology, variations on the familiar "noble savage" ideal. With its alternation between aversion and awe, "Moki Land" anticipates the ambivalent attitude that continued to characterize the travel film genre of the 1900s and 1910s. In fact, ambivalence was the predominant disposition of travel representations at that time.

In addition to ambivalence, travelogues in their multiplicity fostered a visual culture of repetition. Holmes's lecture was but one of many representations of this particular location. After the mid-nineteenth century, the Hopi were represented not only in travel lectures but also in engravings, magazine stories, photographs, and, ultimately, motion pictures. (Holmes and Depue claimed to be the first to shoot motion pictures of the Hopi Snake Dance at Oraibi, as well as of the Grand Canyon.) Other photographers, including John K. Hillers, Edward S. Curtis, and Kate Cory, also photographed the Hopi in this era. Holmes's own lecture gestures toward this repetition with an image of photographers at the Snake Dance with a

HOPI HOPEFULS

FIGURE 1.3 "Hopi Hopefuls," Burton Holmes, "Moki Land," *Burton Holmes Travelogues*, vol. 6 (New York: McClure, 1908), 263.

caption reading, "The Photographic Battery" (fig. 1.4). Each of these many forms of representation had different purposes. Explorers' accounts territorialized the "new" land for the powers-that-were in the East; scientific accounts strove to fit the region into a geological and cultural logic; photographers monumentalized the land's sublime natural splendors; and travel accounts promoted the region for tourism. Yet despite their various uses, these different forms also shared many characteristics, such as a focus on singular oddities that created an image of the American West as a parade of natural wonders. Of interest is the *piling up* of these accounts, the compulsion to repeat and reproduce images of this place and these people in

THE PHOTOGRAPHIC BATTERY

FIGURE 1.4 "The Photographic Battery," Burton Holmes, "Moki Land," *Burton Holmes Travelogues*, vol. 6 (New York: McClure, 1908), 298.

every possible medium. This form of repetition compulsion was perhaps an unconscious effort to master cultural difference, but it is hardly a stretch to speculate that these mechanically reproduced images might also have functioned as an attempt to repress some of the guilt of nation building.

Alongside these speculations, one is left to wonder how the images were perceived by their original viewers and readers. Were the stereotypes perceptible as stereotypes? Did the repetition ever come to seem clichéd? Although we lack readers' and spectators' accounts of Holmes's lectures, it is clear that by including "The Photographic Battery," Holmes himself was pointing out the phenomenon of repetition. Indeed, Holmes's lectures are quite self-conscious in their theatricality. He regularly makes rhetorical gestures toward the constructed nature of his presentations, using theatrical metaphors such as, "Let us draw aside the protecting curtain of distance" (as quoted earlier), which give the impression that one is listening to (or reading) a staged fiction, even though the lecture's content—and especially its photographic slides—simultaneously assert its status as nonfiction.[63]

The Hopi were not the only ones subjected to these multiple representations, of course. At the turn of the twentieth century, the entire American West was the focus of a great deal of interest. Certain specific locations came to stand for the West as a whole: a handful of national parks and Indian reservations served to construct a generic image of the West as a land of natural wonders and supposedly fading tribal cultures.[64] I return to the subject of travel images of the West in the final chapter of this book, but for now, Holmes's rhetoric is important as an ideological model. Pinney has posed the question, "How do local visual traditions mediate modernity in ways that are independent from and critical of European modernity?"[65] For the Hopi, who banned photography of their villages and religious ceremonies beginning in 1915, the answer became a refusal of representation.[66] The Hopi prohibition of photography is a direct rebuttal of modern Western visualizing technologies. But for Holmes and his audiences, these modern technologies of vision were precisely the focus of interest. In fact, a crucial part of the travelogue's rhetoric, and an element that is often overlooked in discussions of the travelogue's imperial project, is the turning of the camera on the ways of the Western world—or, in the case of Holmes, the turning of the camera on himself and his fellow travelers.

While much of the "Moki Land" lecture is devoted to describing Hopi customs, then, Holmes also pays a great deal of attention to his own traveling party's experiences. Using a breezy humor and a casual, relatable tone, Holmes describes their itinerary and meals. He informs his audience that their food came in tin cans, which were known as "air-tights," wryly explaining in the present tense (which creates a sense that the listener/reader is experiencing the trip with him), "We breakfast, dine, and sup on air-tights, and before every meal all hands are set to work with old knives and scissors, for the rare can-opener is usually missing. . . . A heap of empty tins marks every halting-place of every caravan."[67] A panoramic photo depicts the traveling party "en route to Moki Land" (fig. 1.5), displaying their horses and buggies in a line framed against what appears to be a desolate landscape.

These images of Holmes's traveling party function to clinch the fact that

Photograph by H. C. Vroman, Pasadena   EN ROUTE TO MOKI LAND

FIGURE 1.5 "En Route to Moki Land," Burton Holmes, "Moki Land," *Burton Holmes Travelogues*, vol. 6 (New York: McClure, 1908), 231.

Holmes actually took the trip; that he and his fellow travelers were *really there*. Holmes is clearly visible in many of the images, although the captions in his published lecture do not point him out. For example, in the image captioned "'We Ourselves' at Volz's Store" (fig. 1.6), Holmes can be seen second from the left, wearing a hat and tie. These images also function as a point of identification for Holmes's audience. Significantly, there are several women in Holmes's traveling party, and while they are infrequently mentioned, their presence would seem to indicate that travel to this part of the West is now modern and convenient enough even for ladies. Showcasing female travelers to assert the convenience of modern tourism was a common travelogue strategy in the 1910s. Moreover, the inclusion of women here is a gesture toward the many women in Holmes's audience of lecturegoers and readers, who are thereby directly invited to participate as vicarious travelers in the theater.

In keeping with the common practice of using travel experiences as a way to describe the self, Holmes obliquely expresses the emotions he felt during his journey. Near the beginning of the lecture he describes "the sense of freedom, the exhilaration of this boundless region," explaining in his characteristically loquacious manner that "it has been said that it is impossible to despair on horseback. This is more than ever true in Arizona, where the air, the light, the clear, sharp distances, and the level, limitless desert form an environment that uplifts the senses and makes for perfect happiness."[68] He concludes his lecture by exclaiming, "If you would know one of the most wholesome joys of life, go buy a saddle and a bridle, a bronco, and a blanket, and forgetting all the petty things of life ride away into this Sahara of our glorious southwest, and there find the true meaning of such words as

Photograph by H. C. Vroman, Pasadena

"WE OURSELVES" AT VOLZ'S STORE

FIGURE 1.6 "'We Ourselves' at Volz's Store," Burton Holmes, "Moki Land," *Burton Holmes Travelogues*, vol. 6 (New York: McClure, 1908), 240. Holmes is reclining second from the left.

space — exhilaration — freedom!"[69] Here Holmes's tourism has a therapeutic, even antimodern function, cleansing the woes and anxieties of modern urban life: The American West has become a playground for middle-class tourists.

Holmes's travelogues work to distinguish the "old" world from the "modern" world, as we have seen. Holmes was fond of staging moments of contact between these two categories, with the effect of emphasizing the boundary between them. Toward the end of "Moki Land," for example, Holmes and his party have returned to Arizona one year later, this time to the Navajo Reservation, and he shows the Navajo a motion-picture show. Switching to ostentatious third-person narration, Holmes describes the encounter:

> The Indians beheld a miracle. The same white men come again, one year later, bringing strange instruments and a big white sheet. . . . Then, after night has fallen, half a thousand red men, crouching in the sand, behold upon that white surface huge pictures in which men seem to live and move. They view the moving multitudes in the streets of far-off cities; they *see* the railway trains that they have merely heard about; they see themselves performing deeds which they know were performed twelve

months before. But what astounds them most is the appearance in life upon that screen of tribesmen who have died during the intervening year, or others whom they know are far away. As each familiar figure passes, the dumbfounded spectators start to utter cries of consternation, then clap their hands over their mouths and try to smother the incipient yells, so that the ghosts shall not become frightened and disappear. Strange to relate, no curiosity at all is excited by the projecting instrument, but the canvas screen is minutely examined by the nonplused Navajos who finger it and rub their cheeks against it, as if to detect some sign of life or of sorcery in the white fabric.[70]

With this encounter, the "primitive" Navajo are suddenly brought into contact with modern technology. Of course, Holmes's description cannot be verified, and he is most likely adjusting the facts to suit his point. In narrating this encounter, Holmes underscores the essentialized difference constitutive of the primitive/modern binary that structures his lecture. In fact, such scenes of encounter became a trope of travelogues, documentaries, and adventure films. A similar moment appears in the film *Among the Cannibal Isles of the South Pacific* (1918), for example, when Martin and Osa Johnson show films to the "savage cannibals" they encounter. More famously, this type of scene was restaged in *Nanook of the North* (Robert Flaherty, 1922), when Nanook encounters a phonograph and bites the record, performing his (fabricated) "confusion" about modern technology. In these examples, what is presented as the height of novelty is actually already a travelogue convention.

Some moments of Holmes's lecture veer away from his careful essentializing of this geographical space as premodern, when he places it within the dime novel (and soon-to-be film genre) myth of the western. The published version of "Moki Land" reproduces a few filmstrips from the motion pictures he showed in the live version of this lecture. One of them features "Rattlesnake Jack," a female cowboy the traveling party met along the way, in a staged chase scene with several Navajo Indians (fig. 1.7).[71] In quintessential travelogue fashion, geography is transubstantiated into spectacle. Also, as we see, Holmes's travel lectures revel in the anecdotal. A little information is given, but never with much depth, so that the lecture skims from incident to incident in an attempt to amuse and distract the audience. Anecdotalism is a particular characteristic of such turn-of-the-century forms of instructive entertainment.

RATTLESNAKE JACK PURSUED BY A BAND OF NAVAJOS

FIGURE 1.7
"Rattlesnake Jack Pursued by a Band of Navajos," Burton Holmes, "Moki Land," *Burton Holmes Travelogues*, vol. 6 (New York: McClure, 1908), 327.

Ultimately, Holmes contradicts himself by trying to have it both ways. "Moki Land" is a pristine and changeless landscape, yet the land is peopled with tourists who take pictures and bring back stories about their visits there. Holmes's travel narrative propagates familiar stereotypes about the "primitive" and "unchanging" Indians, but he also shows how much they are a part of modern visual culture, even turning them into film spectators. His travel lecture simultaneously propagates and undermines familiar stereotypes, both making and undoing the myth of the frontier by constructing the American West as a tourist playground. Despite the rigid opposition between the "primitive" and the "civilized" at work here, modernity repeatedly intrudes on the world of the primitive. Holmes established an enduring travelogue tradition of ambivalence and contradiction.

From Lecture to Cinema

Holmes's travel philosophy—a liberal-humanist tolerance of difference that relies on stereotypes and propagates imperial ideologies—was a defining influence for scenic films of the 1910s and beyond. Holmes's stated ideal of "making all mankind acquainted" can be seen as the Progressive Era's version of cosmopolitanism.[72] It is my contention that this ideal was absorbed by travelogues in a variety of media and that it took new forms when translated into film. Illustrated lectures were not only some of the first exhibition contexts for scenic films; they also embody some of the same formal elements as the films. Both the lectures and the films are multimedia experiences, involving images (either still lantern slides or moving film images), text (either spoken or presented in intertitles), and sound (a live lecture or live music). And, of course, the content of both is the same: views of places described and visualized for a (usually) foreign audience. These images draw from previously existing formulas about the places they aim to document, and at the same time they contribute to the always ongoing reformulation of perceptions about different locations and cultures. In other words, both the lectures and the films take place in a complex and fluid intermedial culture of travel images. Despite these important similarities, certain key elements of the films are fundamentally different from the lectures, in particular the narrator function and the graphic effect of represented movement. There are also important differences in their industrial basis. Illustrated lectures were largely created by and identified with individual lecturers, whereas travelogue films found a place within a larger and more highly capitalized film industry.

The term "travelogue," adopted from the lecture circuit, was very much in circulation during the early cinema era. So, however, were a variety of other terms. Before the rise of the feature film in the mid-1910s, motion pictures were saturated with the effusive and unstable terminology that characterizes any new technology. Other terms used in the American trade press to designate travel films included "scenic," "nature study," "panorama," "travel picture," "travel subject," "natural scenic film," and even "stereopticon pictures illustrated." In fact, the beginning of the twentieth century saw an explosion of new words spawned by the film industry. Projectors were called phantoscopes, polyscopes, magnascopes, and mutoscopes; projection was referred to as images "thrown upon the screen"; filmmaking was called motography. Many of these terms faded away within a decade or two, but the word "travelogue" remained. In the nickelodeon era, the most common generic name for travel films was "scenic," which emphasizes the intensely visual nature of the genre as well as its pleasing, entertaining function as scenery. While the term "scenic" is more precisely attuned to this historical moment, I favor "travelogue" because it is historically accurate and persists in our vocabulary to this day—as, indeed, the travelogue genre persists—whereas an archaic term such as "scenic" no longer carries the generic meaning it once did. In short, "travelogue" resonates in a way that "scenic" does not. In this book, I use "travelogue" and "scenic" interchangeably, alternating between contemporary resonance and historical resonance.

I define travelogue films as nonfiction motion pictures that represent *place* as their primary subject. The place can be anywhere and of any size—from a continent to a neighborhood—but place is the dominant element. After our consideration of Holmes's imperial rhetoric, we might amend the dictionary definition of travelogues—an illustrated lecture about places and experiences encountered in the course of travel—to state that they are images of local places and people made by outsiders. Yet although travelogues are typically thought of as presenting "foreign" views—that is, views of a place far distant from the audience—in fact, many travelogues also display places nearby. A nickelodeon audience sitting in a theater in Chicago, for example, might just as likely have viewed a film about Chicago as a film about Stockholm or Egypt. Travel is always relative; therefore, I prefer to stress the concept of *place* as central to the genre rather than distance. The word "place" generally refers to a particular location fixed somewhere on the Earth's surface. But as geographers tell us, "Place is also a way of seeing, knowing and understanding the world."[73] This is what distinguishes place from space, which is a more abstract concept involving volume and area: "Place stands for both an object (a thing that geographers and others look at, research and write about) and a way of looking."[74] This dual nature of place is a key part of travelogues, which both document a real location and present an idea about that location: Travel films show a place and a way of looking at that place. This is very much in keeping with the dynamic of landscape, another dual concept that involves both a prospect and an idea of that prospect. As Malcolm Andrews puts it, "Landscape, which has long meant either the real countryside or the pictured representation of it, is in effect the combination of the two, or the dissolving of the two together."[75] An alternative, if more obscure, term for these films might be "landscape films."

Movement is the second concept central to my definition of travelogue films, and movement is a key element that sets the films apart from the lectures. All motion pictures are filled with some sort of graphic motion, of course, but travel films take this movement as their very subject. Most travelogues are filled with motion in every shot, such as a camera pan or a "tracking shot" in which a camera moves through space on a moving vehicle, or with image movement, such as a crowd of moving people or a shot of crashing waves. In addition, travel films turn motion into a metaphor by showing scenes of "faraway" places without requiring the journey that would be necessary to go there. It is perhaps somewhat contradictory that films featuring images of places—films that do not actually journey—are known as travel films. The travelogue's "window-on-a-world" model tends to omit journeys in favor of displaying places; thus, the root word "travel" signifies not voyaging but experience itself.

To conclude this chapter, I turn to a cinematic example that provides a more concrete illustration of the travel film's particular articulation of place through movement. I have chosen this example—*Hawaii, the Paradise of the Pacific*—because it was also produced by a traveling lecturer, Lyman Howe. This film was shown in different kinds of venues: both nontheatrical (as part of Howe's illustrated lectures) and theatrical (as part of the variety film shows of the 1910s). And like Holmes's "Moki Land," *Hawaii* illustrates the travelogue's tendency to focus on regions of internal empire. *Hawaii, the Paradise of the Pacific*, produced by Howe in 1916, names the place documented in its title, as many travelogues do.[76] In addition, the title immediately indicates what version of Hawaii the film will present: a paradise, which by implication exists outside of time and history. Hawaii was a U.S. territory when the film was made, but none of the island's political or social history is presented in this film. Travelogues have an inconsistent relationship with time in that they seem to locate places outside time, yet they also contain temporal markers of modernity such as railroads.

The film begins with an intertitle announcing "A Ride over the Hilo Railway" (fig. 1.8), followed by an extreme long shot, tinted orange, of a train on a trestle bridge crossing a gorge. Movement is thus signified in the first shot with the image of the train, one of the most commonly shown vehicles in early travelogues. As the train crosses the bridge, an automobile enters the frame and crosses the gorge on the same bridge: a modern conveyance literally following in the tracks of an older means of transportation. The technology locates this vision of Hawaii squarely within the contemporary world—a world filled with bridges and trains and automobiles—but rather

FIGURE 1.8 "A Ride over the Hilo Railway," *Hawaii, the Paradise of the Pacific*
(Lyman Howe, 1916). Courtesy EYE Film Institute Netherlands.

than revealing any social or cultural history, technology here simply facili-
tates the visual penetration of a timeless paradise, a world filled with lush
plant life and beautiful gorges.

The nine shots that follow, all tinted orange or green, continue the trip-
along-the-railway theme. In the film's second shot, taken from the front of
the train, we see tracks curving in front of us and watch the screen darken as
we enter a tunnel. Just as quickly, we emerge from darkness, and once again
tracks stretch in front of us as we experience the kinetic feeling of moving
through space, following the cinematic tradition of the phantom ride. The
third shot also emphasizes movement, but the shot has been taken from the
side of the train, so we see a panorama of Hawaiian foliage as the train moves
through space. A couple of high-angle shots display trees and rivers as the
train traverses a series of gorges; another couple of shots show the seashore
with waves lapping at beaches as the train passes by. In one extreme high-
angle shot, we see several men perched precariously on wooden planks jutting off the side of the railway bridge.

Even in these first several shots, notable patterns emerge. Every shot is
filled with movement of some kind—either generated by the train, which
creates a kind of tracking shot, or by something in the image, such as waves

and water. Yet despite these kinetic effects, no spatial connections are made between shots. Rather than stressing movement through a coherent space by means of continuity editing, a practice that was well established in fiction filmmaking by this time, *Hawaii* shows a series of landscape views without making spatial connections between shots. For example, while shot eight moves from right to left along the seashore, shot nine moves from left to right through the same terrain. While the shots do cohere around a unified theme — a ride on the Hilo Railway — their organization resembles a *collection* rather than a single cumulative unit. The effect is rather like viewing a series of postcards or snapshots in a photo album.

This particular print of the film (which is approximately nine minutes long and apparently is incomplete) contains four "segments."[77] After the first segment focusing on the railroad, several shots show natives fishing in the ocean. The third segment features a series of portraits of "Hawaiian types," according to the intertitles: people filmed according to the conventions of popular ethnography at the time (figs. 1.9–1.11). An intertitle announces we are about to see a "107-year-old native"; it is followed by an image of an old man smoking a pipe who looks decidedly younger than 107 (figs. 1.12–1.13). The "freakishly aged native" was a common trope of early travelogue films, although one suspects that the ages given in these instances are fabricated. Finally, the film concludes with several striking images of men surfing, taken from a camera mounted on a canoe bobbing in the waves near them. These clusters of shots constitute something similar to what we call segments in narrative film, yet *Hawaii* is decidedly non-narrative. Instead, each cluster of shots (or segment) sits alongside the other clusters of shots, with equal importance but without narrative progression. A shared geographical locale unites all of the shots and segments, but there is no progression of any sort, no movement closer in or farther away from things, no narrative development, no discernible geographical route. Also, no narrator figure is depicted within the film, and the intertitles provide scant information. Unlike a lecture by Holmes, which might follow a tour structure, the disjointed anecdotalism of individual shots in *Hawaii* (the film) renders Hawaii (the place) a decidedly fragmented paradise.

By focusing on the Hilo Railway, the film presents a settler's view of the area rather than a native's view of the area. In fact, *Hawaii, the Paradise of the Pacific*, like many early travelogues, was sponsored partly by a transportation company, the Great Northern Steamship Company.[78] In 1916, the Hilo Railway was famous for being the most expensive railroad in the world. The line

FIGURES 1.9–1.11
"Hawaiian
Types," *Hawaii,
the Paradise
of the Pacific*
(Lyman
Howe, 1916).
Courtesy EYE
Film Institute
Netherlands.

FIGURES 1.12–1.13 "A 107-Year-Old Native," *Hawaii, the Paradise of the Pacific* (Lyman Howe, 1916). Courtesy EYE Film Institute Netherlands.

had first been built to service the sugar mills of the agricultural industrialists of the region, but it quickly became a route for tourists visiting the Kilauea volcano. When a new line called the Hamakua Division was built between 1909 and 1913, many trestles and tunnels had to be constructed to traverse the dramatic terrain—thus, the railroad's enormous expense and its visual drama. These expenses bankrupted the Hilo Railway, which was reorganized as the Hawaii Consolidated Railway in 1916, the year the film was made. According to one description, "Targeting tourists in addition to cane transport, the Hawai'i Consolidated Railway ran sight seeing specials under the name 'Scenic Express.' Passengers were treated to spectacular views of the rugged Hamakua Coast. . . . Not for the faint of heart, these trips included a stop on the tallest of the trestles, where passengers disembarked to admire the outstanding scenery. Back in the train, they enjoyed carpet, wicker furniture, and a menu including consommé en tasse, tongue, and pot roast."[79] This kind of tourist experience (minus the pot roast) is precisely what the film captures, adopting the gaze of an outsider as the camera documents the natives. Yet while the viewer of the film is interpellated as a tourist, actual viewers in the 1910s may not have been tourists.

In lacking a strong authorial presence, when shown in commercial theaters travelogues such as *Hawaii, the Paradise of the Pacific* make literal Roland Barthes's notion of the "author function." Barthes wrote, "A text is made of multiple writings, drawn from many cultures and entering into mutual relations of dialogue, parody, contestation, but there is one place where this multiplicity is focused and that place is the reader, not, as was hitherto said, the author."[80] Following Barthes, I argue that early travelogue films invite the spectator to imagine herself or himself in the role of traveler, or Author. It is as though, just by watching a travelogue, the spectator is hailed as One Who Travels. In providing a vicarious travel experience for film audiences, these films open themselves up to the spectator's projections, fantasies, and reveries. Or, as Barthes famously put it, "The birth of the reader must be at the cost of the death of the Author."[81] While we can only speculate about audience responses to *Hawaii*, many spectators would have experienced identification or dis-identification with the film and the people it depicts. Some might have pictured themselves as tourists in the landscape, while others might have envisioned themselves living as natives. A curious spectator might have been someone who wanted to know *more* about the place being shown, one for whom these fragmented images were not enough. A resistant spectator might have wondered about the people being shown:

Why were their names not given? Had they been paid to appear in the film? The landscape itself was also ripe for resistant readings. Why did the film not mention Hawaii's status as a U.S. territory? Who built the railroad? The possibilities are almost endless, but actual historical responses by spectators are impossible for us to know. We are left only with observations based on the surviving film. The lack of a narrator figure in films such as *Hawaii, the Paradise of the Pacific* created a potential for a wide range of audience responses, encouraging spectators to engage with the films in ways that were not circumscribed by a narrator's guiding voice.

CHAPTER 2

"THE LIVING PANORAMA OF NATURE"

Early Nonfiction and the American Film Industry

> It was the scenic picture that gave cinematography
> its start.
> —H. F. HOFFMAN, 1910

> The work of the moving picture maker falls in
> two classes—actual events and acted imitations
> of events.
> —NICKELODEON, 1909

"The all-star drama is the latest in pictures," an editorial published in the *Nickelodeon* in 1910 cautioned exhibitors who favored fiction films, "but the scenic picture is the greatest, after all." This unnamed editorialist railed against scenic films' reputation for "obsolescence" and sought to prove that exhibitors who blindly followed the fiction film trend were missing out on an important business opportunity: "The well-rounded drama is undoubtedly the highest form of motion picture art, as an art. To its development is largely due the amazing growth of the picture theater as a form of amusement. But it does not, cannot, satisfy all the desires of an audience. [Neither it], nor any other artificial production, can supersede the living panorama of nature."[1]

This writer praises dramatic films but then just as quickly denigrates them as "artificial productions," contrasting the drama with the scenic film's realism, its presentation of "the living panorama of nature." This evocative expression is broad enough to encompass multiple nonfiction genres: not just travel films but also nature films, topical films, and, arguably, anything shot *en plein air*. Perhaps unintentionally, the writer invokes a classic Aristotelian distinction between artifice and nature. He does not question that distinction, which functions here as a given absolute; instead, he continues the drumbeat of support for one particular nonfiction genre: "Scenic and travel pictures will satisfy a yearning that nothing else at home will satisfy."[2] This "desire" and "yearning" for images of travel is naturalized as common sense. More significantly, the editorial (along with the broader discourse of which it is a part) signals that nonfiction played a significant role in early cinema. It is the contention of this book that what we now call "nonfiction" film— genres such as scenics, industrials, nature films, science films, and topical films—played a more central role in early cinema than in any other phase of film history, occupying an important place as a component of the variety format.

All nonfiction confounds traditional dichotomies between the artificial and the natural, or fiction and fact; early nonfiction film, however, does so in particularly interesting ways.[3] Nonfiction film still functions as a repository of truth in our culture today, but the category of "truth" itself has changed quite radically since the early 1900s. As historians have asserted lately, "While the opposition between art and nature is itself a major leitmotif throughout the history of the West, the forms that this dichotomy takes are themselves far from stable or constant throughout the centuries. On the contrary, the divide is continuously challenged and reassessed."[4] What we see in discussions of early nonfiction film is a reassertion of this popular distinction without a theorization of its larger meaning, which results in some confusion about the role of cinema in the early years: Was it a recording device or an art form?

The cinema emerged out of nonfiction. Film was not renowned as a storytelling medium in its early years; it took some time before filmmakers were able to develop a cinematic language that enabled narrative. Instead, for the first decade of film history, nonfiction was the most frequently produced kind of film. During the second decade of film history, nonfiction continued to be important even while the new techniques of fiction filmmaking were being developed. The early development of film narrative has been explored at length by scholars in recent decades, but in the rush to account for the emergence of fiction film, historians have tended to overlook an equally important story about the fate of nonfiction in early cinema. Between 1895 and 1917, as the film industry sprinted and stumbled on its way to becoming a profitable, organized business, travel films were transformed from a dominant genre of a marginal media into a marginal genre in a dominant media.

Travel films — or "scenic views," as they were first called — were the most numerous film subjects in the late 1890s, and this dominance continued into the new century through 1903.[5] Contrary to what some film historians have implied, nonfiction films, and the travelogue in particular, did not disappear with the rise of the multi-shot story film circa 1903–4. While it is true that nonfiction subjects became marginalized as the cinema shifted toward narrative (in 1903, as Charles Musser claims, or in 1906, as Tom Gunning argues), in fact, travelogues, industrials, and other nonfiction genres persisted on film screens alongside comedies and melodramas throughout the nickelodeon era.[6] Although the emergence of more sophisticated fiction subjects transformed motion pictures from a novelty into a major cultural force, nonfiction also played a crucial role in shaping early cinema. In fact, like early fiction films, the various nonfiction genres grew into their own multi-shot forms and persisted in film programs into the 1910s and beyond. From the onset of the nickelodeon era around 1905 until about 1915, nonfiction films were regularly shown in nickelodeon theaters and in the earliest movie palaces alongside comedies and dramas, as well as song slides, as part of early cinema's variety format. While it is true, as Stephen Bottomore has put it, that "the long-term trend was for the star of fiction to wax and for nonfiction to wane," this shift did not occur overnight. It happened gradually over the course of the cinema's tumultuous first couple of decades.[7]

I want to clarify that "nonfiction" is a contemporary term, used by today's film scholars, whereas "educational" was the preferred term for such films in the 1910s. The term "nonfiction" did not exist in the silent era; moreover, the term "documentary" was not widely used (at least not in English) until John Grierson introduced it in 1926, and it is worth emphasizing that early nonfiction film should not be viewed within a later documentary framework.[8] Likewise, before about 1908, the concept of "educationals" did not yet have traction in the film industry. I use the term "nonfiction" for concision, but I do not want it to imply coherence that did not exist in the jumbled world of early non-story films. I will return to a discussion of early fiction versus early nonfiction later in this chapter.

During the transformative early years of the film industry, nonfiction subjects — and scenic films in particular — were a contentious topic. Even though most early nonfiction films no longer exist, their place in the industry can be reconstructed from the thousands of articles and film reviews published in journals such as *Moving Picture World*, the *Nickelodeon*, and *Moving Picture News*.[9] Analysis of these trade journals reveals a running debate about travel films in early cinema's "transitional era," roughly from 1908 to 1915. Perhaps surprisingly, this dispute did not often focus on the nature of nonfiction's difference from fiction film, which was an unsettled issue at the time. Rather, the debate centered on the relative popularity or unpopularity of nonfiction film genres and their potential to function as commercial, profitable subjects. While nonfiction's status waxed and waned throughout the early cinema period, the trade press shows that a concerted effort was made to promote nonfiction genres in the years 1910–13. During these years, as the film industry worked to clean up the cinema's bad reputation as a form of cheap amusement, nonfiction films began to be marketed as "educational." Certain influential figures in the film industry, in particular Thomas Edison and George Kleine, along with many anonymous voices in the trade press, allied themselves with educators and reformers who were heralding the importance of education in the Progressive Era. The reformers' discourse intersected with (and differed from) the film industry's profit motive in various interesting ways.

Early cinema cannot be adequately understood without a consideration of nonfiction film. Early nonfiction genres complement our understanding of the early film industry as a dynamic field of competing practices. Like early fiction film, early nonfiction was a complex intermedia phenomenon that drew on preexisting cultural conventions. The proliferation of early nonfiction genres demonstrates the degree to which nonfiction, non-narrative films played a culturally significant role in the early years of cinema. In this chapter I present a brief history of early nonfiction film as it was produced, distributed, and exhibited in the United States, with an analysis that shifts between nonfiction film in general and the scenic film in particular. My focus on the scenic film, the most frequently produced early nonfiction genre, is meant not to minimize the importance of industrials, science films, nature films, and the like but merely to gain some focus on this broad topic.[10] As we shall see, nonfiction genres were more numerous than fiction genres in this era.

I first discuss the various ways film historians have divided early cinema into phases, arguing that early nonfiction presents a challenge to currently accepted ideas about the developmental stages of early cinema. Next, I discuss nonfiction's emergence, development, and persistence between the years 1895 and 1915, with a focus on its transition from the single-shot "actuality" film to specific multi-shot genres. I then analyze the phenomenon of genre in early cinema and discuss the fluid boundaries between fiction and nonfiction at this time. I conclude with a consideration of the "popularity" of early nonfiction genres. In an era before the commercial value of nonfiction had been determined, some felt that so-called educationals represented the moneymaking future of the industry. There were indeed some nonfiction film "hits" in the era, although the debate about the scenic film's popularity, I argue, ultimately reflects the unstable nature of the film industry in the 1910s. While early film businessmen were busy debating the commercial value of these films, what they were actually doing was grappling with their inability to know and control the spectator.

Nonfiction Film and the Long Birth of Cinema

Film historians today agree that cinema cannot simply be reduced to "silent" and "sound" periods, for the so-called silent era was one of the most volatile and swiftly changing periods in film history. In the 1980s and '90s, film historians began dividing silent-era cinema into three phases: the early film period (1895–1907), the transitional or nickelodeon era (1907–17), and the "mature" silent-film era (1917–27). While this is useful for its correspondence with important shifts in the film industry, it has a generalizing quality that all such periodizations naturally have: in reality, historical developments do not fit so neatly into ten-year spans of time. Moreover, this three-part periodization has been questioned by some of the very historians who use it, who note reservations such as, "Every period of American cinema could be seen as a 'transitional' one."[11] The tripartite division is certainly an improvement on earlier film histories, however, which tended to view the entire silent era up to 1927 as a static entity.

More recently, André Gaudreault and Philippe Marion have proposed that cinema was essentially born twice: first, in its early and steadfastly intermedial phase (pre-1908) when it emerged by poaching from other preexisting forms; and second, when it became institutionalized (1908–27) and "gradually [found] its personality, through a more or less unique process of managing the irrepressible intermediality that is always present in it."[12] This characterization is useful for the way it stresses early cinema's position as one of many different forms in a complex intermedia landscape, although we should note that the periodization remains virtually the same in this schema as in the tripartite schema (minus the "transitional era" phase of the earlier model, which to my mind is the most interesting phase for early nonfiction). The term "intermedial" suggests that early cinema drew from other popular forms such as vaudeville, magic, and fairy shows: Early cinema was a medium that could not exist without other media.[13] As such, the cinema's emergence was quite literally parasitical on these other forms, and even after it found its own identity, it continued to reinterpret these other media. The history of the scenic film clearly demonstrates this inter-media principle, as it was "born" directly out of the tradition of the illus-trated travel lecture. Scenic films, other nonfiction genres, and fiction film poached from different sets of preexisting traditions. Rather than adapting various forms of live stage performance, as early fiction films did, scenic films adapted nontheatrical media such as postcards, stereoscopy, and illus-trated travel narratives in newspapers and magazines. In addition, unlike the dramatic traditions reinterpreted by early fiction film (farce, melodrama), scenic films reinterpreted aesthetic traditions such as the picturesque, the sublime, and the beautiful.

More broadly, some film historians refer to all cinema before 1917 as "early" cinema, and that which came after as "classical" cinema. Indeed, in large part due to the influence of *The Classical Hollywood Cinema*, by David Bordwell, Janet Staiger, and Kristin Thompson, the year 1917 now holds the status of an important turning point in silent-era history.[14] While these vari-ous divisions are obviously more useful than the overly general term "the silent era," at the same time they remain imprecise when one takes a look at developments outside the realm of film narrative. Because these divisions have been described by historians focusing on fiction film, they are not en-tirely appropriate for early nonfiction. The year 1917, for example, is not the watershed for nonfiction that it was for fiction film, whose crystallization into its "classical" form by that year is identified mainly by stylistic changes that did not take place in nonfiction at that time.

When one examines early cinema from the perspective of nonfiction, 1915 is arguably more important than 1917. There are two primary reasons for this. First, 1915 is the first full year of the First World War, which disrupted the flow of films from Europe. My research has shown that the number of nonfiction films released in the United States dropped off significantly in 1915.[15] And second, 1915 marks the final turn away from single-reel short films toward multi-reel features, which began in 1913 but was irrevocable by 1915. Indeed, Tom Gunning has suggested that we might better call the transi-tional era the "single-reel" era, "to avoid the assumptions implied by calling it 'transitional.'"[16] Likewise, Domitor, the international society for the study of early cinema, focuses on the cinema's beginnings to 1915 and therefore locates the end of early cinema two years earlier than do Bordwell, Thompson, and Staiger. But despite falling off in number, travelogues and other nonfiction genres did not die out after 1915 — or after 1917, for that matter. Because travel films did continue to play on commercial film screens throughout the 1920s and beyond — in much the same form, although in smaller numbers — perhaps an even more significant year of change for the genre was 1927, the year of the commercial adoption of synchronized sound. The addition of a speaking narrator was arguably the greatest stylistic change for travelogues since the advent of multi-shot films in the early 1900s.

Yet another significant moment for nonfiction was 1923, the year Eastman Kodak introduced the 16 millimeter (mm) film gauge. While other small gauges were already in use, such as Pathéscope (28mm) and the 22mm format for the Edison Home Kinetoscope, it was the hugely successful 16mm gauge that enabled the large-scale success of educational films.[17] The 16mm format was economical (about one-sixth the price of 35mm) and nonflammable (unlike most 35mm, which used a highly flammable nitrate film base until 1952). It also did not require a booth or licensed operator for projection The development of 16mm film was highly significant in fostering the emergence of nontheatrical distribution to schools, where nonfiction film shorts led a thriving parallel life throughout the rest of the twentieth century, continuing through the ascendance of video in the 1980s.[18] But once again, because the emergence of 16mm film does not reveal much about the history of narrative feature film, it is rarely mentioned in traditional film histories. The year 1923, then, could be seen as the beginning of nonfiction film's institutionalization — its successful "second birth," if you will, after an abortive "second birth" in commercial theaters in the early 1910s. Viewed from this perspective, this book might be seen as the story of nonfiction's short-lived "second birth" — or better yet, "second emergence," to avoid the essentialism of the "birth" metaphor. Finally, one might alternatively view 1922 as a watershed year for nonfiction film because the most famous early documentary, Robert Flaherty's *Nanook of the North*, was released that year. However, as I aim to demonstrate, many of the trends consolidated by that renowned film — feature length, blending of nonfiction and staged elements, experimentation with a "slight" narrative, and emphasis on the heroic struggle of a "distant" and "primitive" people — were already prominent in the nonfiction film culture of the 1910s.

As my account of all of these different periodization issues is meant to demonstrate, attention to nonfiction film presents a different vision of early cinema history. My intention is not to replace one history with another but to question the need for such categorizations in the first place, which, for all of their sophisticated historiographical underpinnings, still produce a teleology in which one very complicated and messy phenomenon is replaced by another institutionalized, streamlined, and implicitly more "mature" second phenomenon. My point is that nonfiction film challenges this very teleology. Nonfiction films flourished in commercial theaters before 1915, but they did not go away once classical cinema took over the theatrical marketplace. The short format persisted on commercial screens and in schoolrooms and, later, on television and the Internet. Travelogues still exist today, occupying a minor but persistent position in the media industry. Nature films, news films, science films, and a whole host of nontheatrical genres have found a long life in the wings of the commercial media machine. Many of these marginal genres, in turn, have proven hugely influential for experimental film. This demonstrates the importance of addressing the history of media from the margins. Scenic films and related early nonfiction genres such as the science film, the nature film, and the newsreel constitute a system distinct from the classical cinema that came after them, the documentary styles developed later, or the fiction films of their day. Early travelogues serve as an example of a nonclassical, non-narrative, non-feature film practice, a mode that achieved a fair amount of stability within its own system during its brief heyday during the transitional years of early cinema. Perhaps surprisingly, these films forged some of the aesthetic conventions that were later more fully developed by avant-garde film. The irony is that travelogues were not self-consciously oppositional, and in fact if the rhetoric surrounding them displays any self-consciousness, it is a desire to be more normative or more popular.

From Actualities to Scenics

In the first years of the cinema, when nonfiction was more common than fiction, the cinematograph was envisioned as a recording device, and films consisted of a single shot. The earliest films took as their subject matter every aspect of the "living panorama of nature," including animal scenes, street scenes, current events scenes of parades and funerals, views of foreign locales, railroad views, and sports views. Films that recorded the minute movements of nature, such as views of crashing ocean waves, were particularly admired for their mimetic realism. Film scholars call these nonfiction views "actualities" (after the French *actualité*), and this actuality period can be distinguished from what came later by both the brevity of its films and the variety of its subjects. The Lumière brothers famously excelled at making these "real-life" subjects, turning everyday scenes, such as *Workers Leaving the Lumière Factory* (1895), into events of heightened importance.[19] The American Mutoscope and Biograph Company (later Biograph) also produced numerous nonfiction films in the early years: Stephen Bottomore estimates that between 1900 and 1906, approximately 56 percent of that company's films were nonfiction subjects.[20] Although it is difficult to gauge the precise number of nonfiction films produced during the early years of cinema, Patrick Loughney has estimated that among U.S. production companies, "57 percent of titles copyrighted from 1896 to 1906 were actualities, the percentage steadily declining from about 1900."[21] During that period, the cinema functioned not only as a kind of visual newspaper, reporting on important news items of the day, but also as a visual recorder of everyday life, documenting the quotidian practices and places that did not make the headlines. Early cinema attempted to capture all the wide variety of human experience and natural phenomena — notable events, everyday occurrences, natural flora and fauna — on fleeting moments of film.

Before 1908, competition between film production companies was intense, film exhibition practices were not standardized, and new inventions frequently appeared, particularly between 1895 and 1900. Yet some generalities about nonfiction in the early period can be drawn. Travel views were one of many types of actuality films; standardized genres had not yet emerged. As Musser has demonstrated, in this period the exhibitor was the primary creative force structuring film exhibition. The single-shot actuality was not a complete film text unto itself; rather, moving picture exhibitors arranged single-shot films in a particular order, in a sense "editing" the films into a complete program, typically accompanied by a lecture and often composing just one part of a larger show featuring live entertainment such as vaudeville acts. In the earliest years, a discontinuity between film views was stressed. "Exhibitions were initially organized along variety principles that emphasized diversity and contrast even while the selections often built to a climax and ended with a flourish," Musser writes. By 1898, however, programs emphasizing continuity *across* and *between* films had become more common.[22] This was the period in which travel lecturers such as Burton Holmes and Lyman Howe began showing motion pictures in their programs. These programs were typically organized around a single "destination" or tour-oriented travel topic, such as "Scenes and Incidents en Route from Cairo to Khartoum," Howe's program set in Egypt from 1903.[23] Indeed, besides the novelty of motion picture technology itself, foreign views were one of the primary attractions of cinema during this era. However, the actuality film's dominance did not endure; although more actualities than fiction films were produced through 1906, the multi-shot story film became more popular almost as soon as it emerged around 1903–1904.[24]

In the United States, nickelodeons came on the scene in 1905, and by 1907, the film industry was in the full grip of "nickel madness" as five-cent theaters sprang up all over the country. During the nickelodeon era, as the narrative techniques of the story film continued to be developed and refined, the loose denomination of actualities that had constituted all nonfiction production began to be codified into separate genres. These nonfiction subjects, like their fiction-film counterparts, contained up to a dozen shots or more, lasting a total of five to seven minutes. Unlike early story films, however, the earliest nonfiction genre films did not work to develop narratives or themes across a span of several shots; rather, their focus was to present more information. One might say that these earliest nonfiction genre films resembled the earlier actuality films, but they were simply longer. Instead of being "edited" into continuous multiple-shot presentations by a moving picture exhibitor, as the single-shot actualities had been, the longer nonfiction films were edited by the film companies before they were released, making them into stand-alone film texts. Intertitles often did the explaining where a live lecturer had provided commentary before (although lecturers occasionally accompanied nonfiction films in certain commercial theaters). In turn, nonfiction films were presented in a variety program that included other short films that served as a series of contrasts.

In their transformation from single-shot "actualities" to multi-shot genres such as the scenic, the industrial, and the topical film, early nonfiction genres innovated new forms. The most plausibly "narrative"-driven of these nonfiction genres, the industrial film, developed a process-oriented format in which a product's creation was followed from start to finish, as in the film *A Visit to Peek Frean and Co.'s Biscuit Works* (Cricks and Martin, 1906), which shows cookies being produced in a modern factory. Other nonfiction genres such as scenics and nature films rarely followed such a clear narrative progression.

Of the three most common early nonfiction genres — scenics, industrials, and topicals — scenic films were by far the most numerous. Indeed, the transitional era was arguably the travelogue film's apogee. Although it is difficult to pin down the actual popularity of scenics (a problem I will discuss

PLATE 1 Frame enlargement, *The Oasis of El-Kantara* (Éclair, 1913). Courtesy EYE Film Institute Netherlands.

PLATE 2 Poster
for *Colorful Ceylon*
(Paramount, 1917).
Courtesy Academy of
Motion Picture Arts
and Sciences.

PLATE 3 Poster for
Norway (Paramount,
1917). Courtesy Academy
of Motion Picture Arts
and Sciences.

PLATE 4 Poster advertising *La fauvette et le coucou* (Oliver Pike; Pathé, 1912). Courtesy EYE Film Institute Netherlands.

PLATE 5 Poster advertising *How Wild Animals Live* (Midgar Features, 1913). Courtesy
Academy of Motion Picture Arts and Sciences.

PLATE 6 Cover of Kleine's *Catalogue of Educational Motion Pictures*, 1910. Courtesy Academy of Motion Picture Arts and Sciences.

PLATE 7 Poster advertising *Native Industries in Soudan, Egypt* (Pathé, 1912). Courtesy Academy of Motion Picture Arts and Sciences.

PLATE 8 Cover of *Western Trips for Eastern People* promotional booklet, Great Northern Railway, 1915. Courtesy Washington State Historical Society, Tacoma, Wash.

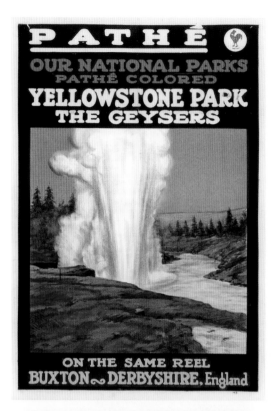

PLATE 9 Poster advertising *Our National Parks— Yellowstone Park: The Geysers* (Pathé, 1918). Courtesy Academy of Motion Picture Arts and Sciences.

PLATE 10 Poster advertising *Picturesque Colorado* (Rex, 1911). Courtesy Academy of Motion Picture Arts and Sciences.

later), they were a highly visible part of the cinema experience at the time. As Charlie Keil and Shelley Stamp write in their introduction to *American Cinema's Transitional Era*, "The years between 1908 and 1917 arguably witness the most profound transformation in American film history to date."[25] The film industry's unsettled quality allowed nonfiction films to occupy an important share of the market, as they had in the early years; because a future in which feature-length films dominated was still unforeseen, nonfiction temporarily obtained a higher status than it came to have in later years.

In addition to the rapid changes taking place in film production, film exhibition was in flux at this time. The nickelodeons were the first theaters designed specifically for motion pictures, but after their initial boom years, they were superseded by the newer and more lavish picture palaces of the mid-1910s.[26] This shift in exhibition venues was neither sudden nor uniform, however. As Eileen Bowser points out, "It should be remembered that the old-style nickelodeons continued to exist in large numbers, particularly in the urban ghettos, and some of them far past 1915."[27]

Although the nickelodeon boom resulted in many flash-in-the-pan businesses, certain elements of the film industry stabilized for a time during the period. From about 1907, as the rush to open nickelodeons reached a fever pitch, through 1915, as the picture palace and the feature film were transforming the business once again, there were two important industry practices that had great consequences for the nonfiction film: the variety format and the split reel. Films had long ceased to be available in single-shot increments, but nickelodeon owners still retained some ability to design the program their viewers saw based on their selection of short film subjects. The variety format—several short films of varying genres—continued to be the bread-and-butter program of the dedicated film house.[28] Film shows ran between a half-hour and one hour in length and were composed of five to ten short subjects. Each of these single-reel films was in turn accompanied by advertising slides or song slides, which were shown as the projectionist changed reels.[29] Most theaters printed paper programs for their film shows, which changed daily or several times a week, but surviving programs from the era are extremely rare. Although this book focuses on nonfiction in the United States, theater programs from the nickelodeon era are so unusual that at this juncture I will turn to an example from a theater in Hull, England, from 1913, whose surviving program demonstrates that the variety format was also characteristic of British film shows (figs. 2.1–2.2). The travel film shown at the Prince's Hall in Hull, *The Sandmore District*, appears in

FIGURE 2.1 Film program (front and back), Prince's Hall, Hull, England, 13 January 1913. Courtesy Academy of Motion Picture Arts and Sciences.

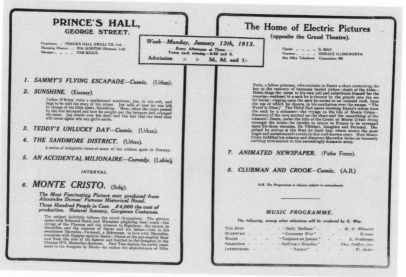

FIGURE 2.2 Film program (inside), Prince's Hall, Hull, England, 13 January 1913. Courtesy Academy of Motion Picture Arts and Sciences.

the first half of the program, interspersed with three short comedies and a drama. This short film, featuring "a series of delightful views of some of the wildest spots in Norway," would have offered a contrast with the comedies that preceded and followed it. Although a travel film was not guaranteed to be projected in all film shows, the genre's existence was in effect assured by this variety format.

Understanding the variety format is crucial to comprehending how scenic films were received in commercial theaters. While travel films excel at creating a conventionalized sense of natural beauty and can be powerful in short doses, a long program of only scenic films would have been a completely different experience. Within the context of the variety program in which they were shown, these films might have served as a pleasant, idyllic interlude. As one reviewer said about the experience of watching a travelogue titled *Scenes in the Celestial Empire* (Eclipse, 1910) as part of a variety program: "This picture followed a series of films that had stirred one's sentimental nature and it was as welcome." Another reviewer had this to say about the industrial film *Sabot Making* (Unique, 1908): "To those who have tired of the 'knock-down-and-drag-out' comedy film and the forced melodramatic stories, it is bound to be an interesting variation. The scenes are laid amid picturesque surroundings and the characteristic peasant workmen who turn the crude blocks of wood into shoes make up an odd and altogether interesting company. There are entirely too few subjects of this light but entertaining and educational sort." Still another reviewer described the nonfiction film *Sevres Porcelain* (Gaumont, 1909) with curt praise: "The film runs only a few moments, but works in well among miscellaneous subjects."[30] Film shows organized around this variety principle by definition needed to include different kinds of film subjects. In the transitional era, nonfiction films — and travelogues in particular — served as part of the backbone of the variety format, a useful contrast to the comedies and melodramas that made up the bulk of the program. Not every theater included scenic films, but many of them did, and it was the variety format that secured this inclusion.

Once the film industry shifted to features, travelogues persisted but served a somewhat different purpose. In the 1920s, travel subjects were often shown before the feature, becoming more like a prologue than a discordant jolt of variety in the middle of the program. The variety principle was streamlined and made less dissonant in the feature film era. "Variety" in the era of the feature film was provided by a variation between the scenes and sequences of a single film rather than between films. In effect, the feature

FIGURE 2.3 George Kleine, split-reel advertisements, *Moving Picture World*, 6 January 1912.

film sequence came to replace the individual single-reel film. Scenes set in interiors could be contrasted with scenes using outdoor locations the next moment, and feature filmmakers learned to vary tone between scenes (e.g., comedy in one scene contrasted with melodrama in the next) to provide a kind of emotional variety for the spectator.

After the variety format, the second most important factor that ensured the inclusion of travel films in nickelodeon programs was the distribution of films on single, one thousand–foot reels.[31] During this period, well over a thousand scenic films were released in the United States, usually as part of a split reel, sharing their reel with a comedy or a drama.[32] Publicity from the period, such as an advertisement by George Kleine from 1912 (fig. 2.3), makes this split-reel release format quite clear. In each of the three films featured in the ad, the travel film occupies approximately one-fifth of a thousand-foot reel, although scenics often constituted up to half of a split reel. Rarely were scenic films longer than five hundred feet (which clocks in at a little over eight minutes in length, running at the silent film speed of about sixteen frames per second). The most common combination was a comedy and a scenic (shown in two of the three examples in fig. 2.3), although other possibilities can also be found, such as scenic and drama or even, occasionally, scenic and scenic.

The split reel effectively ensured the persistence of travelogues in variety film programs. However, as multi-reel feature films such as *Quo Vadis?* (Enrico Guazzoni, Cines, 1912) and *Cabiria* (Giovanni Pastrone, Itala, 1914) became hugely popular, the industry began to move away from programs made up of single reels toward multi-reel features. The shift away from single reels necessarily disrupted the regular place of the scenic in the variety film program. As one commentator wrote in *Motography* in 1913: "While split reels, as an American institution, have not entirely disappeared, lingering still in the old combination of comedy and scenic, they have lost their importance to the manufacturer."[33] This statement is somewhat imprecise, like all trade press commentary, because evidence shows that single reels (and, by extension, split reels) were still regularly used by many American theaters as late as 1915.[34] However, by the end of the 1910s, the split reel had indeed faded away.

The rise of the feature film in the mid-1910s contributed to the increasing marginalization of scenics and other nonfiction genres. When multiple-reel features emerged, there was less need to "fill" one thousand feet of a single reel with a nonfiction film; instead, sustained narratives began to balloon the length of films to two, five, or even seven reels. The role of the nonfiction film within the industry changed irrevocably with the end of the single-reel era, from the backbone of the variety format to the prologue before the feature. As Richard Koszarski has written, scenic films "appeared as frequently as animated cartoons on 1922 theater screens. . . . Little was written about these films at the time, and next to nothing is known of them today. Yet their influence in shaping audiences' perceptions of nonfiction material may have been significant."[35] Scenic films were the nonfiction genre that persisted most strongly into the 1920s and beyond, but without the variety format they were no longer an essential component. Instead, they became locked into a "novelty" status, marketed with other short films as "the spice of the program," as the slogan of the company Educational Pictures proclaimed.[36]

In addition, the increase in feature film location shooting absorbed the travelogue's scenic function to some extent. This shift can already be seen in the film program reproduced as figures 2.1–2.2. The Selig film *Monte Cristo*, the longest film on the program, advertises its "Natural Scenery" as a particular attraction. Scenic backgrounds and establishing shots were more regularly included in features to add realism to the narrative, providing more opportunities to view natural landscapes than fiction films had done earlier. Finally, as I have mentioned, the First World War was yet another major factor contributing to the demotion of travel films in commercial theaters. The war disrupted the production and distribution of nonfiction films, many of which were manufactured by European companies.

Thus far, I have been discussing scenics and other nonfiction genres as they were exhibited in commercial motion picture theaters, but, in fact, nonfiction films were shown in two very different kinds of venues: theatrical and nontheatrical. Often the exact same films were shown in both types of venues, as shown in chapter 1. Theatrical exhibition refers to dedicated movie houses such as nickelodeons and, eventually, picture palaces. On the nontheatrical side, films were shown in lecture halls, churches, and a variety of other public venues in the 1910s; in fact, cinema began in such nontheatrical venues as vaudeville houses and fairgrounds.[37] Gregory Waller has argued that the various and diverse venues that exhibited early film might best be described as "multi-sited cinema."[38] In this book, I am primarily concerned with exploring the travel film's place inside the nickelodeon theater as one nonfiction genre among many within a spectrum of competitive commercial entertainment. Examples of travelogue exhibition in early nontheatrical contexts could easily fill another book, although such evidence is more difficult to track down because the nontheatrical realm was infrequently discussed in the profit-obsessed early film trade press (and indeed the term "nontheatrical" was not used by the film industry until the 1920s).

The point I want to stress is that these different kinds of venues provided very different moviegoing experiences. Obviously, the same film would have produced different effects depending on the type of venue and program in which it was shown. As the distributor George Kleine wrote in a speech in the 1920s, "The current use of the term 'non-theatrical' films usually applies to places and methods of presentation rather than to the character of the films shown. Almost any subject may be presented in a theatre. A clean theatrical film may be shown in school or church."[39] When shown in public halls or churches, travel films often made up the entire program as part of an old-style travel lecture focusing on a single place or region or presenting a "tour around the world" program. Many such venues emphasized the educational nature of their programs and aimed at a kind of niche audience that sought out this kind of instructive entertainment. When shown in a nickelodeon, however, travel films were just one genre among many in the variety format. Another important kind of venue that straddles the divide between the theatrical and the nontheatrical is the vaudeville theater. Travel films were popular in such venues in the 1890s, and travel lectures continued to be programmed at some theaters — such as the Keith and Proctor theaters — into the 1910s.[40] While these were not venues built specifically to show motion pictures, vaudeville theaters were not "nontheatrical," either. This blurred boundary is just one more example of the complexity of film exhibition in this era.

Early Nonfiction Genres

Genre may be a venerable category that cinema studies adopted from literary studies, but genre continues to inspire new questions for film scholarship. While there are many ways to focus on film genre — theoretical or historical, iconographic or thematic, production-based or reception-based — to a certain extent, genre ultimately is a construction imposed by the critic. Rick Altman has pointed out that in the critical rush to look for systems of meaning, "two generations of genre critics have done violence to the historical dimensions of genre."[41] There is a difference between genre as a marketing tool, in which the producers and consumers of films define the categories, and genres as formulated by critics, which are imposed from outside the industry. Genres produced for marketing purposes have commercial and pragmatic goals and are characterized by their flexibility or even messiness, whereas genres defined by critics aim to locate consistent systems within films, which tends to produce a clarity that never existed. So while I have been referring to films as "travelogues" or "scenics," I have been projecting a certain amount of generic consistency onto them that did not exist at the time they were produced. Now I will turn to the term "scenic" as a specific marketing label within the film industry and contend with the complexity of nonfiction genres as they initially appeared to exhibitors and spectators.

Although it is in the nature of film genre continually to fluctuate, genre before the rise of the feature film in the mid-1910s was radically different from what we think of as genre today. Early cinema genres were extremely diversified and fall into a completely distinct taxonomy from today's film genres. To understand the proliferation of nonfiction genres in the early 1910s, we must begin with the inconsistent generic labels of the actuality era. A catalogue for the American Mutoscope and Biograph Company from 1902, for example, lists the following film categories: comedy, vaudeville, trick, sports and pastimes, notable personages, railroads, scenic, fire and police, military, parades, marine, children, educational, expositions, machinery, miscellaneous.[42] Note that generic terms proliferate around nonfiction topics. In 1902, the date of the catalogue, nonfiction dominated film production (especially at Biograph); thus, the numerous categories seem warranted. The logic here has generated categories as varied as the columns in a newspaper. This heterogeneous list of film categories does not necessarily indicate confusion or lack of organization; rather, it was simply the most useful way to group films at the time.

Each of the categories from the Biograph catalogue has its own description, and the reasoning behind the generic divisions is understandable, if somewhat arbitrary. For example, the division between "railroad" and "scenic" films may seem like splitting hairs, but the definitions make the distinction clear:

> Railroads: The Biograph has always been famous for its railroad views. The greatest sensation ever produced in moving pictures is our wonderful picture of the Empire State Express, the celebrated train of the New York Central & Hudson River Railroad. Our cameras, working at a speed of from 30 to 40 pictures a second, have a capacity for this class of work which is not to be found in the smaller machines. We have covered the picturesque side of railroading all over the civilized world, and we point with pride to the completeness and comprehensiveness of our list. We have travelled in special cars from the Atlantic to the Pacific, all over Great Britain and the Continent; we have the armored train on the South African Veldt, and the daily express arriving at Shanghai, China. A large proportion of these views have a stereoscopic value which must be seen to be appreciated.[43]

According to this description, railroad films are all about motion. The railroad genre also clearly highlights technology, and this extends even to the explanation of motion-picture cameras "working at a speed of from 30 to 40 pictures per second." Railroads are evidence of "civilization" in this description; geographical locations are mentioned, but the emphasis is on how technology has changed that geography. In contrast, Biograph's definition of the scenic film emphasizes a sense of place:

> Scenic: Under this head come many pictures of strong local interest; — street scenes, along the great water highways, in the mountains, and on the plains. Our Niagara Falls series is particularly strong; embracing views of the giant cataract from all of the more interesting points, with several turning panoramas covering the whole extent of this wonderful phenomenon of nature, from the beginning of the upper rapids, across the

Canadian and American Falls and as far down as the cantilever bridge. It will be noted also that the foreign subjects include most of the places visited and admired by tourists. The Chinese Philippine [*sic*] views are all very fine pictorially and photographically. The New York street scenes are without exception very typical of Metropolitan bustle and activity.[44]

Rather than motion and technology, scenic films focus on the natural world: mountains, plains, Niagara Falls. Yet street scenes in New York also get prominent attention, indicating that "scenic" did not only mean natural scenery but could also include urban scenery.

This distinction between scenics and railroad films was not operative for very long. By 1907, the railroad category of films had disappeared—or, rather, had been absorbed by the scenic category. In general, nonfiction genres became more streamlined as the film industry became more standardized, though the process was uneven. The process of generic streamlining continued until the various nonfiction genres eventually became subsumed—in commercial theaters, at least—by the term "documentary" in the 1920s. In nontheatrical venues such as schools, the variety of early nonfiction genres continued to flourish for decades. For example, a catalogue of educational films published by the University of California, Berkeley, extension in 1936 lists 16mm films for rent under such categories as nature study, geography, general science, health and hygiene, agriculture, industry, and civics and citizenship.[45]

As the film industry began to stabilize around 1908, in its "second birth," there were still an astonishing number of nonfiction film categories. For example, a list of some of the categories in *Nickelodeon*'s regular "Record of Current Films" column includes scenic, sports, nature study, trick, scientific, topical, industrial, acrobatic, and historical (fig. 2.4). Each category was not listed in every issue, and the types of film seem to have drifted from one category to another over the months. But the point is that generic classifications proliferated around nonfiction, while fiction films were classified simply into two categories—comedy and drama—a division that remained relatively stable. Early nonfiction genres were hybrid in nature; genres such as the scenic, the industrial, and the topical film regularly contained overlapping content. But once we understand the commercial goals of genre as a marketing tool, it becomes apparent that, as Gunning puts it, "rough and ready divisions which seem arbitrary from the viewpoint of genre criticism . . . were most likely serviceable and pragmatic."[46] Although film classifica-

FIGURE 2.4 "Record of Current Films," *Nickelodeon*, 18 March 1911, 317.

tions clearly followed a system, that system was not rigorous or scientific. Rather, it was conceived to suit the goals of commerce, which were rapidly changing.

The reason that a paradigmatic travelogue such as *Picturesque Waterfalls in Spain* (Gaumont, 1911) was classified as scenic is clear: The title alone makes apparent the film's focus on place, natural landscapes, and picturesque beauty. It is less clear, however, why a film such as *Carnival of Japanese Firemen in Tokio* (Pathé, 1910) was classified as scenic. The film's title certainly indicates an emphasis on the place depicted, but Japanese firemen would not seem to be a traditionally "scenic" subject. The film might have included some "scenic" shots of Tokyo streets, but no copy of the film is known to exist, so I could not view it and check for such shots. The film's description, published in the trade press, is not very helpful: "an excellent picture of interest, inasmuch as it shows how different are the customs of the Orient to those we ourselves know."[47] Judging from this description, the film would appear to be "scenic" because of the customs shown rather than because of any scenery pictured. Another possibility is that the film's classification as "scenic" was simply a mistake made by the person compiling the list of films for *Motography*.

In fact, I have found that the concept of "scenic" also frequently included general views that did not necessarily involve nature or landscape, in a sense harking back to the open concept of the actuality film of the 1890s. At times, the classification seems to have been used indiscriminately when referring to just about any "real-life" scene, from *Hospital for Small Animals* (Éclair, 1911) to *The Chicago Stock Yards Fire* (Imp, 1911), both of which were listed in the trade press as scenics.[48] It seems that virtually anything in the world could be scenic as long as it was rendered as a nonfiction subject — indeed, the very word "scenic" at times seems synonymous with the idea of nonfiction in this period. Perhaps more than anything else, we should understand "scenic" to be a nonfiction sensibility.

A similar fluidity can be found in other classifications, such as sports films and industrials. *Hunting Sea Lions in Tasmania* (Pathé, 1910), like many "hunting" films, was listed as a sports film, even though the setting in Tasmania would also appear be an important scenic component. The sports category also included films such as *Athletic Sports in India* (Pathé, 1910), *Winter Sports in Lucerne* (Pathé, 1911), *Salmon Fishing in Canada* (Solax, 1911), and *Bear Hunting* (Great Northern, 1910). However, just when a systematic pattern seems to have emerged, more classifications arise to challenge this uniformity: *Hunting Bats in Sumatra* (Pathé, 1910) was classified as a nature study. And while we might expect *Hunting Bears in Malaya* (Pathé, 1912) to be a sports film, instead the film was listed as a scenic.[49]

The same was true for industrial films, which described production processes — such as *Making Bamboo Hats in Java* (Eclipse, 1911). Although the generic boundaries of the industrial film were relatively stable, sometimes these kinds of "process" films were listed as scenics, as was *Pineapple Cannery in China* (Pathé, 1911).[50] Judging from the titles, there is no discernible reason that a pineapple cannery in China would be more "scenic" than an "industrial" view of the production of bamboo hats in Java. It would seem, in fact, that both films might simultaneously be scenic and industrial. In fact,

I believe this generic instability was simply a product of the shifting practices of the industry at the time, which was in a state of tremendous flux. In sum, although some distinctive patterns emerge, generic categories were extremely fluid. This should not be surprising, however, for the system of classifying films' genre in this period—as in other historical periods—was not scientific but commercial, working in the service of an industry.

While the various nonfiction genres shape-shifted throughout the nickelodeon period, the overall trend was a standardization and reduction of generic categories. The emergence of the classification "educational" exemplifies this trajectory. This category had appeared before the transitional era (e.g., in the Biograph catalogue from 1902), but it gained new force in the early 1910s as the film industry began to appropriate "uplift" rhetoric to justify itself to its critics. By October 1911, *Motography* had begun separating nonfiction from its regular film review section, "Recent Films Reviewed," creating a new column, "Current Educational Releases." "Educational" was an umbrella term that gathered together all kinds of nonfiction films, including scenics, industrials, and topical films, under its mantle. For instance, *A Trip to Mount Rainier* (Pathé, 1912) was classified as an educational film, although previously it might have been called a scenic. And yet, confusing the picture is the fact that these more specific categories did not disappear once the "educational" category gained traction; instead, they stood alongside each other well into the 1910s.

As more nonfiction was beginning to be labeled "educational," it seems puzzling that earlier divisions between scenic, industrial, and topical remained. However, I suggest that the "educational" label was a nascent attempt to differentiate nonfiction from fiction. In addition, the educational category was certainly a marketing tactic, an attempt to capitalize on the educational rhetoric being used by reformers to promote nonfiction film at the time. Perhaps the category "educational" should stand as yet another development on the way to the idea of "documentary" as it emerged in the 1920s. Standard histories of documentary have rarely, if ever, dealt with the history of early nonfiction film, despite the fact that canonical early documentaries such as *Nanook of the North* draw directly from conventions established by early travel films. It is time to give these many early nonfiction genres their due as important precursors of documentary film.

The opposition between fiction and nonfiction, one of the more rigidly observed distinctions of classical cinema, was not clearly drawn in the early film era. As Keil has written, "Distinctions between fact and fiction are marked by instability throughout the first twenty years of cinema's existence."[51] There were many hybrid films in this period that combined nonfiction elements with a fictionalized narrative. One of the best-known examples of this (and not coincidentally, a film about travel, although such mixing was common in films of all subjects) is Edwin S. Porter's *The European Rest Cure*, released in 1904 by the Edison Manufacturing Company. This thirteen-shot film includes many staged shots of a family taking a vacation around Europe, preceded by intertitles announcing their activities (e.g., "All Aboard," "Doing Paris," "Climbing the Pyramids of Egypt"), interspersed with actuality footage of a ship leaving New York City (figs. 2.5–2.6). Anne Friedberg provides a thorough, shot-by-shot analysis of the film, so I will not dwell on it here.[52] I simply want to mention that in *The European Rest Cure* Porter was saving time and money by reusing actuality footage from other Edison films, a common practice at the time.[53] In effect, Porter harnessed the "reality effect" of nonfiction footage to create a sense of realism that was not accomplished by the film's highly artificial staged scenes, whose painted backdrops humorously underscore that the film was not shot on location.

There are many other early examples of hybrid fiction–nonfiction films. A review of *Charlie and Kitty in Brussels* (Pathé, 1910) makes this hybrid style quite clear: "The rambles of two mischievous kids gives the camera an opportunity to show some good views of the Royal Palace, City Hall, and other points of interest in Brussels. Scenes of the country are also displayed."[54] Significantly, the film was classified as a comedy. *Through Snow to Sunshine* (Lubin, n.d.), from about the same time, provides another example:

> This is a kinetographic record of a bridal tour, started in the deep snows of Philadelphia, and terminated in the sunny delights of a Florida winter. Jacksonville, St. Augustine, Palm Beach and Miami are visited and the tropical beauties of those pleasant spots are shown. There is a little drama thrown in. The husband has never met his brother-in-law, and yielding to a temptation to tease her young spouse, the bride leads young hubby a merry little chase for a few feet of properly licensed film. The reel is a splendid example of how harmless and how interesting a moving picture can be when a manufacturer uses gumption enough to make it so. Lubin has done splendidly, and should be encouraged.[55]

The bridal tour was a fairly common narrative structure for these hybrid films. The frequency of fiction–nonfiction hybridity in the early film era indicates not that audiences were unsure of the difference between the two

FIGURE 2.5 Actuality footage, *The European Rest Cure* (Edison, 1904).

FIGURE 2.6 Staged footage, *The European Rest Cure* (Edison, 1904).

categories but that audiences were well able to distinguish between what counted as "real" and what counted as "staged," especially when the difference was underscored by mise-en-scène, as it was in *The European Rest Cure*.

The many "straight" nonfiction films that do not highlight their fictionalization so self-consciously present a different problem for analysis. Early "ethnographic" films make this question central. Edward S. Curtis's early feature film *In the Land of the Head Hunters* (1914) is a hybrid fiction–nonfiction film.[56] Curtis filmed the Kwakiutl Indians of the Pacific Northwest but created a narrative for his footage through the means of a melodramatic story. This strategy of restaging was later copied by Flaherty in *Nanook*. As Alison Griffiths explains in her analysis, "Curtis sought to distinguish [his film] from what he saw as fake film of Native Americans produced by commercial companies."[57] Even though *In the Land of the Head Hunters* was long heralded as an early documentary, its use of staging and its ethnographic inaccuracies mark it as more of a fictionalized film to viewers today. Rather than imposing a rigid distinction between fiction and nonfiction on an era in which that distinction did not yet exist, my point is that the very category of nonfiction contains many fictionalizing tendencies, but those tendencies are usually masked. I discuss the travelogue's "fictionalizations" at length in other chapters; in this chapter about the early film industry, I simply want to establish that fiction and nonfiction categories were not carefully distinguished.

"Depend upon These Frenchmen for at Least One Interesting Travel View a Week"

The history of scenic films defies the auteur theory. Unlike in later eras when the film director became a prominent figure, in the early film period the production company was the most important brand name. Although the actual personnel involved in making the films occasionally have been identified, authorship for the majority of travel films is still an open question.[58] While travel filmmakers such as Félix Mesguich, Burton Holmes, and Oscar Depue eventually published memoirs, these tend to be vague and anecdotal accounts.[59] Holmes, for example, hardly mentions filmmaking at all in his autobiography, focusing instead on his lecturing career, although he does include a photograph of himself inspecting a film can in "one section of my movie vault."[60] All of this is to say that at this point, the practices of travel film production are still largely unknown. Who decided which locations to film? Were executive decisions handed down by the production companies, or did filmmakers choose what they filmed? It seems likely that personnel working at the production companies, rather than the filmmakers out in the field, made the final editing decisions and wrote the intertitles, but I have not focused on unearthing specific information about these practices, which undoubtedly varied from company to company. These are questions that can be answered only by further research.[61]

Setting aside the issue of individual personnel, we are left to survey the names of the companies that produced these films. While many early film companies made travel films, several manufacturers specialized in the genre. French companies in particular had a reputation for their output of scenics. Eclipse, Gaumont, and, especially, Pathé Frères were renowned for their travel films. One reviewer remarked that "between Gaumont, Pathé, and Eclipse it is hard to award the palm for scenics. If Pathé stirs a more intellectual pleasure, the others certainly stir a more esthetic."[62] In Italy, Ambrosio and Cines produced many scenic films. The Charles Urban Trading Company was the most notable producer of scenics and other nonfiction genres in the United Kingdom.[63] Nordisk in Denmark (known as Great Northern in the United States) also produced a number of scenics. Although travelogue production was not as great in the United States as it was in France, it was still common. The Edison Manufacturing Company and the Selig Polyscope Company in particular produced numerous travel films and other nonfiction subjects.

In fact, most early film companies made at least some scenic films at one point or another. Centaur, Éclair, Essanay, Itala, Kalem, Nestor, Powers, Rex, Solax, and Vitagraph are some of the other companies that released one or more scenic films in the United States during the years 1910–14.[64] If we broaden this out to include related nonfiction categories such as nature films and industrials, then the list grows even larger; in effect, almost all production companies made some nonfiction at this time.[65] Even the smallest, most short-lived companies associated with the National Film Distributing Company made nonfiction, and as usual, travelogue films dominated this nonfiction production. For example, Aquila, an Italian company whose films were distributed in the United States by National, released *Views of Monviso* on 9 February 1912. The company's own terse description attests to the travelogue's formulaic nature: "Another travel film of the Alps. We see the sources of the river Po. Water falls, stone bridges, stone huts and mountain lakes add to the picturesque scenes, while as a closing view we see the crest of the Monviso Mountain."[66]

Even companies that are not remembered for their nonfiction output released nonfiction films in this period. For example, Bison released the

416-foot film *Rattlesnakes* on 26 April 1910, and Imp released the 970-foot *Fruits and Flowers* on 19 May 1910, both of which were classified as nature studies.[67] That these companies, known for their fiction output, produced a small amount of nonfiction should not be surprising, however, for scenics and nature films were not difficult or expensive to produce, especially if shot at a nearby location. Many companies that released only a few travel films made "local" scenics, such as *Feeding Seals at Catalina Island* (Essanay, 1910), which was shot soon after Essanay established its studio in California in 1910.[68] Other film companies not known for their nonfiction output sometimes released scenics that were shot while crews were on location for fiction films — for example, Kalem's *Ancient Temples of Egypt* (1912).[69]

Despite all of this, a few companies dominated travelogue film production, and they were largely responsible for developing scenic views into a coherent and established film genre. The most important of these companies — Pathé, Gaumont, and Eclipse — were French. The American trade press frequently noted that scenic production was dominated by the French. Referring to Pathé, a reviewer in *Variety* stated in 1909: "Depend upon these Frenchmen for at least one interesting travel view a week."[70] In 1910, the *Nickelodeon* editorialized about the lack in the United States of a company that could produce scenics of equivalent quality:

We would almost venture the opinion that the old-established house of Pathé, with all its experienced dictators, has realized the public attitude toward educational and nature subjects ahead of some of its contemporaries in this country.

Of course the Pathés have been making educational films ever since they started making films at all, and we have been privileged to see some of them in this country. But they have come only spasmodically and at comparatively long intervals. Practically all the scientific subjects we get are imported, and we are willing to get more of them. If it is the intention of the big French producer's American branch to increase its allotment of technical subjects, even at the expense of a few dramas and comedies, the market will benefit by the change. All the impetus the educational field needs is another big producer who will aid in maintaining on the American market a definite number of specialized releases each week.[71]

In fact, Pathé's releases did not come quite so "spasmodically" as the article indicates, for their educational films were already appearing regularly in the United States. But the larger point rings true: The production of scenics in this era was dominated by the French. This certainly had to do with French national and cultural traditions. Richard Abel cites the secular educational system in the Third Republic as one factor that may have served as a model for Pathé's historical films, and it seems likely that this also would have influenced the company's production of travel and other nonfiction subjects. Abel writes, "Specifically, this [secular educational system] involved the interplay between visual illustrations and verbal captions, probably based on popular engravings, in the new French primary school textbooks on history."[72] The Progressive Era's educational movement in the United States was also exploring theories of visual education, and it similarly had a hand in influencing educational films in the American context, as chapter 3 will explore. Despite the French or European origin of many of these films, they expressed something that transcended national boundaries to become popular in the international film market.

In 1907, European films dominated the releases in the United States. In fact, there was a general shortage of film prints, with exhibitors clamoring for more new material to satisfy their growing audiences as the nickelodeon craze grew. As Musser has stated, this shortage "opened up tremendous opportunities for foreign producers. . . . Only one-third of the films released in the United States during 1907 were American-made. The other two-thirds were European."[73] At the time, Pathé was the largest film production company in the world, so it should come as no surprise that its scenic films were a common presence on U.S. film screens. Abel has found that in 1907, Pathé was selling almost twice as much film on the American market as all of the American companies combined.[74] While American film production gained market dominance by the early 1910s (in the United States, but not yet worldwide), European imports continued to play a major role in U.S. film exhibition through 1914. Indeed, it seems likely that American production of scenic films in this period was inspired by and modeled after European scenic films.

The formation of the Motion Picture Patents Company (MPPC) in December 1908 had a major effect on the distribution of scenic and other nonfiction films in the United States. After this (and through the first half of the 1910s), films were released either by "licensed" companies affiliated with the MPPC, or by "independent" companies that were not affiliated with the MPPC.[75] Travel films were distributed on both the licensed and the independent film circuits, but nonfiction was more common among licensed film releases, primarily because of Pathé's output and George Kleine's importation of Eclipse's films and other European films. The major production companies in the MPPC — including Pathé, Eclipse, Selig, and Edison (the MPPC was often referred to as the "Edison Trust") — released the majority of the travel and nonfiction films in the United States during the 1909–15 period. As I have noted, however, independent production companies such as Éclair, Ambrosio, Itala, Great Northern, Imp, Solax, and Powers also released scenic films, as did the even smaller companies of the National film circuit, but those nonfiction releases were not as numerous or regular as the films produced by the members of the Edison Trust. Alongside Pathé, which distributed its own films, the most important U.S. distributor of European nonfiction films was George Kleine. The next chapter examines his efforts to promote educational films in the nickelodeon era.

The task of filling out a variety program that changed daily or a few times a week was not easy, and exhibitors had to rely on films of varying quality to fill screen time. The term "filler" emerged in the trade as a label for poor-quality or mediocre films, and the application of this term to travel films tells us something about the ambiguous status of the genre in this period. Travelogues were typically marketed with hyperbolic words of praise by boosterish voices in the trade press, but at the same time they were sometimes described by reviewers as "fillers" or as "filling out a reel." For example, a brusque review of the nonfiction film *Montana State Fair* (Vitagraph, 1914) noted: "on the same reel [as a comedy called *Their Interest in Common*] and a good filler."[76] However, nonfiction was not the only kind of film to be called "filler," as a review of *The Cheese Box* (Gaumont, 1910), a "comedy founded upon the substitution of an odoriferous cheese for a box of bon-bons," reveals: "It has no particular qualities to recommend it, and although it draws a laugh, [it] will be forgotten as soon as it is off the screen. It is short, however, and serves as a very good filler."[77] What is interesting here is that the exhibitor's imperative to fill screen time seems more important than any commercial imperative to present high-quality films. These films' mediocrity is not such a drawback that the footage becomes a liability. The overall experience of the variety program (and the live music) was ultimately more important than any individual title, although, as we will see, exhibitors and audiences certainly did pay attention to individual films. The notion that certain types of film served as "filler" underscores the extent to which watching films in the nickelodeon era often served merely as a way to spend one's time; the consumerist ideal that each film should be valuable did not emerge until much later in film history. The variety format — and the quick turnover of film programs—by definition seems to have demanded a certain amount of "filler." If one's goal as an audience member was simply to pass some time, "fillers" met the requirement quite adequately.

Travelogues were not always just filler, however, and many of their reviewers are so full of praise they veer into purple prose. For example, a reviewer of *An Oasis in the Desert* (Gaumont, 1911) exclaims, "One realizes in viewing this beauty spot brought into being by a streamlet gushing out of the desert sand how much of life and natural beauty is due to the presence of water. What a weary, stale, flat, improfitable world we should have without it!"[78] This particular scenic film seems to have been inspirational—for the reviewer, anyway. Moreover, not all scenic films were released as the bottom half of a split reel; some, such as the 544-foot *Customs of the Buddhists in India* (Pathé, 1910), dominated their reels. Still others, such as the nine hundred-foot *A Glimpse of Neapolitan Camorra* (Ambrosio, 1911) commanded a reel all their own.[79] Clearly, the status of scenic films was still being negotiated by the film industry, which experimented with various release lengths well into the transitional era.

Not only were travelogues more than just "filler," they also often had relatively long shelf lives and were reused over the years. Unlike fiction films—and especially unlike topical or newsreel films—travelogues did not become outdated. Thus, we find examples of travel films being reused and recycled in various exhibition formats, especially in schools. In 1912, the General Film Company issued an educational catalogue for nontheatrical use that listed many travel films that had been regular commercial releases just a year or two earlier. Several complete film programs are suggested at the back of the catalogue in the section titled "Suggestions as to How Motion Pictures May Be Applied to School Work."[80]

A few nonfiction-film makers also were trying to make multi-reel "features" by the mid-1910s. For example, Midgar Features released the six-reel nature film *How Wild Animals Live* in 1913. An advertisement for the film promised "6000 feet of live, thrilling, gripping animals in their natural state, photographed by naturalists (not hunters) who depict the Romance and Adventures, Tragedies and Joys of animal life."[81] More famously, film footage was shot during two separate expeditions to the South Pole in the 1910s. The first footage was shot by the photographer Herbert Ponting, who traveled with Captain Robert Falcon Scott in 1910–12; the second was shot by the photographer Frank Hurley, who traveled with Sir Ernest Shackleton in 1914–16. Footage from the second expedition was released in 1919 as a lavish one hundred–minute feature film titled *South: Sir Ernest Shackleton's Glorious Epic of the Antarctic*.[82] Some footage from the first expedition was released in the early 1910s, but it was not released as a feature film until 1924 under the title *The Great White Silence*. It also was later recut and released, with added sound, in 1933 as *90 Degrees South: With Scott to the Antarctic*.[83] Of course, the feature-length documentary film had emerged by the 1920s with the 1922 release of *Nanook of the North*, along with *Grass: A Nation's Battle for Life* (Merian C. Cooper and Ernest B. Schoedsack, 1925), and the more sensationalistic *Simba: The King of Beasts* (Martin and Osa Johnson, 1928).[84] As I have already suggested, however, the feature-length documentaries of the 1920s were a distinctly different phenomenon from the nonfiction films of the transitional era, when short films still ruled the day.

Debating the Popularity of Scenics

Nonfiction held a different status in early cinema than in the classical and post-classical eras. In the early years, nonfiction was arguably more central to the film industry than at any other point in film history. Nonfiction's place in the early film industry was not settled however, but rather a subject of contentious debate. In general, this debate broke down into two camps: those who argued that nonfiction subjects were unpopular and not commercial enough and those who argued that nonfiction subjects were very popular and, in fact, represented the future of motion pictures. The commentary of those in the first camp—mostly exhibitors and reviewers—tends to display a commercial anxiety that appears under the guise of populist rhetoric. Some exhibitors believed that scenics, industrial films, and scientific pictures were not popular with their audiences because they were not immediately entertaining. Certain exhibitors complained, for example, that "scenics don't go."[85] In contrast, the commentary of those in the second camp—some exhibitors and reviewers again, but more frequently educators and reformers—tends to display a kind of utopian wish, also appearing under the guise of populist rhetoric, though of a different kind. One writer remarked in the *Nickelodeon*, "We are still insisting that the educational subject is the most valuable and the most popular." Another claimed, "The average exhibitor does not realize what a tremendous demand there is for just such subjects as these."[86] These reform-minded writers tried to use the logic of the marketplace to argue that educational films would be extremely popular if they only were given a chance. The contradiction, it seems, was that travelogues appeared to fit into an educational agenda, and yet they also clearly made appeals to the popular taste for the exotic, presenting images of foreign lands as spectacle.

Travelogues were numerous during the 1890s, 1900s, and 1910s. Their level of popularity, however, is more difficult to pin down. Because it was engaged in a struggle to discover what audiences would pay to see, the early film industry was particularly obsessed with the question of film's popular appeal. Thus, discussions about travel films in the trade press center on questions about the genre's popularity. "Popularity" was a way to characterize the travelogue's commercial function; the concept of popularity embodied both financial and cultural stakes. While the trade press is an unreliable source of empirical evidence about early cinema audiences, it does provide many rich examples of the contradictory public discourse surrounding nonfiction film. Some reviews indicate that travelogues were perennial favorites, while others make fun of the genre's formulaic qualities. Alongside this lies the industry's own promotional rhetoric, as well as the words of the garrulous cinema reform movement, which illustrate the complex ways in which nonfiction films were manipulated in the service of the sometimes complementary, sometimes competing commercial and reform interests. Although this knot of competing rhetoric is tricky to unravel, this much at least is clear: Travelogue films enjoyed a persistent if limited commercial appeal throughout early cinema's transitional era.

The issue of class becomes important here, and the class makeup of nickelodeon audiences continues to be a subject of debate.[87] Travelogue films were certainly a significant part of nickelodeon programs, but what does this imply about their popular appeal? If nickelodeons were filled with immigrants and the urban poor, as the cinema's own mythology would like to have us believe, does it mean that travel films appealed to a "low-class" taste, despite the genre's familiar "high-class" moniker? If nickelodeons were filled with a more heterogeneous mixture of members of the "lower" and "middle" classes, as recent scholarship has indicated, then what implications does this have for the travelogue film's so-called high-class appeal? Perhaps travel films were a genre that could transcend class divisions. Or perhaps scenics and other nonfiction genres were simply filler in the variety program, ignored or, at best, tolerated by nickelodeon patrons. Regardless of how audiences responded, the fact remains that thousands of nonfiction films were produced, and they were indeed a frequent presence on the screen.

Whether the films were understood as "high-class" or as "filler," audiences had to contend with nonfiction.

Many reviews in the trade press were enthusiastic about nonfiction in general, and about travel films in particular. One reviewer wrote, "Gaumont's scenic subjects are always welcome."[88] Reviews containing positive statements, such as this one of *Colombo and Its Environs* (Pathé, 1910), were not uncommon: "If the Pathé firm would turn out more educational and natural scenic films, its output would be more appreciated by the American audiences. This latest colored picture will be enjoyed anywhere, as it shows the streets of Ceylon, India, with their motley crowds, curious vehicles and ox teams. Men and women of that Oriental section appear in native garb. The photography is excellent."[89] Here the value of foreign views goes unquestioned: What audience would not want to see moving pictures of foreign lands? From this perspective, curiosity about exotic foreign lands is naturalized as the most neutral kind of interest. However, as I explore throughout this book, the taste for the exotic is bound up with a host of complicated desires and disavowals.

The review of *Colombo and Its Environs* mentions color—and, indeed, the most successful travel subjects were often color films. Many films from the period included applied color such as tinting, toning, or stencil coloring.[90] Color is partly a practice carried over from the travel lecture tradition, in which lantern slides were often hand-painted. Color was an important component of postcards and chromolithographs, two other key precursors to the travelogue. The colors in the films often eschew naturalism in favor of sensationalism, and in fact there was a debate about the artificiality of color at the time, which many saw as false or garish. As Joshua Yumibe has demonstrated, "The rapid expansion of nineteenth-century colour technologies transformed much of the aesthetic discourse into polemics in which the technological reproduction of colour exemplified the degradation of colour."[91] Mass audiences, however, clearly responded to color films, as many reviews testify, and color in nonfiction film can be seen as a part of the democratization of education that these films represent.

Some exhibitors did indeed find commercial success with nonfiction films, as a group of letters from exhibitors found in the George Kleine papers attest. An exhibitor at the Bell Theatre in Chicago wrote to Kleine in 1910: "Your Urban Eclipse and Gaumont scenic subjects have certainly won a home with our audiences."[92] Still another exhibitor, the proprietor of the Majestic Theatre in Ault, Colorado, wrote:

I desire to thank you in behalf of my patrons for your importation of Gaumont's "Vale of Aude." It is the first and only picture that has ever been applauded in my M. P. Theatre here. My only regret is that it was too short by far. The applause last night was terrific & my business exceeded the night previous fifty percent.

Here's hoping that you keep on getting such good things, as they are needed as much now, as never before in the film industry, when so many manufacturers or [sic] selling "feet."

I am a customer of the Colo. Film Exchange, Denver and have a standing order with them for all Gaumont & Urban Films, portraying scenic or industrial scenes.[93]

These exhibitors, it should be emphasized, did not specialize in presenting "high-class" lecture programs filled exclusively with travel films, but instead ran dedicated film theaters that depended on variety film programs. This makes their comments all the more significant, for they would seem to offer evidence that scenic films stood out amid the other films on their programs and had strong popular appeal.

Contradicting these reviews and various statements extolling the genre's popularity, however, one can find occasional proclamations about how unpopular travelogues were, as in an advertisement by Méliès from 1914 (fig. 2.7) that read: "In the past we have catered to an imaginary demand for travel and education pictures. In the future our travel releases will be few and far between. . . . In other words, we are now 'out of the rut' and 'in the running.'"[94] In 1913, Méliès released a run of apparently unsuccessful scenics that were filmed during Gaston Méliès's trip to Southeast Asia in 1912–13.[95] However, this example should not lead one to conclude, as does Eileen Bowser, that travelogues were a generally unpopular genre. Indeed, throughout Bowser's otherwise extensive history of this period, scenic films barely garner a mention.[96] If the genre was so bankrupt, why did travelogues persist through the 1910s and beyond? Despite some failures and regular proclamations that the genre was outdated, travelogues remained a persistent genre into the 1920s. In terms of the failure of the Méliès films, it would seem that not all scenics were alike after all, and exhibitors and spectators could tell the difference between a "high-quality" scenic by Pathé and a film from this poor-quality series by Méliès. Indeed, an extant print from the series, *Ruins of Angkor, Cambodia* (1912), is filled with excruciatingly slow pans and shots that contain little movement.[97]

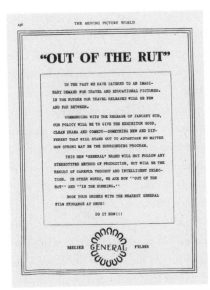

FIGURE 2.7 "Out of the Rut and into the Running," Méliès advertisement, *Moving Picture World*, 14 January 1914, 436–37.

Announcements of the unpopularity or demise of the travel genre circulated periodically alongside the more regular proclamations of its popularity. There was a great deal of uncertainty about which genres were the most appealing to motion picture audiences, but I suggest that the educators and exhibitors of early cinema were defining their debate along the wrong lines — or, rather, their debate about the *value* of travel films was entirely appropriate for their own needs (reforming the mass public, making a profit off the mass public), but their discussion does not reveal much about the *experience* of watching a travelogue film. In fact, it seems clear now that the conflict was not actually between the forces of education and entertainment; rather, the conflict was a fight to know and control the spectator. The reformers and exhibitors missed the point with their debate about what might be the most "popular" as film audiences were viewing scenic films in a variety of ways that did not necessarily correspond to what film businessmen or educational reformers envisioned.

Turning from these anecdotal reviews and testimonials, there is some evidence that a few nonfiction films in this period were "hits." One of the best known is *The Fly Pest* (Urban, 1910), which garnered quite a bit of press during the spring of 1910. Classified as a scientific film, it was shown in nickelodeons and "used by various societies in illustrated lectures on the dangers of the common house fly" as part of a large-scale effort by reformers to educate the public about health and sanitation.[98] *The Fly Pest* struck a chord with audiences: it was both educational and a great popular entertainment. One article compared it to another runaway nonfiction hit, *Roosevelt in Africa* (1910), noting that "no two moving picture films ever made have received so much free advertising as these two. In practically every city, town or village where the 'Fly Pest' was run or is being run, the local papers have given it space varying from an inch of type to over two columns. . . . Even in as big a city as Chicago the *Daily News* gave a column and a half to the story of the picture, the comments of the audience and the educational value of the subject."[99] At a time when the motion picture's role as a new medium was still being defined, certain films were able to break through as media events. This same article explained, "At present there are but two general classes of moving pictures which may be counted upon to get newspaper publicity. One classification is *educational* subjects—the ones that really carry a message to the people. Perhaps it would be better to call them scientific subjects. The other classification is *current events*—whether they be quasi-historical like 'Roosevelt in Africa,' or sporting, like the Jeffries–Johnson fight pictures or the world's series baseball films."[100] Current events films—otherwise known as topicals and eventually called newsreels—were indeed a popular form of nonfiction for many years.

But this kind of nonfiction is quite different from the appeal of the scenic film. Were scenics able to inspire the same kind of enthusiasm as these topical films, which seem to have coasted to success due to their novelty value? The appeal of scenic films—the fascination of natural beauty and foreign lands—may not have had the topical component of big news events, but their appeal was constant. Certainly, not all travel films were the same, as the failure of the Méliès films demonstrates. But despite a certain basic level of consistent appeal, it does appear that certain scenics managed to stand out more than others. Letters to the distributor George Kleine indicate that *Trawler Fishing in a Hurricane* (Eclipse, 1910) was an unusually popular scenic film. An exhibitor in Long Beach, California, sent fifteen cents to order Kleine's film catalogue and wrote, "I wish to speak of a recent Urban release 'Trawler Fishing in a Hurricane,' I ran this picture 3 days, it brought me more business than even 'The Fly Pest,' you can not give us to [*sic*] much of these kind of pictures, a subject in your catalogue 'The Life of a Wood Ant' would certainly be a drawing card."[101] To a contemporary ear, this praise for a film about wood ants almost sounds like sarcasm, but it was not: *The Life of a*

Wood Ant is duly listed in Kleine's *Catalogue of Educational Films* for 1910.[102] *Trawler Fishing in a Hurricane* also got rave reviews in the trade press and seems to have been a minor hit. At least one other exhibitor also wrote in to praise the film, and a review in *Variety* praised *Trawler Fishing* as "one of the best scenic pictures yet produced."[103] Apparently, the film's dramatic ocean scenery was quite appealing. Unfortunately, it has not survived, so we cannot examine it for qualities that might have made it so compelling.

Despite these occasional exceptions, nonfiction films by and large were not runaway commercial successes. Rather, they were defined by their formulaic qualities, their *typicality*. Audiences knew what to expect from a scenic film or an industrial: the shape of certain nonfiction genres remained the same, even if their content — from Egypt to Ecuador, from gold bars to Gouda cheese — might vary. Some reviewers even made fun of the formula. A review of *The Park of Caserta* (Urban-Eclipse, 1910), for instance, begins: "The Park of Caserta, wherever that is, certainly has its full share of fountains, for that's about all the picture shows." Another reviewer complains in a review of *The Wonders of Nature* (Kalem, 1909): "The camera man must have roamed all over the Western state [Idaho] looking for water falls. When he found one that struck him as particularly impressive he became hypnotized with a desire to photograph it from every angle and point of vantage. In one instance the screen held different views of Twin Falls for ten straight minutes. The pictures were undeniably beautiful, but ten minutes is a long time to watch water falling over a precipice without any more enlivening incident."[104] One measure of a genre's success, however, is the level of parody it inspires. (I discuss the history of picturesque parodies in chapter 5.)

Nonfiction was arguably more important in early cinema than at any other time in film history. Before fiction films had perfected their union of the artificial and the natural with the development of conventions of cinematic realism, nonfiction genres were the primary films in which audiences could experience "the living panorama of nature." The classic division between "natural" (unstaged) films and "artificial" (staged) films was drawn differently in this period than it came to be drawn later. Early nonfiction's often conventional depictions of "nature" were sustained by a series of early film industry practices — the variety format, the split reel — that kept them in the public eye long after the new innovations of narrative filmmaking were developed in the early 1910s. Nonfiction films may have rarely made the headlines that fiction films did, but their ubiquity in early cinema should not be overlooked by film historians.

CHAPTER 3

"THE FIVE-CENT UNIVERSITY"
Educational Films and the Drive to Uplift the Cinema

> Motion picture theaters can add largely to
> their receipts if they make a point of showing
> an educational film at least once a week.
> — OLIVER PIKE, 1910

> The eye gate opens almost a royal road to learning.
> — *MOTOGRAPHY*, JULY 1911

In 1912, the *New York Evening Journal* ran an editorial whose headline proclaimed, "The Power of Moving Pictures: They Will Educate, through the Eye, Hundreds of Millions of Children."[1] The existence of the editorial itself is unremarkable—at the time, a heated public discussion about the merits and drawbacks of the new motion picture medium was being carried out in the pages of American newspapers. What is significant about this editorial published in the mainstream press is its celebration of film's ability to educate rather than entertain—as well as its curiously invasive formulation of "education through the eye," a common conceit of the era. This article envisions the moving picture audience as a vast population of children in need of education and discipline, a kind of unruly mob who will benefit from the "wonderful lesson in history and in morals" that films can provide.[2] By this time, due to the success of nickelodeons and the continued growth of the film industry, moving pictures were begrudgingly accepted as an entertainment form of growing significance, and with this success came calls to improve the cinema. To use the language of Progressive Era reform, the cinema needed to be "uplifted." Partly in response to these calls, and partly in an attempt to make more money, some early cinema businessmen launched campaigns to remake the film industry as an educational medium. Many of these efforts involved producing higher-quality dramatic films, like those discussed in the editorial, but other efforts centered on promoting nonfiction subjects such as travel films, nature films, and science films. This chapter tells the story of a neglected moment in early film history, a brief period — at its peak from 1910 to 1913 — in which "educational" films were promoted and shown in commercial motion picture theaters.[3] This moment was short-lived. By the mid-1910s, it was clear that feature film dramas, not nonfiction subjects, represented the commercial cinema's path to profits. Despite this ultimate failure, however, for a brief time "educationals" appeared to be one of the best means to legitimate the cinema; some even argued that nonfiction would dominate the future film industry. One writer in the trade journal *Motography* proclaimed: "Of all forms of motion pictures, scenics are the most popular and always will be so." Another declared, "In time they will prove the best drawing and best paying pictures." Still another predicted, "Before long we expect to see every exhibitor clamoring for scenic and scientific subjects even to the exclusion of the mediocre dramatic and comedy pictures."[4] This chapter analyzes the history of this singular moment and its failure — a moment of speculation in which, some said, those who acted first to get on the educational bandwagon were sure to "reap the first profits accordingly."[5]

It is well known that as soon as cinema began to gain viability as a significant entertainment medium, it faced a cultural crisis. As films gained in popularity during the nickelodeon boom, the attention they garnered from Progressive Era reformers, educators, and clergy, most of whom derided this new form of "cheap amusement," grew. One member of the Society for the Prevention of Cruelty to Children, for example, wrote: "The darkened rooms, combined with the influence of pictures projected on the screens, have given opportunities for a new form of degeneracy."[6] As this comment indicates, a great deal of the cinema's bad reputation came not from the films themselves but from the venues in which they were shown: Nickelodeons were castigated as dark dens of vice, where women were molested by "mashers" and young children were exposed to unsavory influences. Given this outcry, early campaigns to reform the cinema involved upgrading theaters with better lighting and promoting them as safe, clean venues for mothers and children.[7] Alongside these concerns about exhibition, film content became a contentious site for the legitimation of cinema.

In response to such criticism, the film industry embarked on a concerted drive for cultural respectability from about 1907 to 1917. Film scholars in recent years have begun to address this important history. William Uricchio and Roberta Pearson have documented the Vitagraph "Quality Films" of 1908–12 (Shakespeare, historical, and biblical subjects), for example, while Rob King has explored the attempts made by the Triangle Film Corporation in 1915–17 to produce a series of "high-class" subjects using well-respected stars hired from the theatrical stage.[8] As Uricchio and Pearson acknowledge, the Vitagraph "Quality Films" were ultimately "dismissed by their own producer."[9] Similarly, King tells a story of cultural negotiation in which, despite these efforts to gentrify the cinema, "the authority of highbrow culture was transfigured and displaced by consumer values."[10] In a study of other institutional efforts, Lee Grieveson has traced the various repressive forces of film regulation and censorship that held sway in the years 1907–14, with a focus on, among other things, the formation of the National Board of Censorship in 1909 and the production of "uplift dramatic films" that would link cinema with the forces of reform.[11] While censorship remained an important issue for decades, these more localized attempts to "uplift" the cinema failed commercially. That such attempts were made at all, however, reveals the contentious dynamic of class and aesthetics in the early film industry.

Movies did eventually come to be seen as an acceptable form of entertainment for "respectable" citizens, but these scattered efforts were not responsible for that broad shift. It was clearly the rise of the feature film and the attendant trappings of classical cinema that brought about the industry's desired "respectability" and concomitant profits: sustained feature-length narratives, high production values, movie stars, expensive promotional campaigns, and an active fan discourse. The stories of these initial, often abortive attempts to legitimate the cinema, however, are crucial for understanding early cinema's complexity and difference. While the studies by Uricchio and Pearson, King, and Grieveson are vital for their depiction of an industry in turmoil, we can deepen our understanding of this complex period by examining how *nonfiction* film fit into these attempts to legitimate the cinema. For it was the so-called educational subjects—nature films, topical films, and, above all, scenic or travel films—that were most uniformly singled out for praise in this period. Although what we would now call nonfiction film was not yet conceptualized as a distinct mode of cinema, the struggle to define and promote it constituted one of the key battles in this era of cultural negotiation.

To understand nonfiction's role in early attempts to legitimate the cinema, we need to distinguish between two groups who undertook the uplift campaign: educators and reformers, on the one hand, whose work was conducted largely outside the film industry; and producers, distributors, and exhibitors, on the other hand, who attempted to direct the future of cinema from inside the industry. Those reformers and educators who defended the cinema—such as, most famously, Jane Addams—argued that moving pictures should be improved, not eradicated. For these reformers, nonfiction films, and travel films in particular, served as one of the few unfailingly defensible kinds of cinema. For example, in 1909, Frederick Starr, a professor of anthropology at the University of Chicago, wrote, "The moving picture is not a makeshift, but the highest type of entertainment in the history of the world. It stands for a better Americanism because it is attracting millions of the masses to an uplifting."[12] At the same time, certain figures in the film industry echoed these cries to uplift the cinema—most famously, Thomas Edison and George Kleine in the United States and Charles Urban in the United Kingdom. However, the goals of the reformers—working in nonprofit philanthropic or educational institutions—were clearly different from the goals of the early film moguls, who, no matter how altruistic their intentions, still worked within a for-profit industry.

Education and Social Uplift in the Progressive Era

During the Progressive Era, a "crisis of citizenship" seemed to be at hand as reformers debated how to resolve social problems caused by immigration, urbanization, and labor unrest.[13] As large-scale immigration radically changed the makeup of the U.S. population, the issue of "Americanization" became a dominant concern of the day. One response to this concern about national identity was the movement to expand public education in the early twentieth century. Reformers joined with business interests to transform the public high school from an elite training ground for the upper middle class into an institution "designed to prepare boys and girls for jobs in the higher reaches of blue collar labor and the lower echelons of white collar work."[14] As a result, high school enrollment grew from 6.7 percent in 1890 to 32.3 percent in 1920.[15] As part of their goal of "Americanization," public schools expanded the "3 Rs" curriculum of the nineteenth-century common school (reading, writing, and arithmetic), by adding lessons on the language, laws, and customs of the United States.[16]

The nascent film industry, eager to justify itself, was quick to argue that motion picture theaters could also serve as a sort of school. As one writer explained in *Motography*, "The schools themselves are for education; but they have no monopoly on education. . . . In short, the educational application of motion pictures depends wholly on the sort of pictures shown, and not on where they are shown."[17] Others in the industry extolled the "Americanizing" force of educational motion pictures for immigrants and children. One account of a screening for eight hundred children at the Bijou Dream Theater in Boston in 1912 lists the film titles shown, which included nonfiction subjects such as *Colorado Springs and Battle Creek*, *Wild Animals in Captivity*, and *A Day at West Point*. The account concludes by stating, "After the last picture was exhibited the children arose and sang 'America.'"[18]

Many of these so-called educational films depicted foreign cultures and geography, and one might wonder how the goal of "Americanization" was served by such films. However, scenic films were also celebrated for achieving another important goal of the Progressive Era: democratization. By making "travel" available to everyone, scenic films achieved a sort of democratic education through media. "One of the greatest of . . . modern equalizers is the cinematograph," opined the writer of *Moving Picture World*'s regular column "The Moving Picture Educator."[19] Or as another writer put it, "You may call it the five-cent university or the dime civilizer, but its influence is real and sure just the same."[20] Over and over again, writers in this period claimed that films were an equal substitute for actual travel and a better substitute than books. "The cinematograph is now not only the equivalent of the opportunities of travel, but more than the equivalent, in that it gives more universal travel in but a fraction of the time required in actual travel," went the typical words of praise.[21] Of course, watching a film is nothing like actual travel, but I have never encountered an early film pundit who pointed this out. Instead, capitalizing on the enthusiasm for this new, remarkably lifelike medium, the film industry chose to promote films as a practical solution to the goals of universal education and democratization.

The reformist spirit of the Progressive Era was hardly uniform. Instead, it encompassed a spectrum of ideologies. Some secular reformers were motivated by utopian beliefs, while others were motivated by the evangelical Social Gospel movement. One concern uniting these various factions of social reform was an interest in the welfare of immigrants and the urban poor, particularly children. As Gregory Jackson has observed in an article on Jacob Riis's well-known stereopticon lectures on New York tenement neighborhoods, which he calls "virtual-tour narratives," "The principal ethos linking secular, progressive reform with Christian Socialism was the perceived need to intervene in childhood poverty."[22] This interest in children's welfare was certainly reflected in the reformist discourse about early motion pictures: one of the most common criticisms of the medium was its perceived negative effect on children. Given the wide range of reformist ideologies, however, it is reductive simply to claim that all reformers were opposed to the cinema, even though there were many repressive attempts to censor and police it. In fact, a significant number of reformist voices expressed hope for the cinema's potential to educate and called for it to be improved rather than eradicated. Jane Addams took this more inclusive view, to the extent that she installed a five-cent theater in her Hull House settlement in Chicago for a two-week period in June 1907. As J. A. Lindstrom has shown, "The films were selected by Hull House administrators and included fairy tales, 'foreign scenes which filled our Italian and Greek neighbors with homely reminiscences,' known stories with moral lessons (such as *Uncle Tom's Cabin*), and actualities of fire and police rescues and happy domestic situations."[23] Addams's belief in film's ability to educate was broad-ranging; her film program's inclusion of not only "moral lessons" but also entertainment (fairy tales) demonstrates this. Likewise the fact that the scenic films on the program were celebrated for activating immigrants' nostalgic memories of their homelands demonstrates Addams's progressive belief in the value of immigrant experience.

The concept of "uplift" can help us understand the broad range of reformist approaches to cinema in the early twentieth century. The term "uplift," so central to Progressive Era discourse, embodies the era's sense of class and culture as rigid hierarchical categories, while the term simultaneously evokes complex and contradictory practices, which is why I believe it has this broad applicability. As Kevin Gaines has shown, the idea of uplift "embraces elite and popular meanings and encompasses the tension between narrow, racial claims of progress and more democratic visions of social enhancement."[24] The concept is perhaps best known today for its usage by African American educators and reformers working to overcome racism in the late nineteenth century and early twentieth. As Gaines's analysis shows, racial uplift ideology involved two competing notions of black citizenship: a "collective social aspiration" that included everyone and an elite notion of citizenship available only to those who embodied bourgeois standards of "temperance, thrift, chastity, social purity, patriarchal authority, and the accumulation of wealth."[25] W. E. B. Du Bois's notion of "the talented tenth"—the idea that one in ten black men had the potential to become a successful leader—illustrates the social stratification inherent in racial uplift ideology.[26] What the progressive and conservative elements of racial uplift ideology shared, however, was a belief that education was the route to uplift. This emphasis on education had the effect of shifting notions of value and status away from biology and race toward the idea that culture was the force most responsible for shaping the individual. The idea of uplift, then, is by definition an evolutionary concept that reinscribes dominant realms of power; however, the goal of uplift was to admit more people into those dominant realms of power. The contradictory power of racial uplift ideology was thus its use of a hierarchical model harnessed to disrupt the traditional social hierarchy.

Other meanings of "uplift" in the Progressive Era can be found in the work of public education reformers. As recent historical research has shown, much of that work was carried out by women's organizations. In this light, the concept of uplift also carries a gendered connotation resembling the "maternalist" dispensation of much women's social reform, which focused its efforts on children, women, and the urban poor. Many female reformers shared the Progressive vision of antiracism activists striving for a better society that could be achieved through effort, education, and uplift. Women, who were literally un-enfranchised before they gained the right to vote in 1920, targeted their volunteer efforts at helping other disenfranchised groups. Volunteers working in settlement houses, for example, most of whom were students from prestigious women's colleges, undertook a broad range of activities focusing on working-class women and children: "to teach the basics of keeping a moral, clean, American home; to offer alternative pastimes that would keep children off the streets; and to provide what they and their mentors saw as cultural uplift."[27] Women's reform efforts, like racial uplift ideology, encompassed multiple political positions. The goal of public education, like the goal of racial uplift, was to include more people within the ranks of the middle class. But again, many of these efforts were disciplinary. The education activist Kate Douglas Wiggin wrote in the first annual report of the National Kindergarten Association in 1911 that public kindergartens were "a philanthropic agent, leading the child gently into right habits of thought, speech, and action from the beginning" and that they could "help in the absorption and amalgamation of our foreign element."[28] As this quote indicates, female reformers were engaged in issues of assimilation and taste that focused specifically on immigrants and children. These concerns were also registered in the discourse surrounding the drive to uplift the cinema. As

Lee Grieveson has shown, "The pervasive rhetoric about cinema replacing the saloon, reforming men, and reinforcing the family drew precisely on this [maternalist] regulatory context, forging a curious and certainly fragile alliance with early feminist maternalist discourse."[29] I am not suggesting that "uplift" ideology, as it appeared in efforts to legitimate the cinema, was necessarily antiracist or feminist — indeed, it was often anything but progressive in these areas. My point is that the rhetoric of uplift was so pervasive that it carried over into the film industry's internal debates, where it was hitched, sometimes uncomfortably, to the commercial prerogatives of business.

Early Nonfiction's Fluid Class Disposition

Historians traditionally have located the cinema's origins in working-class entertainment forms—the circus, the carnival, the burlesque—and they characterize the shifting class dimension of early cinema as a "transition from broad and raucous forms to refined entertainment product."[30] As such, recent scholarly accounts of early cinema's legitimation campaign have focused on the film industry's attempts to appeal to a particular kind of audience: "men and women of refinement and discrimination."[31] Understood in this way, it follows that attempts to import "high-class" influences (Shakespeare, respected stage actors) have been characterized as variously elitist, conservative, or middlebrow gestures. However, while this interpretation asserts that early cinema's uplift campaign was an attempt to eradicate film's association with cheap amusements, the presence of nonfiction in early cinema tells us that the class valence of early film was by no means so clear-cut.

Scenic films and other nonfiction genres were regularly advertised as "high-class" subjects, which indicates, first, that not all film had a uniformly "raucous" reputation in the early years. Charles Musser, for example, uses the term "cinema of reassurance" to describe the film programs shown in the travel lecturer tradition personified by Burton Holmes and Lyman Howe.[32] Musser's groundbreaking book on Howe correctly asserts that "his activities make it impossible to equate film with commercial amusement per se, for Howe did not embrace popular entertainment in the same way as Coney Island and vaudeville."[33] However, rather than using Howe's shows as evidence of early cinema's fluid class appeal — the same nonfiction films were shown in lecture halls and in nickel theaters, after all — Musser instead views nonfiction subjects as unrelenting bearers of conservative ideology. In analyzing one of Howe's early film programs that showed scenes of the United States, Musser writes, "Howe had created what we can call a cinema of reassurance. . . . Nothing critical enters this view of America. All is right within a screen world where all fill their designated roles."[34] Such a declarative analysis denies the wide variety of responses such screenings undoubtedly produced. Musser's claim that travel lecturers such as Howe and Holmes "appealed to an elitist group that was little concerned with novelty outside its own select world" disavows precisely what travel films aimed to provide: novelty outside the spectator's own world.[35] In contrast, I contend that instead of producing complacent spectators, nonfiction could have had more open-ended effects by producing responses that were not necessarily in keeping with bourgeois standards of taste. The travel film's "genteel" prestige by no means excluded its potential appeal to less "refined" tastes, and we must be wary of dividing early films too neatly into categories of "highbrow" versus "lowbrow" culture, which falls into the trap of reifying the era's own class hierarchies. I believe we need to envision early cinema as a fluctuating domain with indefinite class appeal. This mutability is a crucial aspect of mass culture's ability to construct itself as "mass." What has been overlooked in discussions of cinematic legitimation is a more nuanced sense of the class dimension and the aesthetic appeal of early nonfiction film.

Early travel, nature, and science films were not always the "refined" and "genteel" subjects their reputation would lead us to believe. Rare early posters for the nonfiction films La fauvette et le coucou and How Wild Animals Live help to illustrate the different aesthetic appeals these kinds of films could make, even at the level of promotion (see plates 4–5). Posters were not regularly produced for nonfiction films in this period, so the fact that these two posters were manufactured—let alone that they have survived—is remarkable and indicative of the sizable budgets of these films. The films, which were released within a year of each other (and neither of which is known to exist today), featured promotional materials highlighting different aspects of nonfiction film: one emphasizes science, and the other emphasizes sensation. The delicate French poster advertising La fauvette et le coucou (Pathé, 1912) was drawn by the caricaturist Adrien Barrère, who made a number of posters for Pathé from 1908 through the 1920s. The image is a caricature of a John James Audubon illustration, which depicted birds against minimal backgrounds to facilitate the study of their bodies and movements. In contrast, the American poster advertising How Wild Animals

Live (Midgar Features, 1913), with its sensationalistic imagery of animals devouring each other, clearly fits into a graphic tradition derived from the circus. Each film was a (relatively) big-budget attempt to capitalize on the new popularity of animal films, although *La fauvette et le coucou* was a one-reel short and *How Wild Animals Live* was a six-reel feature, an unprecedented length for a nonfiction film in 1913.[36] *La fauvette et le coucou* was directed by Oliver Pike, the renowned British pioneer of nature films, who had secured a distribution contract with Pathé after the success of his independently produced film *In Birdland* (1907), while the director of *How Wild Animals Live* remains unknown.

La fauvette et le coucou was released as part of Pathé's Vulgarisation Scientifique (Popular Science) series, which places it in the domain of the serious educational film. Judging from the poster, the film showed a baby cuckoo bird invading the nest of two warblers (cuckoos are famous for laying their eggs in warbler [fauvette] birds' nests). This emphasis on habitat was relatively new — Pike was one of the first wildlife filmmakers to show animals in their natural habitat rather than in zoos or staged settings — but it later became a major convention of the nature film.[37] This "scientific" objectivity would seem to lend itself to just the sort of educational praise I have been describing. Perhaps more surprising, however, is the reception of the other film. Despite the circus sideshow quality of its poster, *How Wild Animals Live* was praised by reviewers for being "rich in educational values" and for its potential to "bring hosts of new and desirable patrons."[38] Perhaps the "high-class" reputation of early nonfiction functioned as a sort of decoy, adding a veneer of educational respectability to film subjects that were just as sensational as their fictional counterparts. The contrasting graphic techniques of the two posters demonstrate that early nonfiction film was not monolithic in its style or in its mode of audience appeal.

In fact, a crucial dimension of early nonfiction films, which were shown in both theatrical and nontheatrical venues, is that the same film could be made to serve different purposes in different exhibition contexts. In 1910, a nickelodeon exhibitor named H. F. Hoffman described going to a lecture by Burton Holmes consisting "almost entirely of scenic pictures. . . . The audience was immensely pleased, but what made me gasp was that some of the scenes he showed them for $2 had been seen at my theater for five cents over a year before."[39] Obviously, ticket price is a good barometer of the economic class of each venue's patrons. What is significant is that the same films found an audience in both venues. As Hoffman concludes,

I do not want to give the idea that scenic and industrial pictures are the only kinds you ought to exhibit and that the drama should be left out entirely. I do think, however, that at least one straight picture should be in every day's program. The thing should be balanced properly. . . . There are all kinds of tastes in this world and I realize that you cannot please everybody all the time, but this much is true; there are thousands and thousands of sensible business men and their wives who like nothing better than a fine scenic or interesting industrial. This desirable class is being neglected.[40]

Hoffman does not cite the appeal that nonfiction also had for immigrant and poor audiences, but he does acknowledge the wide variety of "tastes" that the nickelodeon's variety format aspired to reach.

When analyzing the early film industry's attempts at "uplift," if we take nonfiction into consideration, the usual story begins to look different. From the perspective of reformers and educators, the problem was that very few early films met the standards of "high-class" taste; therefore, the fact that educational genres had a respectable reputation made them appealing. But from the perspective of a businessman in the film industry, the problem was quite a different one: not how to make films better but how to make better films appealing. How could supposedly "high-class" subjects such as scenics and science films be made to appeal to a broad and mixed audience that included the middle class, working class, and immigrants populating the nickel theaters? Following the spirit of Progressive Era reform, businessmen such as Thomas Edison and George Kleine believed that simply by making them available to all, educational films would prove they had built-in appeal for a wide variety of viewers, including the working class. Rather than a problem of taste, Edison and Kleine seemed to view the key to the educational film's success as a problem of *access*. That is, rather than a trickle-down model of class, which implies that a condescending elite will bring the gift of culture and good taste to the masses, the uplift model follows the democratic logic of the public schools then being championed by reformers, in which the taste of the masses could be "lifted" to resemble that of the elite simply by giving the masses access to educational material. According to the logic of uplift, what needs to be changed is not so much cultural material as the audience's taste.

Given this complex class dynamic, rather than looking for linear movement toward or away from cultural respectability, it seems more accurate to assess the cinema's shifting cultural status as part of the complex nature of mass culture that concurrently registers on different cultural levels in different contexts. For the film industry, the trick was to create a truly *mass* culture: an entertainment product that could appeal across diverse cultural and economic groups. As Uricchio and Pearson argue, "Contra expectations, we have shown that the attribute 'high' is to some extent misleading, in that such cultural figures as Shakespeare and Napoleon were part of most people's everyday experience. Members of all social formations would thus have had intertextual frames for making sense of the quality films."[41] Clearly, this was also true for scenic films and other educational subjects: The same film circulating through diverse audiences had different meaning for different social groups. This creation of a broad, all-encompassing mass culture actually parallels the political goals of Progressive Era reformers (although they probably would not have viewed it this way). For while these reformers were certainly a diverse group who took a variety of approaches to social problems, historians generally agree that "most shared a vision of citizenship built around the ideal of a common social interest that transcended the goals of economic interest groups."[42]

Turning Good Taste into Mass Taste

Class conflict and class identity were pressing concerns for late nineteenth-century and early twentieth-century America, which was unsure how the influx of working-class immigrants would change the country and which was generally preoccupied with hierarchies of all sorts. Film scholars have frequently turned to an Arnoldian paradigm to analyze the class dynamic of early cinema. Uricchio and Pearson, along with Grieveson more recently, have argued that Matthew Arnold's idea of culture as an antidote to social anarchy—his well-known concept of culture as "sweetness and light"—was "taken up by many in the dominant social formations of the United States, who attempted to forge a cultural consensus that would incorporate rather than repress disruptive forces such as workers and immigrants."[43] But while Arnold's ideas played an important role in British and American culture from the 1870s well into the twentieth century (Arnold's book *Culture and Anarchy* was first published in 1869), by the 1910s, other voices of reform were taking up questions of industrialization and immigration in new ways. I do not deny the continuing influence of the Arnoldian tradition in early twentieth-century thought, but if we are to gain a deeper understanding of education and reform discourse in the Progressive Era, we would do well to consider other voices of reform that were active concurrently with early cinema.

The Arnoldian paradigm, usually understood as representing the anti-repressive wing of turn-of-the-century reform discourse, is still quite rigid when compared with some of the other ideas of the Progressive Era (which itself does not look "progressive" by today's standards). Arnold envisioned a nation of rigid class stratification, in which culture functioned as a compensation for the turmoil of modernization. In the Arnoldian paradigm, culture did not change anyone's social status; rather, it marked one's social status. As Lawrence Levine has shown, the late nineteenth century saw the "sacralization of culture," which brought about a new understanding of cultural hierarchy. The plays of William Shakespeare had once been patronized by both elite and popular audiences, but Shakespeare's work began to take on more exclusively elite connotations, while culture in general became more stratified in this era.[44] But things were changing yet again in the early 1900s. Some economists, educators, and social theorists, from John Dewey to Simon Patten, updated the Arnoldian paradigm for the early twentieth century, arguing not only that culture—particularly "high" culture—was a potentially democratizing force, but also that it should be made available to everyone through public education and affordable (emergent) mass culture. Dewey, a philosopher and prominent educational reformer, articulated a complex theory of education through aesthetic experience in *Democracy and Education*, while Patten, an economist, was an early champion of the power of mass culture to relieve the stresses of workers; his widely read 1907 book *The New Basis of Civilization* contains a chapter on how the amusement field was influencing modern life.[45]

This is not the place for a deep consideration of various Progressive Era philosophies. I simply want to indicate that while the Arnoldian idea of culture was popular in the early twentieth century, adaptations of his influential ideas were also in the air. What is clear is that reformers of the era took it upon themselves to ensure that culture would serve an uplifting and educational purpose.[46] The broad and active reform movement of the day, following this "uplift" ideology, wanted not just to mitigate social stresses, à la Arnold, but to "improve" the tastes of the middle and working classes by means of education, thus transforming the nation's social structure.

Class boundaries were shifting in the early twentieth century. As Steven J. Ross explains, while wealthy Americans grew more visible with their conspicuous consumption, "farmers, manufacturers, and small businessmen comprised what scholars call the 'old middle class' . . . [whose] numbers and power were rivaled by the rise of a 'new middle class' of professionals and salaried corporate managers." Finally, a new group of service-sector employees was also emerging whose class identity was yet undefined.[47] While leisure activities were still highly stratified not only by class but by race and ethnicity, the cinema in the 1910s served as a nascent space for mass culture in which working-class and middle-class patrons could comingle. Or, at least, that was the ideal of businessmen such as Kleine, who saw in this expanded audience not so much the improvement of society as an increase in profits.

Early travelogue films were dubbed "high-class" by just about everyone in their day, but the label was repeated so often that it begins to sound like self-congratulation more than an accurate representation of the economic stature of the audience. Nobody would have deemed his own show "low class," after all — at least, not in the pre-irony era of the early twentieth century. Why, then, do we see these constant reassurances about the class status of the travelogue film? Certainly, the travel lectures of Holmes and Howe drew predominantly upper- and middle-class crowds and can perhaps be seen as "reassuring" to some extent, as Musser asserts, although as I tried to show in chapter 1, even Holmes's travel lectures can be read against the grain. "Reassurance" does not tell the whole story. The travel film as experienced outside the lecture hall and inside the nickelodeon, shown amid a variety program to a heterogeneous audience, challenges notions of the travelogue's ostensibly comforting or conciliatory nature. If one pushes some of the travelogue's contradictory qualities just a little bit, the genre's bourgeois, "conservative" characterization does not seem so accurate after all. In fact, the irony of the film industry's and reform movement's support of the travel film is that the genre would seem to embody qualities that many reformers did not like. Travelogues were short; they stressed disjunction and discontinuity rather than the sanctioned bourgeois absorption of attention; and they relied on a frequently exploitive dynamic of exoticism and sensationalism found in foreign locales. Why, then, were they perceived as genteel?

Clearly, using the term "high-class" functioned as a simple commercial strategy, a form of flattering the audience's sense of status. "High-class" also indicates the extent to which class and education combined in the period to signify that which was socially validated. In fact, by the 1910s, a change was under way: Nonfiction's "high-class" label was becoming superseded by the label "educational." This shift marks a transformation from the nineteenth-century notion of static class divisions into the Progressive Era notion that class divisions might be more permeable. Quite literally, "high-class" now began to take on the connotation of "well-educated." The essentialized category of class was being replaced by a more democratic ideal of education.

During the transitional era, the film industry was experimenting to discover which genres would be the most popular and, thus, the most lucrative. As would seem logical, one strategy adopted by the industry was to appeal to the broadest audience base possible, thus maximizing profits. Democratic and universalizing rhetoric was harnessed to advance the cinema's wider appeal. Robert Allen has written that "part of the bourgeois ideology that undergirded the reintegrative project of B. F. Keith, E. F. Albee, F. F. Proctor, and other vaudeville magnates was the denial of class as a determinative social marker and an insistence that, within the walls of the new, capacious vaudeville palaces, everyone enjoyed equal status as a 'patron.'"[48] The cinema, like vaudeville and other popular forms of entertainment at the time, participated in a process that applied the homogenizing ideology of mass culture to an audience that was actually quite diverse. The complex discourse surrounding early cinema demonstrates just how unstable the concept of a mass audience was at the time. Commercial interests fostered a universalist discourse, while at the same time, reformers tried to steer that "universalism" so that it resembled their own bourgeois values. However, the actual outcome was not necessarily so controlled.

The nonfiction film's transformation from spectacle-oriented actualities into a group of "educational" genres was a part of the industry's process of standardization and reorganization. Although that transformation was more rhetorical than anything else—the sensational "attractions" element of travelogues always remained—its force can be felt all over the discourse surrounding the travelogue in the early 1910s. Examples of this "educational" rhetoric are easy to find: "Geography, ethnography, science, industry, archaeology, may all be usefully illustrated by the cinematograph, and every part of the world, all the races of the earth in their native surroundings—the workman at his bench and the hunter in the forest—may be reproduced in a manner that the youthful student will instantly comprehend and never forget."[49] Travel films and other nonfiction genres were seen as the best medium for mass education; because of film's visual nature, no previous knowledge or genteel status was required to understand the educational motion picture.

In the years 1910–13, the trade press undertook a major campaign to convince exhibitors that scenic and educational films were appealing not just to the "better classes" but also to the wider, more heterogeneous film audience made up of working-class and middle-class patrons. Some tried to claim that travelogues would be the most popular genre if only exhibitors would show them more frequently or if only the audience could be taught to appreciate them. One editorial exclaimed: *"The preference of the public is for travel pictures. Make no mistake about this. It is not merely the opinion of* MOTOGRAPHY'S *editors, nor is it the theory of impractical students. It is the statement of the people themselves."*[50] The writer's evidence for this statement, however, is simply one newspaper poll taken in St. Louis at a time that Lyman Howe was presenting a show in town. Howe even "encouraged the test and was profoundly encouraged in its results," indicating that the poll was not in fact such a disinterested sample of what "the public" really preferred.[51] Again, the rhetoric of uplift promised one thing, but the actual practice on the ground was not so neat and clean. But such rhetoric was hardly scarce. *Moving Picture News* fairly shouted in an editorial on educational films published in 1911, "Gentlemen of the film industry, *these are the films that the people want, these are the stories that appeal to the hearts and understandings, and these you should produce instead of many that you are manufacturing."*[52]

George Kleine and the Promotion of Educational Films

Moving from these broad issues of education and cultural distinction, I turn now to the film distributor George Kleine's efforts to promote educational subjects in commercial motion picture theaters. In 1909, as the nickelodeon craze continued into its fourth year in the United States, Kleine began to actively promote travel films, industrials, nature films, and other educational subjects in an effort to shape the emerging film culture. Kleine's attempt to turn "good taste" into "mass taste" is fascinating for a number of reasons: for the attempt itself, for how it failed, and for its larger implications about film aesthetics. Like the efforts of the Triangle Film Corporation to promote "high-class" fiction films, Kleine's efforts to commercialize educational subjects did not succeed. But if we take a longer view, a place for nonfiction was eventually carved out by the visual education movement of the 1920s, which successfully established film exhibition in nontheatrical venues such as schools. What the film industry miscalculated during the Progressive Era was not so much the cultural value of nonfiction films as their commercial potential.

FIGURE 3.1
Portrait of George Kleine.
George Kleine Papers,
Manuscript Division,
Library of Congress,
Washington, D.C.

Although he appears in most early film histories only briefly, usually in relation to his role in the formation of the Motion Picture Patents Company (MPPC), Kleine was one of the most important promoters of nonfiction film in the United States in the nickelodeon era (fig. 3.1). Kleine's papers are held at the Library of Congress, and a close examination of his meticulously kept records reveals that while he was a businessman first and foremost, Kleine's entrepreneurial goals were clearly shaped by reform-minded principles. Although he was once called a "conservative" by no less a figure than Louella Parsons, I interpret his actions in a somewhat more progressive light.[53] Kleine's reformist bent was perhaps a result of his personal background and education. He was born in New York City to German Protestant parents in 1863, which, given the era, probably makes him the son of immigrants (although I have not found evidence to substantiate this). Kleine was educated at the first free public institution of higher learning in the United States, the College of the City of New York, where he received his bachelor's degree at age nineteen.[54] Kleine thus joined an elite, newly ascendant entrepreneurial middle class who came of age at the beginning of the Progressive Era. While it is unclear what he did in the first eleven years after his graduation in 1882, by 1893 he had expanded his father's business, the Kleine Optical Company in New York, by opening a new office in Chicago. He began selling and importing optical machinery such as lenses, cameras, stereopticons, and other projection devices. He was working with motion pictures essentially from the moment they were introduced, beginning in 1896, and by 1900 he had closed out all parts of his business unrelated to moving picture machines and films.[55]

The Kleine firm began importing films from Europe in 1903, first selling them and then renting them. In 1906, Kleine signed a contract with Gaumont for the U.S. distribution of its films and established a film exchange in Chicago. In 1907, the year he cofounded the Kalem film production company, Kleine began distributing films from the Charles Urban Trading Company in the United Kingdom, which included the important French films from Eclipse, known in the United States as Urban-Eclipse. By 1908, Kleine was importing and distributing films from a dozen European production firms, most of which produced at least some nonfiction subjects: Gaumont and Urban-Eclipse were the most important of these (fig. 3.2). In January 1912, due to problems with Gaumont, Kleine switched to distributing films from the Italian Cines Company, which also produced nonfiction films.[56] Gaumont subsequently opened an American office and distributed its own films through the independent circuit. As an importer of films from Europe, Kleine was a promoter of nonfiction almost by default, even if that was not his original intent. But he became particularly dedicated to promoting educational film subjects, probably in part for cultural reasons (he was now a member of the so-called elite), and certainly for business reasons. The import business was profitable, after all: One report states that Kleine Optical imported almost $1 million worth of foreign films in 1907 alone.[57]

Although Kleine had a complex business relationship with Thomas

FIGURE 3.2
Import ad. George Kleine Papers, Manuscript Division, Library of Congress, Washington, D.C.

Edison over the years, he was one of the major negotiators involved with the formation of the MPPC in December 1908, which Edison spearheaded to protect the patents on cameras and projectors held by the Edison Manufacturing Company (fig. 3.3). Kleine was also vice president (and later president) of the MPPC's distribution arm, the General Film Company. As a founding member of the MPPC, Kleine, alongside Pathé, was the main supplier of imported nonfiction titles to licensed theaters in the United States.[58] The MPPC was founded for business reasons—to limit competition and control the industry—but it also claimed loftier reformist goals, among them the promotion of educational film. According to one contemporary newspaper account, "The Patents Company [has shown its] determination to absolutely eliminate all matter that does not possess either educational or

FIGURE 3.3 Founders of the Motion Picture Patents Company, 18 December 1908. Kleine is second from the right, in the front row. Courtesy Academy of Motion Picture Arts and Sciences.

cleanly amusing value."[59] The MPPC even proclaimed as much on some of its advertisements, using the slogan "Moral, Educational and Cleanly Amusing."[60] To encourage this policy, educational subjects were not subjected to the same rental restrictions as other kinds of film. In addition to being regularly released to licensed theaters alongside fiction films, they could be delivered to unlicensed lecturers or schools.[61]

The term "educational" was still being defined, but it primarily referred to nonfiction subjects. Kleine wrote to Charles Urban in 1909, "It is the intention of the Motion Picture Patents Co. to give a liberal interpretation to

FIGURE 3.4 Advertising "the best films of Europe for the American market." George Kleine Papers, Manuscript Division, Library of Congress, Washington, D.C.

the word educational, but in no case are dramatic, sensational, comedy or other films of that character to be included."[62] Despite giving lip service to nonfiction exhibition in schools, no organized network for nontheatrical distribution existed in this period, and Kleine committed most of his resources to promoting educationals in *commercial* theaters.[63] Educators regularly approached Kleine attempting to obtain films at low prices, but Kleine was a businessman first, not a reformer or an educator. He wanted to commercialize the nonfiction film, and he complained about those educational and religious institutions that "tried to get something for nothing," even calling the nontheatrical users "parasites."[64]

Kleine played up the cultural capital of the films' European origins in his advertisements to exhibitors, pointing out that his were "the best films of Europe for the American market" (fig. 3.4). As Richard Abel has shown, Kleine's rival distributor of nonfiction in the United States, Pathé, "may well have benefited from the turn-of-the-century American belief that France was 'the center of civilized . . . consumption.'"[65] As Abel demonstrates, any perception of "foreignness" was a double-edged sword in a period that was also suspicious of the perceived "immorality" of foreign influences. But imported nonfiction films were largely spared this perception, being so inseparably tied to their "educational" significance.

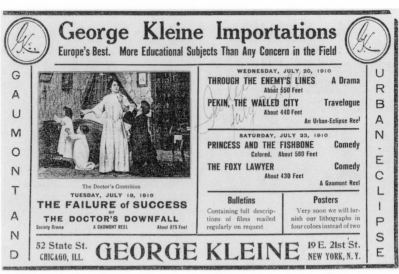

FIGURE 3.5 Advertising "More Educational Subjects Than Any Concern in the Field." George Kleine Papers, Manuscript Division, Library of Congress, Washington, D.C.

Kleine was indeed responsible for distributing "More Educational Subjects Than Any Concern in the Field," as one of his advertisements claimed (fig. 3.5). During the years 1909–13 alone, his company imported 385 different educational film titles. According to his own estimates, about fifty prints of each subject were distributed in the early years, and about twenty prints of each subject were distributed by 1913. This means that he distributed somewhere in the neighborhood of 12,000–19,000 prints of foreign educational subjects.[66] Kleine estimated that these films were viewed by 3 million–6 million people during this period.[67] Kleine believed that educational films might not be profitable at first, but he hoped this unprofitability might be turned around. He explained in a letter to Charles Urban in 1910, "At the best, the time and money that we put into the pushing of Educational and Industrial films will not be repaid for some years to come if at all."[68] Kleine's willingness to experiment with film subjects that many thought unmarketable sets him apart from many other businessmen of his day. Clearly, his motivation was not merely profit, although profit would have been a welcome result.

Kleine took several innovative steps to promote educational films. Most famously, he published a book-length *Catalogue of Educational Motion Pictures* in April 1910. This publication followed in the footsteps of Charles Urban in the United Kingdom, who had been releasing catalogues promoting his Urbanora educational films since 1903. Kleine's and Urban's catalogues are some of the earliest gestures the film industry made toward promoting educational films in commercial theaters.[69] The publications were aimed at exhibitors, not film audiences, and they made a significant impact on the film industry from behind the scenes. The catalogues are just as important as the films they describe, not only for the way they signify an attempt to institutionalize educational film, but for how they go about marketing educational films to the commercial industry.

As a side note, one can see by comparing the catalogues that many of Kleine's film descriptions were lifted directly from Urban's catalogue of 1908. Film descriptions provided by production companies were regularly published in the trade press, so one might assume that the descriptions in Kleine's and Urban's catalogues were furnished by the production companies, but as it turns out, Urban employed a writer named Clegg to write many of his descriptions. For a brief moment, a scandal emerged as Clegg and Urban publicly accused Kleine of plagiarism.[70]

Kleine's *Catalogue* in 1910 was the first large-scale effort to promote educational films in the United States. The front cover, lavishly printed in color, nicely encapsulates Kleine's approach to educational films (see plate 6). The Latin inscription at the top of the image, *disce videndo*, roughly translates as "learn by seeing." Behind the GK logo, presented on a background of stars and stripes, is an arrangement of flags representing the countries from which Kleine imported his films: Italy, the United Kingdom, and France. (The flag of Switzerland is also included, but I have not found evidence that Kleine imported any Swiss films.) A classical proscenium with columns frames curtains that have been pulled back to reveal an image of Niagara Falls. One would normally expect to see a dramatic scene framed with such pomp and circumstance, but instead it is a scenic image of thundering nature that takes center stage, suggesting Kleine's main argument: that educational films could be entertaining. A list of sixteen educational film genres encircles the columns on the left and right, containing categories such as "travel," "surgery," "zoology," and "mining." The overall effect of this elaborate image is to impose a confident tone of educational expertise.

The catalogue was a direct attempt to advertise educational film titles to commercial theaters. Kleine wrote: "I did not look upon this book as being different in kind from the innumerable catalogues which we have issued in the past with the purpose of selling goods, but gave it as much importance as possible to further the main object, which is to increase the popularity of Educational films among Exchanges and exhibitors."[71] The publication of the catalogue in 1910 was perhaps an attempt to capitalize on—or to boost—what the trade press was reporting as an increase in demand for educational films that year. "Within the past year there has been a change in the attitude of theater managers in general toward films of the educational class. The call for the lighter type of educational films is at the present time not only emphatic but widespread; little by little the demand for heavier subjects is increasing," Kleine explained in the trade press.[72] The catalogue itself is dedicated to Thomas Edison, "the most democratic of men," and reproduces a letter of support from Edison himself by way of an endorsement from the famous inventor.[73] The catalogue also reproduces in full the influential article of praise for motion pictures by Frederick Starr (mentioned earlier), which was reproduced widely in the motion picture trade press when it appeared in 1909.

Following the characteristic instability of genres in this period, the films listed in the catalogue are divided into inconsistent if not completely haphazard categories. (These divisions are different from those in Urban's catalogues.) For example, the "Classified Index" at the back lists seven different categories in which one can find travel films: "Dances (Barbaric)," "Ethnology," "Geography," "Hydrography," "Marine," "Panoramic," and "Scenic." All of them note, "See under TRAVELOGUES," although one should note that "Dances (Civilized)" includes the instruction "See under FINE ARTS."[74] The (uncredited) editors of the catalogue seem virtually to have given up on the difficult task of classifying films, explaining, "To find any Educational Subject by TITLE see under the following GENERAL ALPHABETICAL INDEX. Do NOT rely on TITLES as sufficient data to judge a film by. READ ALL LIKELY SYNOPSES VERY CAREFULLY."[75] Indeed, as Oliver Gaycken has suggested, Kleine's organizational logic in the catalogue can be likened to "a modern cabinet of curiosities" linked only by qualities such as wonder and anomaly.[76]

Kleine's papers are filled with letters of praise for the catalogue. One admiring letter writer sent a newspaper clipping gushing that Kleine's catalogue "indicates that there is scarcely a thing under the sun that hasn't been photographed for the film shows."[77] Kleine also took it upon himself to write to a number of educators for their responses to the catalogue. "What do you think of the Moving Picture film as an educator? Nothing would please us more than to have an expression from you, whether we sell you anything or not," he wrote.[78] While he was most likely seeking supportive statements that he could use in advertising, this also demonstrates that Kleine was a unique kind of businessman. Like many early film moguls, Kleine was a kind of prospector, looking to strike it rich not with comedies or with film stars but with educational subjects.

In addition to issuing this important catalogue for commercial exhibitors, Kleine tried advertising nonfiction in the same way that fiction films were publicized. This strategy was unusual enough to attract attention in the *Nick-elodeon*, which reported that it hoped the "innovation [would] elicit comment from the trade."[79] Posters were typically issued only for fiction films, but as the Kleine Company, "in pursuance of its always progressive and 'uplift' policy," explained in 1911:

> We are trying an experiment in posters and would like to have your opinion as to its value.
>
> On March 11th we will issue a Gaumont reel which will contain a story film called "His First Sweetheart," 560 feet in length; and a scenic film "Beautiful Gorges of the Tarn," 415 feet. Instead of illustrating the story film, we are issuing a poster reproducing one of the scenes in the scenic film.[80]

The *Nickelodeon* published a follow-up story two weeks later claiming that exhibitors had had "a change of heart toward scenics" due to a sudden discovery of the genre's profitability.[81] As in many stories in the trade press, this claim is unsubstantiated. Despite ample evidence in print of the campaign to promote educational films, the dearth of surviving evidence from exhibitors makes it difficult to ascertain the actual effects of this short-lived campaign.

While I have not been able to locate any of Kleine's nonfiction posters, Kleine's advertisements in the trade press are themselves illustrative. Many of his advertisements demonstrate that nonfiction subjects were released on split reels, paired with fiction films. Although Kleine's advertisement describes *The Volcano of Chinyero* as "Scientific and Beautiful," for example, at 158 feet and released on a reel with two other short subjects the film would likely have had only a brief and fragmentary impact (fig. 3.6). The same is more or less true of all Kleine's nonfiction subjects — and, indeed, of all nonfiction subjects more generally released to commercial theaters on split reels. Education was the watchword, but it was not necessarily the result. Another Kleine ad describes *Tropical Java of the South Sea Islands* as "about 312 ft. of Education," as though education is a commodity that can be sold by the foot.[82]

Any connection between watching these films and being educated by

IMPORTED BY

George Kleine

52 State St., CHICAGO   19 E. 21st St., NEW YORK

Week of April 9, 1910

VINTAGE AT LANGUEDOC
About 374 feet
Educational and Artistic

THE STUBBORN LOVER
About 452 feet
A truly laughable courtship
A Comedy

VOLCANO OF CHINYERO
About 158 feet
Scientific and Beautiful

April 11
Gaumont
1 Reel
Approx.
Length
984 Feet
Get the
Posters

THE LOOK-OUT
About 678 feet
Romantic and thrilling. A Drama

A RAMBLE THROUGH THE ISLE OF SUMATRA
About 241 feet
An interesting trip. A Travelogue

April 12
Urban-
Eclipse
1 Reel
Approx.
Length
949 Ft.
Remember
the
Posters

Mephisto at a Masquerade
About 486 feet
Colored beautifully
Mystery and Comedy.   A Farce

Touring the Canary Isles
About 478 feet
Choicest points of interest in a
wonderful little country.
A Travelogue

April 16
Gaumont
1 Reel
Approx.
Length
964 Ft.
You will
want the
Posters

Each Subject is Described at Length on Another Page of this Issue

 A POSTER FOR EACH REEL

FIGURE 3.6
Advertisement for
Kleine's weekly releases
for 9 April 1910.
George Kleine Papers,
Manuscript Division,
Library of Congress,
Washington, D.C.

them may be unsubstantiated, but it is everywhere asserted in Kleine's promotional materials. One advertisement promoted *O'er Crag and Torrent* as "well worth any one's time," for instance.[83] Another described *Immigrants' Progress in Canada* as an "enthralling illustration of the first five years' actual experience of a Canadian immigrant" (fig. 3.7). These advertisements reverse the usual order of things, in which the fiction film gets the frame enlargement. Here, the scenic films are reproduced, with varying degrees of visual impact: *A Sea of Clouds* is featured in an advertisement with a landscape shot (fig. 3.8), as were *The Monastery in the Forest* and *The Mountain Lake* in other ads.[84] Likewise, *Modern Railway Construction* gets the visual treatment in its advertisement, not the fiction films, as one might expect (fig. 3.9). These efforts by Kleine were the most sustained attempt to market educational films to commercial venues in the United States in this period. Other companies and other businessmen (such as "Colonel" William Selig) also promoted educational films, but Kleine's efforts went the furthest. The only other early film mogul in America to approach Kleine's enthusiasm for educational films was Edison, whose efforts at promoting nonfiction films were more sporadic and sensationalized.

Related Efforts by Thomas Edison

Kleine and Edison both campaigned for educational cinema, but their approaches differed. Despite his up-to-the-minute excitement about technology, Edison's educational philosophy was in some ways old-fashioned: He believed in rote memorization and seems to have harbored few reservations about the way films might encourage passive spectators. Edison issued a series of well-circulated statements beginning in 1911 about the value of film as an educational tool, asserting that films would someday replace textbooks in the nation's schools. For example, he claimed, "I can teach more accurate geography in half an hour to a class of young pupils by moving pictures than a pedagogue can in a month."[85] For Edison, visual education was as simple as putting images before pupils' eyes, and film served as a transparent window on the world.[86] His beliefs squared with many of the ideas of the Progressive Era education movement in America, which was forward-looking in its openness to new visual technology but still relied on "well-established ideas, such as the ancient hierarchy of the senses that placed vision above hearing, touch, taste, and smell," as Gaycken has pointed out.[87] Kleine's beliefs, by contrast, arguably fall on the more progressive side of the spectrum: For him, education was not simply a matter of putting practical

A FEATURE WEEK
Commencing May 1, 1910

THREE GREAT FILMS

Each Subject is Described at Length on Another Page of this Issue

 A POSTER FOR EACH REEL

THE MONEY BAG Drama. About 610 Feet.

A drama that holds the interest throughout, without the introduction of highly sensational feature.

THE BANKS OF THE DANUBE Scenic. About 331 Feet.

In this interesting and educational picture, we are suddenly transferred from our own home to Austria-Hungary.

Gaumont Reel
About 941 Feet in Length
Tues. May 3

Urban-Eclipse Reel

About 984 Feet in Length

Wed. May 4

CALLED TO SEA Drama. About 584 Feet.

A thrilling, pathetic, realistic and perfectly photographed drama containing all the elements that lend themselves to certain popularity.

IMMIGRANTS' PROGRESS IN CANADA INDUSTRIAL ABOUT 400 FEET

An enthralling illustration of the first five years' actual experience of a Canadian immigrant in the Great North Western Prairie Wheat Belt.

Gaumont Reel

About 919 Feet in Length

Sat. May 7

CALL OF THE FOREST Drama. About 571 Ft

Richly toned, truthfully costumed, strongly enacted; the film will surely please the people.

GIGANTIC WAVES Scenic. About 348 Feet.

Masterfully toned and tinted scenes lend additional charm to this unique subject which presents superb water effects on the wild rockbound coast of the Gascogne Gulf.

EVERY FILM IN THE WEEK IS GOOD

IMPORTED BY

George Kleine

52 State St., CHICAGO   19 E. 21st St., NEW YORK

FIGURE 3.7

Advertisement for Kleine's weekly releases for 1 May 1910. George Kleine Papers, Manuscript Division, Library of Congress, Washington, D.C.

GEORGE KLEINE

FILMS

WEEK BEGINNING MAY 7, 1910

Each Subject is Described at Length on Another Page of this Issue

Release for Tuesday, May 10, 1910

Two subjects by GAUMONT

A LITTLE VAGRANT
about 852 feet

Introducing remarkable child acting

A SEA OF CLOUDS
about 134 feet

Taken among snow capped peaks of the Alps

Release for Wednesday, May 11, 1910

Two Subjects by URBAN-ECLIPSE

On one reel

ROOSEVELT IN CAIRO
about 354 feet

"The Man Who Never Stops" in Egypt.

PURGED BY FIRE
about 541 feet

A strong story of retribution

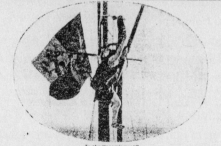

In the "crow's nest"

Saturday, May 14, 1910. GAUMONT   about 997 feet

CHRISTOPHER COLUMBUS

The remarkable feature subject you have read about

There is a standard size poster, in colors, for each reel released

Are you on our mailing list? If not, send your name and address today.

IMPORTED BY

George Kleine

52 State St., CHICAGO   19 E. 21st St., NEW YORK

FIGURE 3.8

Advertisement for Kleine's weekly releases for 7 May 1910. George Kleine Papers, Manuscript Division, Library of Congress, Washington, D.C.

FIGURE 3.9 Advertisement for Kleine's May 1910 imports from Gaumont and Urban-Eclipse. George Kleine Papers, Manuscript Division, Library of Congress, Washington, D.C.

information before the eyes of the student; it also involved the emotions, as I shall explain. Furthermore, in contrast to Kleine, who attempted to commercialize educational cinema in theaters, Edison focused his efforts on promoting motion pictures in schools.

In 1913, Edison gave a demonstration of nonfiction films to a group of prominent educators at his laboratory in West Orange, New Jersey. At the time, he claimed to have made a list of up to one thousand subjects that were to be produced as educational films, but only fifty to sixty of them had yet "been put into scenario form," six of which were screened before this panel of experts. This demonstration of film's educational power was conducted in the manner of a classic Edison publicity campaign, and it received substantial press coverage. Edison's demonstration was generally well received by his audience of educators. Henry H. Goddard, of the Vineland Training School for the Feeble-Minded, wrote that motion pictures were "a time saver, because the student can get in a brief time information that would require much longer if obtained in the usual way." Goddard argued that information obtained via motion pictures was "much more accurate" than printed information. However, it was precisely this belief in film's ability to transparently reproduce reality that also came in for criticism. Leonard P.

Ayres of the Russell Sage Foundation wrote that "the new educational motion pictures are a most convenient ladle for the pouring-in of information. Under this form of their misuse, the function of the pupils would be to sit in a darkened room while the elements of knowledge were passed before them on a screen." To Ayres, classroom films had the potential to produce passive spectators rather than active learners. Significantly, one of the more optimistic audience members was John Dewey. While he expressed reservations that motion pictures produced passive spectators, he also wrote that "some subjects are much better adapted for purposes of conveying information in an intelligent way than others." Dewey singled out geography films and nature films as the two genres best suited to this kind of visual instruction: "In nature study there is no doubt that many operations may be selected for observation which will tend to make children more observing of what is going on around them."[88] For Dewey, film had multiple possibilities: It could render its viewers passive or it might make them "more observing." While Edison was enamored of cinematic technology, it was not so much the technology that was at stake for these educators as the content and context of educational films.

The disconnect between the concerns of educators and the concerns of Edison the businessman can be seen in a publicity photograph that was circulated in conjunction with the press coverage of the demonstration (fig. 3.10). In the image, Edison sits surrounded by a group of ten boys and young men who represent a kind of imaginary audience for his educational motion pictures. As a caption puts it, the "great wizard" does not hesitate to "scrap" any film that his all-male audience dislikes. Edison's publicity machine thus vouches for the popular appeal of his educational films and attempts to market his film product as both "clean" (played up by depicting the boys as "censors") and entertaining. However, educators, as we have seen, were concerned not with the films' potential popularity or market value but with their educational value. This clash between market value and educational value was not resolved until a stable nontheatrical distribution network was established for classroom films in the 1920s.[89]

Despite giving lip service to establishing educational films in schools, Edison did make some overtures to the commercial film market, as well. In 1917, Edison's company launched an ambitious educational series consisting of more than sixty-five fiction and nonfiction film subjects (released in twelve installments) called the Conquest Program, which was distributed to commercial theaters. Kleine and L. W. McChesney, the manager

MR. EDISON AND SOME OF HIS CENSORS.

The great wizard submits his new educational films to the criticism of his "gang"
and doesn't hesitate to "scrap" anything that doesn't "get over to them."

FIGURE 3.10 Publicity photo for Thomas Edison's demonstration of educational films in 1913, *Literary Digest*, 4 October 1913, 576.

of Edison's Motion Picture Division, engaged in an interesting discussion of catch phrases with which to publicize the films. By this time, Kleine was losing faith in the marketability of educational films, for he wrote in 1917, "I dread placing the brand 'Educational' on them, or any other curse that will repel the masses. Even 'Films for the Whole Family' implies a degree of cleanliness that may lead to the inference of weakness or a wishy-washy quality. . . . It may be different in local advertising, and it is certainly a good thing when the appeal is made to women's clubs, civic bodies, etc."[90] Despite great efforts, the Conquest Program series was not a success, and at the end of 1917, Kleine wrote to McChesney, "Whatever the main reasons in detail that are given, it is an established fact that [Conquest pictures] lack earning power. Isolated cases of high enthusiasm from either exhibitor or public do not effect [*sic*] the general results sufficiently to make them a financial success."[91] It seems that by 1917, these "isolated cases of high enthusiasm" had ceased to impress Kleine, although they had so encouraged him several years before.[92]

By the time educational films found nontheatrical success in the 1920s, Edison and Kleine were nearing the end of their careers. Some members of the visual education movement even scolded Edison in the 1920s for his crude formulation of educational cinema, explaining that "Edison did the budding cause much harm by his wild statement to the effect that films could replace textbooks in our schools within a decade." Films should be "*supplements*, not *substitutes*," they explained.[93] But it was the efforts of these early film moguls that had opened the door to the classroom film's success in the 1920s and beyond. Kleine had been correct about film's potential usefulness for education, but he was wrong about the venue. Edison had been correct about the venue, but he was wrong about how long it would take for schools to embrace educational films.

The Campaign Fails

In the end, the campaign to uplift the cinema was not successful in the ways that Kleine and Edison had envisioned. Educational cinema did not prove to be the financial boon that some had predicted, and in the meantime feature-length narrative films appeared on the scene, effectively neutralizing efforts to promote the short nonfiction film as the future of commercial cinema. As Scott Curtis has pointed out, the alliance between reformers and the film industry was short-lived: "As soon as it became apparent that the vast majority of the viewing public was more interested in narrative entertainment, the companies brushed off the reform societies' efforts to influence the product directly."[94] As the feature-length film became clearly established as the commercial future of the film industry, reform-minded businessmen had to give up their dreams of commercial educational cinema and focus instead on promoting the films in schools. Travel films continued to be manufactured, but the idea that they might become one of the most popular genres was dashed for good. Some even sensed this fate by the early 1910s, when the travel film was still arguably at its peak. A letter George Kleine wrote in 1912 outlining some of the issues he would discuss in an upcoming meeting with Cines, whose films he distributed, is revealing in this respect: "POPULARITY OF CINES FILMS: The consensus of opinion among exhibitors is favorable to Cines' dramatic and spectacular films, tolerant of scenics, and opposed to comedies."[95] While this letter refers only to Cines's scenics and not to those of other companies, it does give some indication of the genre's popular appeal, even as seen by one of its major supporters: Scenics were *tolerated*, but if they disappeared, they might not be missed. Kleine was already disappointed by the genre's lack of runaway success and seems to have foreseen that the big money to be made in the future would be in feature films, as his importation of the huge Italian multi-reel hit *Quo Vadis* (Cines, 1913) would soon prove.

Much later in his career, Kleine wrote an eight-page "account of the early years of [the] Motion Picture history based upon my own points of contact" that goes into some detail about educational films:

> Attached to this brief is a memorandum reciting the titles and lengths of so-called "Educational" films (which would today be classed as "non-theatrical"), which we had imported from May 1909, to January, 1913, a total of 335 different subjects ranging in length from 2,000 to 125 feet. During the early years of this period the average number of prints sold was over forty of each subject, but the demand gradually lessened and in 1913 had fallen to about twenty prints.
>
> We were entirely dependent upon the moving-picture theatre for our market. As these subjects were as welcome as a bitter pill to a child, we had to sugar-coat the dose by tying them to another type of film, usually a popular short comedy or drama, and then these twins were not sold separately.[96]

In this account Kleine expresses a belief that audiences would not have watched educational films at all had they not been forced to; he seems to remember the earlier years with some bitterness. There are some indications that his memories are not totally accurate, however, for throughout his letters and papers he repeatedly remarks that educational films had been scorned in the past but now were appreciated—as he does at times even in this account. Yet his overall dissatisfaction seems to stem from the fact that nonfiction films were never as hugely popular as he thought they should be. Finally, although Kleine's catalogue of 1910 garnered a lot of press attention, Kleine wrote to Edison in 1921 that the "catalogue brought little or no business and has been obsolete for many years."[97] By 1928, Kleine had sold his remaining prints of educational and scenic films to Metro-Goldwyn-Mayer and the International News of New York.[98]

Despite his lack of success with educational films in commercial theaters, however, Kleine began by the 1920s to sense a different future for these subjects in smaller gauges distributed to the nontheatrical market. "Your own experience, and knowledge of the attempts of others, to popularize so-called educational films from time to time demonstrated that the field was not profitable," he wrote to Edison. "Of late, however, the purchase and use of smaller projecting machines have increased greatly. . . . The field is not only potential but seems to be actual and immediately before us."[99] This time he was correct, as the emergence of distribution networks for 16mm film, publications such as *Educational Screen*, and new educational series such as those of Eastman Teaching Films in 1928 demonstrate.

Aesthetics of Educational Film

Although the films were marketed as educational, their visual impact was clearly a selling point for the commercial trade. Scenic films in particular were typically reviewed in terms of their visual beauty, a point that was not overlooked at the time. To quote again from the *Motography* editorial "Current Educational Releases": "Anything that is beautiful and appeals to the better emotions is educational. . . . The human craving for scenery is unquestionably the strongest of any purely aesthetic demand of our natures. Men spend thousands of dollars traveling in search of nothing else but scenery."[100] Travel films, then, are a nonfiction genre that provides a different way to think about the aesthetics of cinema and its relation to education. First, this is a somewhat nontraditional concept of art cinema, whose aesthetic power is derived not from bourgeois forms such as the theater or the novel (as was attempted by Vitagraph and Triangle) but, instead, from a notion of experience itself. Second, the discourse surrounding early educational films can thus be connected to the more progressive strain of the reform movement — one that follows the ideas set forth by educational reformers such as Dewey, who spoke at length about this idea in *Art as Experience*.[101]

Kleine's thoughts on this matter can be ascertained in one of his lectures. Despite his reputation as a sober man of business and a promoter of films for the "better classes," Kleine also had enthusiasm for art and democratic ideals. He wrote:

> One of the popular sports of the Intelligentzia [*sic*] of today is to berate the general public for its lack of intelligence. . . . The low mentality of moving picture audiences is considered established by the popularity of many inane and stupid stories, vulgar comedies and melodramas, their worship of the Stars and persistent neglect of the Good, the True and the Beautiful in pictures.
>
> I do not agree with this view. Whatever deficiency there may be is rather of culture than of the mind. The pictured Good and the filmed Beautiful are interesting to an audience when they appeal to its own specialized kind of culture. We may even be paradoxical and say that ap-

proval of sublimated honor and virtue becomes most pronounced and noisy with audiences whose sense of honor and aesthetics are supposed to be nascent or atrophied.[102]

In an era dominated by racism and social Darwinism, this opinion is markedly egalitarian. Defending the filmgoing immigrant "masses" who were typically derided, Kleine argues that all classes can be united under the banner of "the pictured Good and the filmed Beautiful." This ideology is in step with the more liberal wing of the Progressive Era educational movement that strove to create critical citizens educated through experience rather than dutiful citizens who learned their lessons by rote memorization. Kleine stopped importing films from Europe in 1914 because of the onset of the First World War, and he ultimately gave up his quest to commercialize nonfiction films. Although he failed, his efforts led the way for the visual education movement of the 1920s that was to find success — if not profits — by distributing nonfiction *outside* the commercial theaters, in schools.

CHAPTER 4

"ATOP OF THE WORLD IN MOTION"
Visualizing the Pleasures of Empire

I n late 1912 and early 1913, New Yorkers could watch a two-hour film of
life in Alaska and Siberia at Weber's New York Theatre on Broadway and
29th Street. *Atop of the World in Motion*, filmed by Beverly B. Dobbs, was
warmly received in the trade press, which dubbed it "one of the masterpieces
of practical, interesting, and educational cinematography."[1] Ten years before
Nanook of the North, this film featured a polar bear hunt and a walrus hunt,
along with scenes of gold mining, fur trading, and a July Fourth celebration
on the bank of the Snake River in Nome, Alaska. At the time, multi-reel
features were still quite new, and *Atop of the World in Motion* would have
been one of the first multi-reel nonfiction films (fig. 4.1). Accompanied by a
live lecture by Mr. Dobbs, this feature demonstrates the travel film's debt to
the illustrated lecture tradition. It also exemplifies early cinema's impulse to
document the world far and wide: This was one of numerous films of polar
exploration to be promoted in the years 1911–13, when several polar expeditions were under way. The film's title, *Atop of the World in Motion*, serves as an
apt description of the era's compulsion to capture the entire world in moving
pictures—a desire to fix the world as an image, atop which the viewer might
metaphorically stand.

Into a world already saturated with representations of travel, travelogue
films emerged as the newest, most modern form of all travel media. Within
a few years after cinema's emergence in the mid-1890s, a vast number of
places on nearly every continent had been "cinematographed." As Emilie

Weber's New York Theatre Success

[SOME FEATURE] **BEVERLY B. DOBBS** [SOME FEATURE]

"ATOP OF THE WORLD IN MOTION"

(The Original Alaska-Siberia Motion Pictures)

330 PERFORMANCES WHITNEY OPERA HOUSE, CHICAGO

Last Chance   STATE RIGHT BUYERS   Last Chance

Films Withdrawn From the Market Jan. 15th

Will Soon Be Seen in London, Berlin, Paris, and All of the Principal Cities on the Continent

To Close All Sales   ☞ Sacrificing Remaining Territory ☜   To Close All Sales

A Wire Will Bring You Rock-Bottom Prices

JOSEPH CONOLY   Suite 702   1482 Broadway, New York City

FIGURE 4.1 Advertisement for *Atop of the World in Motion* (1912), *Moving Picture World*, 18 January 1913, 305.

Altenloh wrote in 1914, "Today, hardly anything happens in the world . . . that is not swiftly captured on film and shown to a cinema audience in the whole world."[2] While no complete inventory of locations documented by early cinema exists—indeed, such a list would be impossible to compile—a loose survey of film titles conveys a sense of the scope of this vast new representational enterprise. Travelogues depicted cities (e.g., *Berlin* [Pathé, 1910]), regions (*The Auvergne Mountains, Central France* [Lux Film, 1912]), nation-states (*In Japan* [Selig, 1911]), continents (*In Africa* [Imp, 1910]), and even, on occasion, hemispheres (*Life and People South of the Equator* [Great Northern, 1911]). As this selection of titles demonstrates, early travelogues manifest a hierarchical tendency to document European places with the most specificity. However, there are many exceptions to this tendency, as shown by titles that focus with some specificity on Asian and African locales, such as *Pekin, the Walled City* (Eclipse, 1910) and *Life in Senegal, Africa* (Gaumont, 1910). Likewise, some (though fewer) titles generalize about European locales, such as *In Old England* (Kalem, 1914) and *Eastern Europe* (Pathé, 1911). It should hardly be surprising, however, that there are no films titled "Western Europe" or "Life and People North of the Equator." Even though the motion picture camera was understood as a highly realistic recording device, it still reflected the preconceptions of those behind the apparatus. Some films emphasized the exoticism of their subject matter, such as *Curious Scenes in India* (Edison, 1913) and *Strange Places and Quaint People in New York* (Kalem, 1912), while others focused on the common-places of life in a foreign land, such as *Every-Day Life in Malacca* (Pathé, 1911). Many films focused on people and their customs—for example, *Dutch Types* (Pathé, 1910), *Arabian Customs* (Gaumont, 1911), and *Jewish Types in Russia* (Pathé, 1910). Still others depicted natural landscapes, highlighting rivers (e.g., *On the Banks of the Ganges* [Pathé, 1910]), mountains, caves, and, especially, waterfalls. Industrial films, too, were often as much about place as about the production of a commodity, as shown in titles such as *Butter Making in Normandy* (Pathé, 1910) and *Making Bamboo Hats in Java* (Eclipse, 1911). Unfortunately, because most of these films no longer exist, it is not possible to examine the specific ways in which the promise of each title is played out in every film. But the titles alone are enough to make the point that the entire world was filmed by early cinema.[3]

As soon as motion picture technology became available, filmmakers set about capturing the globe on film, not only because they could, but because they believed it was their prerogative. Like map making, the acquisition of images was an attempt to fix the world in a particular order. Yet for all their totalizing implication that documenting the entire world is possible, early travel films present incomplete, provisional, and often badly translated versions of knowledge about the places they depict. Made by a variety of early film companies based in many different countries, the films are diverse and do not present a coherent message about geography or power. Nonetheless, they assume a great deal of authority in describing the world for their viewers, confident in their own privilege to define other places and other people. In short, travelogue films are deeply implicated in power relations. Activities such as map making, census taking, photography, and descriptive writing were all undertaken by colonial powers as part of their effort to know and control their territories. Travelogue films may have mimicked such colonial strategies, but as commercial films, they were not engaged in the enterprises of state control. Rather, they presented generalized and popularized versions of imperial ideology, and they remained open to other uses.

In focusing on travelogues released in the United States that were produced by European and North American film companies, one of this book's tasks is to analyze how the Western world spoke *about* and *for* other places and other people, as well as places and people "nearby." These films often reveal more about the speaking subject—the uncredited filmmakers and their ideologies—than they do about their subject matter. While nonfiction films certainly were being made by non-Western filmmakers in the early years of cinema, these were almost never released in the United States. In fact, foreign films produced by companies outside Europe and the Soviet Union were not released in the United States with regularity until after the Second World War, and even then, it was unusual.[4] (In the silent era, a few Japanese-language and Spanish-language movie houses in Los Angeles catered to immigrant populations, but more research is needed to ascertain how many Japanese and Mexican films were shown in those theaters and how widespread that kind of business might have been in other U.S. cities.[5]) Early film audiences in theaters worldwide may have been able to look at images of places located around the world, but these viewers were treated to a visualization that was European and North American in its point of view. What these films show us is how the Western world visualized the globe during the early years of cinema, before the First World War. It is crucial to understand, however, that this Western mode of visualization was exported around the world and viewed by spectators in many different regions, making for a complex web of possible reception contexts. Viewers in Paris may not have watched Mexican films in the 1910s, but viewers in Mexico certainly watched French travelogues, for example. Early travel cinema is thus an example of Western representation and global reception.

Because most of these films are unknown and difficult to access today, this chapter analyzes the travelogue's aesthetic and political dimensions by looking closely at archival films, accompanied by copious illustrations. The films depict what Edward Said called the "pleasures of imperialism," showing colonial territories and lands of internal empire as spaces apart from the malaise of the European bourgeoisie. Said summed up the mythology of the white European experience of the colonies in his analysis of Rudyard Kipling's novel *Kim*: "Isn't it possible in India to do everything? be anything? go anywhere with impunity?"[6] This attitude underpins early travel films, and my argument centers on the cinematic specificity of the travelogue's imperial vision. I argue that imperial ideology takes on a new dimension in cinematic form because of the mechanized movement of the film image. As scholars have argued regarding photography, "However hard the photographer tries to *exclude*, the camera lens always *includes*."[7] The reality captured by moving pictures thus has even more potential to exceed the intentionality of its makers. As a recording technology, film indiscriminately documents whatever is framed by the camera lens, which must necessarily contain elements in excess of the filmmaker's intentions. In travel films, that excess often appears in the form of discomfort on the part of people being filmed as they shift awkwardly before the camera or glance self-consciously in many directions. I discuss several examples of such discomfort in what follows.

Certainly, the encyclopedic ambition to document the world was not new in the early twentieth century, but cinema was new. Travelogues heralded a new form of sensory perception of the world: not direct experience but experience through media. To understand what was new about this perceptual experience, we must understand the travelogue's aesthetic dimension. In this chapter I begin by describing the early travel film's characteristic form and style; unlike other forms of travel media, cinematic travelogues are characterized by an aesthetic that combines fragmentation with movement. I then analyze the travelogue's focus on "exotic" locations, including not only colonial territories but also regions of internal empire. The chapter concludes with accounts of the filmed subjects of travelogues looking back at the camera, focusing on how such encounters, rendered in motion and unfolding in time, are frequently uncomfortable. I argue that the look at the camera is one way in which travel films destabilize the impulse of collecting, recording, and consuming that undergirds the genre.

The Explicit Look: Early Nonfiction and the "View Aesthetic"

After nearly a century of neglect, one of the first important critical encounters with early nonfiction films occurred in July 1994, when the Nederlands Filmmuseum (now the EYE Film Institute Netherlands) held a workshop at which more than fifty film scholars and archivists were invited to view new restorations of nonfiction film from the 1910s. During the recorded discussions that took place at the workshop (at which I was not present because it took place before I began researching this subject), several film scholars commented on nonfiction's apparent lack of stylistic development over the years. When compared to the editing innovations that were being developed in fiction film, the travelogue seemed to be formally stagnant. Ben Brewster argued that travelogues in particular seemed to be an "ahistorical form," in the sense that "they don't seem to exist in the regime of stylistic pressure that was clearly there for fiction filmmakers."[8]

In contrast to Brewster, I contend that travelogues were not stylistically dormant in this period; rather, they developed along different lines from fiction films. This was partly a result of having strong prior conventions to draw from in the illustrated travel lecture tradition. Stephen Bottomore made this point at the workshop: "[Nonfiction] was based to some extent on art forms which were there already — photography, magic lantern shows — whereas dramatic films had less of a base to work from at the start."[9] Nonfiction's continuity over many years also demonstrates just how well suited its form was for presenting information. As Tom Gunning has written: "Accounting for this apparent lack of radical transformations should not lead us to think of the nonfiction film as somehow stagnant . . . in relation to fiction film. . . . One could attribute the relative lack of development in the nonfiction film to the fact that the existent modes of film style remained entirely *effective* for the genres then practiced . . . there was little motivation for transformation."[10] Nonfiction film style did not change much before the 1920s not because filmmakers were avoiding stylistic innovation, but because the films' style was adequate to fulfill their needed function. The "collection" editing structure I describe later, for example, was an entirely effective editing style for the travelogue and can be seen as one alternative to the continuity style of editing that later came to dominate narrative filmmaking practice. In contrast to nonfiction, fiction film form was not fulfilling its promise in the early years, and new forms had to be innovated before the fiction film could find its audience. Clearly, early nonfiction film needs to be analyzed on its own terms.

Watching a travelogue is like flipping through an album of snapshots or postcards. Each individual shot is emblematic in some way — so much so that if single shots were to be dismantled and made to stand alone, like a postcard or a single-shot actuality film, many of them would make sense by themselves. They might need some contextualization in the form of a caption or a title, in the way that postcards contain captions identifying places shown, yet the individual shot alone would be enough to epitomize the location through the logic of synecdoche. This is in direct contrast with fiction films, in which individual shots — or even narrative segments — rarely could stand alone to make any kind of emblematic sense if removed from their narrative context. As Walter Benjamin writes, "For the first time, captions become obligatory. And it is clear that they have a character altogether different from the titles of paintings. The directives given by captions to those looking at images in illustrated magazines soon become even more precise and commanding in films, where the way each single image is understood seems prescribed by the sequence of all the preceding images."[11]

In a scenic film, the viewer is presented with a series of fragmentary images of a place, an accumulation of separate images whose connective logic is not one of narrative or character but one of location. The editing principles of early nonfiction are distinct from the new techniques of continuity editing that were then being developed for fiction film; here we find not a principle of continuity but a principle of *collection*. Almost any early nonfiction film will serve to illustrate this principle of editing based on the idea of collection. I turn to the Cines film *The Velino River and Falls (Central Italy)* as an example because it focuses on landscape rather than figures, which is helpful for isolating certain formal characteristics. In fact, the film is entirely composed of landscape shots. Each shot stands alone as a view, but cumulatively the shots convey a patchwork sense of the place being documented. The film was released in the United States by George Kleine on 14 January 1913 as part of a split reel including the fiction film *A Fisher-maiden's Heart*. According to his business records, Kleine purchased twenty-four prints of the film for distribution.[12] *The Velino River and Falls (Central Italy)* was described in *Motography*'s "Current Educational Releases" column as "showing many picturesque views of the Velino River as it wends its way between its grassy banks, and finally plunges over the beautiful falls."[13] Notably, the print of the film at EYE is titled simply *The Velino River*, which underscores the fact that U.S. release titles often featured additional geographic information to assist viewers with locations that might be unfamiliar to them. While the film's written description seems to indicate a kind of forward progression—the river "wends its way," moving along in an almost narrative progression until it "finally plunges" in a kind of dramatic denouement—the film itself barely gestures toward such a progression.

The print held by EYE contains ten shots (not counting the intertitles).[14] Without exception, every shot is an extreme long shot: images of trees, mountains, waterfalls, the river, and a lake. One panning shot does capture the image of a town, and another includes a small boat being rowed in the distance, but overall this is a film without people. Every formal element is designed to enhance the sense of idealized natural beauty: Five of the ten shots are framed by either an oval or a circular matting. This kind of matting was a common convention in scenic films; it has the effect of isolating the image, quite literally making it picturesque, or like a picture. Including this kind of matte frame is akin to putting the image in quotation marks: the frame self-consciously calls attention to the image as a view. A frame enlargement from a similar film, *Scenes along the Pescara River, Central Italy* (Cines, 1913) also demonstrates this circular matting (fig. 4.2).[15]

Gunning has discussed this tendency of early nonfiction to underscore the

FIGURE 4.2 The "view aesthetic" in *Scenes along the Pescara River, Central Italy* (Cines, 1913). Courtesy EYE Film Institute Netherlands.

act of looking, dubbing this phenomenon the "view aesthetic." As Gunning writes, "Early actuality films were structured around capturing something visually, capturing and preserving a look or vantage point. In this respect the "view" clearly forms part of what I have called the "cinema of attractions," the emphasis found in early cinema upon the act of display and the satisfying of visual curiosity. . . . To my mind the most characteristic quality of a "view" lies in the way it mimes the act of looking and observing."[16] The travelogue's view aesthetic is certainly a component of the "cinema of attractions"; the very concept of the tourist attraction should remind us of this connection. This kind of view aesthetic sensationalizes its own visuality. Gunning writes, "While my description of 'views' may sound simple to the point of tautology—a film showing something—the films themselves are far from simplistic." This "miming" of the act of looking—foregrounding the looking that takes place in the representation—is not the same thing as just looking by itself. The view is a representation of looking and as such has a double significance: Like landscape, the view represents the thing or place being shown, and it represents the act of looking at that thing.

An additional key aspect of the view aesthetic that I want to stress is its unstated presumption of a point of view, for of course there can never be a view from nowhere. This visual curiosity is not neutral; it carries with it a great deal of ideological baggage about geography, gender, and race. These films "reveal the ambiguous power relations of the look so nakedly," Gunning asserts, that they have been repressed in traditional histories of nonfiction film. "These 'views' stage for us the impulse towards 'just looking' so important to our modern era; and we have learned in the work on visual culture over the last decades that 'just looking' is never *just* about looking."[17] It is this dimension specifically—the way in which the "view aesthetic" reveals the power relations inherent in cinematic looking—that opens up possibilities for resistant readings of the films. This visual explicitness was not understood as perverse, as, say, the explicitness of pornography (whose history also dates back to early cinema) was understood, but it has the curious ability to lay bare the desires of the look that are masked by continuity editing.[18] This excessive form of looking is one of the travel film's most significant stylistic dimensions.

Fragmented Worlds: The Collection Principle of Editing

In addition to its explicit staging of the act of looking, the travelogue film (and early nonfiction more generally) is characterized by a distinct regime of editing techniques, which emphasizes discontinuity at every turn. Each shot of *The Velino River and Falls* features a different subject—a waterfall amid lush foliage, a stretch of river, another waterfall just visible in the distance on a hillside—creating an effect of generalized picturesqueness. The first shot is preceded by an intertitle announcing "the river's current," and the second announces "the first waterfall," giving some sense that the film might follow the river as a kind of structural progression. This conceit is immediately dropped, however, as the film continues with a series of apparently arbitrary shots of the landscape. The fourth shot, which an intertitle announces as "the Piediluco Lake," is of slightly longer duration than the rest. Tinted yellow, the shot is a slow pan to the right, showing a town at the edge of the lake at the base of a small mountain. Compositionally, the shot resembles a standard landscape painting; the water fills the bottom third of the frame, and the shore fills much of the top half, with the sky becoming more visible at the top as the camera pans right along the edge of the mountain. To a viewer unfamiliar with the location being shown, as most Americans would have been in 1913, each of these discrete shots with so little commentary from the intertitles creates the effect of a generalized prettiness.[19] The shots are generic in their subject matter—waterfalls were a favorite topic of scenic films—and yet specific in the place they show. Each shot could feasibly stand alone;

cumulatively, the shots add up to little more than a miscellaneous collection. Yet the singularity of each shot gets subsumed by the more general sense of place uniting the film—the Velino River—and the generalized beauty the film works so hard to construct.

Although the basic principle of early nonfiction editing is discontinuous, organized around the idea of the collection, one can often find examples of a few shots edited together to provide a limited sense of "continuity." In these cases, however, that continuity is sustained for just two or three shots. These clusters of shots make up rudimentary "segments," although such segments still function as stand-alone units, essentially bumping up against other shots or segments rather than being bound inextricably into that place in the film. These segments typically cohere around a theme, as in the convention of "native types" imagery, which I discuss later in this chapter. Sometimes the limited sense of continuity is spatial: It is also common to find two or three different shots taken from varying angles at the same location in a travel film. In other instances, one can find a localized stretch of editing that creates a sense of movement into or out of a place, rather like a zoom in or out, but achieved via cuts rather than a zoom, as in the four concluding shots of the film *Kuala Lumpur* (Pathé, 1912).[20] This kind of editing makes connections between just a few shots, constructing a small cluster of shots that serve as a unit. The cluster of shots is different from a fiction film segment, for these clusters do not construct any sense of narrative progression, and they are shorter than the segments in classical filmmaking, which are typically assembled from a dozen or more shots. And yet these shot clusters function as "segments" in that they create a momentary sense of continuity between shots located in the same space and focusing on the same object.

If the logic behind the editing of multi-shot travelogues is that of the collection, then that collection might be assumed to resemble a tour—yet early travelogues rarely follow a clearly defined tour itinerary. In contrast to the narrative-driven travel lecture that serves as their model, most travelogue films lack even the barest narrative gesture of a journey. The films simply present a series of images joined together by the unifying topic of place. The film *Picturesque Japan* (Éclair, 1913), for example, does not present any discernible narrative logic.[21] This twelve-shot film (not counting intertitles) is a series of discrete shots joined together, lacking even the vaguely narrative journey-along-the-river convention that the *Velino River* film began to hint at. Also unlike that film, *Picturesque Japan* uses no matte framings, although it has been colored with a more sedate set of tints (uniformly amber-colored

FIGURE 4.3 Frame enlargement, *Picturesque Japan* (Éclair, 1913). Courtesy EYE Film
Institute Netherlands.

shots with blue intertitles). The film focuses mostly on people and Japanese
culture rather than on scenic landscapes. The first several shots, taken in a
park, feature groups of children at "a popular festival," as the intertitle tells
us. Shot five shows "the toy salesman," a man with a huge wooden hutch on
his back filled with toys, who turns to model his toy cabinet for the camera, smiling, as a group of people look on. Two more shots are located in
the city, showing a "theatre street in Tokyo," and some men looking into a
shop window who are clearly posing for the camera. Next we are suddenly
in the country as an intertitle announces "How people travel in the mountains of Japan"; the subsequent shot presents a man being carried in a litter
by two other men, with his wife walking several paces behind along a dirt
road. Other shots present a similarly diverse selection of images: a man on
a "Japanese swing," a country woman with her infant posing for the camera
in a rare medium shot (fig. 4.3), and paper fish decorations blowing in the
wind. These shots do not appear in any particular order—in fact, they could
be reassembled differently to achieve basically the same effect. No cumulative result is derived from any connections the film makes between shots.
Instead, the film is structured as a collection of views, each view interesting

for itself. Again, the effect is rather like looking at a photo album: One sees glimpses of a place, but no overarching, uniform argument narrativizing that place. The difference, of course, is that this "photo album" is filled with moving images.

Other films, such as *Rocks and Waves* (Gaumont, ca. 1911), display no sense whatsoever of time unfolding. *Rocks and Waves* is simply a series of shots of water crashing on a rocky seashore; there are no figures, and there is no shot progression moving toward or away from the scene being filmed. This film is similar to a much earlier title, *Rough Sea at Dover* (Birt Acres, 1895), which was one of the most popular early British actuality films. ("Rough sea" postcards were also popular at the time.) However, *Rough Sea at Dover* is a single-shot, black-and-white film, while *Rocks and Waves* is a multi-shot, color-tinted film. In the 1910s, Gaumont specialized in this kind of nature film showing scenery abstracted from its geographical context. Gaumont made a series of river films, along with films with titles such as *A Sea of Clouds* (1910), *Sunset* (1910), and *Autumn Leaves* (1911).[22] Significantly, each of these films was classified as a scenic. These titles are more generic than the clearly located titles that were also produced by Gaumont at the time, such as *The City of Amalfi, Italy*, which can be said to have a loose "tour" structure. In the variety programs that dominated nickelodeon theaters, this kind of non-narrativity might have served as a break from the fiction films on the program, functioning as a chance for the audience to rest or experience a different kind of attention.

Industrial films, arguably the most "narrative" driven of the early nonfiction genres, do present shots in a specific order following the production of a commodity from start to finish, but this progression is entirely different from the narrative progression we think of in fiction films. *Harvesting Coconuts in America*, for example, concerns itself with both place and process.[23] Unlike in the cinema of narrative integration, the story told by this film is the decidedly undramatic "story of a cocoanut." In a series of tableau-like shots, we first see a man climb a tree and throw down some coconuts (fig. 4.4). On the ground a man drinks the milk from a coconut, followed by a traditional picturesque shot of the water at sunset. There are a few more shots of a man laying out pieces of coconut, and finally another man makes a basket out of a palm frond. There really is no "story" here—we do not follow a single coconut from planting to harvesting to eating, for example. Neither is there a sustained depiction of "process," since each shot shows the coconut being used differently. The only fully detailed example of "process," the final

FIGURE 4.4 Frame enlargement, *Harvesting Coconuts in America* (a.k.a. *The Story of a Cocoanut* [Selig, 1912]). Courtesy EYE Film Institute Netherlands.

shot in which a man makes a basket, simply serves as another example of the variety of uses being depicted.

The collection system of editing functions rather like a series of visual anecdotes. The collection structure might be compared with a string of pearls, each view functioning as a little imagistic gem, followed by another, and then another. The collection system of editing harks back both to the program of single-shot actualities of the late 1890s, as well as the tradition of illustrated travel lectures. However, the key component of the lecture tradition was the live narrator who would have made the images fit together with narrative cohesion—depending, of course, on the content of the lecture or the skill of the speaker. Because travelogue films shown in commercial theaters usually lacked the live narrator of travel lectures, the sense of flow in the presentation of information was much more open-ended. Intertitles took the place of lecturers in cinema to some extent, but travelogues from before the 1920s contain relatively few intertitles, especially when compared with the garrulous verbiage one reads in the lectures of John Stoddard and Burton Holmes. Scenic film intertitles were simple, mostly place names and sparse descriptions to underscore the images, which carry most of the informational significance in each film. Occasionally one encounters an interjection of humor, but this is rare in nonfiction films before the 1920s. The collection principle is a resolutely non-narrative form of editing that is quite unlike anything one encounters in fiction films.

Discontinuous Knowledge: Travelogue Movement

Film scholars such as Anne Friedberg and Giuliana Bruno have argued that a "mobilized gaze" is central to cinematic representation. As Friedberg points out, "The *mobilized gaze* has a history, which begins well before the cinema and is rooted in other cultural activities that involve walking and travel."[24] The cinema quite literally presents motion because filmic images move, but travel films expand this movement well beyond the way it is experienced in fiction films. The cinema's mobilized gaze brings something new to the experience of mobility: Representations of movement begin to substitute for actual movement. More than other early film genres, travelogues enacted this virtual mobility. Travelogue films exemplify a vicarious view of the world in which more and more experiences have become mediated. In this new modern world, vision and experience come to be represented in increasingly mechanized, technological forms. Travelogues produced a new kind of tourist spectator, a consumer of represented travel rather than an actual traveler.

The two primary forms of camera movement in motion pictures are movement in which the camera remains stationary (the pan, the tilt) and movement in which the camera itself moves (the tracking shot). Travelogue films consistently use both kinds of camera movement. In fact, it is rare to find a shot in a travelogue film that does not move in some way. If the camera is not moving, then the image itself is filled with movement, such as a cascading waterfall or people walking through a landscape. Plentiful movement was perceived by reviewers to be a mark of quality. A film titled *In Morocco*, for example, was praised for this quality: "The pictures have plenty of motion in all except the fortress, where only one or two moving figures are in range of the camera."[25] A dynamic kineticism was one of the travelogue film's primary appeals. In fact, camera movement was one stylistic element that scenic films developed before fiction filmmaking: Dramatic camera movement was not adapted by narrative films until later in the 1910s.

The pan is the most paradigmatic travelogue shot; very few travel films do without it. Pans allow the camera to survey the landscape, quite literally creating a panoramic effect. Pans work very well with the extreme long shot, which is the travelogue's most common framing distance. Together, the pan

FIGURE 4.5 Frame enlargement, *Amalfi* (Cines, 1910). Courtesy EYE Film Institute Netherlands.

and the extreme long shot are used in just about every travelogue film from this period. Often such shots begin travel films, as in the elegant opening shots of *Amalfi* (Cines, 1910; see fig. 4.5). Once again, this formal element can be traced to pre-cinematic influences: The panning long shot is reminiscent of the popular moving panoramas exhibited in the nineteenth century. Camera tilts are much rarer in travelogues. This is most likely because a tilt up or down does not serve as well to capture a landscape. Tilts can sometimes be found, however, as in the film *Ruins of Angkor, Cambodia* (Méliès, 1912), which displays a noticeable tilt up and down to film one of the tall spires of Angkor Wat.

Tracking shots taken from a moving train play a particularly important role in travelogue history.[26] The phantom ride tradition continued in travelogues of the 1910s. Phantom rides, popular in the 1890s, consisted of landscape views shot out of the front of a moving train, simulating the experience of travel for the viewer.[27] *From Spiez to Loetschberg, Switzerland* (Eclipse, 1913) is just one example of a nickelodeon-era phantom ride, featuring many shots taken from a moving train (fig. 4.6).[28] These images of moving through space create an effect of virtual movement, as though the spectators themselves are on the train moving through the landscapes being shown. As one

FIGURE 4.6 Frame enlargement, *From Spiez to Loetschberg, Switzerland* (Eclipse, 1913).
Courtesy EYE Film Institute Netherlands.

reviewer described another phantom ride titled *The Foothills of Savoy* (Gaumont, 1910), "Nothing could be simpler. A camera has been placed on the front end of a passenger train climbing the foothills of a range of mountains. The scenery is extremely beautiful."[29] The railroad is important in these films not just as a means of conveyance that provides mobility for the camera but also institutionally: Railway companies were some of the most important early sponsors of travel films. They often provided access to filmmakers, but even more (as I discuss in chapter 7), they financed films that promoted various railroad destinations.

Cinematic movement, a primary concern of classical film theory addressed in the writings of Jean Epstein, Germaine Dulac, Louis Delluc, Sergei Eisenstein, and others, engages the spectator in ways that are unique to the medium and distinct from the effects of still photography. Like Friedberg and Bruno, Gunning has lately called for a renewed focus on cinematic motion in film historiography and theory. For these writers, "Cinematic rhythm as a product of editing, camera movement, and composition; the physical and emotional reactions of film spectators as shaped by visual rhythms . . . were all linked to cinema's ability both to record and create motion."[30] Attention to the cinema-specific properties of motion, Gunning argues, can help us rethink key issues related to film aesthetics and spectatorship.[31] Gunning develops an argument (drawing upon Christian Metz) that cinematic motion has a participatory effect in that the audience actively participates in the here and now of movement on the screen in a way that is quite distinct from our encounter with still photography, which, because of its stasis, seems to represent a past time.[32] Because it demands more of the spectator's attention and delivers an experience that is perceptually richer, cinematic movement can be said to involve the viewer's participation more fully. Gunning develops this theory of cinematic movement from Henri Bergson, who wrote, "Action is discontinuous, like every pulsation of life; discontinuous, therefore, is knowledge. . . . The mechanism of our ordinary knowledge is of a cinematographic kind" — knowledge apprehended in a series of static instants, just as the cinema presents a series of static images.[33] Movement and fragmentation are certainly qualities found in all cinema, but they are particularly important components of the travelogue system.

While it is true that Bergson was skeptical about cinema and its positivist impulse to record all of life, recent scholarship has been turning to Bergson's work in order to rethink cinema's construction of time and space.[34] In her study of the "Archives de la Planète," a vast private effort to document the entire world in photographs and film funded by the French banker Albert Kahn from 1909 to 1931, Paula Amad documents the friendship between Bergson and Kahn, his former pupil. Amad persuasively argues that although "at first glance the Kahn Archive seems like an affront to everything Bergson stood for . . . the Bergsonian heritage of Kahn's films also discloses a significant point of contact between the Archives de la Planète and avant-garde film culture."[35] Amad provides the helpful insight that Kahn's work might be understood as "a banker's vision of Bergsonism."[36] We might revise and extend this observation to propose that early travelogue films, in their complex and contradictory presentation of the exotic and of everyday life, can be understood as the film industry's Bergsonian vision, containing both life-denying and life-affirming potential. While this book is not the place for a sustained engagement with Bergson's theories of perception and experience, especially given that others such as Amad have so thoroughly covered this ground lately, the utopian element of Bergson's thought provides an important underpinning to my claim for the fundamental ambivalence of the early travelogue film's system of representation. I return to questions of cinematic experience and audience participation in the final section of this chapter, when I discuss the effects of the look at the camera. But before that, it is important to place ideology alongside this chapter's consideration of film form.

Internal Empire: Invented Traditions

Travel films tend to focus on "exotic" locations—either regions of internal empire within Europe or colonial lands. But these are not the only places documented by travelogues; urban modernity was also a focus of these films, as I will show. Nonetheless it is crucial to examine the films' construction of the exotic, for this will help us to understand their particular social and political valence. Travel films purported to present realistic geographical knowledge about locations around the world. Today, it is a well-accepted critical axiom that such "knowledge" was partial, contingent, and implicated in dominant power relations. In the remainder of this chapter, I discuss the cinema-specific aspects in which travel films took up imperial ideologies and I return to questions of film form to suggest a few ways in which these cinematic techniques in some cases could actually undermine those very ideologies.

A number of early travel films were made in the Pyrenees, an important travel destination in the nineteenth century. Often contrasted with the better-traveled Swiss Alps, the Pyrenees became a popular destination during a craze for mountaineering in the 1860s. They were the first foreign destination for Gustave Flaubert, who went there in 1840 at age eighteen and soon after published an account of his experience. The influential French naturalist writer Hippolyte Adolphe Taine published *Voyage aux Pyrénées* in 1855, an account of the area illustrated by Gustave Doré (fig. 4.7).[37] Many guidebooks about the region were published, including the popular *A Guide to the Pyrenees* by the British mountaineer Charles Packe, who wrote, "[Englishmen] are all very loud in protesting that the inundation of our own countrymen, who meet you at every turn, is one of the great drawbacks to the pleasure of a summer tour through Switzerland. Why, then, do we not give the Pyrenees a trial?"[38]

A film known as *A Car Ride in the Pyrenees* (Pathé, ca. 1910) follows what was already a well-traveled path for moneyed tourists and sportsmen. The film, however, reached a much broader class spectrum than the tourists who visited the region. It seems probable that some viewers in the United States might never even have heard of the Pyrenees before encountering these

FIGURE 4.7
Hippolyte Taine, *Voyage aux Pyrénées* (Paris: Librairie Hachette, 1860). Illustration by Gustave Doré. Mountaineering Collection, Special Collections Department, University of Colorado Boulder Libraries.

images on the movie screen. The film depicts a group of tourists traveling by motorcar to various sites of interest.[39] The tourist party is made up of four women and two men, one of whom carries a bullhorn and serves as a tour guide. All appear well fed and well clothed—the embodiment of the European bourgeoisie. Their nationality is unstated, but they are clearly visitors; performing their tourism for the camera, they point and look at the sights around them with awe, without ever looking at the camera. They drive past a mountain village with ramshackle buildings and stop to peer at a series of waterfalls. In one shot, they stand in a riverbed under a high bridge and wave at a passing train, figures carefully composed so that all are visible (fig. 4.8). The film emphasizes the ease of voyaging by automobile, demonstrating that

FIGURE 4.8 Frame enlargement, *A Car Ride in the Pyrenees* (Pathé, ca. 1910). Courtesy EYE Film Institute Netherlands.

even ladies can travel comfortably this way. The film is also careful to depict the multitude of exotic sights to be seen, as if to assert that the convenience of auto travel does not negate the singularity of the experience.

Unconcerned with its audiences' level of familiarity with each subject, travelogue films work to construct a picture of exotic visual delights, regardless of location, enjoyable by all. What counts as exotic in this Pyrenees film are the rural villages the auto passes through and the waterfalls the tourists visit—in other words, spaces signifying the past and nature. This is in keeping with the conventions of exoticism in this period, in which colorful and unfamiliar sights seem to reside outside the domain of the modern. Yet it is the modern conveyance of the auto that has enabled the tourists to visit here, and it is the railroad to which they point. Moreover, tourists are themselves quintessentially modern figures. In fact, the tourists in this film serve the function of picturesque lead-in figures, who within the conventions of landscape illustration help guide the eye (and the sensibility) of the viewer into a foreign scene. Such lead-in figures "are inserted on the threshold of the painting"—or in this case, the film—in "the transition space between observer and observed. They 'sit in' for the European observer," as W. J. T.

Mitchell has said.[40] In this film, the tourists can be seen as stand-ins for the spectators in the audience. The audience is meant to feel that it shares a point of view with the figures in the film, as we see in the film's use of point-of-view shots: One sequence includes an alternation between shots of ladies looking through binoculars and shots of waterfalls framed with a binocular-shaped black matting. This matting serves to create a different kind of eye-line match, one that not only emphasizes the act of looking and foregrounds the shared point of view, but also includes the viewer as a third term in the eyeline match (figs. 4.9–4.10). The audience literally sees what the tourists in the film see, rendering the film a more interactive, almost three-dimensional experience. This might have felt enabling for the many cinema patrons who would not have fit into the demographic of the bourgeois tourists depicted in the film.

As *A Car Ride in the Pyrenees* demonstrates, "the exotic" could be found not only in faraway lands but "nearby" within Europe. Indeed, a great many travelogues focus on regions of internal empire, complicating traditional notions of center and periphery. For example, in *The Auvergne Mountains, Central France* (Lux Film, 1912), a series of frontal long shots shows rural villagers practicing various crafts, each individual or group of individuals represented as a particular "type" of craftsperson (fig. 4.11).[41] This film also includes the "aged native" convention, announced by an intertitle that reads, "A 100-year-old cobbler." The implication is that these traditional crafts are dying out; the region is presented as a picturesque and nostalgic image of the old country. A review of the film explains, "Many of the interesting industries of the inhabitants of the quaint little towns and villages which lie snugly hidden in the valleys are reviewed, we are introduced to some of the picturesque characters of the district and pay a visit to the cattle fair held at Murat, a town celebrated for the manifold small trades it is engaged in."[42] This "quaint" region filled with "picturesque characters" is presented as an image of the old world; its outmodedness is precisely the point.

What we might call the trope of disappearance is repeated in many other nonfiction films, from travelogues such as *Hungarian Folklore* (Pathé, 1913) to industrials such as *Cork Production in France* (Cines, 1913). While these are certainly real images of existing places and people, they also participate in the modern practice of "invented tradition." First theorized by Eric Hobsbawm, invented traditions are "responses to novel situations which take the form of reference to old situations, or which establish their own past by quasi-obligatory repetition. It is the contrast between the constant change

FIGURES 4.9–4.10 Emphasizing point of view: black matting to simulate binoculars, *A Car Ride in the Pyrenees* (Pathé, ca. 1910). Courtesy EYE Film Institute Netherlands.

FIGURE 4.11 "Coppersmiths," *The Auvergne Mountains, Central France* (a.k.a. *Picturesque Auvergne* [Lux Film, 1912]). Courtesy EYE Film Institute Netherlands.

and innovation of the modern world and the attempt to structure at last some parts of social life within it as unchanging and invariant that makes the 'invention of tradition' so interesting."[43] It is not that these traditions did not exist but that they are presented in an a-historical manner that seems to render them timeless. As Hobsbawm claims, it was particularly in the decades before the First World War that these invented traditions appeared, and travelogue films clearly played a part in constructing such images of nostalgic internal empire.

I adapt this concept of "internal empire" from the term "internal colonialism," which was influential in the 1960s for critics and activists involved in the struggles for decolonization, particularly in Latin America. According to one definition from that era, "An internal colony constitutes a society within a society based upon racial, linguistic, and/or marked cultural differences as well as differences of social class. It is subject to political and administrative control by the dominant classes and institutions of the metropolis. Defined in this way, internal colonies can exist on a geographical basis or on a racial and cultural basis in ethnically or culturally dual or plural societies."[44] In addition to its application for analyzing societies in the developing world, the concept played an important role in analyses of the social position of racial and ethnic minorities in the United States during the 1960s and '70s. Taking the concept one step further afield, Michael Hechter applied the model of internal colonialism to the United Kingdom in an influential study in 1975, arguing that the "Celtic fringe" of Scottish, Welsh, and Irish national identity functions as a series of internal colonial regions within the dominant British state.[45] While many regions of internal colonialism have been (and continue to be) engaged in separatist struggles (Kurdistan, the Basque region), I use the term more broadly to refer to any area within an established nation-state marked off as "traditional" or "primitive."

Of course, since the 1970s, a great deal of work has engaged with questions of nationalism and empire in new ways. So what is the purpose of returning to the idea of internal colonialism now to describe travelogues from the early twentieth century? Certainly it is not to make literal comparisons between colonial nation-states and internally dominated regions, which manifest different economic, military, cultural, and spatial dimensions. Rather, travelogues demonstrate the need to move away from nationalist-based models of power toward definitions of geography and identity based on smaller, regional boundaries. Moreover, the idea of internal empire seems uniquely descriptive of many tourist destinations, which were some of the most frequently documented travelogue subjects.

Rather than use the term "colonialism," I prefer to call these regions glimpsed by travelogues "spaces of internal *empire*," following Michael Hardt and Antonio Negri's description in which "in contrast to imperialism Empire establishes no territorial center of power and does not rely on fixed boundaries or barriers. It is a decentered and deterritorializing apparatus of rule that progressively incorporates the entire global realm within its open, expanding frontiers."[46] While Hardt and Negri argue that this model of empire characterizes our contemporary globalized world, I find their description apt (though not exact) for early travelogues (thus, I do not capitalize the term as they do), whose international scope of production, distribution, and reception functioned as a kind of globalized media *avant la lettre*. Early travel films particularly focus on locations of internal empire, for such locations were (and are) often some of the most popular tourist destinations. For my purposes, regions of internal empire do not necessarily have clear geographical boundaries; rather, films of internal empire are defined by a specific type of imagery, including traditional crafts, rural or wilderness landscapes, and native types. In travelogues, internal empire is not so much real geography as an image.

Colonial Travelogues: Landscapes and "Native Types"

Of course, in addition to regions of internal empire, many early travelogues focused on colonial lands. And despite the diversity of colonial travel film locations, the films are noteworthy for their repeated use of specific conventions. Colonial travelogues echo the broad colonial discourses of surveillance, appropriation, and aestheticization analyzed by David Spurr.[47] Rather than remap those discourses, which have already been thoroughly analyzed by others, I focus on the specifically cinematic conventions these films used both to represent and disavow colonial power.

As I have emphasized, travelogues tend to follow well-trodden paths. *L'Oasis d'El-Kantara* (Éclair, 1913) portrays the area known as El Kantara in Algeria, which was already famous in the late nineteenth century as a North African Eden and a popular stop on tourist itineraries. Often called the "Gate of the Orient" and renowned for its bridge, gorges, oasis, and three villages (known as the white, black, and red villages), the area was featured on many turn-of-the-century postcards. Like most travelogues, then, the film depicts a region that had already been pictured many times. Indeed, an entire set of Orientalist representational traditions had been forged in the nineteenth century; what Peter Dunwoodie has called "the famous Orientalist triad of palm tree/camel/caravan" was already in place.[48] This tradition was fostered by the multitude of travel books published in the nineteenth century, many of which first appeared as installments in the illustrated magazines. In the case of Algeria, the region had first been made familiar to French readers by the French painter and writer Eugène Fromentin, who published two well-known travel books about the region. Fromentin was just one of many French writers and artists to represent the new French colony in the nineteenth century. Dunwoodie points out that Fromentin's representations of Algeria "produce a fictional vision grounded in a mythical past which veils the harsh realities of the present, [creating] a space in which European superiority can parade its 'openness.'"[49] A similar process is at work in travelogue films such as *El-Kantara*.

There are at least two extant prints of this film—one at EYE and another at the British Film Institute (BFI). The BFI print appears to be complete and consists of six intertitles (in English) with accompanying footage.[50] The information and imagery presented in the film are minimal: One sees the requisite oasis, gorges, and "red village," along with a number of children scrambling for coins that the filmmakers have tossed to them. After the

FIGURE 4.12 Frame enlargement, *The Oasis of El-Kantara* (Éclair, 1913). Courtesy EYE Film Institute Netherlands.

film's main title card, the BFI print contains an intertitle announcing, "The mountain passes which are the gates of the desert," making reference to the area's "gateway" reputation. (The area takes its name from a famous bridge; *el-kantara* means "the arch" in Arabic.) The shot that follows (which is missing from the EYE print, as is the first intertitle) pans from left to right across a mountain landscape as a railroad train emerges from a tunnel. This image follows the travelogue's aesthetic principle of movement in every shot. Another intertitle announces, "An oasis of 90,000 palm trees," followed by a second panning shot of the landscape, this time in the opposite direction (from right to left), creating a dynamic contrast with the camera movement in the preceding shot. The composition of this shot follows some of the conventions of picturesque illustration. Foliage protrudes from the right of the frame; a lead-in figure squats in the foreground at the right; and the viewer's eye is led down the path of the stream receding at the center of the frame, emphasizing the depth of the landscape (fig. 4.12).

The film concludes with a medium shot of two girls embracing each other and smiling for the camera, clearly following the directions of the (unknown) filmmaking personnel (see plate 1). This final image is captivating,

FIGURE 4.13 Frame enlargement, *Indian and Ceylonese Types* (Éclair, 1913). Courtesy EYE Film Institute Netherlands.

but it also fits into a longstanding representational tradition in which "primitive" or "exotic" landscapes are populated with outsider figures—women, children, or the poor. These two girls fit into all three categories. This tradition, which John Barrell has called "the dark side of the landscape," is a key trope of the picturesque.[51] While the cheerful raggedness of these young children may have been real, as the photographic image attests, it also fits into a larger ideological project of making what seems exotic also appear harmonious. The fact that this ideology may have been unconscious on the part of the filmmakers does not blunt its force.

In contrast to the European tourists shown in travelogues such as *A Car Ride in the Pyrenees*, who are granted point-of-view shots, the people encountered in exotic foreign lands are treated as specimens—or, in the parlance of the day, "types." *Indian and Ceylonese Types* (Éclair, 1913) presents a series of "native types" posing for the camera in a series of shots that emphasize racial and cultural difference. The roughly four-minute film contains fourteen shots, each of which is a separate tableau of people posing for the camera, ranging from individuals, to small and large groups, to crowds (fig. 4.13). The film enables and encourages a kind of gawking that might not have been available to the viewer if he or she were actually there. In keeping with the relentless categorization of people that characterized this era, the film draws distinctions between some of the different ethnic and regional populations of Sri Lanka. Intertitles announce "Tamil inhabitants," "Kandyan people," and "Sinhalese." Qualities that an early twentieth-century European or North American viewer would find unusual are played up. We see a palm reader, a beggar, a number of scantily dressed children, and a group of well-dressed officials eating with their hands. Ceylon was, of course, a British Crown Colony (and separate from British India) at the time the film was made; today, it is the location of a major separatist struggle on the part of the Tamils. Ceylon was featured in the many guidebooks for European travelers in India in the nineteenth century, but the film conflates the two different regions and cultures of Ceylon and Southern India.

The film overlays its exotic imagery with two conventional tropes of popular Western representation: the pretty young girl and the three graces. The smiling pretty young girl is a travelogue cliché—such images are often positioned as the final shot, as we saw in *El-Kantara*—and in *Indian and Ceylonese Types* there are not one but two subsequent shots of a pretty young girl in close-up, each smiling for the camera. The three graces, a convention drawn from classical Greece and popular during the Victorian era, is another travelogue stock shot, and the film contains just such a grouping of three young women in a medium long shot smiling for the camera (fig. 4.14). The duration of this take (along with the act of posing itself) clearly makes the women uncomfortable. The shot lasts for sixteen seconds on-screen, and while the women remain good-natured (they are clearly being given instructions from off-screen), the shot captures their discomfort as one of them shyly covers her face with the hem of her sari and another covers her face with her hand.

There are several possible ways to interpret this shot beyond its meaning as an iconic image of the three graces. One is to view it as evidence of the filmmaker's coercion of his subjects and the awkwardness of the colonial encounter, which is clearly registered by the long duration of the take. (The subjects' discomfort is not captured in the same way by a still photograph.) A rejoinder to this interpretation, however, is to point out that the film company that edited the film chose to include the shot, which indicates that the discomfort was perhaps not subversive after all. In fact, such shots of people (most often women or children) giggling uncomfortably before the camera appear frequently in travelogue films—so much so that I would list them as yet another convention of the genre. What we might call the motif of un-

FIGURE 4.14 The three graces, *Indian and Ceylonese Types* (Éclair, 1913). Courtesy EYE Film Institute Netherlands.

ease before the camera is a travelogue staple. We might speculate that such shots of embarrassment were included to confer authenticity on the film, anticipating a long tradition of including superfluous details or "mistakes" in nonfiction film. Such awkward moments function as "reality effects," asserting the truthfulness of the imagery.[52] For me, the shot functions in both ways simultaneously—as an example of the reality effects of nonfiction, but also as an example of the tension of the colonial encounter. One further significance can be found in the film's exhibition context: Such scenes of discomfort restage the tension of colonial encounter before the audience in the theater, and here we come to the most important—but unknowable— dimension of this shot's meaning: the viewer. It would be up to the sensibility of the spectator to produce one or the other of these readings or to come up with a different reading altogether. Today, one wants to interpret this moment of unease as an oppositional image—perhaps even opposition that was intentional on the part of the women pictured. Regardless of how it was interpreted, the ambiguity of such scenes is palpable.

The representation of native "types" is one of the most distinctive conventions of early travel films, a convention that became outmoded a few decades later. Types — or stereotypes — provided one of the principal frameworks through which people in the era understood racial and cultural difference. In fact, "types" are a kind of modern updating of the destitute figures that were common in the European picturesque aesthetic tradition. But the rhetoric of "types" was also drawn from the emergent discipline of anthropology. As Robert J. C. Young writes, "Type came into widespread use in the 1850s because it neatly brought together the implications of both species and race while dispensing with the theoretical and terminological difficulties of both."[53] In other words, typology is a form of popular scientific knowledge that validates an imperial hierarchy. The types idea fits into a concept of difference as permanent and unchangeable, fixed in time. The types depicted in *Ceylon* are not granted much subjectivity; types are creatures at which one gawks, like people on display at a World's Fair or animals in the zoo. Yet these types, when represented in moving pictures, often manage to convey a sense of their subjectivity anyway, despite the odds stacked against them, through their expressions of uneasiness, or through more defiant expressions of resistance.

Although the word "ethnographic" was not used to title or promote travelogues, the films clearly drew from conventions of ethnographic representation to forge a kind of popular ethnography. The published description of *Native Industries in Soudan, Egypt*, a 1912 Pathé industrial film set in the then-British colony of Sudan, for example, illustrates the educational film's quasi-ethnographic interest in different cultures, as well as its limited ability to comprehend different cultures. "The natives of Soudan perform their many and varied labors before the camera giving one a knowledge of their habits, customs, and the crudity of their implements. There is an entertaining fascination in watching them work."[54] A poster for this film survives today, representing the natives as generic brown bodies at work, rather than individuals with names and a culture with a history (plate 7).

Popular ethnography can also be seen in the frequent references to scientific anthropometry in travelogues. Anthropometry was a nineteenth-century "science" that dealt with the measurements of the human body, comparing physical sizes, shapes, and proportions across races. Travelogue films adopted the conventions of anthropometric photography, showing portraits of individuals frontally and in profile. In the film *Moroccan Shoemakers* (Pathé, ca. 1915), for example, one witnesses a fascination with facial features that exceeds the film's attention to the local craft of shoemaking, its purported subject. In one shot, a man shown in a medium close-up poses for the camera, turning his head from the side to face front, then back to the side again, clearly obeying the instructions of the filmmaker standing outside the frame (figs. 4.15–4.17). We are given no information about this man beyond his photographic image. The shot allows the film spectator to gawk at his physical features in a way that would be less possible in a real-life encounter; it also provides an extended view of his head attire from all sides. Frame enlargements cannot convey the complex awkwardness captured in such encounters. As the man's eyes dart back and forth looking at the (invisible) filmmaker and the camera, a nervous smile flits across his face. Once again, multiple interpretations of this moment of unease are possible. The man is objectified by the camera, yet his discomfort is clearly recorded. His discomfort marks this shot as real, yet it also has the effect of mitigating or undermining the shot's objectification of him.

This sort of quasi-scientific portraiture appears frequently in travel films from the 1910s, and I have even found examples of anthropometry in films from the 1920s, although by that time it had become outmoded in the discipline of anthropology. Anthropometry was most often used to portray people of color in some location far away from Europe, although the convention was also used for European peasants, as in *South Tyrolean Folkloristic Dress* (Pathé, ca. 1920). As early as 1905, in fact, the convention was already being parodied in a comic film from Pathé titled *Types Français*, which features a vaudeville performer impersonating a gallery of French character types. (This film may have been based on a series of satirical lithographs by Honoré Daumier, also called *Types Français*, first published in 1835.) The quasi-scientific gesture of anthropometric portraiture is merely a loose reference to the actual nineteenth-century practice of anthropometry, which usually posed its subjects in front of a backdrop grid to facilitate measurements. It is not the travelogue's goal to collect empirical scientific data; rather, the anthropometric convention validated as "scientific" what was little more than a voyeuristic curiosity about racial difference.

I have been describing the objectifying nature of travelogues, which proceed from an imperializing logic that validates the Western world as the master of all it sees. While this logic may have been mostly unconscious, it structures every aspect of these films. As Spurr writes, "There is nothing especially conscious or intentional in [the use of colonial rhetorical tropes]; they are part of the landscape in which relations of power manifest themselves."[55] The travelogue places its spectator in an ideal viewing position, as someone who can gawk from the comfort of his or her theater seat. Even so,

FIGURES 4.15–4.17
Anthropometric
portraiture,
*Moroccan
Shoemakers*
(Pathé, ca. 1915).
Courtesy EYE
Film Institute
Netherlands.

FIGURE 4.18 Frame enlargement, *In Egypt* (1920, Pathé). Courtesy EYE Film Institute Netherlands.

the uneasiness of the filmed subjects is impossible to miss. Moreover, the people in travelogue films not only express their discomfort; they also frequently stare back from the screen.

The Look at the Camera

In many places, travelogues open up to oppositional readings when the figures refuse to be "picturesque," but instead return the look of the camera. As is well known in film studies, the look at the camera is one of the primary taboos of classical filmmaking. And yet in travelogue films, this look is ubiquitous—in fact, someone looks directly at the camera in almost every travelogue film I have seen. Sometimes this look is posed, as in the "types" sequences just discussed; other times this look is accidental, as when a person just happens to pass through the area being filmed, and looks at the filming taking place. The final shot of *In Egypt* (Pathé, ca. 1920) is a stereotypical image of a veiled Islamic woman, and yet this woman is looking into the camera with a gaze of remarkable intensity; indeed, she might be casting the evil eye on the camera (fig. 4.18).[56] The woman's glare refuses the film's fetishistic desire to possess her; her stare undermines the film's attempt to capitalize on her geographical, cultural, racial, and gender difference. As

FIGURE 4.19 Frame enlargement, *Stockholm* (production company unknown, ca. 1912).
Courtesy EYE Film Institute Netherlands.

I have explained, travelogues frequently conclude with a kind of hyper-picturesque cliché (a sunset, a smiling child, a smiling woman), but because of her angry look, this woman is able to sabotage the travelogue's conventional concluding shot. Although the subversive potential of this shot may be limited (she still serves to fulfill the film's need for an image of a veiled Islamic woman, and she remains absent from the space of the theater), the woman's intense look at the camera hardly renders the film's conclusion reassuring for the spectator.

In contrast, *Stockholm* (production company unknown, ca. 1912), serves quite a different purpose (fig. 4.19). This black-and-white film is mostly a phantom ride through the modern city of Stockholm, shot from the front of a moving vehicle. But the camera movement does stop at times, and for one very brief shot one sees a man standing at the docks holding what appears to be an eel. The man smiles at the camera, holding the eel out to the camera in a friendly gesture. He does not indicate any feeling of discomfort but, rather, seems to enjoy the novelty of being filmed, although there is still a certain awkwardness about the interaction. Of course, the travelogue's power dynamic with this man is quite different from its relationship to the

FIGURE 4.20 Frame enlargement, *Venice and Its Monuments* (Éclair, 1914). Courtesy EYE Film Institute Netherlands.

veiled Egyptian woman; this man in fact fits the position of the travelogue's own implied tourist spectator (Western, white, male, urban).

A third example of the rupturing power of the look can be found in *Venice and Its Monuments* (Éclair, 1914). The man looking at the camera has not been posed (fig. 4.20); rather, he walks into the frame from the bottom left and stares at the camera with an expression of surprise and curiosity on his face. Such shots of people staring at the camera apparatus are extremely common in travelogue films. In this exchange, one is aware that the look has been initiated by the man in the image, rather than by the filmmaker. (This look is not truly "accidental," however, because the shot was consciously left in during editing.) This is but a quick moment of rupture: A man looks back at the camera, and the film audience might feel a jolt of recognition in the theater. This man's stare is perhaps less loaded with transgressive significance than that of the woman in *In Egypt*, but it disrupts a sense of this film as a hermetically sealed world.

Finally, in my fourth example, from the film *South America* (production company unknown, ca. 1920), one can see a direct trace of the filmmaker's presence: his arm and hand are visible entering from the left side of the

FIGURE 4.21 Frame enlargement, *South America* (production company unknown, ca. 1920). Courtesy EYE Film Institute Netherlands.

frame adjusting the pose of the people he is filming (fig. 4.21). This kind of trace is extremely rare, for the travelogue filmmaker almost always retains the privilege of invisibility as the camera stares at everyone else. Here, one can finally see some physical signifiers inscribed on the body of the filmmaker: He is wearing a suit and what appears to be a wedding ring, and his hand is visibly pale, contrasting with the darker skin of the indigenous men being filmed. This shot, which is very brief, is all the more remarkable for the exchange of gazes going on. The filmmaker's hand restrains one man in the front center of the frame, and the man stares back at the filmmaker's invisible face outside the left of the frame. On the left side of the frame there is another man staring directly into the camera, or perhaps at the person behind the camera turning the crank. Finally, in the background a few other men look on, one with a huge grin on his face. Such an image would make for a remarkable snapshot, but it moves by so quickly on the movie screen that it would have been noticed only by extremely attentive viewers.

All of these looks at the camera stage two encounters: an encounter at the moment of production between the filmmaker/camera and the person being filmed, and an encounter at the moment of exhibition between the person in the image and the person looking at the image. Of these two encounters, only the first occurs in a unified space, yet the second encounter is the one that concerns me here. The look at the camera was a topic of interest to film scholars in the 1980s as part of a broad theorization of the cinematic gaze that was then state-of-the-art. I suggest that the analysis of the returned gaze can still yield significant insights for early nonfiction film. Mark Vernet argued in 1989 that the look at the camera is both utopian and nostalgic: "The look at the camera is the emblematic figure of this nostalgia, of this encounter that could have taken place. It does not mark an actual encounter between the character and the spectator: it signals its past possibility and its present impossibility, thereby intensifying that division in the spectator that simultaneously makes him or her a believer and a skeptic."[57] The returned gaze catches the film spectator in the act of voyeurism. By calling attention to this voyeurism, travelogues emphasize the fact that the spectator's travel experience in the theater is a fantasy. This unmasking of fantasy might have several effects: It might activate a nostalgia for a failed encounter, or it might activate a spectator's critical faculties. This look begins to undo one of the travelogue's primary myths: It reveals the encounter with difference to be a representation only. When filmed subjects stare back at the viewer from the screen, one realizes that this is not a real encounter but a mediated, virtual experience. Nobody has actually traveled but the man behind the camera. Vernet writes that the look at the camera is "an ambiguous, doubled, perverse look that simultaneously expresses desire and its condemnation, invitation and rejection, project and renunciation of projects."[58] The look at the camera sabotages the travelogue's confident assertion of its ability to record the entire world, instead liberating the subversive potential contained within its seemingly iron-clad system.

In the 1990s, some film scholars rejected the idea that the look at the camera might have the potential to rupture the system of cinematic voyeurism. Of the Edison film *What Happened on Twenty-Third Street, New York City* (1901), in which a woman's skirt is blown up by wind from a city grate (at which point she laughs and briefly glances at the camera), Lauren Rabinovitz writes, "The woman who looks back is hardly transgressive since her look is so fully recoupable and recuperated." Moreover, the woman has been "easily co-opted as a conspirator into her own sexual objectification, while her audience—both men and women—are taught about the exercise of sexual surveillance as power within the regime of the real."[59] While it may be true that a mere look at the camera is hardly enough to undo the power dynamic of a whole system of cinematic looking, perhaps at this point we can draw some insights from each side of this debate. We might return to the cinema's essential quality of movement, and its potential for interactivity, to find a new answer.

These looks at the camera, like all other moments in a travel film, are actually discontinuous images, fragments of the real world presented as part of a grandiose new technology, cinema. The travelogue system purported to represent all aspects of life in all corners of the globe, yet it necessarily failed at this task. In its global striving, the travelogue system reveals its imperial ideologies—but it would be naïve and ahistorical to expect early travel films to somehow stand apart from the imperialism of their day. And given that cinema is defined not only by images but also by spectators, there are too many contingencies and gaps on the other side of the cinematic equation—reception—to make these films hold tight to their normative meanings. In fact, the very predictability of these films allows one to spot their ruptures more readily. As I shall discuss in the following chapter, travelogues draw upon the aesthetic convention of the picturesque to smooth over conflict with a veneer of harmony—and yet the bumps underneath frequently remain visible. The movement inherent in cinema allows what Bergson called the "pulsation" of life to appear.[60] Flashes of mechanized movement enable the spectator to read against the grain between the dynamic clash of images on screen. The experience of the returned gaze cannot be matched by any other medium—not even by still photography—because this look moves.

CHAPTER 5

SCENIC FILMS AND THE CINEMATIC PICTURESQUE

Travelogue films are deeply bound up with the aesthetic of the picturesque. Films were often titled with the word: *Picturesque Andalusia, Picturesque Japan, Picturesque Rocks of Baume-les-Messieurs, Picturesque Colorado, Picturesque India*, and the list goes on.[1] Likewise, the word appears in many descriptions and reviews of scenic films; it seems that virtually everything becomes "picturesque" when it appears in a travelogue. For example, *Scenes in Korea* (Selig, 1912) is described in the release flyer as "another picturesque travel picture, giving glimpses of the life and habits of these Oriental people." *Sheep Shearing in New Mexico* (Selig, 1912) is likewise described as "An Interesting Educational Film with Picturesque Features."[2] "Picturesque" is not a neutral term; rather, it carries with it aesthetic and political implications derived from a visual tradition that, at the dawn of the twentieth century, was already more than one hundred years old. The picturesque was a uniquely commodifiable category, and its persistence in all sorts of media — literature, painting, photography, and, ultimately, cinema — was enabled by a process of popularization as it was made over by many generations to suit the needs of a growing consumer culture. As I demonstrate in this chapter, in the early twentieth century, the picturesque was a mode of the marketplace. By this time, the word was frequently used as an advertising term, as though picturesqueness were just the thing needed to guarantee a good time at the cinema. I devote an entire chapter to this aesthetic's history and incarnation in early cinema because its lineage helps us to understand the travel genre's stylistic appeal and class valence.

Of course, the mere repetition of an adjective is not necessarily significant in itself; after all, there are other keywords that appear frequently in the travelogue schema: beautiful, scenic, scenes, views, panoramas, types, and more. But the unrelenting repetition of the word "picturesque" in this era and in this genre suggests that it was symptomatic of something larger. As I will demonstrate, before the First World War, the picturesque still contained some cultural capital derived from its long lineage as an aesthetic category that emerged in the eighteenth century. The picturesque is a vast and far-reaching aesthetic convention encompassing all kinds of imagery both "high" and "low," from landscape paintings by Thomas Gainsborough and J. M. W. Turner to popular nineteenth-century magazine illustrations by artists such as Harry Fenn and Thomas Moran, to postcards, tourist brochures, and chromolithographs. Indeed, the style continues to thrive in commercial visual culture today, even if the word is rarely used. Consider images from British heritage films, *National Geographic* magazine, and programs on the Travel Channel, to name just a few examples. In the era before the First World War, as the Western world was on the brink of losing its innocence, the picturesque still had some meaning, but it was a depleted category — reduced almost entirely to a sign of commodification.

It is tricky to pinpoint the precise meaning of the picturesque in the 1900s and 1910s, because the term was used in several different ways. "Picturesque" most often referred to scenic landscapes, as in the advertisement for a film called *Picturesque Darjeeling, India* (Edison, 1912), which "well . . . deserves the name" (see fig. 5.1). Mountains have an important significance in the history of landscape representations, and the description of Mount Everest lending "a touch of awe and majesty" indicates that this film is reaching for the infinite. The commercial trappings of the advertisement, however, significantly inhibit any sublime effect. Indeed, from a certain perspective, the picturesque can be seen as a commercialized form of the sublime. Rather than overwhelming the viewer with awe, the picturesque instead soothes the viewer with idealized landscape imagery. The picturesque was not only reserved as a description for landscapes, however; it was also used as a descriptive term for native or destitute figures, as the description of *Picturesque Darjeeling* makes clear: "As picturesque as the scenery are the people whose habits and customs have stayed stagnant in the onward march of civilization." Aestheticizing Otherness in this manner was a way to remove

Picturesque Darjeeling, India

In the Himalayan Mountains

SCENIC—RELEASED JULY 13, 1912

No. 7077. About 300 feet. Copyright, July, 1912. Code, Vorschuhen

PICTURESQUE Darjeeling, for well it deserves the name, is delightfully located in the Himalayan Mountains. The scenic portion of this picture is exceptional and leaves nothing to be desired. A view of the snow range including Mt. Everest, the highest mountain in the world forty-five miles away, lends a touch of awe and majesty as these mighty earthworks rear their summits higher and higher until at last passing through the clouds, the peaks are crowned with ice and snow.

Another view equally as imposing was taken above the clouds which appear like a great rolling sea of soft white fleece, parting now and then, enabling one to see far below into the dizzy depths of valley space.

As picturesque as the scenery are the people whose habits and customs have stayed stagnant in the onward march of civilization. A market scene with hundreds of natives trading and bargaining also a general view of the town give a fair conception of what there is and what goes on in the land of Allah.

Pictures of such people as a wandering minstrel, Tibetan women dancing, mountaineers dancing and an aged pair of Bhutanese dancers, add an unexpected touch of humor with their queer steps and gestures. Some boys of Darjeeling are shown playing a native game in which they juggle a ball from one to the other, only using their feet. This is a "stunt" that would make a professional stage artist take notice.

H. G. PEARSON of Somerville, Mass., has recently featured "Church and Country" and "How Washington Crossed the Delaware" in his local newspaper advertising. In one case he printed the entire synopsis and in the other the cast of characters. The following letter received from the very successful manager reads in part as follows:

"It might interest you to know that the Young Men's Club which is associated with the Baptist Church in Melrose recently gave its first moving picture show. Out of six films chosen for this performance three were Edison films. There is not a church in Melrose whose minister has not a good word for good pictures—what a change from five years ago."

FIGURE 5.1
Release flyer for *Picturesque Darjeeling, India* (Edison, 1912), from *Edison Kinetogram,* 1 July 1912, 11. Courtesy Academy of Motion Picture Arts and Sciences.

any social or political context that might inhibit the spectator's enjoyment. Moreover, whatever is deemed picturesque also tends to signify a quality of "pastness," particularly when the place depicted is a faraway colonial land. These "stagnant" people are emissaries from the past who persist in the present, just as these idealized landscapes seem frozen in time, rather like a series of snow domes.

The application of the term "picturesque" to figures can also be seen in a promotional flyer for *Life and Customs of the Winnebago Indians* (Selig, 1912; see fig. 5.2), which asserts, "On the whole, the picture is wonderfully entertaining, remarkably instructive and delightfully picturesque."[3] This hybrid fiction–nonfiction film used nonactors performing idealized versions of native lifeways and customs. (This is the same technique Edward S. Curtis

Life and Customs of the Winnebago Indians

An interesting and picturesque educational picture depicting the manners, sports,
and pastimes of these famous northwest red men

Produced by GEORGE L. COX

THOSE TAKING PART

Bucks.	Squaws.	Bucks.	Squaws.
CHIEF OLGALALAFIRE	Lilly Chipmunk	DARK CLOUD	Newanos
CHIEF WILLIAM THUNDER	Gowawassa	LITTLE EAGLE	Laughing Water
CHIEF BUFFALO HEAD	Panesa	LITTLE BEAR	Fawn Face
LITTLE CLOUD	Watawasa	RUNNING FOE	Silver Moon
BIG MOON	Watmana	BLACK HORSE	Starlight

THE Winnebagos were the most powerful and intelligent of the migthy Siouan family that were left in the middle west after their forbears, the Sioux, had drifted farther west to give war to the fast encroaching white man. For many years the Winnebagos roamed through Illinois, but at present their largest settlement is in the Black River Falls district of Wisconsin. While they are essentially "woods" Indians, they have taken a keen interest in farming. They still prefer to live in wigwams, although their tribal characteristics incline towards the modern methods. The Winnebagos are not a vanishing race, and their standards of morality and education place them among the highest type of modern Indian.

In this exceedingly interesting educational picture the manners, customs, sports and pastimes of this proud and haughty tribe are shown in a series of intimate picturesque scenes. One scene shows them at their bead weaving. Another view shows their adeptness at canoe making and repairing. Still another scene gives us an idea of their strange games. Their renowned ceremonial dances are also shown. On the whole, the picture is wonderfully entertaining, remarkably instructive and delightfully picturesque.

SELIG

Copyright, 1912, by The Selig Polyscope Co.

FIGURE 5.2 Release flyer for *Life and Customs of the Winnebago Indians* (Selig, 1912). Courtesy Academy of Motion Picture Arts and Sciences.

used in *In the Land of the Head Hunters* in 1914 and that Robert Flaherty used for *Nanook of the North* in 1922.) Even though this description does allude to the Winnebagos' historical loss of territory, the film, we are assured, is "delightfully picturesque." Once again, the word seems to guarantee a form of placidity: What is deemed picturesque is the way in which the Winnebago are presented as remnants of the past, their "life and customs" under threat, despite the fact that they are "not a vanishing race" and are labeled "among the highest type of modern Indian." These contradictions are not a problem for the picturesque, which smooths over any objections or discontinuities that might threaten.

Outside its descriptive application to landscapes and figures, the term has a peculiarly redundant quality. The word "picturesque" is used two other places in this particular advertisement, each time as a surplus adjective. The film is "an interesting and picturesque educational picture" and shows "intimate picturesque scenes." In both of these instances, the word "picturesque" might have been cut with no diminishing of the phrase's basic meaning. So why was the word used? "Picturesque" essentially functioned as an advertising term in this era. In addition to serving as a kind of pledge of political detachment, "picturesque" carried genteel connotations and thus it was meant to attract middle-class audiences interested in "high-quality" pictures. Perhaps more than anything, "picturesque" denoted a generalized sense of something pleasing. In this sense the picturesque in the early twentieth century can be seen as a bland sign of commodification, much the way words such as "amazing" or "extreme" are used today. The sheer ubiquity of the term demonstrates that "picturesque" was a keyword of commodity culture in the early twentieth century, a seemingly blank adjective that signified "you will like this" to the emergent middlebrow consumer.

The critical consensus today, simply put, is that the picturesque is politically retrograde. The picturesque relentlessly aestheticizes the world, depoliticizing it and structuring it in terms of a set of reductive conventions that can be easily understood. As such, the picturesque is seen as a form of knowledge in the service of the dominating classes in imperialistic Western culture. Linda Nochlin puts it most succinctly: One of the functions of the picturesque is "to mask conflict with the appearance of tranquillity."[4] The suppression of social and historical conditions in the interest of entertainment has been one of the picturesque's primary roles. However, my aim is not solely to explore the ways in which the picturesque has been a repressive force, for this effect has already been well analyzed by many scholars, although rarely in the context of cinema. (One exception is Giorgio Bertellini's *Italy in Early American Cinema*, which provides an insightful account of the picturesque as a representational strategy in early cinema, especially as it relates to depictions of Italian immigrants.[5]) My aim is also to focus on how the picturesque came to serve as a commercial style for early nonfiction film, and how it often contradicts itself in cinematic form.

The question for this chapter is not so much "How is the picturesque a distorting mode of representation?" as "Why was the picturesque so useful for early travelogues?" Ultimately, I argue that the picturesque might be read against the grain as a potentially disruptive aesthetic, not *despite* but *because of* its impulse to soothe, which very often shows its seams. This has to do with certain aspects of cinematic form—specifically movement—but it is also bound up with history. By the early twentieth century, when it was adopted by cinema, the picturesque had come to appear untenable as an aesthetic concept, even if it served a commercializing function for the film industry. As Gary Harrison and Jill Heydt-Stevenson have observed, "The picturesque adapts to serve and sometimes to subvert the various ends of its users, thus promoting emancipatory and democratic, as well as repressive and aristocratic, spatial practices."[6] In this chapter, I briefly summarize the origin of the picturesque in eighteenth-century aesthetic theory in order to analyze its function in early travelogue films. While the concept was worn out by the 1910s, it contained fluid possibilities for reinterpretation in the cinema.

Early cinema's connection to nineteenth-century media such as vaudeville is well established, and I analyzed the travelogue's connection to the illustrated travel lecture tradition in chapter 1. But early cinema's links to larger aesthetic categories have proven more elusive. One of the most influential theorizations of early cinema aesthetics has been Tom Gunning's notion of early cinema's fairground aesthetic, the "cinema of attractions" that "directly solicits spectator attention . . . supplying pleasure through an exciting spectacle . . . that is of interest in itself."[7] Gunning later expanded this argument to describe the "aesthetic of astonishment" underlying these cinematic attractions, which offers the viewer a "moment of revelation" that connects early cinema to magic as well as to the fairground. The spectator's response is key to these twin concepts of "attractions" and "astonishment": "The spectator does not get lost in a fictional world and its drama, but remains aware of the act of looking, the excitement of curiosity and its fulfilment."[8] For Gunning, this awareness by spectators is akin to later avant-garde practices of distantiation: The audience is not absorbed or deluded by cinema but instead remains self-consciously aware of film as an illusion and even delights in the knowledge of that illusion. As I discussed in chapter 4, early nonfiction's "view aesthetic" is a component of this dynamic of attractions.

While I share Gunning's interest in linking early cinema with later avant-garde practices, I approach an avant-garde sensibility by way of the decidedly rear-guard terrain of the picturesque. When compared with the dynamic "attractions" aesthetic of the fairground, the picturesque looks determinedly stodgy. Yet it is my contention that early cinema updated the picturesque in the early 1900s because it was particularly suited to mechanical reproduction. This means not that the picturesque was "radicalized" in modernity but that it was well suited to the modern marketplace and easily adaptable to cinematic qualities of motion, framing, and repetition. The picturesque found its way into most scenic films—and into many fiction films as well, such as in the panning landscape shot that opens D. W. Griffith's *The Country Doctor* (1909). Cinema contributed motion to the tradition of picturesque representation, thus introducing an entirely new dimension to this familiar way of perceiving the world. In addition, traditional picturesque destitute figures were reinvented by their meeting with the modern science of anthropology to produce a new understanding of "Other" peoples. Often carrying an implication of refinement or culture, and functioning as the flip side of early cinema's sideshow "attractions" mode, the picturesque seemed to function as early cinema's "highbrow" aesthetic. Yet, as I suggest throughout this book, supposedly respectable styles could have unintentionally subversive potential. Finally, early cinema's appropriation of the picturesque demonstrates not so much a developed and intentional style as what André Gaudreault and Philippe Marion have recently called "a *filmed* style," borrowed from other pre-cinematic media.[9]

In their own way, contemporary critics were also quite concerned with cinema aesthetics inasmuch as they debated film's potential—or lack of potential—to become an art form. While early cinema was denigrated by most critics as a lowbrow form of entertainment, by the 1910s a few forward-looking writers were able to see cinema as a medium that contained exciting potential for new aesthetic experimentation. In the United States, Vachel Lindsay and Hugo Munsterberg both famously wrote early books of film criticism that celebrated the new medium. Munsterberg claimed in 1916 that film embodied a "new form of true beauty," while Lindsay had asserted vehemently a year earlier that "THE MOTION PICTURE ART IS A GREAT HIGH ART, NOT A PROCESS OF COMMERCIAL MANUFACTURE."[10] These early film critics focused their analyses on fiction films, despite the prevalence of nonfiction at the time—an oversight that anticipated the disregard for nonfiction that was continued by generations of film critics.

The enthusiasm of these writers is perhaps understandable, as their approval was a counterbalance to the dismissal of cinema coming from many other voices at the time. Their enthusiasm is also a tempered but symptomatic version of the general rhetoric surrounding the cinema in its early years, which is characterized by just such a split between grumbling naysayers and breathless supporters. Rather than falling into one or the other side of a predictable binary, however, I suggest that travel films fall somewhere in between. Neither an aesthetically bankrupt style of "cheap entertainment" nor an inherently radical new art form, early travelogues instead poached from previous aesthetic traditions to forge a style of instructive entertainment that we might better understand as middlebrow. I do not use the term "middlebrow" with the pejorative force that is usually implied. Rather, I use it descriptively, as a barometer of the way early travelogues fit into the larger constellation of cinema as a distinct kind of mass culture that was incorporating new and broader demographics into cultural consumption. To understand how the picturesque was used by early cinema, it is necessary to understand the picturesque's meanings when it was still a vital and debated term. I contend that the picturesque had become a commerical, middlebrow style by the early twentieth century. When it emerged more than one hundred years earlier, however, it contained more genteel associations as a taste and a pastime of the gentleman traveler.

The emergence of the middlebrow is usually located in the interwar years, with the start of the Book-of-the-Month Club in 1926.[11] Without taking time to trace the meaning of the various kinds of "brows" of the 1910s, I simply want to assert that middlebrow culture was already under construction in the years before the onset of the First World War.[12] As we have seen, early educational cinema was championed as part of a campaign to "uplift" its working-class audiences. Historians have argued that the Arnoldian (or genteel) tradition died out after the First World War, but Joan Shelley Rubin contends that it continued, "albeit in chastened and redirected form, throughout the 1920s, 1930s, and 1940s," as the middlebrow. While the focus of my argument is not to nitpick about terminology—the picturesque certainly fits into the genteel tradition, just as it continued into the era of the middlebrow—what I hope to gain by also associating the picturesque with a "brow" one step removed from elite culture is a sense that the picturesque was always an aesthetic for amateurs, despite being marketed as a "high-class" style in early cinema's promotional campaigns. A review of the term's origins will help clarify the picturesque as a neophyte's sensibility.

Theories of the Picturesque

The picturesque has never been a monolithic or undisputed concept.[13] Literally, the term means "like a picture," and it initially referred to any subjects thought to be suitable for painting—landscape in particular. The aesthetic originated in late eighteenth-century England as a means of inducing edifying sensations in the viewer: Aesthetic appreciation was then coming to be seen as derived from the viewing subject's sensibility rather than from his or her reason. It originated out of a reverential appreciation for nature and retained some sense of high moral purpose. Reverend William Gilpin, the first major theorist of the picturesque, wrote, "Nature is but a name for an *effect*, / Whose *cause* is God"; thus, the first, eighteenth-century version of the picturesque could be appreciated only by the so-called man of taste.[14] As such, the picturesque was eminently suited to preserving social hierarchies, as it validated a particular kind of masculine, upper-class ideal. Women, too, could appreciate the picturesque—there are many examples of women going on picturesque tours, usually in the company of a man— yet such cultivation was clearly thought to lie outside the abilities of most human beings; the "man of taste" was a privileged, elite subject position.[15] Despite the fact that the picturesque worked to shore up various hierarchies, it was from the start connected to tourism, a practice that was already shedding its highbrow connotations by the nineteenth century. In fact, the picturesque grew directly out of travel accounts such as Gilpin's *Observations on the River Wye* and Thomas West's *Guide to the Lakes*.[16]

Gilpin, a clergyman and amateur sketch artist, first described and popularized the picturesque in his series of travel books about Wales and the Lake District in northwestern England; he then attempted a more systematic theorization of picturesque practices and aesthetics. More philosophical theorizations quickly followed in the 1790s and beyond, written by Uvedale Price and Richard Payne Knight.[17] Scholars generally agree that Gilpin's concept of the picturesque differs from that of Price and Knight, and Gilpin's loose amateur musings are usually seen as less sophisticated than the rigorous treatments of Price and Knight. Kim Ian Michasiw, however, argues that Gilpin's foundational version of the picturesque is more unruly and potentially transgressive than the tamed variety that followed in the footsteps of Price and Knight. Michasiw points out that in Gilpin's writing, odd or accidental elements of landscape "remain anomalous, ambiguous, destabilizing. . . . Gilpin's position asserts the contingency and fragility of the picturesque order while the later theorists insist that true taste can deal with any object the world presents."[18] In other words, Gilpin's picturesque is less totalizing than later versions; its attempts to impose aesthetic order on a chaotic world occasionally fail. Important for my argument here is the idea that at its very inception, the concept of the picturesque contained within itself the seeds of its own undoing; in trying to imbue new landscapes with

a veneer of enchantment, the picturesque could lead an unwitting spectator into potentially disruptive foreign territory, leaving the traveler suddenly
alone to face an Otherness that might never have been approached without it.

Despite their disagreements, all of these eighteenth-century theorists of
the picturesque were themselves building on the same aesthetic treatise:
Edmund Burke's hugely influential *Philosophical Enquiry into the Origins of
our Ideas of the Sublime and Beautiful* (1757). Burke's *Enquiry* did not deal
explicitly with the category of the picturesque, but it was immensely influential for picturesque theory, both aesthetically and ideologically. Malcolm
Andrews writes: "The important stress in the *Enquiry* is on the sensationist
interpretation of both the Sublime and the Beautiful. Beauty is not determined by such hallowed Renaissance criteria as proportion, utility or 'fit-
ness,' for these are intellectual judgements. Beauty and Sublimity seize the
mind before it can collect its thoughts."[19] Reason has thus been supplanted
by sensibility. This "seizing the mind," an immediate, almost unconscious response, would become the key to commercialization in twentieth-century
mass culture, yet at first it was thought to reveal an elite sensibility. Not
everyone was believed capable of such discernment.

It has often been pointed out that Burke's writing, and his notorious political conservatism, were reactions against one of the most crucial shifts
into modernity: the rise of the bourgeoisie.[20] Picturesque theories of the
eighteenth century fall in line with Burke's elitism, resembling as they do an
essentialist defense of upper-class taste. It is perhaps ironic, then, that the
picturesque ended up becoming such a popular commercial style. Teasing
out the contradictory implications of Burke's individualist aesthetic sensa-
tionism coupled with his antipopulism would require a careful historical
examination that is outside the scope of this study.[21] Suffice it to say that
Burke's *Enquiry*, written at the beginning of his career, did draw on a certain
"vogue of feeling" for individual sensation (as opposed to "timeless" classical
values) and thus can be seen as unwittingly contributing to the rise of indi-
vidualistic bourgeois aesthetic values.[22]

It is important to understand that the picturesque is *not* the same thing
as the sublime—nor was it, at least at first, the same thing as the beautiful. The picturesque emerged as a third term alongside "the sublime" and
"the beautiful" in the 1790s through the writings of Gilpin, Price, and others.
For Price, "Picturesqueness appears to hold a station between beauty and
sublimity." That is, it aspires to grand meaning yet retains a more pedes-

trian pleasant quality—although he is careful to point out that the picturesque is not always beautiful but can also encompass that which is "terrible, ugly, or deformed."[23] The terms "sublime," "beautiful," and "picturesque" are frequently conflated today, but they carried distinct resonances when they emerged. Therefore, a quick review of historical definitions is in order.

In the strict Burkeian sense, the sublime is "whatever is fitted in any sort to excite the ideas of pain, and danger, that is to say, whatever is in any sort terrible." Qualities such as vastness, magnificence, strength, and infinity are indicative of the sublime. Furthermore, Burke wrote that "the passion caused by the great and sublime in *nature* . . . is Astonishment; and astonishment is that state of the soul, in which all its motions are suspended, with some degree of horror."[24] For Burke, the quintessential sublime experience would be to feel physically overcome with emotion (feeling your heart jump into your throat) while standing on a mountain precipice or at the edge of a crashing ocean. This terror, astonishment, and horror are to be contrasted with the much more tame aesthetic of the beautiful, "that quality or those qualities in bodies by which they cause love, or some passion similar to it." The effect of the beautiful is not as strong as the effect of the sublime because, Burke argues, "the ideas of pain are much more powerful than those which enter on the part of pleasure."[25]

Next to vastness, the most important quality of the sublime for Burke is obscurity. Immanuel Kant expressed the "obscure" aspect of the sublime more explicitly than Burke: For Kant, the sublime is not a picture but a state of mind, an emotional response conjured up by images, sounds, or experiences. The sublime is a feeling of awe, of insignificance in the face of the infinite; it cannot be represented: "What is sublime, in the proper meaning of the term, cannot be contained in any sensible form but concerns only ideas of reason, which, though they cannot be exhibited adequately, are aroused and called to mind by this very inadequacy, which can be exhibited in sensibility."[26] Strictly defined, then, the sublime is always unrepresentable. But there is a long tradition of representations of the sublime, which we can understand not as literal representations of sublimity but, rather, as representations of the *idea* of sublimity.

As conventional, mass-produced images striving for realism, travelogue films by definition cannot be sublime. But, of course, travelogue films are not attempting to exemplify Burkean or Kantian aesthetics. When they depict vast mountain vistas or high waterfalls, the emotional response they inspire is always at one remove, making the viewer wonder what it might be like to be there rather than making the viewer fear for her life standing on the edge of a precipice. In an important sense, as Kant pointed out, attempts to represent the sublime often fail—and sometimes even humorously so, because the attempt can so easily appear ridiculous. Realist representation, in contrast, can more directly and easily capture beautiful or picturesque qualities. In a passage on imitation, Burke dwells on the aesthetic implications of realism. Imitation brings pleasure, he writes, and "it is by imitation far more than by precept that we learn every thing; and what we learn thus we acquire not only more effectually, but more pleasantly. This forms our manners, our opinions, our lives. It is one of the strongest links of society; it is a species of mutual compliance which all men yield to each other. . . . Herein it is that painting and many other agreeable arts have laid one of the principal foundations of their power."[27] Realism traditionally has been understood as a spur to knowledge; in this analysis, it makes learning more pleasant. Perhaps most important, imitation is "one of the strongest links of society," something that binds a society together, "a species of mutual compliance which all men yield to each other." This assertion describes the function of a kind of cultural imaginary, a shared set of values that influences perceptions as well as actions. In fact, this language runs very close to that of the Progressive Era reformers who celebrated visual education for its powers to form a more cohesive American society.

As just such a realistic form, the picturesque, unlike the sublime, was easily and immediately adopted as a representational style. Gilpin wrote that "a strong *impression of nature* will enable us to judge of the *works of art*. Nature is the archetype."[28] Picturesque "likeness" was often found in the natural world through the use of a device known as a Claude glass, a small, convex mirror named after the French painter Claude Lorraine that eighteenth-century tourists frequently carried. Aided by travel guides such as Gilpin's *Observations on the River Wye* or West's *A Guide to the Lakes*, these picturesque tourists went out into the natural world to identify landscapes that seemed particularly scenic. Once identified, the tourist would hold up his or her Claude glass to fix the scenery as a picture, viewing the landscape as reflected in the mirror. As an optical device for capturing and framing natural landscapes, the Claude glass is an important precursor to the camera.[29] Most important, the Claude glass, like photography, reduced actual landscapes to a miniature, manageable size.

One of the pleasures of the picturesque was a recognition of certain artistic qualities in the natural world, a kind of associationism encouraged by the earnestly literal picture-making device of the Claude glass. The picturesque in nature could be appreciated only by those who already had some knowledge of art with which to compare it; thus, the picturesque depended on and fostered connoisseurship. Once natural landscapes were recognized as picturesque, or like a picture, the next step for a picturesque connoisseur was often to sketch it, transforming nature that already seemed like a picture into an actual picture. Rosalind Krauss has observed this circularity in picturesque aesthetics, noting that "landscape becomes a reduplication of a picture which preceded it." As part of her larger argument about the modernist myth of originality, Krauss extends this observation to make a point about this paradox that produces singularity by means of formulaic repetition: "Although the *singular* and the *formulaic* or repetitive may be semantically opposed, they are nonetheless conditions of each other: the two logical halves of the concept *landscape*."[30] What Krauss here implies I want to make explicit: This paradoxical production of singularity (or exoticism) through repetition (generic conventions) is what makes the picturesque so uniquely suited to commodification in modernity. With its stress on that which can be *pictured*, the picturesque is a sensation strictly attuned to the eye. Barbara Stafford writes that during the reign of the picturesque, "Nature came to be looked upon pictorially—that is, as a series of pictures created to stimulate automatic aesthetic enjoyment."[31] This automatic element cannot be stressed enough: A viewer does not have to work to appreciate the picturesque. What could be better suited to the commodity form?

In the late eighteenth century, qualities associated with ruinousness and decay became picturesque: rough terrain, old buildings, winding roads, wild foliage, bedraggled cattle, and most notoriously, beggars and peasants, figures representing the rural poor. Ruins were appreciated for the way they served as emblems of the past, their decay in the present serving only to mark their evocation of a romanticized past. According to Uvedale Price:

> A temple or palace of Grecian architecture in its perfect entire state, and with its surface and colour smooth and even, either in painting or reality, is beautiful; in ruin it is picturesque. Observe the process by which time, the great author of such changes, converts a beautiful object into a picturesque one. First, by means of weather stains, partial incrustations, mosses, &c. it at the same time takes off from the uniformity of the surface, and of the colour; that is, gives a degree of roughness, and variety of

tint. Next, the various accidents of weather loosen the stones themselves; they tumble in irregular masses, upon what was perhaps smooth turf or pavement.[32]

Thus, the picturesque served as a contradictiory construction of pastness in the present. A few pages later in the same essay, after discussing which animals possess picturesque qualities (his amusing list includes Pomeranians, shaggy goats, wild deer), Price writes: "In our own species, objects merely picturesque are to be found among the wandering tribes of gypsies and beggars; who in all the qualities which give them that character, bear a close analogy to the wild forester and the worn out cart-horse, and again to old mills, hovels, and other inanimate objects of the same kind."[33] In this analysis, real social conditions are transmuted into aesthetic pleasantries, ethnicity and economic class become exotic. In this regime, social subjugation signifies obsolescence, which in turn functions as picturesque. This is where the picturesque meets the ethnographic: early travel films delighted in finding examples of the "past" existing in the present and regularly featured "primitive" peoples costumed in native dress performing premodern local customs.

This derogatory stance was not without controversy at the time, and criticisms of the picturesque, mostly centered on its belittling view of poverty, surfaced early in the nineteenth century. One of the most eloquent critiques came from John Ruskin, a figure who was also immensely influential for nineteenth-century tourism. (Ruskin's *The Stones of Venice* [1851] was popular as a tourist guidebook, as was his *Mornings in Florence* [1877].) In "On the Turnerian Picturesque," Ruskin makes a distinction between high and low forms of the picturesque: The "low school of the surface-picturesque [is] eminently a *heartless*" ideal, whereas the "true or noble picturesque [demonstrates greater] sympathy . . . with the object."[34] For Ruskin, J. M. W. Turner is the exemplar of this high picturesque, while the "lowness" and "heartlessness" Ruskin identifies would seem to be a fair categorization of the picturesque vernacular operating in much popular media in the early twentieth century. This distinction between high and low anticipates the division of culture into highbrow and lowbrow later in the century. Like the practice of tourism, which has long enabled its detractors to reinscribe cultural hierarchies, the picturesque appears to be an aesthetic mode that encourages the drawing of cultural distinctions—although in practice it often muddies those distinctions. In fact, by falling somewhere in the middle, the picturesque confounds divisions between the obviously "high" and the obviously "low."

In a footnote to his essay on the picturesque, Ruskin quotes from his private diary, describing a walk he once took in Amiens along the Somme: "As I looked to-day at the unhealthy face and melancholy mien of the man in the boat pushing his load of peats along the ditch, and of the people, men as well as women, who sat spinning gloomily at the cottage doors, I could not help feeling how many suffering persons must pay for my picturesque subject and happy walk."[35] In this account, the picturesque does not prevent Ruskin from taking a critical, active view of what he sees. Indeed, it is the very picturesque impulse to take such a walk that leads him to perceive these downtrodden social conditions, of which he might otherwise have been unaware. In this way, I argue, the picturesque contains within itself the seeds of its own undoing.

In addition to harboring a potential for critique, picturesque idealization was understood as a fabrication from the start. Gilpin intended his sketches to illustrate picturesque ideas rather than actual places. Thus, his method of depicting nature was to idealize. He wrote:

> Most of the sketches here offered to the public, are *imaginary* views. But as many people take offence at *imaginary* views; and will admit such landscape only as is immediately taken from nature, I must explain what we mean by an *imaginary* view.
>
> We acknowledge nature to be the grand storehouse of *all picturesque beauty*. The nearer we copy her, the nearer we approach perfection. But this does not affect the *imaginary view*. When we speak of *copying nature*, we speak only of particular *objects*, and particular passages — not of *putting the whole together* in a picturesque manner; which we seldom seek in nature, because it is seldom found.[36]

Despite its inspiration from nature and foothold in realism, Gilpin acknowledges that picturesque representation is a construction. He writes in the same essay, as in his other essays, of the need to subordinate detail to the service of "embellishing the *general effect*." The imaginary view is created for larger, generalizing purposes, and small details serve merely to heighten the reality effect. Idealization was not problematic for Gilpin; rather, it helped him get closer to the divine perfection he sought in the world around him. After the advent of photography, however, questions about idealization and falsification became centrally important to aesthetic theory, which interro-

FIGURE 5.3 William Gilpin, "View of Beaulieu River"; with wooded banks, watercolor (1791). © Trustees of the British Museum.

gated photography's status as either a realistic documenter or a fabricating distorter of truth.

Some picturesque techniques were explicitly theatrical in nature. One of the most important compositional elements of Gilpin's picturesque is the concept of side screens and front screens, which he discusses in *Observations on the River Wye*: "Every view on a river, thus circumstanced, is composed of four grand parts; the *area*, which is the river itself; the *two side-screens*, which are the opposite banks, and mark the perspective; and the *front-screen*, which points out the winding of the river."[37] Gilpin's watercolors provide clear examples of how to create picturesque sketches by means of such screening conventions (fig. 5.3). He continues:

But the views on the Wye, though composed only of these *simple parts*, are yet *infinitely varied*.

They are varied, first, by the *contrast of the screens*. Sometimes one of the side-screens is elevated; sometimes the other; and sometimes the front. Or both the side-screens may be lofty; and the front either high, or low.

Again, they are varied by the *folding of the side-screens over each other*;

and hiding more or less of the front. When none of the front is discovered, the folding-side either winds round, like an ampitheatre; or it becomes a long reach of perspective.[38]

Picturesque representation is revealed quite literally to be a staged construct, as Gilpin's text resembles set description. This kind of staging is dominant in travelogue films. I have found many cinematic examples that are striking in their compositional resemblance to Gilpin's static picturesque, and I discuss several of these films in the sections that follow.

Commercialization and Parody

Despite a radically changing social context, the picturesque persisted throughout the nineteenth century and into the twentieth. William Marshall, a British writer on the picturesque in the eighteenth century, wrote a statement in 1795 that still rings remarkably true for the travel film of the 1910s: "One great end of Landscape painting is to bring distant scenery, — and such more particularly as it is wild and not easily accessible, — under the eye, in a cultivated country."[39] By the early twentieth century, however, the definition of what counted as "wild" had expanded in scope. Or, rather, the picturesque now required a greater degree of "wildness" to seem so: Mere English country landscapes were no longer enough. The picturesque appetite now required images of Asian and African landscapes to fulfill its desire for difference; English beggars, although still of interest, no longer sufficed to fill the figurative demands of the picturesque, and even Italian *banditti* seemed overly familiar, so that now images of veiled North African women or South American peasants were also needed to fill out the impression of quaint Otherness, as in films such as *In Egypt* (Pathé, ca. 1920) and *South America* (production company unknown, ca. 1920).[40] As Nochlin puts it, "The picturesque is pursued throughout the nineteenth century like a form of particularly elusive wildlife, requiring increasingly skillful tracking as the delicate prey—an endangered species—disappears farther and farther into the hinterlands."[41] Clearly, the picturesque was a form of Western viewing, even if it was experienced or appropriated by those who did not necessarily share a Western point of view.

The picturesque persisted through a variety of vastly different cultural practices in the nineteenth century. A very rough set of examples would include the growing phenomenon of tourism (with its accompanying fledgling industry in the form of travel guides such as *Baedeker's*), literature such as Ann Radcliffe's *The Mysteries of Udolpho* or Lord Byron's *Childe Harold* (which was often read as a sort of travel guidebook in itself), and the landscape paintings of artists such as John Constable and Turner. The picturesque legacy has frequently been traced in such canonical artworks. Less explored, however, are the numerous amateur picturesque artworks, which were certainly more common. In this light, it is interesting to note that Gilpin himself was an amateur artist, and his *Observations on the River Wye* was the first of his several books to be illustrated with his own sketches and watercolors.[42] Ann Bermingham has written that "by the turn of the [nineteenth] century the word *picturesque* had become so overused that it had become virtually meaningless."[43] But if the word was "meaningless," then why did it persist? And why do we still find the picturesque a century later in early cinema? Certainly, Gilpin's techniques were not without their lasting appeal, for when one juxtaposes his sketches with travelogue images, the similarities are striking. In fact, rather than joining the chorus of elite voices deriding this overly familiar, commodified style, it seems more useful to trace the picturesque's influence on commercial art forms such as cinema and search for reasons for its enduring appeal.

Despite some important continuities, it is a long way from Edmund Burke to the picturesque vernacular of the late nineteenth century and early twentieth. However, I do not intend to construct a solely depreciating model of picturesque taste, from theory to practice. In fact, not only was picturesque tourism already popular in the late eighteenth century, but, as we have seen, picturesque aesthetics were actually *derived from* touristic practices. Thus, there was always a popular practice of picturesque consumption alongside the theoretical writings, the theory and the practice influencing each other in complex ways. In addition, Andrews points out that the audience for the picturesque was relatively heterogeneous from the start: "The vogue for the Picturesque may have had its origins in a predominantly patrician or squire-archical interest-group (the Grand Tourists, the landowning commissioners of landscape paintings from Wilson and Lambert); but as the popularity of Picturesque tourism grew so its devotees expanded in social range (barristers, journalists, clergymen [such as Gilpin], shopkeepers, clerks)."[44] The picturesque was always a muddle—an imprecise term that "can designate an experience, a method, a view or an object" that appealed to a wide spectrum of people, from elites to the nascent middle class and, eventually, even the working class who frequented moving pictures.[45] Perhaps most interesting is that the picturesque, from the start, was precisely an aesthetic for amateurs.

The picturesque was important for chromolithography, a method of mass-market color printing that was hugely popular in the nineteenth century. Millions of chromos were printed, sold, and hung on middle-class parlor walls in the United States from the 1840s to 1900 and beyond. Chromos were mostly copies of famous oil paintings, as well as landscapes, still lifes, pictures of animals, and religious imagery. They were one of the most important forms of democratized art culture in the nineteenth century. By the late nineteenth century, chromos were derided by many as artificial, cheap, and ugly, an opinion that reached a famous articulation in the Edwin Lawrence Godkin article "Chromo-Civilization," which compared the supposedly debased morals of the era to the debasement of high culture signified by chromolithographs.[46]

As Peter Marzio has shown, women were the primary consumers of chromos. In *The American Woman's Home*, Catharine Esther Beecher and Harriet Beecher Stowe endorsed chromos for their educational power in much the same way that nonfiction films would be endorsed fifty years later. They wrote of chromos, "Surrounded by such suggestions of the beautiful, and such reminders of history and art, children are constantly trained to correctness of taste and refinement of thought, and stimulated — sometimes to efforts at artistic imitation, always to the eager and intelligent inquiry about the scenes, the places, the incidents represented."[47] Like travelogue films, chromos tended to simplify what they represented and strove to avoid offense at all turns. Yet despite what seemed an old-fashioned style by the end of the nineteenth century, they did make a great impression on children and adults who otherwise would not have been exposed to art. Even Billy Bitzer, D. W. Griffith's legendary cameraman, recalls in his autobiography the impression a chromolithograph of Jean-François Millet's "The Angelus" made when it hung in the family parlor during his childhood, giving it partial credit for his interest in light and shadow.[48]

Criticism of the chromo as a democratic force stemmed from elite voices who resisted the expansion of art education and taste to the masses who had previously been excluded from such realms. In an analysis of synaesthesia and art education, Joshua Yumibe points out that the work of the prominent chromolithographer Louis Prang did not calcify preferences in taste but, rather, "at its most utopian, purported to educate the working classes by distributing art and thus transforming it ('republicanizing' it) through technical reproduction."[49] Chromos picked up on the aesthetic of the picturesque and arguably contributed to the picturesque's continuing transformation from an elite taste to a democratic taste by adopting its formulaic subject matter. Another way to put this would be to say, following Lawrence Levine, that both the picturesque and chromolithography became demoted together as culture became more stratified — or "sacralized" — in the late nineteenth century.[50]

Over the course of decades of usage, the picturesque became a popular style, a mass-culture shorthand for anything visually pleasing. Through increasing commercialization, the aesthetic lost any edge of rigorous associationism and elitist connoisseurship and came to stand for all that was tame and unchallenging. The publication of the book *Picturesque America* in the early 1870s marked another significant milestone in the popularization of the picturesque. In her study of that publication, Sue Rainey once again repeats the claim that the picturesque was already an outmoded joke, stating that by the end of the nineteenth century, the idea of the picturesque seemed like an exercise in nostalgia: "For most of these citizens of the new century, especially the urban dwellers, the phrase 'picturesque America' could call up an image like [a] satiric cartoon as readily as a cascading waterfall."[51] However, from a different perspective, *Picturesque America* indicates not the style's outmodedness but its commercial viability, especially when we consider that outmodedness was one of the constituitive elements of the picturesque in the first place.

Or perhaps everyone was already in on the joke. Early film reviewers — at least, those who were not busy championing the educational value of travelogues — seem to have enjoyed poking fun at the high-mindedness of travel film style. In a review of *Wonders of Nature* (Kalem, 1909), as noted in chapter 2, a writer for *Variety* complained that the cameraman must have "roamed all over the Western state looking for water falls" and that "ten minutes is a long time to watch water falling over a precipice without any more enlivening incident."[52]

In fact, the picturesque was parodied all along. One famous text from the early nineteenth century, William Combe's *The Tour of Dr. Syntax, in Search of the Picturesque*, illustrated by the British caricaturist Thomas Rowlandson, lampoons Gilpin himself (fig. 5.4).[53] In Mark Twain's well-known tourist parody *The Innocents Abroad*, published in 1869, a group of American tourists enjoy magic lantern travel slides aboard their ship to Europe. The lecture is advertised to "show the passengers where they shall eventually arrive," but comically enough, "the first picture that flamed out upon the canvas was a view of Greenwood Cemetery!"[54]

DOCTOR SYNTAX
TUMBLING INTO THE WATER.

FIGURE 5.4 "Tumbling into the Water" (1817), from William Combe, *The Tour of Dr. Syntax, in Search of the Picturesque* (London: Methuen, 1903).

Parody films were made early on, as well. In addition to Edwin S. Porter's *European Rest Cure*, many other parodies were made that no longer survive. A review of a film titled *Motoring around the World* (production company unknown, 1908) describes a "burlesque of the difficulties of auto racers from New York to Paris. . . . The [auto] is swallowed by a whale who obligingly carries it to the other shore and restores it to dry land."[55] Similarly, the animated film *Johnny's Pictures of the Polar Regions* (Pathé, 1910) is said to feature a pair of explorers who "seem to have made their journey in motor boats which travel through the ice-floes at a reasonable speed, coming through the Metropolitan Subway, passing all sorts of trained seals and walrus, and various igloos, one of which is labeled post cards, another telegraph office, the third New York Herald, and finally reaching the pole the two explorers find it housed in a spacious igloo with an Esquimau taking tickets at the door for which he charges one franc fifty centimes."[56] Other reviews show that *Johnny's Pictures of the Polar Regions* was a parody of the rivalry between the explorers Frederick Cook and Robert Peary, who each claimed to have reached the North Pole in 1909. The film was perhaps not so humorous as it sounds, however; *Variety* reported with dry understatement, "The Union Square audience laughed once or twice."[57]

The predictable nature of travelogues makes them an easy target for ridicule and parody; likewise, whoever is doing the ridiculing benefits by appearing more sophisticated than the naïve consumer of such a humdrum style. While parody films have been interpreted to mean that the picturesque had become too formulaic, the fact that this parodic attitude was common from the start demands a different interpretation. We can better understand the picturesque as a style that is precisely about what it means to be a cliché—that is, "formulaicness" is one of the travelogue's chief generic traits. After all, travel accounts always have seemed predictable and hackneyed, even in the early nineteenth century. In an interesting discussion, Linda M. Austin has analyzed the "touristic shame" experienced by some nineteenth-century tourists, who were painfully aware of the cultural skepticism about touring.[58] Yet this skepticism and these parodies have never slowed the practice of tourism or the production of travelogues, which only continued to increase in the modern era. Nor did the satires stop: A number of excellent cartoon parodies of travelogues were made in the 1930s, such as *The Isle of Pingo Pongo* (Tex Avery, 1938), *Aviation Vacation* (Avery, 1941), *Cross Country Detours* (Avery, 1940), and *Crazy Cruise* (Avery/Bob Clampett, 1942).[59] Perhaps predictability has always been one of the pleasures of the picturesque. In its adaptability and propensity for self-parody, the picturesque was uniquely well positioned for resucitation by early cinema.

Picturesque Techniques in Cinema

Scenic films appropriated picturesque representational strategies in two ways: by depicting picturesque subject matter (pastoral scenes, peasants, ruins, and places familiar from picturesque tour itineraries), and by using picturesque compositional strategies such as side screens and composition in depth. But the films transformed picturesque conventions by rendering them in cinematic form, which means adding movement and the fragmentation of editing to an aesthetic that was previously quite static. The films also transformed the aesthetic institutionally. What had once been a style or a practice that supposedly marked those who appreciated it as elite now became a sign of commercial value in a rapidly industrializing new media business. This transformation marked the picturesque's saturation point but also heralded its demise: In its guise as a term of the mass-culture marketplace, which always must remake itself, the picturesque necessarily became outmoded as the new century wore on.

Numerous travelogues depicted the familiar itineraries of British picturesque travelers, such as two films by Eclipse from 1911: *The Beautiful Wye Valley, England* and *The Thames from Oxford to Richmond*. A print of the second of these films still exists.[60] *The Thames from Oxford to Richmond* was released in the United States on 15 March 1911. Imported by George Kleine from Urban-Eclipse in the United Kingdom, the film was released on a split reel with an Eclipse drama called *Redemption*.[61] It was reviewed in the *Nickelodeon*, with the slightly different title *The Thames from Oxford to London*: "An exceedingly enjoyable scenic. The beauty of the scenes and their suggestions of English life and character, give the film a deep and profitable interest. It is unusually long for a scenic, but a large audience followed it with close attention, without any indications of uneasiness or boredom. The old bugbear that was supposed to roost on scenic and educational subjects has, we hope, emitted its last croak."[62] The film's destination point, Richmond, has been renamed London in this review, presumably for the benefit of an American audience that might not have been familiar with the borough in southwest London. The area was part of the county of Surrey before 1965; thus, it was not a part of London at all when the film was made. At 472 feet, the film is not actually "unusually long for a scenic," as the writer claims. The film opens with two street scenes in Oxford, followed by a blue-tinted image of a sightseeing boat pulling away from its dock. (All of the film's water views are tinted blue, and all land views are tinted amber.) Subsequent shots present views along the river's shore filmed from a moving boat, which gives the viewer the perspective of a passenger on the sightseeing boat just shown. Other leisure boats speed by; we pass country estates and well-dressed people eating at waterside restaurants.

 The Thames from Oxford to Richmond uses many conventions of picturesque representation. One extreme long shot, for example, composed with a bridge in the distance, exemplifies several specific picturesque techniques (fig. 5.5). At the beginning of the shot, a tree blowing in the wind functions as a picturesque side screen jutting into the right of the frame. The water recedes into the center left of the image, following a picturesque emphasis on depth of composition and a curved (rather than straight) body of water leading the viewer's eye into the center of the frame. Picturesque "local type" figures—children playing along the shore—populate the left of the frame as the boat passes by. Despite its leisurely pace, the film presents very little information about the specific buildings and bridges shown, instead conveying a fragmentary kaleidoscope of the landscape traversed. After the shot just described, as the boat continues to approach the bridge, there is a cut

FIGURE 5.5 Frame enlargement, *The Thames from Oxford to Richmond* (Eclipse, 1911).

FIGURE 5.6 "Windsor Castle Changing Guard," *The Thames from Oxford to Richmond* (Eclipse, 1911).

to a medium shot as the boat passes underneath. Focusing on the bridge in this way might seem to indicate that it is an important structure, but the film does not name it. This moving-through-space effect creates a kind of visual drama; crossing under a bridge feels like an event. This event could not be captured by still photography, and it is the addition of movement that allows the film to mimic the experience of being there. But to depict movement through space, that space must be fragmented into bits, otherwise the film would move too slowly. Thus, the film condenses time by fragmenting space, rendering the traditionally contemplative experience of the picturesque much more unsettling. A few shots after the bridge undercrossing, an intertitle announces: "Windsor Castle Changing Guard." The film presents only two shots of the changing of the guard, however, and does nothing to explain the significance of either the castle or the event itself. As is common in travelogues, the shot is less interesting for its official subject than for what was inadvertently captured along the way—in this case, a group of children passing by (fig. 5.6).

Many of the travelogue conventions I have been discussing are present in *The Thames from Oxford to Richmond*: a "tour" structure, some sort of movement in every image, color tinting. The editing follows the "string of pearls" arrangement I described in chapter 4, but in this case, that conceit is literal: The Thames itself has long been compared to a string of pearls. This area along the Thames was known for its scenic beauty, and Richmond was a residence of several English monarchs. In fact, *The Thames Illustrated: A Picturesque Journeying from Richmond to Oxford*, a popular book first published in 1897, had already documented this exact route, which was a popular journey for boat tours in the Victorian era (fig. 5.7).[63] In films depicting European pleasure tours such as *The Thames from Oxford to Richmond*, the picturesque does not need to mask a colonial context, but it does provide an interpretive framework that dulls any potentially dark or unsettling imagery. The Thames's history of flooding is not mentioned; nor is its relatively recent use in the nineteenth century as a sewage dump. Perhaps more relevant, all economic relations are suppressed in the film. When workers are shown, usually passing in the background or hovering around the edges of the frame, they serve as picturesque adornment for the sightseeing experience.

Gaumont made a series of films on French rivers in the early 1910s that also illustrate picturesque principles in cinematic form. *L'Orne* (1912) consists of a series of images that—whether intentionally or not—directly mimic Gilpin's eighteenth-century picturesque illustrations. The landscape

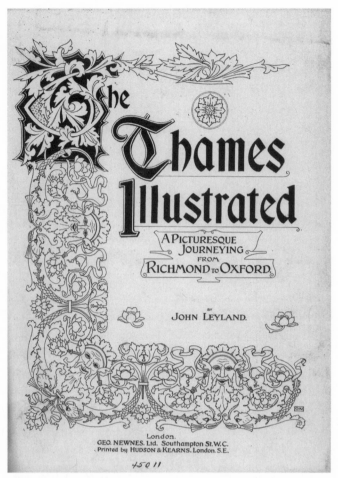

FIGURE 5.7 *The Thames Illustrated: A Picturesque Journeying from Richmond to Oxford*, by John Leyland (1901).

in *L'Orne* is carefully composed and framed, although since the filmmaker remains unknown at this time, we cannot know if he intended to emulate picturesque conventions.[64] Nonetheless, picturesque values were so widely circulated that it hardly matters what the filmmaker intended, for the result surely demonstrates a continuity with the picturesque tradition. The print I viewed contains ten shots. After a title card, the first shot presents a crudely drawn map of France illustrating the location of the Orne River. Nine shots of river scenery follow, each of which is a slow left-to-right pan of the river landscape. Many of these shots feature picturesque side screens that guide the viewer's eye into the pictorial depth of composition at the center of the

FIGURE 5.8 Frame enlargement, *L'Orne* (Gaumont, 1912). Courtesy EYE Film Institute Netherlands.

frame (fig. 5.8). A few houses are visible on the banks of the river, but there are no people; for the most part, this is a film of trees and water. It is also a film about the more abstract visual elements of movement and color, which are arguably more important than the Orne River being depicted. Movement is present in every shot: Leaves sway gently in the wind; the water shimmers and flows; and the camera pans from left to right. The film's scenic aspect is amplified by green and blue stencil coloring; rather than enhancing the "realism" of the river, these colors instead have a non-naturalistic effect, lending the river an otherworldly aspect, as though it were one step removed from reality. All of these elements—movement, color, trees, and water rather than human figures—work to create not a documentary transcription of the actual Orne but an idealized space that invites the viewer's eye into an unpopulated natural playground. In this sense, the film is "like a picture" of a fantasy place. Other Gaumont river films such as *A Boat Trip through the Gorges of the Ardeche* (1910) and *On the Banks of the Yerres* (1912) depict tourists enjoying themselves amid the scenery, thus providing the spectator with lead-in figures to aid in imagining oneself in the scenery. But *L'Orne* presents an empty space that encourages more open-ended reveries about what it would be like to be there.

The picturesque effect described by Nochlin as "masking conflict with the appearance of tranquility" is more conspicuous in films about colonial locales. Pathé's *Kuala Lumpur: Capital of the Malay States* (1912) is a good example of this effect. The film depicts the capital city of this British colony as a picture of cleanliness and beauty, but does not show anything about local culture or ways of life. Unlike many other travelogue films extant today, the print seems to be complete, retaining its opening and closing images; it is composed of ten shots, plus intertitles.[65] As its title card indicates, Kuala Lumpur does indeed appear to be "One of the Most Picturesque Cities on the Peninsula of Malacca, South Asia." But to achieve this effect, the film excludes people from its picturesque vision, choosing instead to show a series of well-manicured public spaces, such as "the government building" and "the lake in the botanical garden," as the intertitles tell us (figs. 5.9–5.10). The lake is shown in an excruciatingly slow pan, which includes a quintessentially picturesque bridge and its reflection in the water. Lushly blooming plants and flowers are shown in the hothouse, and the film concludes with a close-up of pink flowers with a bee crawling on them (fig. 5.11). As is common in travelogue films, shots such as the final close-up of the flowering bush could have been taken anywhere, they signify not necessarily "Kuala Lumpur" but, rather, a generalized, clichéd sense of picturesque beauty. Pathé's stencil coloring process contributes much to the feeling of picturesqueness, adding a striking palette of colors—pinks, greens, and blues—to the landscape. The only figures in the film are peripheral, mere window dressing for the larger idea of this city as a pleasant place. In the one shot that does include people as its subject, introduced by an intertitle as "Native mowers in the botanical garden," the people are undifferentiated figures, a group of six men moving rhythmically to cut the grass together, shown in a long shot that renders their faces indistinguishable (fig. 5.12). Kuala Lumpur is presented as a place of quiet beauty; of clean, sparsely populated, tamed spaces. Any hint of dissatisfaction with colonial rule is banished from this film.

"The picturesque is found any time the ground is uneven," Roland Barthes wrote in *Mythologies* in 1957.[66] Picturesque travelogue films convey a sense that one is seeing something that is "like a picture": self-conscious idealization is built into the concept. But while this much is clear, it is less clear what kind of viewing experience the picturesque aesthetic created for the spectator in the cinema. Was this idealization perceptible to early film audiences? As I have been suggesting, the soothing, masking effects of the picturesque can rupture when presented in moving rather than still images.

FIGURE 5.9 "The Government Building," *Kuala Lumpur: Capital of the Malay States* (Pathé, 1912). Courtesy EYE Film Institute Netherlands.

FIGURE 5.10 "The Lake in the Botanical Garden," *Kuala Lumpur: Capital of the Malay States* (Pathé, 1912). Courtesy EYE Film Institute Netherlands.

FIGURE 5.11 "A Flowering Bush in the Park," *Kuala Lumpur: Capital of the Malay States* (Pathé, 1912). Courtesy EYE Film Institute Netherlands.

FIGURE 5.12 "Native Mowers in the Botanical Garden," *Kuala Lumpur: Capital of the Malay States* (Pathé, 1912). Courtesy EYE Film Institute Netherlands.

Chapter 6, the most speculative chapter in this book, will address questions of spectatorship, suggesting that despite their formulas and stereotypes, travelogue films could actually provide viewers with moments of wonder and reverie that transcended the iron cage of their clichés. The picturesque may have functioned as a middlebrow aesthetic, but it was still accessible — in theory, at least — for strange and minor uses. Moreover, viewing films in the often raucous, variety-oriented nickelodeon theaters of the 1910s was hardly a soothing, middlebrow experience. Viewers may not yet have been practiced at reading films against the grain, but all of the ingredients were in place, ready to be discovered by the avant-garde viewing practices of the 1920s.

CHAPTER 6

"A WEIRD AND AFFECTING BEAUTY"
Watching Travel Films in the 1910s

Travelogue films were praised for their realism and their ability to educate. Yet their appeal arguably lay more in the realm of aesthetics and the various perceptual and emotional effects they could produce for the viewer. An article about a film of the South Pole from 1911 describes some of the genre's affective qualities. According to James B. Crippen writing in the *Nickelodeon*, the film *Dr. Charcot's Trip Toward the South Pole* (Eclipse, 1911) begins in a conventional fashion but quickly moves away from the familiar into a more wondrous domain: "The first polar picture is of an ice-bound sea—a phrase often met with in geography books, but understood in quite a new light by means of this picture. It is a bleak and forbidding picture, with its heaving ice-floes and angry waters darting and swirling between every crack and fissure, but the picture has a weird and affecting beauty. One begins to realize what Arctic exploration means, and to admire the temerity of men who pit themselves against such crushing and formidable forces."[1] A familiar notion of an "ice-bound sea," thanks to this film, is "understood in quite a new light." The attempt to represent the "bleak and forbidding" Antarctic landscape is relatively new—polar expeditions reached a peak at the time of early cinema—but more important, the means of representation is new.

What the writer seems to find remarkable is the *motion* of this moving picture, the "heaving ice-floes and angry waters darting and swirling between every crack and fissure." No medium other than cinema could represent movement in this way, and, as I have been suggesting, attention to the cinema-specific dimension of travel films is an important key to understanding the genre. Moreover, this description begins to indicate some of the limitations of the written language to capture the aesthetic quality of moving images. This writer, clearly moved, must use words to describe the film's visual power; his description of the film's "weird and affecting beauty" cannot identically reproduce the force of the images. Instead, his choice of words only stokes the reader's desire to see the film (which is not known to exist today). Herein lies some of the significance—and difficulty—of early travel films. In this highly conventional genre, some films can achieve peaks of affective force. It is a genre that reaches for the sensational and the exotic, yet it is bogged down by its own formulas and the baggage of its historical precursors. Above all, it is a visual genre that uses the cinema-specific quality of movement to produce its aesthetic effects.

Clearly, clichés and stereotypes are the travelogue's stock in trade. An editorial in *Motography* in 1911 explained it this way: "The experts discovered one very interesting thing. What people liked to see on the screen—it did not matter what country they belonged to—was something that agreed with their preconceived notions."[2] But there is more to the story than this. Travelogue films were regularly praised in early film reviews for their ability to expose viewers to new realities—for "making all mankind acquainted," to borrow Burton Holmes's phrase. The genre was also remarked on for its beauty and ability to move the spectator. As I show in this chapter, I have found evidence that nickelodeon audiences, who were known for being boisterous, sometimes fell silent when travelogues came on the screen. While this evidence can be variously interpreted, I argue that it reveals the possibility that audience members fell into a state of poetic reverie. While reverie itself is not without perilous components, implying on the negative side passivity or a state of becoming mesmerized, *poetic* reverie, I argue (following Gaston Bachelard), can have more positive or even utopian implications.

So what was the appeal of early travelogue films? Were they simply an affirmation of received ideas and prejudices about the world, giving the audience an illusion of mastery and omniscience? Or did they present the world in ways that were contradictory and potentially disruptive? As I have already pointed out, the few scholars who have discussed travelogues—such as Charles Musser, who labeled them a "cinema of reassurance"—have usually argued the former point. My analysis acknowledges this dimension but emphasizes the second interpretation: Despite their formulas, or perhaps even *because* of their formulas, travelogues could also open up possibilities for resistant readings. Several questions remain, however. How did such a formulaic genre actually move audiences emotionally? Did they produce passive or active spectators? Were they simply boring? I argue that travelogues are a fundamentally ambivalent genre, one that could produce many different responses, perhaps in the same spectator and perhaps even over the course of watching one film. Travelogues may represent an old-fashioned aesthetic, but they are also redeemable as a particular kind of affective experience.

The visionary filmmaker and theorist Jean Epstein wrote in 1921, "An idea thought to be used up, empty and old is projected against another just as finished, and from the shock of their decrepitude a young spark is born."[3] This chapter argues that early travelogues had the potential to produce just such sparks. Centering on questions of spectatorship and travelogue affect, I place travelogues within a larger discourse of the critique of modernity. In the fast-moving new image culture of the early twentieth century, travelogues functioned as a contradiction: a mass-market space for contemplation. In speculating about the travelogue's capacity to enable experiences of wonder, insight, and poetic reverie, I aim to rehabilitate the early travelogue from its bad reputation as an instrument of bourgeois complacency. While travelogues certainly could serve that function, they also contained the potential to disrupt such complacency. Both sides of this dynamic are crucial to the genre's dialectical function as a form of minor cinema, one that spoke in a major language but remained open to minor uses.

Spectatorship and the Early Travel Film

The "founding myth" of early cinema in the United States—that its audiences were comprised of immigrants and the working poor—has been complicated lately by revisionist scholarship.[4] The net result of this empirical research and debate has been to reaffirm that urban nickelodeon theaters were indeed patronized by diverse audiences composed of mostly working-class patrons. New scholarship has demonstrated the significance each theater and neighborhood had on audience composition: Different kinds of audiences were drawn to different kinds of theaters, which in turn showed different kinds of movies. While I have not undertaken empirical research about specific theaters in specific cities for this book, that approach would certainly yield more precise information about spectatorship and early nonfiction film. At this juncture, however, I simply want to speculate about the range of possible meanings travelogues might have had for early cinema spectators. In so doing, however, I find myself back with some of the original evidence that forged the myth of early cinema in the first place: rose-colored accounts of working-class nickelodeon audiences. This evidence demands a good deal of skepticism, but it can still lead to some valuable insights.

One important article in this vein is Mary Heaton Vorse's "Some Picture Show Audiences," published in *Outlook* magazine in 1911. Vorse was a well-known writer, labor activist, and suffragette whose article is sympathetic to the working class, albeit in a sentimental fashion (which was, of course, a dominant mode of reform rhetoric at the time). Vorse writes, "You cannot go to any one of the picture shows in New York without having a series of touching little adventures with the people who sit near you, without over-hearing chance words of a *naïveté* and appreciation that make you bless the living picture book that has brought so much into the lives of the people who work."[5] Vorse writes of meeting a "moving picture show expert, the connoisseur" who visits the movies every night. She quotes this man as telling her: "W'en I goes to a show, I likes to see the woild. I'd like travelin' if I could afford it, but I can't; that's why I like a good travel film. A good comic's all right, but a good travel film or an a'rioplane race or a battle-ship review—dat's de real t'ing."[6] Vorse concludes that cinema functions as "the door of escape," and because of cinema, "life holds some compensation, after all." One of the best kinds of film, she concludes—"de real t'ing"—is the travel film, for it provides working people "a chance for once to look at the strange places of the earth."[7]

Clearly, Vorse's article is not helpful as evidence of who was actually in the audience, for her writing is filled with generalizations and probable fabrications, or caricatures at best (such as the so-called connoisseur she quotes, using dialect to mark him as different). In short, she fictionalizes, even though her article functions as a piece of journalism. However, given the scant evidence about early motion picture audiences, Vorse's article is invaluable for capturing a sense of how audiences were perceived at the time. Vorse's heartfelt defense of the working class, and her endorsement of cinema as "a chance for once" to enter the "door of escape," suggests that we would do well to take early cinema seriously as a mode of leisure that gave audiences access to what had previously been enjoyed only by the elite.

This insight carries implications not only for economic class but also for gender. As scholars such as Kathy Peiss and Lauren Rabinovitz have shown, the cinema was one of several new kinds of mass entertainment that helped shift leisure from a homo-social world of men-only activities to a hetero-social world of mixed men's and women's leisure in the early twentieth century. The cheapness of nickelodeons meant that "a few nickels could be eked out of the family budget to enable a mother and her children to attend a weekly show."[8] Moreover, the theaters were places where women could safely leave their children, and "many seem to have thought of the nickel theaters as day care centers."[9] The cinema's formation of a new mass audience brought diverse populations together for the first time. Large groups of people who had been excluded were now included in a cultural experience that spoke directly to them. The nonfiction part of early cinema programs gave these social groups access to a different kind of cultural experience, a geographical and social mobility that was otherwise unavailable. At the same time, the cinema incorporated previously established working-class and ethnic forms of leisure. As Sabine Haenni has shown, early cinema was "less a vehicle of assimilation and homogenization than a medium for establishing and regulating emotional connections with newcomers in the United States—for promoting highly regulated, heterogeneous collective identities . . . ethnicized cinematic cultures recast mass culture as a nuanced space where differences of class, race, gender, and ethnicity may get transformed but not erased."[10] The formation of this new heterogeneous mass public is one of the most significant aspects of early film spectatorship.

Miriam Hansen's work on the public sphere describes how early cinema constructed a new kind of mass audience. As Hansen points out, one key political question raised by issues of early film spectatorship is "whether and to what extent a public sphere is organized from above—by the exclusive standards of high culture or the stereotypes of commodity culture—or by the experiencing subjects themselves, on the basis of their context of living."[11] Certainly, in an important sense, travelogue films imposed standards of culture from above, reproducing "elite" aesthetic concerns and commodifying the travel experience in terms of leisure. At the same time, the open-ended nature of early travelogue films could make them available for alternative uses. Drawing from the public sphere theory of Oskar Negt and Alexander Kluge, Hansen explains that the concept of an alternative public sphere, as drawn from "a rather complex theory of experience in the tradition of Adorno, Kracauer, and Benjamin, [envisions] experience as that which mediates individual perception with social meaning, conscious with unconscious processes, loss of self with self-reflexivity; experience as the capacity to see connections and relations . . . ; experience as the matrix of conflicting temporalities, of memory and hope, including the historical loss of these dimensions."[12] Travel films would seem to reproduce precisely this complex dimension of experience, albeit an experience that is restricted to the space of the movie theater. The travelogue's alternative use value disappears later in film history with the rise of the feature film and especially with the transition to synchronized sound. But in this early period, travel films can be evaluated in just this way: "The reciprocity between the film on the screen and the spectator's stream of associations becomes the measure of a particular film's use value for an alternative public sphere: a film either exploits the viewer's needs, perceptions, and wishes or it encourages their autonomous movement, fine-tuning, and self-reliance."[13]

Offering evidence for a spectator experience defined from above, a well-known article about early cinema audiences from the *Saturday Evening Post* in 1907 claimed, "Civilization, all through the history of mankind, has been chiefly the property of the upper classes, but during the past century civilization has been permeating steadily downward."[14] But seen from a slightly different perspective, nickelodeon theaters were also interpreted in a more open-ended manner. Another article, also from 1907, explains that nickelodeon theaters "offered harmless diversion for the poor. They were edifying, educational, and amusing. They were broadening. They revealed the universe to the unsophisticated."[15] Audience comments about travel films can also be found in the motion picture trade press, as in one article that quotes a Persian immigrant saying, "I like them because I learn so much from them without knowing the English language."[16] Even if we take this commentary with a grain of salt, the trajectory of these statements as discourse is revealing. It would seem that from the reformer's perspective, "culture" was a disciplinary force, but from an audience's perspective, "culture" could be empowering.

The Discourse of Armchair Travel

The discourse about travel films has not changed much over the years. People have always said that travel films are appealing because they make it possible to travel without actually traveling. As we have seen, early travelogues were regularly celebrated for making travel available to those who could not afford actual travel. Writers in the trade press repeatedly emphasized that the experience of cinematic travel was just as good as the real thing. As one commentator explained, "Everyone knows the value of travel in broadening the mind and in enlarging the sympathies. To look at good pictures of distant peoples and scenes is to be a stay-at-home traveler, and to enjoy many of the advantages of real travel without its dangers and trials."[17] Another writer in the trade press explained that, although motion picture dramas might be artistic, they could not truly satisfy the audience's desires:

> As an exhibitor, if you are successful enough to "make your pile" in a few years and become sole master of your own time, what will you do with your money? "See the world" is the first reply that comes to your lips. You will want to travel; you will want to visit the old country, if there is a place that you can affectionately call the old country. You will want to see the big, strange cities of other lands; the mighty mountains and almost as mighty works of ancient man; the queer peoples of queer corners of this old round earth of ours. Did you ever stop to think that that same question asked of anybody would elicit practically the same answer? That almost every one of your five or ten cent patrons has somewhere within him, or her, a great longing to see the world?
>
> You have in your power the only possible substitute for tedious and expensive travel in seeing the world. You alone can take your friends around the world in easy and comfortable stages, collecting for each trip a sum so insignificant that it would hardly carry the traveler out of town.[18]

This anonymous editorial, one of many such examples, emphasizes the ubiquity of the desire to travel that cuts across class lines, naturalizing a desire for the foreign as the most neutral, commonplace sort of impulse. The article also emphasizes the cheapness of motion picture travel, a benefit that everyone can enjoy, a universal and democratic form of entertainment. The armchair traveler no longer has to wait until he or she has "made a pile," because travel can now be experienced by anyone in the moving picture theater.

In 1909, the *Nickelodeon* published what it called a "ringing panegyric" about the marvels of cinematic travel. Delivered by Frederick Starr, a professor of anthropology at the University of Chicago, the testimonial makes clear the travelogue's emerging status in the film industry, as well as some of the presumptions shaping this new visualization of the world. Starr wrote with an enthusiasm and verbosity resembling that of Burton Holmes:

> I have seen Niagara thunder over her gorge in the noblest frenzy ever beheld by man — I have watched a Queensland river under the white light of an Australasian moon go whirling and swirling through strange islands lurking with bandicoot and kangaroo — I have watched an English rail-

road train draw into a station, take on its passengers and then chug away with its stubby little engine through the Yorkshire Dells, past old Norman Abbeys silhouetted against the skyline, while a cluster of century-aged cottages loomed up in the valley below, through which a yokel drove his flocks of Southdowns. I have been to the Orient and gazed at the water-sellers and beggars and dervishes. I have beheld fat old Rajahs with the price of a thousand lives bejeweled in their monster turbans, and the price of a thousand deaths sewn in their royal nightshirts as they indolently swayed in golden howdahs, borne upon the backs of grunting elephants. I saw a runaway horse play battledoor and shuttlecock with the citizens and traffic of a little Italian village, whose streets had not known so much commotion since the sailing of Columbus. I know how the Chinaman lives and I have been through the homes of the Japanese. I have marveled at the daring of Alpine tobogganists and admired the wonderful skill of Norwegian ski jumpers. I have seen armies upon the battlefield and their return in triumph. I have looked upon weird dances and outlandish frolics in every quarter of the globe, and I didn't have to leave Chicago for a moment.[19]

This effusive text was first published in the *Chicago Tribune* as an expensive full-page advertisement in February 1909. It was reproduced several times in the next few years in the trade press, and it is featured at the beginning of George Kleine's influential 1910 *Catalogue of Educational Motion Pictures*, even before an endorsement by Thomas Edison. Starr himself was a sometime filmmaker and travel lecturer, so he was certainly invested in travel films, although his endorsement served to boost not just travel films but the entire motion picture industry.

I quote Starr's verbiage at length because it echoes the Holmesian version of cosmopolitanism. Starr's endorsement also underscores two of the travelogue's key effects: the leveling of many very different places by comparison and equivalence, and the multiplication of signs into an ever expanding description of places, objects, peoples, cultures. The combined effect of all this leveling and description is vise-like, flattening the globe so that it spreads out into a pancake of more and more words and images. Starr adopts the rhetoric of picturesque convention by highlighting ancient ruins ("old Norman Abbeys silhouetted against the skyline") and the typology of popular ethnography ("fat old Rajahs with . . . the price of a thousand deaths sewn in their royal nightshirts as they indolently swayed in golden howdahs"), both of which seem somehow familiar, despite their professed novelty. His description moves from the familiar North American and European world into the exotic world of the "Orient," his descriptions becoming more general along the way.

Throughout his description, Starr interchanges the verb "I have seen" with "I have been," which is the element in all of this that garners the most excitement: Travelogue films make it possible to consume this worldwide "outlandishness" without actually traveling. This new form of mechanically reproduced travel is quite unlike any experience previously available. Despite being touted as educational, in fact it hardly mattered what location was shown; what mattered was that the film was a travel film.

Starr is a curious figure whose career straddled the domains of academe and popular culture. Like Holmes, Starr epitomizes the values of instructive entertainment that reached a peak in this era. Appointed to the University of Chicago in 1892 by William Rainer Harper to help design a program in the newly emerging field of anthropology, Starr was known for his accessible lecture style, and he made many efforts to popularize anthropology. He published frequently in journals and newspapers such as the *Atlantic Monthly*, *Chicago Tribune*, and even the *Ladies' Home Journal*. An outspoken opponent of imperialism, Starr was a prominent member of the Anti-Imperialist League. A controversial professor at Chicago until his retirement in 1923, Starr was one of the earliest anthropologists to undertake field research as part of his work. He frequently gave lectures on anthropology to the public, often with the assistance of lantern slides. In 1909, he added moving pictures to his presentations. For example, in April 1909 Starr gave a series of three public lectures accompanied by moving pictures at the Music Hall in Chicago's Fine Arts Building. The lectures focused on Mexico (1 April), Samoa and Fiji (8 April), and the Panama Canal (15 April).[20]

Some of Starr's films were eventually released to commercial theaters by the Selig Polyscope Company. A flyer for *In Japan* (1911; see fig. 6.1) bills the film as "educational" and "refreshing" and presents Japan as a land "whose Civilization has Advanced so Rapidly In Recent Years."[21] This film was released on a split reel with *Seeing Cincinnati*. While I have not been able to determine the exact nature of Starr's arrangement with Selig (who approached whom first, how much money was involved), I have discovered that the Selig company did train Starr's camera operator, Manuel Gonzales, who had accompanied Starr on many research trips before 1909 and who had already shot most of Starr's photographs before he started making films. Starr's dab-

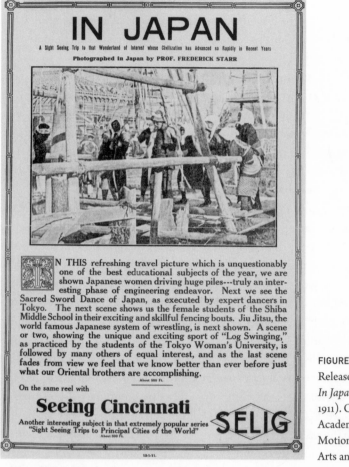

IN JAPAN

A Sight Seeing Trip to that Wonderland of Interest whose Civilization has Advanced so Rapidly in Recent Years

Photographed in Japan by PROF. FREDERICK STARR

N THIS refreshing travel picture which is unquestionably one of the best educational subjects of the year, we are shown Japanese women driving huge piles---truly an interesting phase of engineering endeavor. Next we see the Sacred Sword Dance of Japan, as executed by expert dancers in Tokyo. The next scene shows us the female students of the Shiba Middle School in their exciting and skillful fencing bouts. Jiu Jitsu, the world famous Japanese system of wrestling, is next shown. A scene or two, showing the unique and exciting sport of "Log Swinging," as practiced by the students of the Tokyo Woman's University, is followed by many others of equal interest, and as the last scene fades from view we feel that we know better than ever before just what our Oriental brothers are accomplishing.

About 500 Ft.

On the same reel with

Seeing Cincinnati

Another interesting subject in that extremely popular series "Sight Seeing Trips to Principal Cities of the World"

About 500 Ft.

SELIG

FIGURE 6.1
Release flyer for *In Japan* (Selig, 1911). Courtesy Academy of Motion Picture Arts and Sciences.

bling in filmmaking demonstrates the overlap between education and entertainment in this era.[22]

From the perspective of the discourse about vicarious (or virtual) travel, travelogues serve a compensatory function: not quite as good as the real thing, perhaps, but fulfilling a perceived lack in the spectator's real life. This is related to the representational logic that Jonathan Culler has identified as central to the phenomenon of tourism. For Culler, tourist attractions function only as signs of themselves. "The tourist is interested in everything as a sign of itself, an instance of a typical cultural practice: a Frenchman is an example of a Frenchman, a restaurant in the Quartier Latin is an example of a Latin Quarter restaurant, signifying 'Latin Quarter Restaurantness.'"[23] This doubling of the semiotic function is fundamental to tourism, a characteristically modern way of understanding the world. Culler is in agreement with Guy Debord and others who understand "the modern quest for experience as a quest for an experience of signs."[24] This semiotic equation makes even more sense when applied to representations of travel instead of actual travel. In the early 1900s, one would have been more likely to envision travel as a series of *representations* of faraway places familiar from photographs, postcards, and moving pictures than as actual tourism.

Yet while this semiotic analysis of travel is compelling, it does not account for the actual experience of travel, whether real or virtual. Travelogues may indeed function as signs of themselves, but people clearly found meaning in them nonetheless; travel films are not *simply* hermetically sealed signs of themselves. To focus on the emptiness or virtual quality of represented travel is to overlook the *affect* of virtual travel. For all of their compensatory function, then, travel films can also be understood in a different light. I believe that travelogues created a unique kind of travel experience for the movie spectator that was different from the experience of actual travel but significant in its own right. Some contemporary commentators seem to have been aware of this, remarking, for example, that cinematic travel could be "superior to taking the actual trip because the camera catches scenes impossible to the keenest observation of the traveler."[25] The implications here are significant: *Superior to taking the actual trip,* the experience of watching a travel film is something new. Travelogues constitute an experience that is *not* identical with the experience of the place itself. Travel films create geographies that exist only on the screen. If a film viewer *had* done some traveling in the early 1900s, perhaps as a tourist but more likely as a migrant, her or his experience probably would not have accorded with the idealized set of pictures displayed in travel films.

The Global Reach of Early Cinema

It has often been remarked that early cinema was an international industry. As film historians have shown, within months of the first public screenings in late 1895, cinema was being exhibited around the world. The first Lumière cinématographe program in India was projected at Watson's Hotel in Bombay on 7 July 1896 (for an exclusively white audience). A Lumière show appeared in Rio de Janiero on 8 July 1896. Lumière films were shown in Mexico City beginning on 15 August of that year; in Maracaibo, Venezuela, on 28 January 1897; and in Osaka, Japan, on 15 February 1897. Shows featuring Edison's Vitascope projector often followed soon after, and sometimes the Edison screenings preceded the Lumière screenings. The Lumière company specialized in travel views, but Edison also made them. Because films were shown internationally from the start, it is too simple to impose a binary in which travel views of "non-Western" lands were consumed by "Western" viewers. In fact, different kinds of spectators all over the world watched different kinds of travel views of locations all over the world. It is by no means a simple thing to ascribe fixed meaning to these images, because the contexts in which they were viewed were so diverse.

The quick global dissemination of Lumière films is well established in film history. Less discussed is the international dimension of cinema screenings during the transitional era. Early travel films in fact constitute a kind of early globalized media. While area studies are perhaps the best place for fully researched accounts of individually located histories, a survey of the American trade press reveals traces of this transnational film export and exhibition business. *Motography* ran a series of short items describing worldwide cinema exhibition in February 1912, including descriptions of moving picture shows in Norway, Spain, Syria, Scotland, Morocco, and Turkey, among other locations. Colonial film shows appear to have been racially segregated—as was the case in the United States at the time. The Philippines, a U.S. colonial territory in 1912, contained nearly fifty moving picture theaters, according to one account: "The front seats, which are benches, are occupied by the natives, who view [*sic*] with each other in getting as close to the front as possible. The building is divided, the back part having good seats occupied by the better class of Filipinos and Americans. The cost to the natives is five cents and to foreigners is ten cents."[26]

This series of articles, which focuses on the potential for U.S. film companies to develop their export business in these markets, does not make systematic mention of the kinds of films shown in each of these countries, although one reporter remarks that in South Africa, "a majority of the scenic films come from the Continent."[27] Another reporter surmises that, for the Russian market, "It seems very probable that if scenes from the city and country life of various parts of the United States could be shown they would be popular. For instance, a series of pictures presenting the views that an immigrant would see on his way to the United States and after landing there would probably be well received. Such views would be of interest not only to those who at some future time intend to emigrate, but also to those who have friends in the United States or are interested in the country for other reasons."[28]

Speaking of the "drama" of the growing motion picture industry, an

American writer noted: "One trait of this drama is its internationalism. Probably more than half of the motions given in this country come from France. On the title curtains of Broadway the Gallick cock frequently crows the name of that enterprising French firm [Pathé], which, by the bye, sent a cinematographic expedition a year ago into Libya. From Paris comes the newest phase of motions."[29] Travel films marked a new era of understanding the world visually. They made foreign locales more visible than ever before, encouraging a new curiosity about other places and other lifestyles around the world. In its utopian guise, the travelogue film seemed to represent a new modern era of cosmopolitanism. Indeed, it was the very *legibility* of these new moving images that was celebrated, a legibility that transcended language barriers and educational barriers.

Another example of travelogue exhibition in a non-Western context provides specific film titles to consider. In 1912, the Japanese film company Fukuhodo purchased the rights to the British Kinemacolor process in Japan and East Asia. Among the various genres it produced, Kinemacolor specialized in the scenic film, which was considered an excellent format for showcasing the spectacular aspects of its color process. The Japanese rights to Kinemacolor were absorbed by a new company, Toyo Shokai, the next year, which released several color films in Japan in 1913, including some films made by British Kinemacolor and some scenes filmed by Fukuhodo's cameraman Noboru Tamai. According to Hiroshi Komatsu, these Kinemacolor programs included films such as *The Ruins of Egypt*, *Ramble in Paris*, and *Autumn Scenes in Japan*, and "every review of the programmes was favorable."[30] Kinemacolor ceased to be profitable in Japan after the outbreak of the First World War in the summer of 1914, which increased the cost of raw film stock. (Kinemacolor required twice the usual amount of film.) But its brief heyday in the Japanese film market in 1913–14 establishes conclusively that travelogues produced by both European and Japanese companies were shown to Japanese audiences at that time.

This admittedly lean evidence allows me to venture a few hypotheses. First, the imperial logic of travelogues was opened up to other, nondominant populations by two important characteristics of early cinema: the global flow of film distribution and the mass exhibition context of early theaters, which combined people from different demographics into one diverse audience. Second, the diversity of these reception contexts makes it impossible to conclude that travelogues were interpreted the same way by every spectator. All spectators were free to read these films against the grain, no matter where they were located, for while the practice of spectatorship is shaped by geographical location and ethnic or gender identification, it is ultimately determined by the viewer's sensibility.

Last Century at Marienbad

By the 1920s, a new wave of cultural critique began to move well beyond the reformers' debate about cinema in the 1910s. As I discussed in chapter 3, that debate hinged on the question of film's status as an art form and a social influence, and moved between a rejection of cinema as a "lowbrow" form of entertainment and a celebration of cinema as a tool of democracy and civilization. The reformers' debate certainly continued in the newspapers and popular press well into the twentieth century, but alongside that, a new group of theorists emerged who examined cinema from a philosophical and historical perspective. For this group in the 1920s, the dominant assessment of culture was pessimistic; sociologists and critical theorists such as Georg Simmel, Max Weber, Georg Lukács, and others viewed modernity as a lapsed condition; those who wrote about cinema tended to view it as a symptom of this decline. As I discussed in the introduction, however, there was a countertrend to this assessment, represented by Walter Benjamin, that began from this critical position but moved beyond it to argue that cinema contained redemptive potential. I want to briefly turn now to the work of the theorist Siegfried Kracauer, who also made a case in the 1920s for cinema's possibilities as a disjunctive, reflexive, and ambivalent medium.

Siegfried Kracauer's 1927 essay "Photography" provides a critique of modern culture as a "flood" of images. As we have seen, this flood was already a characteristic of visual culture in the late nineteenth century, but with the advent of cinema, the flood increased. Kracauer wrote:

> The aim of the illustrated newspapers is the complete reproduction of the world accessible to the photographic apparatus. They record the spatial impressions of people, conditions, and events from every possible perspective. Their method corresponds to that of the weekly newsreel, which is nothing but a collection of photographs. . . . Never before has an age been so informed about itself, if being informed means having an image of objects that resembles them in a photographic sense. . . . But the flood of photos sweeps away the dams of memory. . . . In the illustrated magazines, people see the very world that the illustrated magazines prevent them from perceiving. The spatial continuum from the camera's per-

spective dominates the spatial appearance of the perceived object; the resemblance between the image and the object effaces the contours of the object's "history." Never before has a period known so little about itself.[31]

Cameras capture the world's photographic face, Kracauer asserts, but these images act as a kind of decoy, preventing viewers from seeing the "very world" they depict. The aim of these images, Kracauer stresses, is the "complete reproduction of the world." This completeness is fundamental — one or two images cannot produce this effect (and for Kracauer, paintings do not produce this effect either), but the "flood" of photographic images people are subjected to overwhelms the viewer. Kracauer mentions newsreel films as a corollary of the still photograph's deception, and one imagines he would make a similar claim for travelogues. Photographers and cameramen of the early twentieth century were engaged in a project to reproduce the entire world — or, at least, all that was "accessible to the photographic apparatus." Secure in their belief that such a reproduction was possible, early motion picture photographers went on a crusade to capture the globe. Kracauer sums up this point by observing that "the world itself has taken on a 'photographic face.'"[32] For Kracauer, what gets swept away by this flood of images are memory and historical perception.

Miriam Hansen has made a compelling argument that Kracauer's critique, particularly in the "Photography" essay, does not stop at merely diagnosing the cultural problems presented by modernity in general and photography in particular. As she points out, for Kracauer, "from this condition, there is no way back, either conceptually or ontologically, to an unmediated state of being."[33] Rather, as for Benjamin, for Kracauer the only route toward overcoming these conditions is through mass media itself: "Kracauer's investment in photographic negativity is fueled by photography's potential to point up the disintegration of traditional and reinvented unities."[34] As Hansen explains, Kracauer made a case that photographic and cinematic technologies such as framing and editing had the capacity to defamiliarize and "'stir up,' mobilize, and reconfigure" the elements they depicted. "Combining photographic contingency with cinematic montage, film can 'play' with 'the pieces of disjointed nature' in a matter 'reminiscent of *dreams*.' In other words, similar to the oneiric imbrication of the remains of the most recent and ordinary with the hidden logic of the unconscious, film could animate and reassemble the inert, mortified fragments of photographic nature to suggest the possibility of a different history."[35]

FIGURE 6.2 Frame enlargement, *Life and Times in the Bohemian Baths of Marienbad, Karlsbad, Franzensbad* (Bavaria-Film-Straubing, 1911). Courtesy EYE Film Institute Netherlands.

A German film from 1911 titled *Leben und Treiben in den böhmischen Bädern Marienbad, Karlsbad, Franzensbad* (*Life and Times in the Bohemian Baths of Marienbad, Karlsbad, Franzensbad*), which I call *Marienbad* for the sake of brevity, documents just the sort of modern alienation identified by 1920s critical theorists. For all its ostensible celebration of the modern spa experience it depicts, the film also provides a remarkably ambivalent and even critical picture of European modernity. The film presents a series of disjunctive scenes of fashionable, modern Europeans on holiday.[36] It begins with a few landscape panoramas of Marienbad and views of parks with fountains. After these opening landscape shots, the film quickly moves to its main focus: images of people milling around the various curative baths of the region. We see shot after shot of crowds: big crowds at the "Cure House," more crowds at the "Franz Josef Spring," crowds of people waiting in line for glasses of water at the "Schlossbrunnen Spring," and so on, as announced by the simple intertitles I have just quoted (fig 6.2).

The curative waters of what was then the Austro-Hungarian Empire had become popular spa destinations in the late nineteenth century. By the turn of the twentieth century, many guidebooks had been published, and the local spas and mud baths had reached international renown. (The parody film *The European Rest Cure* [Edison, 1904] makes a reference to European spas with its staged scene at a German bath house.) Mark Twain wrote about his visit in 1892 in "Marienbad—A Health Factory." His description of the approach by train evokes a clear contrast between the old world and modernity: "A couple of hours from Bayreuth you cross into Bohemia, and before long you reach this Marienbad, and recognize another sharp change, the change from the long ago to to-day; that is to say from the very old to the spick and span new; from an architecture totally without shapeliness or ornament to an architecture attractively equipped with both. . . . It is like jumping out of Jerusalem into Chicago."[37] Twain draws a specific contrast between the opulent modernity of Marienbad and the poor soil of nearby Bavaria, but his larger point illustrates one of the most consistent oppositions constructed by travelogues: an opposition between the old world and modernity.

Given the lack of a first-person narrator in *Marienbad*, the viewer is free to speculate on her own about the meaning of these scenes. The crowds are well dressed in the garb of the Edwardian bourgeoisie. The women wear buttoned-up blouses, full-length skirts, and the colossal, feather-adorned hats that were then fashionable. The men wear three-piece suits and hats, and most of the children wear sailor suits. Many people hold water tumblers in their hands, because, of course, the water was the draw for most visitors to this spa region. These well-dressed crowds are collectively seeking a curative health experience, but the images do not convey a sense of community or shared experience. Many of the people in the film gawk at the camera. The people interact less with each other than with a mechanical apparatus—a common effect when the camera is present in nonfiction film, to be sure. But it is hard not to notice the lack of joy or amusement on these faces—with the exception of the children, who seem to be enjoying themselves, at least. One is reminded of Henri Lefebvre's notion of the work-leisure dynamic: "We work to earn our leisure, and leisure has only one meaning: to get away from work. A vicious circle."[38]

Marienbad certainly invites interpretation as a film about alienation, but this conclusion reveals one of the pitfalls of historical analysis: Textual readings are often symptomatic of the historical moment in which they are made. In this case, while I argue that *Marienbad* is a film about modern alienation, I also want to point out how this interpretation is facilitated by my own contemporary perspective. Viewed from a distance of one hundred years, can we understand how such a film might have been interpreted when it was released? One answer would be to turn to accounts of travelogue spectatorship in the 1910s, but, as we have already seen, such accounts are extremely rare. Instead, I want to take a detour through a fictional account of the experience of travel in modernity. Literature does not provide the same kind of evidence as a documented spectator's account, but in the absence of such accounts, literature provides one way into thinking about the experience of virtual voyaging in the early twentieth century.

In its depiction of fashionable European modernity, *Marienbad* seems to capture a spirit of apprehension. The film serves as an apt visual companion piece to Thomas Mann's novel *The Magic Mountain* (1924), a story of invalids in Europe set in the same era that uses illness as a metaphor for the incipient decline of European civilization on the brink of the First World War. Like all travelogues, *Marienbad* works to hail its spectator as one who might travel there. Put another way, travelogues function to create a kind of recognition within the spectator. *The Magic Mountain*, for all its critique of European civilization, contains appreciation for moments of experience that puncture the alienation of modern life. In one important scene, the novel's main character, Hans Castorp, gets lost in a snowstorm in the Swiss Alps above the sanitarium where he has been living. As Hans stands against the side of a remote, locked hut, shivering in the snow as the sun goes down, he gazes into the woods before him and experiences an epiphany inspired by the landscape. He drinks from a flask of port to keep warm and looks out across the tree-filled mountainside, which transforms itself before him into a Mediterranean seaside scene: "Hans Castorp had never seen it before, not even anything like it. He had never vacationed in the south, taken so much as a sip of it. . . . And yet he *remembered* it. Yes, it was that peculiar sense of recognition he celebrated now. 'Ah, yes, that's how it is!' —a cry went up within, as if he had always carried this blue sunshine now spreading before him secretly in his heart."[39] This reverie continues for some time, moving from a pleasant seaside fantasy complete with a beatific mother nursing her child to a horrific scene in which two old women dismember and eat a child. The reverie ends with Hans's awakening to the realization that he has been dreaming.

This scene in Mann's novel nicely encapsulates the experience of reverie that travelogues potentially could inspire in film spectators. Hans looks upon a real landscape, and this inspires him to dream about a landscape he has never before seen. The dream involves recognition, happiness, and rapture, followed by horror. This process is very much like the emotions one might experience in the nickelodeon theater, in which different short films in different genres (melodrama, comedy, scenic, newsreel) followed quickly one after another. Cinematic techniques such as framing and editing brought about fragmented visions of geographic locations around the world. In attempting to map the world in this way, in presenting these place fragments, travelogues were perhaps more successful at enabling the spectator's daydreams than at teaching any real lessons about geography. The films' participation in the standard turn-of-the-century myths of racial and geographical hierarchy distorted the real world, but at the same time, the films also had the potential to trigger a kind of geographical free association driven by the viewer's unconscious. These films may describe a sort of narrating omniscience, but more significantly, they enable the consciousness of the viewing spectator. For film viewers who could not afford actual leisure travel, this experience could have been significant.

Earlier in the novel, Hans and his cousin Joachim take their fellow patient Karen Karstedt to the Bioscope Theater in the Swiss town of Platz near their sanitarium. Mann describes their experience watching a variety program of short films, which featured "all sorts of life, chopped up in hurried, diverting scraps that leapt into fidgety action, lingered, and twitched out of sight in alarm, to the accompaniment of trivial music."[40] Later in the program, a series of nonfiction subjects appear on the screen—so many that Mann's description seems like a memory of multiple film shows, not one: "They now saw pictures from all over the world: the top-hatted president of the French republic reviewing a long cordon . . . the viceroy of India at the wedding of a rajah; the German crown prince on a barracks drill field in Potsdam. They observed the life and customs of an aboriginal village on New Mecklenberg, a cockfight on Borneo, naked savages blowing on nose flutes, the capture of wild elephants. . . . Space was negated, time turned back, 'then and there' transformed by music into a skittering, phantasmagoric 'here and now.'"[41] Mann's description, which I have significantly truncated, actually resembles Starr's description in certain ways, although their interpretations of cinematic travel could not be more different. What for Starr is evidence of civilization's triumph is for Mann evidence of civilization's decadent decline. What these accounts share, however, is a multiplicity of places described, producing in each case a long list of visual attractions. Mann's account emphasizes not any enlightenment produced by all this footage but the audience's exhaustion at the end of the program. "People stared in bewilderment at the face of this charming specter, who seemed to see them and yet did not, who was not at all affected by their gaze, and whose laughter and waves were not meant for the present, but belonged to the then and there of home—it would have been pointless to respond. And so, as noted, their delight was mixed with a sense of helplessness."[42] This cinema scene, set in the pre–First World War era but written after it, looks back at early cinema as a symptom of the alienation effects of modern photographic representation. Janelle Blankenship has written of this passage, "In Mann's text the cinema does not mark 'fullness.' It ushers in an almost shameful encounter with the loss of the German colonies in Africa and the South Seas, which was legally confirmed by the Treatise of Versailles."[43] Already in 1924, five years after the end of the war, early travelogue films can be rendered by a figure such as Mann as an ambivalent site for both enjoyment and "shame."

Sound and Silence

Turning from this fictional account of film spectatorship, we can return to historical evidence of actual spectatorship to examine the important issue of silent film sound. The experience of watching a scenic film contains an important sonic dimension. Like all silent-era cinema, travel films were usually exhibited with some sort of live sound accompaniment. In the early cinema era, these practices were extremely diverse. Lauren Rabinovitz has shown that *Hale's Tours*—illusion rides that showed travel films at the front of a stationary railroad car to imitate a sense of movement—were about more than just the picturesque destination of regular scenic films. They were, she writes, about "the *experience* of being in that place, and that experience was dependent on the sound convincingly linking the motion and visual events of the ride." *Hale's Tours* used a wealth of sound effects, including "steam whistles tooting, train wheels clattering, paddle wheels churning water, automobile horns blowing . . . and other effects associated with whatever activity was being depicted on screen."[44]

By the nickelodeon era, when the exhibition of nonfiction film was becoming institutionalized, musical accompaniment was still in flux, although it is difficult to track down evidence of sound practices in this era. Rick Altman argues that "far from representing a uniform soundscape more or less like that of later theaters, nickelodeons offered their own characteristic economy and their own complex auditory world. More than at any other time during the so-called silent film period, sound practices were in a state of chaos during the nickelodeon period."[45] In the nontheatrical domain, live lecturers were a central component of travelogue film exhibition.[46] In nickelodeon programs, the sound component was usually music, although lecturers were occasionally used in some theaters. The most common musical accompaniment for nonfiction films in the 1910s was the waltz. George W. Benyon wrote in 1921, "It has been the custom to portray all these [educational films] by introducing a waltz as the accompaniment, and regard the problem well solved."[47]

But by the early 1920s, when guidebooks to film music began to appear, musicians were encouraged to abandon the waltz in favor of a wider range of other material. Erno Rapee wrote in 1925, "The scenic picture, by the very nature of its being, as a rule portrays scenery and atmosphere with relatively little action and all it requires for its accompaniment is purely melodious music moving in the same atmosphere as the picture." Rapee, recommends, among other things, Dvorak's "New World" Symphony and Tchaikovsky's Symphony No. 5 for general scenic use. Both Rapee and Benyon make interesting musical recommendations tailored to the specific concerns of the scenic film. Rapee recommends that North American scenics featuring massive rocks and thundering waterfalls can be suitably accompanied by Victor Herbert's "Natoma Selection," a popular opera from 1911 celebrating the "Old Spanish Days" of Santa Barbara, California. He suggests that scenic pictures dealing with water and sea pair nicely with Felix Mendelssohn's "Fingal's Cave" Overture, a Romantic era composition that was responsible for popularizing the real Fingal's Cave in Scotland as a tourist destination.[48]

Benyon called scenics "musical landscape portraits," arguing, "The Scenic always provides opportunity for some real music. This is the one chance in the program given to the musician to show what he can do as a virtuoso. . . . Panoramas are very much alike on the screen, and music alone can lend the required atmosphere as a distinguishing mark."[49] Benyon recommended choosing musical selections "with a view to the characteristics of the countries shown. For India, oriental music, for Japan, Japanese music, or for Egypt, Egyptian music."[50] Benyon's principle of accompaniment is designed to complement and enhance:

> If the waves of the ocean quietly lave the feet of the crags and the Island of Malaita is shown in its noontide listlessness, it would spoil the picture to play a bright Allegretto, even though the music might be most appropriate from the standpoint of atmosphere. That laziness and sense of ennui must be carried out musically to obtain the maximum results. On the other hand, when the business section, the wharves and peopled

streets of Tokio, Japan, are shown, it would be foolish to attempt to fit the lively scenes with an atmospheric Andante. The activity of the Japanese calls for an equal degree of activity in the music.[51]

Benyon's principle of musical complementarity was not necessarily heeded by the musicians of the day, but certainly this level of thought about the musical accompaniment of scenic film indicates the institutionalization of the scenic film's place on silent-era film screens. Benyon concludes his section on scenic films by distinguishing between fiction and nonfiction:

> It is more vitally important to hold the atmosphere of the Scenic than to portray the action in the feature; for the latter speaks for itself, while the former must be determined. The very fact that the program is selected to give variety for the patrons, makes it imperative that the music should change with each picture and emphasize the ideas depicted in the various scenes, whether they be from elemental or animated nature. Of all the pictures presented to the public the Scenic calls for greater ingenuity, more resourcefulness and keener discernment on the part of the leader than any other class of film.[52]

As Benyon points out, the "atmosphere of the Scenic . . . must be determined." This observation supports my claim that travel films could produce extremely open-ended experiences. While we do not have recordings of nickelodeon musical accompaniment to study, we do have some of the films, and they provide ample evidence of the poetic effects travelogues might have on the viewer.

Altman has argued that contrary to film historians' commonplace assertion that "the silents were never silent," nickelodeon theaters were in fact often filled with silence. Smaller theaters sometimes did without music entirely, while more elaborate theaters could afford to hire musicians (or, at least, a mechanical musical device) as a way to attract patrons. "While some nickelodeons provided live musical accompaniment for films," he notes, "substantial evidence confirms that many theaters conceived music only as a separate attraction, alternating with the film rather than enforcing it."[53] While Altman's analysis of the silence of the silents is an important intervention, I am surprised that he does not account for the likelihood that audiences themselves might have provided some noise in the theater. Citing the example of a 1909 *Nickelodeon* article that offered instructions for musical accompaniment that occurred only between films, Altman concludes, "During film projection, ventilating fans would provide the only sound, along with whatever ballyhoo music might bleed through the entrance doors."[54] Certainly, that is what the article in question communicates. But what about the patrons in the theater? From the sound of bodies shifting in their seats to the sound of breathing, laughing, snickering, or sneezing, surely the audience contributed an important sonic dimension to the silent moments in early cinema theaters. Indeed, reformers were apt to criticize nickelodeon patrons for just this sort of clamorous behavior. Audiences often responded vocally to the films they encountered in the nickelodeon theater, with one important exception: scenic films.

My research has found evidence that scenic films were indeed exhibited in complete silence on numerous occasions, although my analysis of this silence is quite different from Altman's. I have found several accounts of audiences who were so entranced by travel films that they fell silent in the theater. "Have you ever watched the average audience closely while the 'weekly' or a beautiful travelogue picture was being exhibited?" asks an article defending travelogue films from 1912. "You do not hear the murmur of voices and exclamations that are generally audible during the exhibition of the ordinary program. The audience is perfectly quiet; you can hear a pin drop. This denotes attentiveness, which proves that the audience is interested."[55] In another account, a writer blames exhibitors for misreading the taste of the film audience: "The average exhibitor has no more idea of what kind of pictures his patrons prefer than he has of their preference in literature between a dime novel and an encyclopedia. If he shows an alleged comic film of the slap-stick variety, and five people in the audience laugh, he concludes that he has found a winner. If he shows a scenic picture so beautiful that the whole audience sits almost breathless while it is run, he concludes from the absence of noise that the picture was no good."[56] Another undercover observer—this time at a screening of the Paul Rainey African pictures—wrote: "There was found a large and seemingly breathless audience. Apart from the spokesman's voice there was not the faintest trace of sound."[57]

In each of these three accounts, audiences were so enraptured by scenics that they fell silent. This response is contrary to the usually vocal audience reaction to the material on-screen. While this silence may denote attentiveness, as one of the above writers concludes, we should not exclude the possibility that it also might indicate boredom. Nonetheless, the silence itself is remarkable. Benyon's *Musical Presentation of Motion Pictures* gives evidence that silence was often a conscious strategy employed by musicians rather than merely a result of a lack of funds on the part of the theater. Benyon devotes seven pages to a discussion of silence used by musicians, and while I do not have space for a full account of that discussion here, I do want to quote him in support of my argument: "Strange as it may seem, silence sometime expresses . . . reverence."[58]

Moving the Spectator: Poetic Reverie

Like real, physical travel, travelogue films are highly experiential. Take the film *Loetschberg*, for example. This "phantom ride" film of a railway line running through the mountains of Switzerland was made by Eclipse around 1913.[59] The film presents the viewer with images of railroad tracks, telephone poles, mountains, and Alpine cabins (fig. 6.3). The bulk of the film is composed of motion-filled landscape shots taken from a moving train, but there are some stationary shots of the train arriving at a station, reminiscent of the famous Lumière film. As the train passes through several tunnels, we experience the kinetic sensation of space moving away at the sides of the frame. The film plays up the sensation of movement, as phantom rides had been doing since the 1890s. In the well-known Hale's Tours, which showed phantom rides inside stationary train cars, the spectator was encouraged to imagine himself or herself aboard the train.[60] When shown in a regular nickelodeon theater, the effect would have been much the same. *Loetschberg* is more about the experience of movement than it is about the specificity of the Loetschberg railway. While it is likely that the film was produced on the occasion of the opening of a new railway line with the full cooperation (or even sponsorship) of the railroad company, to a viewer unfamiliar with this landscape, many of the images might just as well have been pastoral scenes of any mountainous place in Europe.

Again, I want to stress that in presenting motionless voyages for film spectators, travelogues were only updating a long tradition of virtual travel presented in panoramas, dioramas, magic lantern shows, and stereographs. But as David B. Clarke and Marcus A. Doel have pointed out, "There is another kind of stationary trip effected by film, which is arguably much more profound: a journey into the very fabric of space and time itself."[61] While they may have promised a sense of geographical mastery, then, what travelogues actually delivered was a profoundly discontinuous sense of geography. This discontinuity or even incoherence could only be made sense of by the viewer's perception, for coherence was not provided by the films themselves. As Alison Byerly has argued, the panorama (and, by extension, the

FIGURE 6.3 Frame enlargement, *From Spiez to Loetschberg, Switzerland* (1913).
Courtesy EYE Film Institute Netherlands.

travelogue) "alters the spectator's sense of his or her own relation to reality by creating an imaginary projection of the spectator who is transported elsewhere."[62] Forms of virtual travel such as the panorama, diorama, stereoscope, and travelogue may have functioned culturally as forms of knowledge, as though seeing a place were akin to knowing a place, but what they delivered was an experience.

I suggest that travelogue films encouraged a unique kind of spectatorship that we might describe as a form of poetic reverie. Of course, we can only speculate about how early audiences experienced these films. But when viewing them today, I certainly find myself sent off into daydreams inspired by the slow panning shots of landscapes and people posing stiffly for the camera. This dreamlike reception is certainly not the learning experience that educators envisioned; falling into a state of reverie is quite unlike learning a fact-filled lesson about the world's geography. Instead, the spectator in a state of reverie might experience a series of free-floating, subjective associations. Gaston Bachelard defines reverie as "a flight from out of the real" and explains that "reverie puts us in the state of a soul being born."[63] Might we not say, then, that travelogues (and other early nonfiction films) simulate the real world to allow the spectator to leave the real world?

One might analyze this notion of spectatorship as reverie in both negative and positive ways. On the one hand, this dreamlike spectatorship would seem to produce something that is quite the opposite of knowledge: mythification. Exotic places and peoples are presented in these films as though they are disappearing, as though these picturesque scenes of traditional crafts, natural landscapes, and "primitive" peoples might never exist again in such an idealized way. Travelogue reverie thus might appear nostalgic, a fantasy of the premodern world viewed within a framework of loss, a key symptom of what Benjamin viewed as the dreamworld of mass culture. But on the other hand, as we have already seen, Benjamin also viewed mass culture as the only avenue to overcoming the decline of experience in modernity. His metaphor for discovering the revolutionary potential in mass culture was one of "awakening." While poetic reverie might not seem like a form of awakening, it is one step removed from the enthrallment of a passive dream state. And for Bachelard, poetic reverie is precisely *not* a form of dreaming. He writes, "It is a poor reverie which invites a nap."[64] For Bachelard, it is the word "poetic" that is key. "An adjective is going to save everything," he writes. *Poetic* reverie, in the language of phenomenology, describes "a subject who is struck by wonder by poetic images." Poetic reverie puts the subject on the track of "an expanding consciousness"; it allows the subject to envision "hypothetical lives which enlarge our lives by letting us in on the secrets of the universe. A world takes form in our reverie, and this world is ours. This dreamed world teaches us the possibilities for expanding our being within our universe."[65]

As early as the 1910s, some intellectuals had begun to write directly about the cinema's dreamlike form of realism. The French writer Jules Romains said of the film audience: "They are no longer conscious of their bodies. Instead there are only passing images, a gliding and rustling of dreams. They no longer realize they are in a large square chamber, immobile, in parallel rows as in a ploughed field. A haze of visions which resemble life hovers before them. Things have a different appearance than they do outside."[66] Avant-garde artists and writers appreciated travel and scientific films for their magical, mysterious quality, not for the educational knowledge they were supposedly imparting. The French film critic Louis Delluc wrote in 1917, "For a long time, I have realized that the cinema was destined to provide us with impressions of evanescent eternal beauty, since it alone offers us the spectacle of nature and sometimes even the spectacle of real human activity."

Delluc singles out travelogues as films that excel in displaying this kind of beauty, although he complains that "they are far too short."[67]

We might say then, following Romains and Delluc and a long tradition of avant-garde film criticism and spectatorship, that travelogues open up a dreamlike cinematic geography.[68] From this perspective, travel films are more about desire than education, with all of the perilous implications of fantasy and fetishism that implies. Travelogues cater to the desires that lie to some extent behind all travel: a desire to experience someplace (anyplace) different, a desire to leave one's current conditions, a desire for new experiences. Herein lies the genre's appeal: Travelogues presented images of the real world that allowed the spectator to experience a flight from out of the real, a flight toward fantasy. Travelogues therefore encouraged a particular kind of spectator—perhaps not a spectator who watched to better educate herself or himself but a spectator who enjoyed the films because they provided a space apart for poetic reverie. Rather than educating the audience in the traditional sense, early travel films functioned as a school of dreams, presenting strange and obscure pictures that taught lessons not about geography but about desire.

CHAPTER 7

"THE NATION'S FIRST PLAYGROUND"
Wilderness Modernized in the American West

R eviewing a travel film of Austria in 1910, a disgruntled *Variety* critic wrote, "This is another one of those scenic things with mountains, streams, castles, water fronts and all other things that go with this [*sic*] scenery exhibitions. The scenery is pretty, of course, it doesn't take any great amount of intelligence to pick out a pretty spot, and the makers can go on indefinitely turning them out. It would probably be more interesting, however, to show the American public scenes of our own continent."[1] This gesture of mocking travelogue conventions is familiar. As we have seen, the tradition of travel parody is nearly as old as the practice of documenting travel itself. But this review is perhaps more interesting for how it contradicts itself: The reviewer turns a complaint about scenery in general into a nationalistic plea for specifically American scenery. What the writer does not seem to be aware of is that from the beginning, the film industry had been doing just what he suggests: showing the American public scenes of its own continent.

The western United States was one of the most frequent settings for travel films in the first decades of film history. During the earliest years of the cinema, when the medium was still a novelty, single-shot views of the American West were featured in many moving-picture shows, such as *Royal Gorge, Colorado* (Edison, 1898), *Upper Falls of the Yellowstone* (Edison, 1901), *Panoramic View of Moki-Land* (Edison, 1901), and *Gap Entrance to Rocky Mountains* (American Mutoscope and Biograph, 1902).[2] A decade later during the nickelodeon era, travelogues were an established genre, and they continued to highlight the American West with titles such as *Grand Canyon, Arizona* (Nestor, 1912), *Glacier National Park* (Pathé, 1912), and *The Taos Indians at Home — New Mexico* (Selig, 1912).[3] Commercial interests fostered this picturing of the American West: The major railroad companies encouraged the promotion of the West on film beginning in the 1890s, and in the 1910s, they enlarged the practice by subsidizing numerous film productions and initiating a major tourism promotion campaign using the slogan "See America First."[4]

It should be apparent from this brief inventory of film titles that a few specific points of interest — mostly national parks and Indian reservations, or what Mark David Spence has called the "separate islands" conceptualization of the West — came to stand for the vast region of the western United States in early travel films.[5] By extension, and following the same logic of synecdoche, the American West frequently came to signify the entire United States for the rest of the world. While one might presume that these travelogues reaffirmed the popular image of the "Wild West" as an untamed wilderness, what is striking about them, besides their often spectacular landscapes, is their focus on tourists. Even the earliest Edison release set in or near a national park, *Tourist Train Leaving Livingston, Mont.* (1897), features a train heading for Yellowstone "crowded with tourists waving goodbye."[6] This is a film not about the untamed Wild West but about modernity, for to see tourists waving from a crowded train is to witness the modern world. While silent-era travel films did strive to represent the American West as an Edenic garden, then, they also contradicted the myth of the West as a pristine wilderness by depicting a region traversed by trains and peopled with tourists.

This chapter explores the representation of the American West in early travelogues, arguing that these films modernized the image of the western United States for the new twentieth century.[7] The films reinscribed the old myth of the West as a wilderness region replete with natural wonders and exotic native tribes, as it had been so often depicted in nineteenth-century paintings, photographs, and travel narratives. Yet the primary framework in which this myth was understood had shifted from the territorial ideology of Manifest Destiny to the consumerist ideology of recreational tourism. At the same time, then, the films showed the American West as a region ripe for tourism and settlement. By populating these "primeval" landscapes with mediating tourist figures, the films also modernized those landscapes, opening them up to history. The historical imaginary of the Western (Euro-American) world at this time typically drew a line between the essentialist categories of the primitive and the modern. However, in locations of internal empire such as the American West, in which native populations had only recently been displaced and which were still in the process of being settled by Europeans and Easterners, the division between the primitive and the modern was regularly blurred. (It is worth remembering that this new wave of Euro-American settlers was, in its turn, overtaking a previous generation of Spanish Mexican settlers in the region of Alta California, a territory of Mexico until 1850 that included what is now Southern California, Arizona, Utah, Nevada, and part of Colorado.) With the commodification of the U.S. West as a tourist playground in the early twentieth century, the region was made to support contradictory myths in which the frontier coexisted with modernity.

As I have shown throughout this book, supporters of the new motion picture medium were fond of claiming that the cinema made travel accessible to all. The Edison Manufacturing Company's description *A Trip from Colorado Springs to Cripple Creek* (1911), published in the *Edison Kinetogram*, for example, repeats the familiar mantra that "it is no longer necessary to spend hundreds of dollars, time, energy and the fatigue of travel to gaze upon the great wonders of the earth. They are yours for the asking; they cost little and they fascinate much."[8] Similarly, a commentator writing about a new series of films about Yellowstone National Park in 1914 explained: "By these pictures . . . the scenic wonders of the nation's first playground will be brought to the millions of people in the United States who are unable to visit the park."[9] Significantly, Yellowstone is figured in this description not as a wilderness but as a playground. As Bill Brown has shown, "play" was a newly important value at the turn of the twentieth century.[10] The "recreational scene" embodied by sports and the park and playground movements, along with the rise of national parks, was part of a larger reaction to the well-known social changes of the Progressive Era, such as immigration, industrialization, urbanization, and labor disputes. Cinema is certainly a recreational form, and analysis of this cinematic "playground" of the western United States can provide insight into the cinema's complex and contradictory role as a mediator of social and environmental changes.

In tandem with these images of domesticated wilderness, early travel films displayed images of the new, modern American West in growing cities such as San Francisco, Los Angeles, and Denver. This dialectic, in which a mythical wilderness meets dynamic modernity, worked to promote the West as a region that simultaneously signified the past and the present, a destination for both tourism and settlement.[11] As we shall see, although these films vary in geographical location and subject matter, their formula for envisioning the U.S. West remains relatively consistent. A newly modernized vision of the West as a tourist playground dotted with a few growing urban centers emerged in silent-era travelogue films.

American National Scenery

At the beginning of the twentieth century, the world had become a field of competing scenic attractions. Illustrated magazines, stereographs, postcards, and other mass media catered to popular curiosity about foreign lands and colonial territories. Diverse audiences of middle-class and working-class citizens were now provided with a seemingly endless flow of information and pictures from exotic lands they probably would never visit. With the arrival of motion pictures, the cinema became the preeminent marketplace of exotic images. Early travel cinema entered into this crowded field of exotic visual culture, contributing moving images poached from preexisting notions of what foreign views should look like. In the new motion pictures, nineteenth-century pictorial conventions such as the picturesque were reconfigured in more popular and commercial terms. The scenic was now more than an aesthetic ideal: The scenic had become a commodity.

The American entry into this international contest of scenic marvels was its celebrated western landscape. Defensive comparisons between American and European scenery were commonplace at the turn of the century. Clearly, many people perceived the United States as locked in a contest with Europe that was being waged on the level of scenery. Travelogue films explicitly took up this campaign. As a writer in *Motography* explained in 1912:

> If people only realized that in our own country we have mountains more picturesque than those in Switzerland, lakes more beautiful than those of the Emerald Isle, rivers far more interesting than the Rhine, forests that make the Black Forest look like a postage stamp, and magnificent prairies and plains that cover areas as big as many European principalities. . . .
> There are now on the market moving pictures showing the wonders of our own Yellowstone National Park, the beauties of Colorado, the grandeur of the Canadian Rockies, the splendor of our Northwestern territories, and other gems of our wonderlands, which when disclosed motographi-

cally cause the most phlegmatic "yes-but-in-Europe" bug to acknowledge that his own country offers him the best travel "buy" available.[12]

As this passage demonstrates, famous places around the world were being brought into accord with a hierarchy of tourist value, and North Americans were game to have their scenery compete. In his classic study of tourism in the American West, Earl Pomeroy lists a series of similar comparisons: "Colorado was the Switzerland of America, or, in a more daring mood, Switzerland the Colorado of Europe, though along the 'Switzerland Trail of America' one found Eldorado Springs and Boulder, respectively, the 'Coney Island of Colorado' and 'the Athens of Colorado.'"[13] Every place was open to comparison, but only certain places became recreational landmarks. Not just the landscape but also indigenous people became part of a nationalistic American agenda. The photographer and writer George Wharton James wrote in 1915, "The Hopis, Havasupais, Apaches and Navajos are more picturesque than the Swiss, Irish, Serbian or Russian peasants."[14] In this picturesque economy, natives and peasants are valued primarily as props adorning the agenda of national scenery.

The fact that previously unfamiliar regions could be promoted as premiere tourist destinations by 1900 was the result of a more general fascination with the West in the nineteenth century. As Edward Buscombe points out, the idea of "the West" is "essentially a nineteenth-century invention."[15] The American frontier myth conceived of the West as a pristine wilderness, a virgin land ready to be conquered by a virile European-derived society.[16] Many scholars have traced the history of nineteenth-century pictorial depictions of the West as an untouched Eden, from the paintings of Albert Bierstadt and Thomas Moran and the photography of Eadweard Muybridge and Timothy O'Sullivan to the government-sponsored expeditions led by Major John Wesley Powell and Ferdinand V. Hayden and beyond.[17] The U.S. West was well documented in the nineteenth century, and these abundant representations fostered an understanding of the landscape that was explicitly tied to U.S. territorial concerns: The West became the land of scenic nationalism.[18] This practice of marking off a section of national territory for its possession of scenic beauty and traditional culture is entirely in keeping with the construct of internal empire, as discussed in chapter 4.

The West and its representations had become an important part of a larger U.S. imperial project, its scenic grandeur supposedly reflecting the glory of the people who territorialized it, who fostered the myth of Manifest Destiny.

However, the mythology of the West was not immutable; part of its power was that it adapted to changing times. Anne Farrar Hyde describes how the meaning of "the West" shifted over the decades of the nineteenth century. What began as a threatening wilderness filled with incomprehensible desert landscapes, mountains, and rock formations that challenged European aesthetic standards slowly emerged in the second half of the century as a monumental landscape that bolstered nationalistic pride. Hyde writes, "Instead of claiming that the Western United States replicated Europe, many writers [began to use] Europe as a reference point to claim that the far Western landscape was bigger, better, and more wondrous."[19] These kinds of comparisons persisted well into the twentieth century.

Part of the impulse driving these representations of the West was an impulse to preserve landscapes and lifestyles that were perceived to be disappearing. Such nostalgia is more immediately apparent in fictional westerns, and the relation between fiction and nonfiction set in the U.S. West is illuminating. The fictional western, we might observe, is one of the only film genres to be semantically dependent on place: Western stories are by definition set in the American West. Westerns were one of the earliest fiction film genres to regularly use location shooting.[20] As one editorial proclaimed in 1911, American fiction films highlighting natural scenery (along with "scenes of cowboys and Indians") were the most profitable: "This picturesque [is] a real, definite commodity of genuine commercial importance."[21] In addition to being set in the West, another of the fictional western's generic requirements is that the stories must be set in the past. As Robert Warshow put it, "Where the Westerner lives it is always about 1870 — not the real 1870, either, or the real West."[22] The genre is concerned with reenacting the conquering of the wilderness and must be set in a particular place and time to generate national historical resonance. Unlike fictional westerns, however, travel films must necessarily show the West in the present, as it looked at the moment of its filming. Thus, travelogues enunciate in the present tense, but they are very much about a nostalgia for a mythologized past. Rather than working through national identity by means of storytelling, as the fictional genre does, early travel films of the West present spectacular landscapes and indigenous cultures as places to be consumed. In travelogues, the wilderness fantasy has been domesticated, its "majesty" rendered spectacular rather than sublime. These early travel films present tourist-friendly landscapes that exist thanks to the artificial support system of the National

Park Service; they depict tribes contained within the boundaries of Indian reservations who stage traditional dances for the benefit of the camera. Savage wilderness has been reinvented as benign nature.

But in fact, the American West had long been seen as fading away. By the beginning of the twentieth century, academic credence had been given to the idea that the "authentic" West had disappeared. Frederick Jackson Turner famously declared the western frontier closed in his lecture "The Significance of the Frontier in American History," delivered to the World's Congress of Historians at the Columbian Exposition in Chicago in 1893.[23] With this overdetermined proclamation of closure, Turner observed that western expansion itself had shaped the national character. Thus, the bittersweet loss of the old West cleared the way for the myth of the West to be ritualistically reenacted in representations for decades. Unlike fictional westerns, which depict the West as a wilderness on the verge of being conquered, early travelogues show a West that actually *has* been conquered. Richard Slotkin writes: "According to this myth-historiography, the conquest of the wilderness and the subjugation or displacement of the Native Americans who originally inhabited it have been the means to our achievement of a national identity, a democratic polity, an ever-expanding economy, and a phenomenally dynamic and 'progressive' civilization."[24] Depicting the West as a parade of natural wonders, travelogue films commodified the region's landscapes as visual spectacle.

Railroads and the Promotion of the West

Before turning to close analysis of several early travelogue films set in the West, I want to sketch out the connection between early cinema and the railroad. The history of the West—its land, its settlement, the displacement of Indian tribes, and the onset of tourism—cannot be understood without discussing the role of railroads in the region. The connection between the railroad and early cinema has already been well explored by Lynne Kirby, who has shown the extent to which the railroad and the cinema not only resembled each other but were literally enmeshed.[25] Travelogues were often sponsored by railroad companies, who viewed early cinema as just another tool in the available advertising arsenal. By promoting the West through cinema, the railroads stood to gain profits through the sale of tickets to tourists and migrants. Equally important, they stood to gain cultural capital by fostering a particular visual iconography of the West that suited their purposes. Indeed, the representation of the West and the promotion of the West are virtually inextricable: To represent the West usually was to promote the West in this era.

To aid in the construction of the major railroads in the nineteenth century, the U.S. federal government gave land grants to the railroad companies, which then subdivided the land and sold it to settlers. Naturally, the railroads had a stake in promoting the West as a region for settlement to encourage land sales, as well as passenger and freight traffic. Railroad companies quickly became involved in the promotion of both migration to the West and tourism in the West. As a first step in promoting migration, the railroads established special "emigrant cars" in the 1870s with reduced fares; these were attached to freight trains and were notoriously slow. By 1900, the Southern Pacific Railroad had instituted special "colonist" fares, or one-way tickets at reduced rates designed for those relocating to California.[26] The railroads' promotions soon became more wide ranging. As Richard J. Orsi has shown, Southern Pacific, for example, was actively involved in promoting California at international expositions from the 1880s onward. Southern Pacific also gave funding to a variety of booster groups, such as the Immigration Association of California. The railroad's advertising was overseen by the Passenger Department, which by 1900 was issuing huge numbers of maps and booklets promoting opportunities for settlement and tourism in California, Nevada, Oregon, Arizona, and Texas, including the venerable *Sunset* magazine, which it launched in 1898 (and which is still published today). By 1911, the annual advertising budget at Southern Pacific had reached $1.8 million.[27]

Railroad officials quickly embraced all manner of modern marketing and promoted the idea of the scenic West in a flood of advertisements and films. Motion pictures were part of Southern Pacific's advertising strategy from the first decade of the twentieth century. In 1911, *Motography* stated, "For some time the Southern Pacific has maintained a department for the advertising of California, which consisted of a staff of lecturers and motion picture films which were displayed throughout the country at Chautauquas, fairs and resorts."[28] In 1910, the *Nickelodeon* explained that Southern Pacific had hired a motion-picture company to make several films of the Sacramento Valley in California; this scheme, the article states, was costing the company "several thousand dollars."[29] Similar announcements were made in the trade press about scenic films used by the Great Northern Railway to promote Montana, by the Northern Pacific Railway to promote Yellowstone National Park, and by the Denver and Rio Grande Railroad to promote the

Grand Canyon of the Arkansas River in Colorado.[30] The Great Northern Railway actively promoted tourism to the West from the East, as can be seen in the booklet *Western Trips for Eastern People* from 1915, the cover of which shows two fashionable young women holding a camera and a guidebook (see plate 8). It was a common strategy to show women engaged in outdoor pursuits in order to demonstrate how easy and enjoyable it was for all sightseers — even ladies — to engage in wilderness tourism. Thus, women can be seen as modernizing figures — and as figures signifying commodification — in early travelogues of the West.

Great Northern also initiated the highly influential "See America First" campaign in 1910, which was quickly adopted as a general railroad slogan. Intended to lure American tourists away from the European destinations they had so long favored, the campaign brought visitors and their money to the national parks instead. The campaign was such a success that the slogan entered the general parlance of the time. The slogan of the American Film Manufacturing Company, for example, which specialized in fictional westerns, was "See Americans First" — a play on the railroad campaign. One reviewer wrote in 1912 about a film titled *Glacier National Park*, "We heartily commend the Pathé company's apparent purpose of making a series of 'See America First' pictures."[31] Here the issue of nationalism gets an international twist, since Pathé is a French company focusing on American wonders. The motion picture industry played a great role in these promotions, sometimes working with the railroads, which regularly granted free access to trains for filmmakers, and sometimes working independently of the railroads.

It is worth emphasizing how different travel in the western United States was in the 1910s. Although the railroads had made train travel fashionable, it was still out of the ordinary, and automobile travel was even more so. While many people did indeed travel west on the new railroads, it was not until the era of automobile travel really took off in the 1920s that the western United States became accessible to mass tourism.[32] In 1915, the writer Emily Post decided to drive an automobile across the country with her son Edwin. "One would have thought that we were starting for the Congo or the North Pole!" she exclaims in the published account of her trip.[33] Everyone, she says, encouraged her to take the train. Only four main roads traversed the continent, and "once you get beyond the Mississippi the roads are trails of mud and sand."[34] The trip took four weeks, driving mostly at the speed limit of twenty miles per hour, although they occasionally reached a maximum of thirty-five or forty miles per hour.[35] Such an auto trip was rare even for a wealthy writer such as Post. Most tourists to the American West in this era visited by train, but undoubtedly the most common experience of the western United States in this era was in the movie theater.

Despite the difficulty of auto touring in the 1910s, the automobile industry began sponsoring films that promoted it as early as 1913.[36] That year, the American Automobile Association sponsored a transcontinental trip to photograph "attractive scenery . . . from the tonneau of [a Pathfinder] car while it is in motion."[37] In 1918, *Moving Picture World* reported on a series of films about U.S. national parks commissioned by Pathé; the series was filmed by the cameraman Ralph Earle and his wife, who traveled around the country by car: "[Earle's] Buick car [is] the only one which has been in all of the National Parks, and he was accompanied on his trip by his wife, formerly Hazel Brown, once queen of the Tacoma Montamara Festo. The American flag, which graced the car during the trip, is likewise the only one that has been to all of the parks and this is to be sent to the Secretary of the Interior as a souvenir."[38] The experience of Earle—alone in nature with a camera, a beauty queen, and the American flag—underscores the extent to which the car often became an extension of the home and commercial travelogues resembled home movies. This tradition by the travel industry of using nonfiction films for promotion continued well into the twentieth century. As one might expect, the airlines were also sponsoring travelogues by the 1950s.

With their focus on tourism, early travelogue films rarely depict the settler's experience of the West. Nonetheless, the mythologized version of the West was clearly appealing to migrants as well as to tourists, as the railroad companies seem to have understood with their sponsorship of the films. Moreover, in the press coverage of travelogues, tourists and immigrants are frequently conflated. As one article put it, moving picture campaigns aim "to attract the tourist, home-seeker and investor," casting a wide net over all kinds of potentially mobile spectators.[39] The creation of idealized landscapes in travelogue films served multiple purposes, not just the promotion of actual tourism, but also the promotion of cinema itself as a medium that was regularly celebrated as "the next best thing" to actual travel. The contradictory nature of a modern medium (cinema) using modern technology (the railroad) to bring the wilderness experience to the theater did not seem to bother film spectators, who were perhaps willing to suspend disbelief to have a pleasant and affordable virtual travel experience. In fact, despite all this mobility in the early twentieth century, the West's landscapes and locales were consumed as *representations* first and foremost.

Wonders of Nature in the National Parks

With the new embracing of recreation, exercise, and fresh air that characterized the late nineteenth century, nature became constructed as a site of authenticity, a place where people could go to recuperate from the stresses of modern urban life. The cinema emerged just as the national park system was being established in the United States, so it is hardly surprising that national parks were a favorite topic of early film.[40] It is perhaps ironic, however, that the cinema, a quintessentially modern technology, should have become such a significant promotional outlet for the parks, which celebrated wilderness and encouraged fantasies of primeval nature. In fact, it is that very relationship between the modern and the primitive that these films can illuminate for us. Early films of the American West show us a wilderness in the process of domestication. Traditional views of the West's sublime natural landmarks such as Yosemite's Bridalveil Fall or the South Rim of the Grand Canyon, familiar from nineteenth-century paintings and photographs, remain staples of the films, but such views are now often cluttered by frolicking tourists. Something new has entered the iconography of the wilderness in these films. The ultimate quest is still magnificent scenery, but the films are equally invested in representing the *process* of getting to that scenery — the railroads, cars, horse paths, and walking trails the traveler must use to reach the scenery — and the *experience* of viewing the scenery once one has reached it. The films solicit the spectator's attention by providing mediating tourist figures within the landscape, essentially holding the audience's hand while leading it into the spectacular places on-screen. But by making nature easier to access, the ideal of "virgin" wilderness — always a myth in the first place — becomes more difficult to sustain. While this powerful myth has not died out, it has been changed by the onset of modernity. To engage with the fantasy of an unspoiled wonderland, the spectator on some level must pretend that the tourists are not there.

The earliest single-shot films of the national parks alternate between views of pristine natural sights such as waterfalls and views of tourists enjoying the parks. The American Mutoscope and Biograph Company released a series of actualities filmed in Yosemite in 1902, for example, featuring six titles: *Artist's Point, Glacier Point, Cascade near Wawona, Cal., Wawona Big Tree, Coaching Party Yosemite Valley,* and *Tourists Arriving at Wawona Hotel.*[41] Each of the six films consists of a single shot, and each prominently features movement. *Artist's Point* and *Glacier Point* are both landscape views; Half

Dome is visible in both films, along with other bits of the Yosemite Valley's striking landscape, but taken from such an extreme distance that the image is somewhat difficult to make out. These two landscape panoramas create a striking effect of movement and depth, but the specific context of Yosemite remains unseen as the camera pans across a vast expanse of abstracted air and earth. *Cascade near Wawona, Cal.*, by contrast, is a stationary shot depicting movement from the waterfall; without outside knowledge of the subject filmed, one would not know that this image was specific to Yosemite. Finally, *Coaching Party Yosemite Valley* and *Wawona Big Tree* feature another kind of movement: Vehicles filled with tourists move through the frame while the camera remains stationary.

A series made by the Edison Manufacturing Company at Yellowstone in 1899 also alternates between natural wonders and tourists. Films depicting vacationers include *Tourists Going round Yellowstone Park*, *Coaches Arriving at Mammoth Hot Springs*, and *Coaches Going to Cinnabar from Yellowstone Park*.[42] In these three films, very little of the park is visible; instead, vacationers and vehicles are the focus. It might seem strange that the filmmakers went to the trouble of shooting this footage at Yellowstone when virtually none of the park is visible; however, the sightseeing coaches shown in the films are quite distinctive, and at the time they were just as much icons of Yellowstone as the park's geysers.

Other films from the same series—for example, *Lower Falls, Grand Canyon, Yellowstone Park*—focus on geysers and waterfalls.[43] These films feature unique natural landmarks that unmistakably belong to Yellowstone, yet while they show images of nature, they still function as appeals to tourism. Visiting waterfalls was a well-established tourist practice by the late nineteenth century. As Brian J. Hudson has shown, waterfalls have long appealed to leisure travelers who seek to experience "satisfying emotions at the sight of water falling from a height in a scenic natural setting."[44] Such an aesthetic experience of nature is a specific kind of tourist experience, carrying on the practices of picturesque travelers that I discussed in chapter 5. While it might seem that these films of natural landmarks serve as a contrast to the films depicting vacationers, I argue that the films of natural landmarks serve as much to signify tourism as images of tourists in coaches.

These early actuality films must be distinguished from the multi-shot travel films made in subsequent phases of film history. The films in these early series were all sold separately; they could have been combined to make one mini-program about Yellowstone or Yosemite, or they might have been purchased individually and shown juxtaposed with shots of entirely differ-ent subjects or locations. If single films were shown alone, without the other films for contextualization, there would in fact have been nothing on-screen to verify that the views were actually taken at the places they claim to depict. The extreme-long-shot framing and single-shot structure create an almost mystical separation of the images from any existing geography. However, in many early moving picture shows, a lecturer would have been present to ex-plain the subject matter to the audience. These very early films are formally distinct from the travelogues made during the transitional era, which are much less abstracted from their context.

National parks continued to be a favorite subject in the 1910s, and travel films made during the nickelodeon era focused even more on the resort qualities of the parks. Rarely is an untouched natural wilderness depicted; few places appear free from human intervention. One film from the late 1910s, *Paradise on Earth*, for example, particularly highlights Yosemite Na-tional Park as a tourist playground.[45] The film has a distinctly promotional feel, displaying Yosemite's stunning landscapes and celebrating tourism, showing white, middle-class vacationers relaxing and enjoying the nature and fresh air. Groups of tourists on horseback are led by guides down a switchback trail, through a grove of trees, and across a wooden bridge. Cars filled with tourists pass through the landscape. The famous Overhanging Rock at Glacier Point is shown with a female tourist standing precariously atop its rock jutting out over the spectacular valley. Overhanging Rock has been shown in so many travelogues and photos, in fact, that it has become a Yosemite cliché. In more than half of the shots in *Paradise on Earth*, pristine nature is penetrated by tourists who disturb that pristine quality. Signifi-cantly, most of the tourists shown in medium shots are women (some chil-dren are also visible); here again we witness the strategy of showing female tourists to emphasize the ease and comfort of modern travel to the West. In one shot, clearly staged, three young women run into the frame from the left and kneel down at the edge of the Merced River to drink. They lie on their stomachs drinking the river water, laughing and shaking the water out of their leisure clothes as they stand up. The women are just as idealized as the nature depicted, but in a larger sense what is being idealized is the *ex-perience* being shown. In addition, there are several shots of waterfalls in the film with no mediating tourist figures in the frame. These images, like the single-shot views of waterfalls made a couple of decades earlier, have an ab-stract quality, inviting the viewer to meditate momentarily on the spectacle

FIGURE 7.1 Frame enlargement, *Seeing Yosemite with David A. Curry* (Arthur C. Pillsbury, 1916).

of flowing water. The persistence of such shots indicates that dramatic, unmediated scenery remained a travelogue ideal.

By the 1910s, Yosemite was one of the most popular subjects for films about national parks. *Seeing Yosemite with David A. Curry* (Arthur C. Pillsbury, 1916), released a few years earlier than *Paradise on Earth*, features many of the same shots: dramatic natural landscapes, tourists standing proudly atop Overhanging Rock, and female climbers (fig. 7.1).[46] These films certainly show the natural beauty of Yosemite, but they are also striking for the throngs of people they show in the park. Travel to Yosemite, these films seem to beckon, and you, too, can enjoy nature's wonderful regenerative powers. For the film spectator who does not literally travel, the wilderness has become a spectacle. William Cronon has argued that the idea of wilderness is a modern construction, pointing out that "only people whose relation to the land was already alienated could hold up wilderness as a model for human life in nature, for the romantic ideology of wilderness leaves precisely nowhere for human beings actually to make their living from the land."[47] In other words, the contradictory fantasy presented in these films—a "virgin land" populated by tourists—is a product of modern alienation from the land.

Some films from this period do focus more exclusively on landscape without figures. The Pathé film *Our National Parks — Yellowstone Park: The Geysers*, for example, mostly contains images of geysers.[48] *Our National Parks* was released in the United States on 3 March 1918; a full-color poster advertising the film has survived that depicts a landscape scene with a large geyser erupting (see plate 9). The film opens with an extreme long shot of a striking, otherworldly landscape filled with small, steaming geysers. The horizon line falls about halfway up the frame, and the many tufts of steam blowing toward the left of the frame are echoed by the cloudy sky in the top half of the image. The rest of the film shows a series of individual geysers in action, preceded by intertitles providing facts about the geysers, much like a tour guide: this one shoots one hundred feet; that one shoots from fifty to seventy-five feet in the air; Old Faithful goes off once an hour. The movement of the water and steam shown in the shots of geysers is the inverse of waterfall movement. More so than the previous films I have been describing, this film bears some resemblance to pictorial traditions derived from landscape painting. Several shots are carefully framed with picturesque side screens, and the human figures, when visible, are so distant that they function not as tourist "characters" but instead as compositional lead-in figures who help guide the viewer into the scenery.[49] Yet the geysers in *Our National Parks* do not fulfill the traditional aesthetic demands of landscape: They are not pastoral, contemplative, or even allegorical. Rather, the Yellowstone shown in the film is a parade of wonders, a series of famous landmarks, a commercialized landscape. Landscape in the travel film is not sublime; instead, it provokes the wonderment of a fairground attraction.

Over and over, travel films promote the national parks as "wonderlands." Describing a series of films of Yellowstone National Park, a catalogue dated 1907 from the Selig Polyscope Company explains, "By common consent the term 'Wonderland' has been given to the marvelous region which the United States Government has forever dedicated to public use and enjoyment."[50] Similarly, the Biograph catalogue of 1902 describes the film *Artist's Point* as "a turning panorama amid the marvellous scenery of nature's wonderland in the Yosemite Valley of California."[51] The railroad companies regularly used the word; the Northern Pacific Railway, for example, used the concept of "wonderland" as part of a long-term advertising campaign, issuing a series of guidebooks to Yellowstone Park from 1885 to 1910 with various iterations of "Wonderland" in the title.[52] Wonder has long been a valued philosophical category, "a highly prized mode of experience, to be fostered and stabilized," as described by R. W. Hepburn in his classic study.[53] However, in travelogues we see the term turned into a veritable brand name, and I contend that this transformation is brought about by the concept's territorialization as a wonder*land*. In the abstract, "wonder" may be a starting point for knowledge, "stimulat[ing] a person to enquiry," but a "wonderland" is territory ripe for material consumption.[54] "Wonder" also has ties to traditions of nature appreciation: In the context of travelogues set in the wilderness, the term signifies an aesthetic experience of nature. As one commentator wrote in 1896, "There is a fascination in simply standing and watching the falls."[55] But "wonderland," in contrast, would seem to be a concept well suited to the commercial imperative, with its fairground-style appeal to astonishment rather than contemplation, and it operates as a constitutive part of early cinema's function as a visual "attraction." It is this dual quality—nature plus commodification—that typifies travelogues set in national parks. Travelogues depicted the commercial, recreational aspect of the parks, to the exclusion of the parks' other uses, such as conservation and wildlife preservation. In so doing, these films shaped a new mythology in which the western wilderness signified not so much monumental nature as recreational nature.

Figures in the Landscape: Tourists and Natives

I have been arguing that travel films modernize the myth of the old West by populating the region with tourists. But that is only one part of the picture, for travelogues are defined by two opposing kinds of figures: Caucasian tourists and American Indians. While tourists function figurally as stand-ins for the spectator, American Indians appear in a more performative manner. If the tourists are modernizing figures, the Indians are presented as emissaries of a "primitive" human past, dressed in traditional clothing and performing tribal rites for the camera. Such images fit into a well-established tradition of indigenous display, derived from the practice of touring live attractions of native peoples at world's fairs and dime museums. This tradition of live native display began in the seventeenth century (and can be traced even earlier), but it flourished in the nineteenth century.[56] In keeping with its tendency to poach from existing representational traditions, early cinema picked up on this framework, which Roslyn Poignant has described as the tradition of "professional savagery."[57] Indeed, the "savage" trope was one of only a very few lenses through which indigenous people were represented in early cinema.

The other major framework for American Indian representation is the trope of the "vanishing Indian." Alternatively labeled the "vanishing American," the trope of the "vanishing Indian" recurred well into the twentieth century and was a popularization of anthropological concepts.[58] Photographers such as Edward S. Curtis picked up on the convention, as did early cinema. *The Taos Indians at Home — New Mexico* (Selig, 1912), for example, is described as a "panorama of [a] North Pueblo Indian village, showing in detail the modes of living and customs practiced by this almost extinct tribe."[59] As Fatimah Tobing Rony writes, "A central premise of much of anthropology was that the native was always already vanishing, and the anthropologist could do nothing but record and reconstruct, racing against the evolutionary clock."[60] Nowhere were Indian tribes represented as resilient in this tradition. Lurking behind this notion of vanishing was a kind of displaced national guilty conscience. The myth of the vanishing Indian smoothed over the nation's responsibility for its violent origins, hiding the destructiveness of nation building behind a screen of nostalgia.

All of the familiar practices of typage are used in early travelogues of the American West. Little attention is paid to tribal specificity; instead, Indians are presented as generic "natives," posed on horseback or framed in close-up profile shots. The Indians in these films are thus essentialized, made into a-historical "primitives" rather than mobile subjects with a specific culture and history. For all of their efforts to present American Indians as "types," however, this idea of the "professional savage" contains an important insight. This is a form of subjectification, but one that requires authentication by native participation and performance. Although it can be difficult to discern from still images, when one watches these films in their entirety, there is a potentially transgressive aspect to their mimetic realism, embodied in the movement and behavior of the figures, that exceeds the films' efforts to freeze natives in time. While the films are almost entirely controlled by the filmmakers and the film companies that produced them, the Indians arguably maintain a small amount of control in this dynamic, for they are the ones enacting their performance, even if this performance is framed, edited, titled, and marketed by nonindigenous filmmakers out to make a profit.

It is imperative, then, to point out the racist hierarchy that structures these images, but it is also crucial to locate moments in which these films can be opened up to resistant readings. A film from 1917 titled *Glacier National Park*, for example, epitomizes the travelogue's contradictory affirmation and denial of the wilderness myth by contrasting American Indians and tourists.[61] In the existing print, whose title translates as *The National*

FIGURE 7.2 Frame enlargement, *Glacier National Park* (Pathé, 1917). Courtesy EYE Film Institute Netherlands.

Park in America, we are never told which park is being shown, although the locale is clearly Glacier National Park. This remarkable film is more complex than most from the period, traversing the themes of tourism, landscape, and ethnography—subjects that were often treated separately in individual films—and it includes several animated segments. Glacier National Park was founded in 1910, just a few years before the film was made, and the first half of the film depicts the park as a natural paradise for tourists. In one shot, a tourist couple is romantically silhouetted against Two Medicine Lake (fig. 7.2). The shot places the visiting tourist figures in the foreground of a pristine natural scene, displaying both Glacier's monumental beauty and ease of access enabled by the park. Next follow several shots of gigantic glaciers in which the landscape dominates the frame, but in which small figures can be seen hiking in almost every shot. Several waterfalls are also shown, some with tourists hiking and some without. The "MacDermott Waterfalls" are featured in a shot with two "cowboys" chatting in the foreground; these men are clearly acting, otherwise they would look at the camera.

The first half of *Glacier National Park* is dominated by magnificent landscapes populated with tourist figures. In the second half, which focuses on American Indians, the tourists drop out of the scenery. It is as though the "wonders of nature" ideology can accommodate tourists in the landscape, but the "vanishing Indian" trope demands a segregation of tourists and natives. An intertitle announces "Indian types," followed by a series of medium close-up shots of individual men, first in profile and then in frontal portraits, all dressed in full tribal costume (figs. 7.3–7.6). As I have discussed, this kind of anthropometric portraiture was an important visual convention of the scenic film, drawn from the nineteenth-century faux-scientific practice of photographing ethnographic subjects from the front and in profile to allow for later measurements and racial classification.[62] The men are next shown standing in a line, each turning his head to look at the camera (fig. 7.7). This particular shot, with the men turning to face the camera one by one down the line, resembles a chorus line more than a frightening spectacle of savagery. This chorus line resemblance is readily apparent when one views the film in movement; in the still image reproduced here, that resonance is not as evident.

In this section of the film, the men are clearly performing their "Indianness" for the tourist gaze, as though they were characters in a fictional western. However, the performative quality of these shots—and this "chorus line" shot in particular—is so stylized that it opens up easily to interpretation as a self-conscious critique of the "savagery" on display. This shot feels closer to Eddie Cantor's *Whoopee!* (Thornton Freeland, 1930) than to the captivity narratives of the eighteenth century. Having made this observation, one might ask: Who can be credited with this potentially subversive performativity? The Indians? Or the filmmakers, who obviously chose to include these shots in the final cut of the film? The answer is unknown, and perhaps irrelevant, for no matter the intention, what audiences actually saw is this self-conscious performativity. Moreover, the film's animation sequences add a further parodic element. One segment shows an artist drawing an Indian, but when the Indian sees his caricatured likeness, he chases the artist angrily with a tomahawk (fig. 7.8). It does not even require reading against the grain to see this image as a self-critical moment, if a playful one. I argue that this potentially disruptive self-consciousness is part of the film's modernizing imperative. Even as it draws from the residual mythology of the past, it looks forward into the twentieth century.

What all of this playful self-consciousness masks, of course, is the legacy of actual violence behind the settling of the American West and the founding of national parks such as Glacier. As Mark David Spence has argued, the West was shaped by a "dual 'island' system of national parks and Indian

FIGURES 7.3–7.6 Anthropometric portraiture, *Glacier National Park* (Pathé, 1917).
Courtesy EYE Film Institute Netherlands.

FIGURE 7.7 Frame enlargement, *Glacier National Park* (Pathé, 1917). Courtesy EYE Film Institute Netherlands.

reservations" that developed almost simultaneously in the decades after the Civil War.[63] This system, founded on the misconception that national park lands were uninhabited wilderness areas, was established via the forcible removal of American Indians from lands they had inhabited for centuries. To take Glacier National Park as an example, in 1895 the Blackfeet Indians, who had resided in the region for centuries, reluctantly agreed to cede land to the U.S. government, selling off the mountainous portion of their reservation, which would eventually become the national park. When he made the agreement, Chief White Calf of the Blackfeet stated, "Chief Mountain is my head. Now my head is cut off. The mountains have been my last refuge."[64] None of this history is reflected in travelogues, of course, for it would have been bad for business. A more sinister interpretation of the playful self-critique in *Glacier National Park*, then, is that imperial ideology is so secure by the 1910s that it can afford to poke fun at itself.

In fact, unlike at other national parks, at Glacier Indians became a main attraction.[65] After the founding of the park in 1910, Blackfeet Indians were hired as greeters and performers at the hotels run by the Great Northern Railway. Cowboys and Indians escorted park guests from their train to the hotel's front door. Thus, as it turns out, the men featured in *Glacier National*

FIGURE 7.8 Animation in *Glacier National Park* (Pathé, 1917). Courtesy EYE Film Institute Netherlands.

Park are literally "professional savages," for they were actually park employ-ees. The same men appeared in other travelogues, including *Twelve Minutes in Glacier National Park* (late 1920s).[66] The intertitles of that film are even more explicit in guiding the viewer's impressions of the images shown. Be-fore a shot of an Indian man wearing a full headdress, posing in profile and then turning to face front, an intertitle reads: "Among the picturesque chiefs of this vanishing race is Chief Bull Plume." After a second shot of an Indian man, "Chief Turtle" (but of course, all Indian men are chiefs), an intertitle reads: "Probably the most famous living chief is Chief Two Guns White Calf, known the world over as the Indian whose likeness appears on the buffalo nickel." In fact, this man is *not* depicted on the buffalo nickel, but as I have been arguing, travelogues are unafraid to lie, being more invested in spec-tacle than truth.[67] The next shot features another of the figures from the earlier film, the man with the striking round face. Here he is named: "Chief Owen Heavybreast." As one might imagine, these men appeared not only in films but also on postcards, in photographs, and in articles about the park. Certainly, from one perspective, all of these performances and representa-tions served to present Blackfeet Indian traditions, in some limited sense, to outsiders as part of the discourse of twentieth-century tourism. Clearly, however, these traditions have become spectacles, and the park a setting, all in the service of tourist playacting—or, in the case of cinema, spectator fantasy.

Early cinema was ready and eager to document all of the new gimmicks of modern tourism being developed by the railways. Great Northern, which had played a major role in convincing the government to open Glacier National Park in 1910, used the tropes of "virgin wilderness" and the "vanishing Indian" throughout its many elaborate promotional campaigns to lure tourists to the region. In 1913, Louis Hill, the president of Great Northern, shipped a group of Blackfeet Indians to a trade show in New York City and had them camp on the roof of a hotel to stir up publicity for the park.[68] Pathé dutifully filmed the Indians, and *Motography* covered the story:

PATHE PICTURES INDIANS ON TENTED ROOF

On the roof of New York's newest hotel, the McAlpin, twenty-four stories above the hum of busy events of Greeley Square, are camped twelve Indians of the Blackfoot tribe. They are from the reservation in Glacier National park and have been the main attraction at the travel show, held at the Grand Central Palace. One of the number, "Long Time Sleep[,]" is eighty years old and his trip to New York is the first he has ever taken off the reservation.

Up in their tent city, they eat, sleep, promenade, smoke their long pipes and receive a chosen few callers. Among the first to present compliments to Chief John White Calf and his little band, was a Pathé camera man. "Picture taken?" and the chief replied "heap much pleased." So it is that the Pathéplay trade-mark adorns a most novel and interesting series of views of the Blackfoot people in their roof-garden quarters.[69]

The number and variety of representations here is astonishing (a trade paper reports on the filming of a newsreel about an Indian performance staged to promote a national park), but also characteristic of the modern world, in which each spectacle is covered by every medium, and each representation often serves as an advertisement for the medium itself. The meeting of essentialized natives and the modern world is a hyper-spectacularization, as layer upon layer of representation combine to make identity into a performance. As the article would have it, everyone is made happy—"heap much pleased"—by the performance. The material effect of the encounter is an exchange of capital: more tourists to Glacier and more film sales for Pathé. The hidden effect of the spectacle, however, is what the experience must have meant to the Indians who performed it; likewise, one wonders what the film meant to the cinemagoers who watched it as a newsreel sandwiched between a melodrama and a comedy.[70] The racialized primitive and the modern urban world may be inscribed as static, absolute terms in this publicity stunt, but when the two meet, their encounter has the potential to unmask the artificiality of both constructions.

The Modern West

Alongside films of national parks and American Indians, a new image of the American West began to emerge in early cinema — that is, the modern, urban West depicted in travelogues that were set in cities, such as *Glimpses of San Francisco* (Pathé, 1911) and *San Diego* (American, 1912).[71] Although they are contradictory, these two images — the wilderness West and the modern West — worked in tandem to create a pleasing image of the West with something for everyone: a place for recreation, a place for settlement, a place to consume. Although these films of cities are set in the geographical West, they resist visions of the so-called Wild West, instead depicting a region dotted with civilized urban modernity.

As I have already suggested, to represent the West in this era was usually to promote the West. Travelogues documenting Western cities often served to promote both tourism and settlement to the region. *Picturesque Colorado* (Rex, 1911) is a good example of a travelogue with clearly promotional aims. Fortunately, at least two prints of this film exist today, and an excerpted version is now available on DVD.[72] Moreover, unlike most early travelogues, whose productions are entirely undocumented, there is actually quite a bit of documentation of this film's production, distribution, and release. All of these surviving traces indicate that *Picturesque Colorado* was widely distributed and widely seen in the early 1910s.

Picturesque Colorado begins with images of an industrial parade in Denver and a panorama of the city. It then quickly moves to shots of landmarks in other parts of the state. We are shown "Snowballing in July," the famous Georgetown Loop railway, the Garden of the Gods, swimming at Glenwood Springs, and various other locations. Visiting these places in person would take a few days, as the area shown covers several hundred square miles, but the film does not mention distances, choosing instead to play up the region as a single, easy tourist destination. The film also contains a shot of two men and a boy in full costume performing an Indian dance, which pans over to show the cliff dwellings at Manitou; this imagery is loosely alluded to in the film's color poster (although the poster does not depict the actual imagery from the film; see plate 10).[73] The film's strategy for promoting the region is to alternate between images of urbanization and images of wilderness recreation. It is significant that the poster for the film, however, plays up the Wild West stereotype rather than the emerging notion of the modern West.

Alison Griffiths includes a brief analysis of *Picturesque Colorado* in her book *Wondrous Difference*. She focuses on the shot of Indian dancers that I have described and speculates about why the camera operator might have panned away from the dancers to focus instead on the cliff dwellings at Manitou. Griffiths concludes, "The Indian dancers are presented as merely one attraction among many . . . transformed into touristic icons which, like other aspects of modern life, can be consumed quickly, without the need for lengthy contemplation."[74] In the first part of the shot, however, we can see an Indian woman giggling in the left side of the frame, and as Griffith speculates, the laughter might have "undermined the nostalgic tone evoked by the dance" and thus motivated the pan to the cliff dwellings at right.[75] To me, the woman's potentially subversive laughter *and* the representation of Indians as tourist attractions are part of the same ambivalent treatment of place as spectacle. The travelogue is a kind of spectacle-making machine, and this quality marks it as distinctly modern, even though the genre traffics in images of a nostalgic past.

In fact, the film *Picturesque Colorado* was only one component of a larger promotional event: the Greater Colorado Industrial Parade of 18 July 1911, organized by a committee of local business leaders. "One of the best publicity schemes ever devised by a city and state," the parade was carefully timed to open the same day as the convention of the National Association of Real Estate Exchanges then being held in Denver.[76] The parade committee and other business concerns based in Denver raised funds and commissioned the William H. Swanson Film Company to make the film. According to the *Denver Post*, "The Greater Colorado pictures are the result of the combined efforts of the Denver commercial bodies, the labor organizations and many of the fraternal societies, who in July, through the Greater Colorado fair and frolic, raised funds to have the pictures taken, printed and assured of a ninety-day run on the leading motion picture circuits of the country."[77] Another article in the *Denver Post* gives credit for the entire concept to one J. Rush Bronson, who, "although modest, was the original conceiver of the great parade and the moving picture advertisement of Denver and Colorado all over the world."[78] This travel film, then, was instigated by local business concerns, not a film company; from the start, the film was conceived as an advertisement rather than just one of many generic travel subjects generated by a film production company. Essentially, a group of local industries got together and hired what was then one of the larger film companies to document their parade and their community. The film businessman William H. Swanson, who can be seen in a photo of the parade reproduced in the local press, was an owner of motion-picture theaters and film exchanges. He was also the president and director of the Rex Motion Picture Company, the brand name that ultimately went on the film print.[79]

The industrial parade was enthusiastically documented by the local press, which described in loving detail many of the more than one hundred floats that participated, including a float from the Princess Theater, "the largest moving picture house in Denver," along with floats from the carpenters' union and local plumbing, lumber, roofing, floor, paint, and cement companies. These descriptions are fascinating in their own right, but I will quote just a small amount here: the float from the Western Union Telegraph Company "carried a huge globe representing the world, all countries being shown as connected by Western Union wires. At each corner of the float sat typewriters and operators keeping up the good work of sending messages throughout the world." There was also a float from the International Asbestos Mill with "a truckload of asbestos rolls of all textures and dimensions" on display, a float from the local pickle works, and a local meat company, which provided "a characteristic float with a huge ham looming in front."[80]

Sadly, very little of this elaborate industrial parade made it into the final film, although *Picturesque Colorado* seems to have done the job for which it was intended, for it was warmly received by the locals who commissioned it. The film debuted for the press and local businessmen at the Princess Theater on 6 September 1911. A headline in the *Denver Post* proclaimed, "First Showing in Denver Brings Cheers from Business Men." The article states that the film's bird's-eye view of Denver (fig. 7.9) was "realistic and interesting. All of the large buildings downtown, the state capitol, Auditorium, and others were shown to advantage."[81] Not only did the film play well to the local audience, but national reviews warmly praised the film. *Moving Picture News* gushed, "Rex has accomplished with the aid of science what artists have failed to produce."[82] A review in *Moving Picture World* stated:

> "Picturesque Colorado" is a scenic film of fine educational value. It will serve to teach many Americans that there is sightseeing right at home

FIGURE 7.9 "Bird's-Eye View of Denver," *Picturesque Colorado* (Rex, 1911).

that will make a pygmy of the Alps and a streamlet of the Rhine. Best of all, it will teach dwellers beyond the sea something of the glories of our natural scenery and will tend to turn a stream of summer travel toward the awe-inspiring scenes of Colorado and Arizona.

The film, which is lightly tinted, is marked by clear, soft photography. It should have a big sale, as we have had too few scenics of our own country. Let's have more of a similar kind.[83]

The film did indeed reach "dwellers beyond the sea," given that a print with German intertitles survives today at the BFI National Archive in London. As I stated at the outset of this chapter, however, this claim that "we have had ... few scenics of our own country" is untrue, for scenic films of the West were produced with regularity from the 1890s on. Perhaps picking up on *Picturesque Colorado*'s success, the Edison company made three travelogues of Colorado a few months later, including *A Trip from Colorado Springs to Cripple Creek* (released 16 December 1911), *The City of Denver, "The Queen of the Plains"* (released 10 February 1912; see fig. 7.10), and *One Thousand Miles through the Rockies* (released 21 February 1912). The *Edison Kinetogram*'s description of *The City of Denver* explicitly describes that film as an advertisement aimed at potential settlers: "'Young men, go West and grow up with

No. 6970   Copyrighted, Feb., 1912   Released, Feb. 10, 1912
Code, VORHOEFEN   Approx. Length, 575 feet

The City of Denver, "The Queen of the Plains"

(SCENIC)

HAVE you ever been West? No? Then why not have a glimpse of one of its cities, Denver, the Queen of the Plains? And indeed she is a queen perched upon the edge of that great Western prairie and facing those grand old Rockies. A regal queen in all her glory.

Doesn't the subject interest you? That is because you have not seen the picture. It isn't a series of streets and people with a few public buildings thrown in, but a variety of views that fascinate and charm. The stock yards with their hundreds of cattle on their way to your dining table; the buffalos in the park; the hand-maids of the city cleaning their regal queen for her daily task; the public baths, the Municipal Theatre and the public playgrounds all give an added sparkle and interest to this interesting and instructive picture which closes with a magnificent run of the entire fire department of the City of Denver in action.

"Young men, go West and grow up with the country" is an old adage; to-day we say, "Go to a moving picture house and see if you like the West first and then go if you will."

It is well worth your while to see the Queen of the Plains, Denver.

Charles Ogle is one among the many on the photo play stage these days. He has been at the Fresno Photo Theatre in the "Battle of Trafalgar," "Foul Play" and appears again in a leading part as Sir Daniel Brackley in "The Black Arrow."

"The Black Arrow" is probably the greatest one act play produced this year. Over three hundred soldiers are to be seen in the battles of Shoreby and Gloucester.

It would have done Robert Louis Stevenson's heart good, could he have seen this, his first book ever filmed, portrayed in so magnificent a manner. As usual, the Edison players are perfectly rehearsed, while the settings and mediaeval costumes are correct to the last detail.—*Fresno Morning Republican.*

FIGURE 7.10 Release flyer for *The City of Denver, "The Queen of the Plains"* (Edison, 1912), *Edison Kinetogram,* 1 February 1912, 9. Courtesy Academy of Motion Picture Arts and Sciences.

the country' is an old adage; today we say, 'Go to a moving picture house and see if you like the West first, and then go if you will.'"[84] Moreover, representations of the West continued to flourish in non-cinematic media in the era. The Colorado and Southern Railway published a guidebook titled *Picturesque Colorado* from 1899 to 1913. All of these representations are promotional in nature, yet these films and guidebooks were not considered advertisements as we think of them today. Rather, in the early film era, the boundary between promotional and nonpromotional content was unclear.

My final example in this chapter, *Seeing Los Angeles* (Imp, 1912), also depicts the modernizing urban West.[85] Unlike *Picturesque Colorado*, this film focuses on a city rather than a state. Also unlike the previous title, *Seeing Los Angeles* concentrates more exclusively on images of a growing metropolis. The two films share a promotional function, although I have not been able to discern as much information about the production of *Seeing Los Angeles*. Imp is better known for its fiction films, and for staging the famous publicity stunt that introduced the first movie star, Florence Lawrence, to the world. However, like most early film companies, Imp, which was based in Los Angeles (and would soon merge with several other companies to become Universal Pictures), also produced some scenic titles.

Seeing Los Angeles opens with a street scene of a bustling modern downtown complete with trolley cars, bicycles, and throngs of pedestrians (fig. 7.11). These opening shots give the impression that Los Angeles is a prosperous metropolis. Next the film shows a park scene (in Eastlake Park, now called Lincoln Park) featuring well-dressed local residents and swaying palm trees in the background. As the Imp company's description of the film explains, "Los Angeles, Cal., is counted one of the most beautiful and progressive cities in the United States. It is fortunate in its situation, being near the Pacific and under the shadow of picturesque mountain ranges. This picture gives a very good idea of the architectural and commercial features of the city."[86]

The film next shows shots taken at an alligator farm and an ostrich farm. To today's viewers, these ostriches and alligators seem out of place in a film about Los Angeles, but in fact ostrich and alligator farms were one of the area's most popular attractions at the beginning of the century. The travel lecturer John Stoddard mentioned ostrich farms in his lecture on Southern California, and several other motion pictures were made featuring the subject.[87] A Los Angeles Chamber of Commerce pamphlet from 1910 also highlighted the ostrich feather business, which served the ladies' hat industry,

FIGURE 7.11 Frame enlargement, *Seeing Los Angeles* (Imp, 1912). Courtesy EYE Film Institute Netherlands.

stating that "ostriches are raised here for their plumes, and the industry is profitable. There is a large ostrich farm at South Pasadena, near Los Angeles, and a smaller one in the city, also an alligator farm."[88] The farms displayed their animals for tourists in zoo-like settings. An ostrich farm and an alligator farm were operating next door to each other in the Lincoln Heights neighborhood of Los Angeles when *Seeing Los Angeles* was made, and these are most likely the venues shown in the film.

The three concluding shots of *Seeing Los Angeles* show "the fastest trolley car in the world," a hilltop panorama of the city, and the ocean at sunset. The film's scenes are alive with modern excitement: the thrill of the urban crowd, the exoticism of unusual animals, the sentimentality of the ocean at sunset, the extreme speed of the trolley car (remarkable because it is the fastest *in the world*). The images register a consciousness about the rest of the globe: A panorama of Los Angeles unfolds, fitting itself into the greater panorama of the world as a whole. The film was, in fact, exported around the world: It exists now as part of the Desmet Collection at the EYE Film Institute Netherlands. It solicits the viewer's appreciation for Los Angeles as a burgeoning modern metropolis and seems positioned directly against popular notions of the Wild West. The Chamber of Commerce's pamphlet took the same approach to promoting the region, playing down western stereo-types in favor of showing a sleek urban modernity. It states, "Don't imagine when you come to Southern California that you will find here a portion of the 'wild and wooly West.' Southern California is fully on a par with any of the Eastern states, and ahead of some of them, in what our Boston friends refer to as 'culture.'"[89]

Unlike *Picturesque Colorado*, which was a success with local audiences, at least one local Los Angeles audience did not like *Seeing Los Angeles*: "The picture did not seem to fulfill the expectations it aroused. . . . The chief criti-cism [was] that the particular scenes selected were neither the best nor the most characteristic that could have been obtained."[90] I suspect that these local viewers may have objected to the alligator and ostrich farm scenes, since they did not exactly contribute to the image of a modern metropo-lis. Perhaps the audience also objected to such a focus on Lincoln Heights (where the park and the farm were located), one of the oldest neighbor-hoods in Los Angeles, which was known for its tourist attractions in the early 1900s (including the Selig Zoo), but which was already beginning to become peripheral by 1912 as industrialization pushed wealthy residents to other neighborhoods.

Seeing Los Angeles, along with a host of other early travelogues, encour-aged viewers to see the West as part of the modern world. Although one vision of the West dominated many early scenic films — the West as a wilder-ness playground — a competing version of the West was possible even in the early 1910s: the West as a cosmopolitan participant in the modern world. These early films of western cities evince a remarkable optimism and faith in the transformative power of modernity, as though any locale touched by the magic wand of urbanization would bloom into a major metropolis. The re-lease flyer for Selig's *Seeing Spokane* (1912), for example, proclaims, "Another city in that delightful, educational series of sight-seeing trips to principal cities of the world," as though Spokane were sure to become the next San Francisco.[91]

In travel films of the West, then, we see a modernization of myths about the American West. In these films, the West is no longer a barren wilder-ness waiting to be conquered. Instead, it has become a picturesque destina-tion for tourists and immigrants. The explicit empire-building objectives of nineteenth-century imagery have been replaced by the commercial objec-tives of the twentieth century: Travelogue films market western scenery as a commodity. Rather than a frontier in need of taming, the West appears in early cinema as a space for recreation. What is more, cinema audiences could play in "the nation's first playground" without leaving their theater seats. Thus, the true national playground constructed by these films would seem to be not the space of the western landscape, but the space of cinema itself.

REVERIES OF THE SOLITARY WALKER

In this book, I have argued that early travelogue films should be seen as a new form of sensory experience encountered by a diverse range of early moviegoers. I have suggested that travelogues provided a space for poetic reverie in the motion picture theater, encouraging viewers to move beyond their everyday conceptions of dwelling and selfhood and enabling spectators to envision new horizons of experience. Early travel films were a relatively open-ended experience, appearing at unpredictable places in the disjunctive variety format of the nickelodeon theater. Unlike illustrated travel lectures, and also unlike travel films with synchronized sound, travelogues from the early cinema period were freed from the guidance of a narrating voice. As I have argued, this lack of a narrator figure opened up a space in which the spectator could envision herself as the One Who Travels, and in which she might project her own fantasies, desires, or resistances.

Travelogues persisted on commercial cinema screens for many decades, but much of this unbounded quality was shut down as the film industry changed. Travelogues continued to be shown before the main feature in movie houses from the late 1910s until well into the 1950s. The genre remained formulaic, but there were several significant changes soon after the nickelodeon era. These institutional changes—production in a series, voice-over narration—underscore the singularity of the travelogue experience in the first two decades of cinema. During the nickelodeon era, travelogues had been produced in an ad hoc manner as the camera operator traveled; the films were then shipped back to the production company for individual release. Although there was some sense of "brand" identity—to the extent that Pathé was known for its high-quality stencil-colored scenics, for example—travel films typically were not released in a clearly labeled series. As we have seen, directors were not known to film audiences at the time, and the films were not yet associated with particular personalities, as they had been in the illustrated lecture tradition.

By the late 1910s, however, travel films began to be released in series with uniform titles and clearly identifiable logos or personalities. Burton Holmes's travelogue series, distributed by Paramount in the late 1910s and 1920s, is one of the first prominent examples, and many others followed. The coming of sound altered the travelogue's mode of enunciation even more significantly. Once synchronized sound technology became the norm, an unceasing voiceover became the travelogue standard. The well-known MGM series FitzPatrick's Traveltalks from the 1930s and '40s, for example, featured James FitzPatrick narrating throughout each film. Voiceover narration guides the viewer's interpretation of the images to such a degree that little room for thought—let alone reverie—remains. Voiceover narration became a favorite subject of parody in the 1930s and beyond, its bombastic pedagogical tone sounding even more formulaic than the already formulaic images it described. In nontheatrical contexts, travel films have continued to thrive to this day. Travelogues were a major genre of classroom cinema, which became an important presence in schools in the 1920s and '30s after a distinct educational-distribution network was established for 16mm films.[1] Travel films also, of course, are a staple genre of home movies and amateur cinema, and this generic dominance continues even today, in the age of digital video and smartphones.

In addition to this literal persistence as a genre, early travel films were influential in demonstrating the value of location shooting and camera movement, techniques that were adopted by fiction filmmakers in the 1910s. Travel films had fulfilled a scenic function in the nickelodeon's variety film program, but by the early 1910s, scenery began to be integrated into feature films as location shooting became an attraction in narrative filmmaking. Around 1912, stories in the trade press begin to mention scenic backgrounds as a special feature of certain fiction films. An Italian film imported by George Kleine titled *Song of the Soul*, for example, was reviewed with the headline "Superb Human Interest Film" and subtitled with the proclamation "Beautiful Scenic Effects." The review carefully pointed out that "a number of the scenes ha[d] been taken among the ancient ruins of Rome, while others show[ed] a typical Italian seaside pleasure resort."[2] This could almost be a description of a travel film, yet the scenery is framed by a larger narrative. The fact that the film's reviewer paid special attention to the scenery indicates that it was still unusual in 1913.

In fact, during the early 1910s, certain film companies managed to carve niches for themselves by specializing in scenic backgrounds for their fiction productions. Companies such as Selig, Essanay, and Biograph began to establish branches in Southern California at this time, and it is well known that the region's abundant scenery was one of the primary reasons for the film industry's move west. The American Film Manufacturing Company of Chicago, for example, opened a branch in Santa Barbara, California, and became renowned for its use of scenery, particularly in westerns, the company's generic specialty. One review of a film by American, *Quicksands* (1913), points out that the "Backgrounds Are Well Chosen." The review also notes: "The closing scene, in which Kerrigan returns to his tropical paradise and is seen rejoining his island sweetheart, against a background of dashing waves, is as magnificent as anything recently shown in motion pictures. The big rollers come dashing in across the broad Pacific and break in a spectacular fashion against the rock-bound coast, making a background for the love scene that is seldom equaled."[3] Scenic films of crashing waves had been popular during the nickelodeon era (Gaumont specialized in films of rivers and oceans), but in those films, the moving water had remained abstracted and isolated from context. In contrast, the moving water in *Quicksands* became part of the narrative, an added attraction serving as the backdrop for a love story.

Techniques of camera movement were also developed more significantly by the early travelogue film than in early fiction films. As we have seen, early travelogues were filled with camera movement. Pans and tracking shots appear in the majority of travel films. In fiction films before the 1910s, however, camera movement was much less pronounced. Eileen Bowser points out that in the 1910s, as fiction films began to adapt to the needs of location shooting, "films made on distant locations were mostly filmed out-of-doors and reflect the freer positioning of actors and horses and all living creatures deep in space. Because the action spread over a wider range than in a studio, it was more difficult to keep in the center of the frame, and the cameraman had to pan to follow it."[4] In addition to this practical need to pan across an extreme long shot, there was the added dynamism of camera movement that could enhance the excitement of film narrative.

The travelogue's influence can be traced in additional directions. Most obviously, the appeal of the travel film was expanded through a series of popular exploration films in the 1910s–30s such as *South* (Frank Hurley, 1919); Herbert Ponting's films of Captain Robert Falcon Scott's expedition to the Antarctic in 1911, *The Great White Silence* (1923) and *Ninety Degrees South* (1933); and *The Epic of Everest* (J. B. L. Noel, 1924). Likewise, films by Martin and Osa Johnson such as *Among the Cannibal Isles of the South Pacific* (1918) and *Simba: The King of Beasts* (1928) built on travelogue traditions, pairing the genre's use of documentary realism with an extremely sensationalistic, fairground-style appeal. Most famously, Robert Flaherty's *Nanook of the North* (1922) adopted many travelogue techniques, expanding them to feature-film length.[5] Finally, the well-known films of Merian C. Cooper and Ernest B. Schoedsack, such as *Grass* (1925), *Chang* (1927), and even *King Kong* (1933), quite clearly were influenced by early travelogue conventions.[6] Travelogue films have been a major influence within and beyond the boundaries of nonfiction.

Beyond its persistence as a genre in commercial and nontheatrical exhibition formats, and beyond its influence on other forms of commercial cinema (feature films and documentary films), I find the early travel film particularly intriguing for the way it has inspired certain practices in experimental cinema. In recent decades, an important tradition of avant-garde filmmaking has emerged that uses found footage from early nonfiction film. These films recontextualize early nonfiction through juxtaposition, isolation, slowing down, speeding up, and other techniques. *From the Pole to the Equator* (Yervant Gianikian, 1987), *Lyrical Nitrate* (Peter Delpeut, 1991), *Mother Dao, the Turtlelike* (Vincent Monnikendam, 1996), *Decasia* (Bill Morrison, 2001), and *Film Ist* (Gustav Deutsch, 2000–2009) are just some of the films that fit into this tradition.[7] They reinterpret early cinema visually, as I have been reinterpreting it textually.

But to conclude, I want to focus on one film from an era closer to that of the early travelogue and touch on the relationship between early travel cinema, which was an institution of sorts, and a completely unique and little seen experimental film from the 1920s, Oskar Fischinger's *Walking from Munich to Berlin*. Fischinger is associated with the cinematic tradition of abstract animation. He and other filmmakers, such as Viking Eggeling, Hans Richter, Walter Ruttman, and Mary Ellen Bute, strove to create a kind of visual music in the 1920s–40s. These film artists shared an interest in the relationship between film imagery and sound, exploring questions of form, duration, color, and tone. In Fischinger's films, such as the well-known *Composition in Blue*

(1935), we see geometric shapes moving rhythmically in space, accompanied by a rendering of "The Merry Wives of Windsor" on the soundtrack. The relationship between image and sound in that film is one mostly of duplication or mirroring. However, in his later films, such as *Motion Painting No. 1* (1947), Fischinger opened up these sound–image relations to looser and less clear connections.[8]

Fischinger's non-objective films are worth discussing at length, but my interest is in his less well known photographic or "live-action" film *Walking from Munich to Berlin*. According to Fischinger's biographer, William Moritz, there is no record that Fischinger ever showed the film publicly.[9] In 2006 it was released on DVD by the Center for Visual Music.[10] The film's formal brilliance — along with its indebtedness to the travel film legacy — is now widely available for all to see.

Walking from Munich to Berlin is a four-minute, silent, black-and-white film that traces a back-road walking route Fischinger took between the two German cities in the summer of 1927. During the trip, he exposed single-frame images of the landscapes, people, and scenery he encountered. Rather than experimenting with issues of form and color, as was Fischinger's usual practice, the film is a collage of portraits and countryside scenery. It functions within the familiar realm of photographic realism and yet it is no less experimental than Fischinger's animated films, for it explores the fragmentation of time and space by cinema.

To make the film, Fischinger took single-frame images using quick bursts of the camera trigger. The film was not edited; rather all effects were created in-camera. According to Moritz, who closely examined the nitrate print, "Many of the sequences . . . involve hundreds of consistent, even exposures."[11] These single-frame images, unfolding at the rate of twenty-four per second (on the DVD, or ideally eighteen frames per second when projected), spool forth like clusters that resemble traditional film "takes" or "shots" but animated in a more mechanical, jerky fashion. In turn, each "shot" lasts only a second or two on the screen, so that each shard-like moment is bumped up against another and another, images flowing in quick, relentless succession. These shot-like clusters are separated by white flash frames, which enhance the film's otherworldly, even mystical effect. The film moves quickly, almost too fast to be grasped on the first viewing, forcing the viewer to contemplate the very mechanics of cinema.

Presented in conversation with Fischinger's brilliant formal experimentation are the film's images, drawn from a familiar gallery of travelogue iconog-

FIGURE E.1 Frame enlargement, *Walking from Munich to Berlin* (Oskar Fischinger, 1927). Courtesy of the Center for Visual Music.

FIGURE E.2 Frame enlargement, *Walking from Munich to Berlin* (Oskar Fischinger, 1927). Courtesy of the Center for Visual Music.

raphy. There are peasants, children, village streets and pastoral landscapes. A farmer poses for a facial close-up and then a profile shot, just like the old convention of anthropometric portraiture. A village landscape is framed by a picturesque arched doorway; a peasant couple stares back from the screen (figs. E.1–E.2). This imagery is striking, yet it is derived from the travelogue tradition. The film is an accumulation of radiant, considered images that transcend their usual significance as iconic formulas. Fischinger uses a modern form of representation to signify a traditional landscape and way of life. He has liberated the picturesque from its middlebrow cage, making it speak to the modernist avant-garde. This film demonstrates that the picturesque aestheticizing of the world does not necessarily result in tepid representations or passive spectators.

Fischinger made a second "live-action" travel film, *Swiss Trip [Rivers and Landscapes]* (1934), which is currently not available on DVD. *Swiss Trip* was made during another solo walking journey that Fischinger took seven years later, in 1934. The film presents images of landscapes, mostly water and mountains, which connects it to a long tradition of landscape representation in painting, photography, and poetry. *Swiss Trip* resembles *Walking* in its visual style, although it focuses almost exclusively on landscapes and not figures. The film also contains numerous regular-speed shots, however, and, most notably, it was juxtaposed with Bach's Brandenburg Concerto No. 3, which Fischinger also used to accompany his painstakingly produced major work *Motion Painting No. 1* thirteen years later.

Fischinger's walking journeys place him in a tradition that extends back to the Romantic period — that of the solitary walker who discovers a sense of self through contemplation of the world. In the late 1770s, Jean-Jacques Rousseau wrote *Reveries of the Solitary Walker*, an autobiography that describes his version of this kind of experience. I conclude with Rousseau's description of walking, which is also an apt description of the experience of Fischinger's *Walking*: "I came to enjoy this recreation of the eyes, which relaxes and amuses the mind, taking it off our misfortunes and making us forget our sufferings. The nature of the objects contributes greatly to this distraction and adds to its charm. . . . One has only to love pleasure in order to yield to such delightful sensations."[12] This description of walking, which could also be a description of early travelogue film spectatorship, should encourage scholars of early cinema to be attentive not just to film's historical and cultural dynamic, but also to cinematic experience, the element that has always brought audiences into the theater in the first place.

NOTES

Preface

1. Howard Koch, "Script to Screen with Max Ophüls," in *Letter from an Unknown Woman*, ed. Virginia Wright Wexman and Karen Hollinger (New Brunswick: Rutgers University Press, 1986), 200.

2. *Letter from an Unknown Woman* was released on VHS in 1998, and after many years of unavailability on DVD in the United States, it was finally released on Blu-ray in October 2012.

3. Film prints are held at the EYE Film Institute and the Library of Congress. The Library of Congress print is available online under its U.S. release title, *On the Coast of the Bay of Biscay, France*. Search by title at http://memory.loc.gov/ammem /index.html (accessed 12 October 2012).

4. Rick Altman, "From Lecturer's Prop to Industrial Product: The Early History of Travel Films," *Virtual Voyages: Cinema and Travel*, ed. Jeffrey Ruoff (Durham: Duke University Press, 2006), 61.

5. Jeffrey Ruoff, "Introduction: The Filmic Fourth Dimension: Cinema as Audio-visual Vehicle," in Ruoff, *Virtual Voyages*, 14.

6. See Thomas Elsaesser, "The New Film History as Media Archaeology," *Cinémas* 14, nos. 2–3 (2004): 75–117.

7. See Robert C. Allen and Douglas Gomery, *Film History: Theory and Practice* (New York: McGraw-Hill, 1985), 67–76.

8. Rick Altman, *Silent Film Sound* (New York: Columbia University Press, 2004), 22–23.

9. Charles Musser, with Carol Nelson, *High-Class Moving Pictures: Lyman H. Howe and the Forgotten Era of Traveling Exhibition, 1880–1920* (Princeton: Princeton University Press, 1991), 55.

10. On the discourse of cruelty in *Las Hurdes* specifically, see Catherine Russell, *Experimental Ethnography: The Work of Film in the Age of Video* (Durham: Duke University Press, 1999), 38–40.

11. Dudley Andrew, "Praying Mantis: Enchantment and Violence in French Cinema

of the Exotic," *Visions of the East: Orientalism in Film*, ed. Matthew Bernstein and Gaylyn Studlar (New Brunswick: Rutgers University Press, 1997), 243.

12. Walter Benjamin, "Surrealism," trans. Edmund Jephcott, *Reflections* (New York: Schocken Books, 1986), 179.

13. Recent scholarship has also begun to trace early cinema's influence on cubism. See the exhibition catalogue for *Picasso, Braque, and Early Film in Cubism*, ed. Bernice B. Rose (New York: Pace Wildenstein, 2007).

14. André Breton, "As in a Wood," *The Shadow and Its Shadow: Surrealist Writings on the Cinema*, ed. and trans. Paul Hammond (San Francisco: City Lights, 2000), 73.

15. James Clifford, "On Ethnographic Surrealism," *The Predicament of Culture: Twentieth-Century Ethnography, Literature, and Art* (Cambridge: Harvard University Press, 1988), 117.

Introduction

1. "Current Educational Releases," *Motography* 6, no. 4 (October 1911): 156–57.

2. Charles Musser, *The Emergence of Cinema: The American Screen to 1907* (Berkeley: University of California Press, 1990), 145. See also Charles Musser, "The Travel Genre in 1903–04: Moving towards Fictional Narrative," *Early Cinema: Space, Frame, Narrative*, ed. Thomas Elsaesser, with Adam Barker (London: British Film Institute, 1990), 123–32.

3. On Imax travel films, see Alison Griffiths, "Time Traveling Imax Style: Tales from the Giant Screen," *Virtual Voyages: Cinema and Travel*, ed. Jeffrey Ruoff (Durham: Duke University Press, 2006), 238–58. A search for "travelogue" on YouTube currently yields more than 13,000 results (http://www.youtube.com, accessed 23 September 2012).

4. Hans Robert Jauss, "Modernity and Literary Tradition," *Critical Inquiry* 31, no. 2 (Winter 2005): 331, 360.

5. Ben Singer, *Melodrama and Modernity: Early Sensational Cinema and Its Contexts* (New York: Columbia University Press, 2001). Singer isolates three main components of the "modernity thesis": that the cinema is *like* modernity, that the cinema is *part* of modernity, and that the cinema was a *consequence* of modernity: ibid., 102–3.

6. Miriam Hansen, *Babel and Babylon: Spectatorship in American Silent Film* (Cambridge: Harvard University Press, 1991), 84.

7. Walter Benjamin, *The Arcades Project*, trans. Howard Eiland and Kevin McLaughlin (Cambridge: Harvard University Press, 1999). Although it was not published (in German) until 1982, and the English translation did not appear until 1999, Benjamin wrote this text over a period of thirteen years between 1927 and his death in 1940.

8. Susan Buck-Morss, *The Dialectics of Seeing: Walter Benjamin and the Arcades Project* (Cambridge: MIT Press, 1991), 253.

9. W. J. T. Mitchell, "Imperial Landscape," *Landscape and Power*, ed. W. J. T. Mitchell (Chicago: University of Chicago Press, 1994), 10.

10. Nor is this a "surrealist" account of mass culture as a dreamworld. It is important to emphasize that Benjamin found the surrealist emphasis on dreaming to be a romantic notion that valorized the individual's experience over collective experience. He described the emergence of surrealism in the early 1920s as a moment in which "life only seemed worth living where the threshold between waking and sleeping was worn away in everyone as by the steps of multitudinous images flooding back and forth": Walter Benjamin, "Surrealism," trans. Edmund Jephcott, *Reflections* (New York: Schocken Books, 1986), 178. The surrealists found revolutionary energy in the threshold between dreaming and waking, but, as Carlo Salzani has pointed out, "Benjamin's project, to the contrary, is concerned 'to find the constellation of awakening,' to dissolve the modern mythology 'into the space of history'": Carlo Salzani, "The Atrophy of Experience: Walter Benjamin and Boredom," *Essays on Boredom and Modernity*, ed. Barbara Dalle Pezze and Carlo Salzani (Amsterdam: Rodopi, 2009), 143.

11. Kristin Whissel, *Picturing American Modernity: Traffic, Technology, and the Silent Cinema* (Durham: Duke University Press, 2008), 4.

12. John M. Mackenzie, "Empires of Travel: British Guide Books and Cultural Imperialism in the 19th and 20th Centuries," *Histories of Tourism: Representation, Identity, and Conflict*, ed. John K. Walton (Buffalo, N.Y.: Channel View Publications, 2005), 19.

13. Mary Louise Pratt, *Imperial Eyes: Travel Writing and Transculturation* (London: Routledge, 1992), 4.

14. See, e.g., Tom Gunning, "'The Whole World within Reach': Travel Images without Borders," in Ruoff, *Virtual Voyages*, 25.

15. Leslie Page Moch, "Moving Europeans: Historical Migration Practices in Western Europe," *The Cambridge Survey of World Migration*, ed. Robin Cohen (Cambridge: Cambridge University Press, 1995), 127–28.

16. Ibid., 127.

17. Caren Kaplan, *Questions of Travel: Postmodern Discourses of Displacement* (Durham: Duke University Press, 1996), 4.

18. Pierre Bourdieu, *Distinction: A Social Critique of the Judgment of Taste*, trans. Richard Nice (Cambridge: Harvard University Press, 1984), 7.

19. Jonathan Culler, "The Semiotics of Tourism," *Framing the Sign: Criticism and Its Institutions* (Norman: University of Oklahoma Press, 1988), 153.

20. Paul Fussell, *Abroad: British Literary Travelling between the Wars* (New York: Oxford University Press, 1980); Dean MacCannell, *The Tourist: A New Theory of the Leisure Class* (New York: Schocken Books, 1989). The quote is from James Buzard, *The Beaten Track: European Tourism, Literature, and the Ways to "Culture," 1800–1918* (New York: Oxford University Press, 1993), 4.

21. *Times* (London), 12 January 1850, quoted in Piers Brendon, *Thomas Cook: 150 Years of Popular Tourism* (London: Secker and Warburg, 1991), 57.

22. Jeffrey A. Auerbach, *The Great Exhibition of 1851: A Nation on Display* (New Haven: Yale University Press, 1999), 137.

23. See Brendon, *Thomas Cook*, 57–63.

24. C. Michael Hall and Stephen J. Page, *The Geography of Tourism and Recreation: Environment, Place, and Space*, 3d ed. (London: Routledge, 2006), 1.

25. The deregulation of airlines after 1978 and the air fare wars of the early 2000s are two other important developments in the history of increasing access to tourism. On the history of tourist practices, see John A. Jakle, *The Tourist: Travel in Twentieth-Century North America* (Lincoln: University of Nebraska Press, 1985); John Sears, *Sacred Places: American Tourist Attractions in the Nineteenth Century* (New York: Oxford University Press, 1989); William W. Stowe, *Going Abroad: European Travel in Nineteenth-Century American Culture* (Princeton: Princeton University Press, 1994).

26. Sharon S. Kleinman and Daniel G. McDonald, "Silent Film and the Socialization of American Immigrants: Lessons from an Old New Medium," *Journal of American and Comparative Cultures* 23, no. 3 (Fall 2000): 80. In 1890, the total percentage of foreign-born U.S. residents peaked at 14.8 percent. This percentage reached a record low of 4.7 percent in 1970 and by 2009 had risen to 12.5 percent. In short, today's immigrant population mirrors that of the early film era when measured by percentage of total U.S. population: Migration Information Source, http://www.migrationinformation.org/USFocus/display.cfm?ID=818 (accessed 23 September 2012). One major difference, of course, is that the immigrants of today and those of one hundred years ago come from very different regions. The top countries of origin for legal U.S. immigrants today (undocumented immigrants by definition cannot be counted), in descending order, are Mexico, China, India, and the Philippines: Migration Policy Institute, http://www.migrationinformation.org/datahub/countrydata/data.cfm (accessed 23 September 2012).

27. Scott MacDonald, *The Garden in the Machine: A Field Guide to Independent Films about Place* (Berkeley: University of California Press, 2001). See also P. Adams Sitney, "Landscape in the Cinema: The Rhythms of the World and the Camera," *Landscape, Natural Beauty, and the Arts*, ed. Salim Kemal and Ivan Gaskell (Cambridge: Cambridge University Press, 1993), 103–26.

28. Martin Lefebvre, ed., *Landscape and Film* (New York: Routledge, 2006).

29. See Barbara Maria Stafford, *Artful Science: Enlightenment, Entertainment, and the Eclipse of Visual Education* (Cambridge: MIT Press, 1994).

30. For a useful basic history see Nils Buttner, *Landscape Painting: A History* (New York: Abbeville, 2006).

31. Malcolm Andrews, *Landscape and Western Art* (New York: Oxford University Press, 1999), 5, 7.

32. Martin Lefebvre, "Between Setting and Landscape in the Cinema," *Landscape and Film*, ed. Martin Lefebvre (New York: Routledge, 2006), 27.

33. Ibid., 24.

34. According to Lefebvre, when landscape is foregrounded in a narrative film, the story recedes: narrative and spectacle are two modes that cannot exist simultaneously. Setting aside the question of the exclusivity of these two modes (I have

reservations about this claim), Lefebvre's basic point about the different modes of narrative and spectacle is important. This argument resonates with an established line of thinking in film studies about the difference between spectacle and narrative—what Donald Crafton has dubbed the "pie and chase" dynamic of slapstick comedy, or what Tom Gunning has analyzed as the "cinema of attractions" in contrast with the "cinema of narrative integration." See Donald Crafton, "Pie and Chase: Gag, Spectacle and Narrative in Slapstick Comedy," *Classical Hollywood Comedy*, ed. Kristine Brunovska Karnick and Henry Jenkins (New York: Routledge, 1995), 106–10; Tom Gunning, "The Cinema of Attractions: Early Film, Its Spectator and the Avant-Garde," *Early Cinema: Space, Frame, Narrative*, ed. Thomas Elsaesser, with Adam Barker (London: British Film Institute, 1990), 56–62.

35. Lefebvre, "Between Setting and Landscape in the Cinema," 28.

36. For an account of avant-garde filmmaking as a form of minor cinema, see Tom Gunning, "Towards a Minor Cinema: Fonoroff, Herwitz, Ahwesh, Lapore, Klahr and Solomon," *Motion Picture* 3, nos. 1–2 (Winter 1989–90): 2–5.

37. See Fernando Solanas and Octavio Getino, "Towards a Third Cinema" (1969), *New Latin American Cinema*, vol. 1, ed. Michael T. Martin (Detroit: Wayne State University Press, 1997), 33–58.

38. Constantine Verevis, "Minoritarian plus Cinema," *The Deleuze Dictionary*, ed. Adrian Parr (New York: Columbia University Press, 2005), 166.

39. Miriam Hansen's notion of cinema as a form of vernacular modernism is relevant here: see Miriam Hansen, "The Mass Production of the Senses: Classical Cinema as Vernacular Modernism," *Modernism/Modernity* 6, no. 2 (1999): 59–77.

40. Gilles Deleuze and Félix Guattari, *Kafka: Toward a Minor Literature*, trans. Dana Polan (Minneapolis: University of Minnesota Press, 1986), 16–18.

41. Gunning, "The Whole World within Reach," 30.

42. "Ephemeral film" is a term favored by film archivists. According to the Internet Archive, "Ephemeral films are non-fiction films usually made for educational, industrial, or promotional purposes": see http://www.archive.org/details/ephemera (accessed 17 October 2012). "Nontheatrical film" is another important label for such film genres, although that label makes more sense after the early cinema period when the divide between theatrical and nontheatrical film stabilized and these terms became adopted by the film industry. In this book I primarily discuss travelogues as a theatrical phenomenon.

43. I am not arguing that every marginal or short-format film is minoritarian. Certainly, we can understand that the phenomenon of cult films, for example, operates largely by taking a marginal film and raising it to a level of new importance among a particular group of viewers, thus negating its marginal status. (Take, for example, *Freaks* or *Night of the Living Dead*, which rose from oblivion to hold important places in film history.) Films can shift in status from minoritarian to majoritarian (and back again) perhaps more easily than literature because of their status as mass culture.

44. Deleuze and Guattari, *Kafka*, 26.

45. Gilles Deleuze and Félix Guattari, *A Thousand Plateaus: Capitalism and Schizo-phrenia*, trans. Brian Massumi (Minneapolis: University of Minnesota Press, 1987), 55.

46. See ibid., 55–57.

47. Vinzenz Hediger and Patrick Vonderau, "Record, Rhetoric, Rationalization: Industrial Organization and Film," *Films That Work: Industrial Film and the Pro-ductivity of Media*, ed. Vinzenz Hediger and Patrick Vonderau (Amsterdam: Amsterdam University Press, 2009), 36–37. See also Michèle Lagny, "Film History: Or History Expropriated," *Film History* 6 (1994): 26–44.

48. The inclusion of the Desmet Collection on the United Nations Educational, Scientific, and Cultural Organization's Memory of the World Register was announced in May 2011. The press release is available online at http://www.eyefilm.nl/en /news/eye%E2%80%99s-desmet-collection-inscribed-on-unesco%E2%80%99s -memory-of-the-world-register (accessed 23 September 2012).

49. For an excellent account of Desmet's career, see Ivo Blom, *Jean Desmet and the Early Dutch Film Trade* (Amsterdam: Amsterdam University Press, 2003).

50. For more on this subject, see Tom Gunning, "Early Cinema as Global Cinema: The Encyclopedic Ambition," *Early Cinema and the National*, ed. Richard Abel, Giorgio Bertellini, and Rob King (New Barnet, Herts.: John Libbey, 2008), 11–16.

51. All four of these films are in the collection of the EYE Film Institute. I discuss *Glacier National Park* at length in chapter 7.

52. The beginning or ending of a film print was often the first part to be lost (due to its being caught in the projector or trimmed). It is likely that many more such endings would be found if more complete prints existed today.

1. Varieties of Travel Experience

1. *Oxford English Dictionary*, 2d ed., s.v. "Travelogue."

2. X. Theodore Barber, "The Roots of Travel Cinema: John L. Stoddard, E. Burton Holmes and the Nineteenth-Century Illustrated Travel Lecture," *Film History* 5, no. 1 (1993): 82.

3. Charles Musser, *The Emergence of Cinema: The American Screen to 1907* (Berkeley: University of California Press, 1990), 223.

4. For an account of the female travel lecturer Esther Lyons, see Giuliana Bruno, *An Atlas of Emotion: Journeys in Art, Architecture, and Film* (London: Verso, 2002), chap. 4. Female lecturers are occasionally mentioned in the early film trade press. For an interview with the lecturer Bernyce Childs, see "Educational Lectures," *Moving Picture News*, 11 March 1911, 9. This interview concludes with the statement, "Our impression is now . . . that the time is ripe, when such ladies as Miss Childs' services can be secured to give educational talks to the various motion picture houses." See also "Miss Steiner Shows Moving Pictures of Northern Ice Fields," *Moving Picture News*, 4 May 1912, 22.

5. The Magic Lantern Society, an organization of collectors, enthusiasts, and schol-

ars, has published several slide catalogues and history books about the magic lantern. For more information, see http://www.magiclantern.org.uk/publishing .html (accessed 24 September 2012).

6. For an overview of work on this subject, see Peter Hulme and Tim Youngs, eds., *The Cambridge Companion to Travel Writing* (Cambridge: Cambridge University Press, 2002).

7. Jeanette Roan, *Envisioning Asia: On Location, Travel, and the Cinematic Geography of U.S. Orientalism* (Ann Arbor: University of Michigan Press, 2010), 34–35.

8. Tom Gunning, "Moving away from the Index: Cinema and the Impression of Reality," *differences* 18, no. 1 (2007): 35.

9. Emmanuelle Toulet, "Cinema at the Universal Exposition, Paris, 1900," *Persistence of Vision* 9 (1993): 18.

10. Alison Griffiths, *Wondrous Difference: Cinema, Anthropology, and Turn-of-the-Century Visual Culture* (New York: Columbia University Press, 2002), esp. chap. 2.

11. Mark Sandberg, *Living Pictures, Missing Persons: Mannequins, Museums, and Modernity* (Princeton: Princeton University Press, 2002), 9–10.

12. See Barbara Maria Stafford, *Voyage into Substance: Art, Science, Nature, and the Illustrated Travel Account, 1760–1840* (Cambridge: MIT Press, 1984); Vanessa R. Schwartz, *Spectacular Realities: Early Mass Culture in Fin-de-Siècle Paris* (Berkeley: University of California Press, 1998).

13. Eric Ames, "From the Exotic to the Everyday: The Ethnographic Exhibition in Germany," *The Nineteenth-Century Visual Culture Reader*, ed. Vanessa R. Schwartz and Jeannene M. Przyblyski (New York: Routledge, 2004), 314. See also Eric Ames, *Carl Hagenbeck's Empire of Entertainments* (Seattle: University of Washington Press, 2008).

14. Caren Kaplan, *Questions of Travel: Postmodern Discourses of Displacement* (Durham: Duke University Press, 1996), 4.

15. Edward Said, *Orientalism* (New York: Vintage, 1979), 63.

16. Mary Louise Pratt, *Imperial Eyes: Travel Writing and Transculturation* (London: Routledge, 1992), 5.

17. Fatimah Tobing Rony, *The Third Eye: Race, Cinema, and Ethnographic Spectacle* (Durham: Duke University Press, 1996), 82.

18. Ibid., 42.

19. E. Ann Kaplan, *Looking for the Other: Feminism, Film, and the Imperial Gaze* (New York: Routledge, 1997).

20. Griffiths, *Wondrous Difference*, xix.

21. Ibid., xxxi.

22. Catherine Russell, *Experimental Ethnography: The World of Film in the Age of Video* (Durham: Duke University Press, 1999), 55.

23. Christopher Pinney, "Introduction: 'How the Other Half . . . ,'" *Photography's Other Histories*, ed. Christopher Pinney and Nicolas Peterson (Durham: Duke University Press, 2003), 2–3.

24. Homi K. Bhabha, "The Other Question: Stereotype, Discrimination, and the Dis-

course of Colonialism," in Homi K. Bhabha, *The Location of Culture* (London: Routledge, 1994), 66–67.

25. Ali Behdad, *Belated Travelers: Orientalism in the Age of Colonial Dissolution* (Durham: Duke University Press, 1994), 13.

26. Doreen Massey, *Space, Place, and Gender* (Minneapolis: University of Minnesota Press, 1994), 50.

27. David Sibley, *Geographies of Exclusion* (London: Routledge, 1995), 49.

28. Ibid., 121.

29. Ibid.

30. See Eric J. Hobsbawm, *The Age of Empire: 1875–1914* (London: Weidenfeld and Nicolson, 1987).

31. Burton Holmes, *The World Is Mine* (Culver City, Calif.: Murray and Gee, 1953), 7. Much of my brief summary of Holmes's early life is derived from this autobiography. For more on Holmes, see Genoa Caldwell, *Burton Holmes Travelogues: The Greatest Traveler of His Time, 1892–1952* (New York: Taschen, 2006).

32. Trumbull White, "Burton Holmes, the Man and His Work," *A Trip around the World through the Stereoscope*, ed. Burton Holmes (Meadville, Penn.: Keystone View, 1926), 15.

33. White, "Burton Holmes, the Man and His Work," 16; see also Holmes, *The World Is Mine*, 16–19.

34. Holmes, *The World Is Mine*, 147.

35. Ibid., 137.

36. For an extended consideration of the concept, see Rebecca Solnit, *Wanderlust: A History of Walking* (New York: Penguin, 2000).

37. Holmes, *The World Is Mine*, 138.

38. Ibid., 142.

39. White, "Burton Holmes, the Man and His Work," 23.

40. Oscar B. Depue, "My First Fifty Years in Motion Pictures," *A Technological History of Motion Pictures and Television*, ed. Raymond Fielding (Berkeley: University of California Press, 1979), 60.

41. Burton Holmes, "The Stereoscope as a Title Deed to the World," *A Trip around the World through the Stereoscope*, ed. Burton Holmes (New York: McClure, 1901), 9.

42. *Motography* 18, no. 7 (18 August 1917): 330.

43. It will some years before the films in the collection are preserved. For a more complete description of their discovery see the press release at http://www .burtonholmes.org/rediscovery/release.html (accessed 24 September 2012). Currently, more than a dozen of Holmes's films from the 1920s and '30s are available for viewing online at the Burton Holmes Archive website, at http:// www.burtonholmesarchive.com (accessed 24 September 2012). An excerpt from Holmes's film *Among the Geysers of the Yellowstone* (1923) can also be seen on the DVD *Treasures from the American Film Archives, Volume 5: The American West* (2011) (for which I provide the DVD commentary).

44. To download the complete collection of Holmes's published lectures, search

the Internet Archive at http://archive.org/search.php?query=burton%20holmes (accessed 24 September 2012).

45. Charles Musser, with Carol Nelson, *High-Class Moving Pictures: Lyman H. Howe and the Forgotten Era of Traveling Exhibition, 1880–1920* (Princeton: Princeton University Press, 1991).

46. Kaveh Askari, "From 'The Horse in Motion' to 'Man in Motion': Alexander Black's Detective Lectures," *Early Popular Visual Culture* 3, no. 1 (May 2005): 65.

47. Bruno, *An Atlas of Emotion*, 115.

48. Rick Altman, *Silent Film Sound* (New York: Columbia University Press, 2004), 69.

49. Jeanette Roan, "Exotic Explorations: Travels to Asia and the Pacific in Early Cinema," *Re/collecting Early Asian America*, ed. Josephine Lee, Imogene L. Lim, and Yuko Matsukawa (Philadelphia: Temple University Press, 2002), 191.

50. Jeffrey Ruoff, "Show and Tell: The 16 mm Travel Lecture Film," *Virtual Voyages: Cinema and Travel*, ed. Jeffrey Ruoff (Durham: Duke University Press, 2006), 217–37. See also Ruoff's film *The Last Vaudevillian: On the Road with Travelogue Filmmaker John Holod* (1998).

51. Holmes, *The World Is Mine*, ix.

52. See T. J. Jackson Lears, *No Place of Grace: Antimodernism and the Transformation of American Culture, 1880–1920* (Chicago: University of Chicago Press, 1994).

53. White, "Burton Holmes, the Man and His Work," 29.

54. Ibid., 12.

55. Roan, *Envisioning Asia*, 35.

56. Burton Holmes, "Moki Land," *Burton Holmes Travelogues*, vol. 6 (New York: McClure, 1908), 227. Holmes explains later in his lecture that "the name 'Moki'. . . means literally 'dead people,' and was originally a term of derision given by the warlike Apaches and Navajos to these peaceful farmers and home-builders." However, Holmes assures his audience that although they call themselves the "'Hopi,' or 'good people,' . . . the term 'Moki,' once an insult, has almost lost its derisive meaning and is not seriously resented": ibid., 251. An attentive listener or reader might have wondered whether Holmes's disavowal of insult was accurate.

57. Ibid., 228.

58. See Brian W. Dippie, *The Vanishing American: White Attitudes and U.S. Indian Policy* (Lawrence: University Press of Kansas, 1982).

59. Holmes, "Moki Land," 256, 265.

60. Ibid., 278–81.

61. Ibid., 315–16.

62. Ibid., 319–20.

63. Ibid., 228.

64. Along with "Moki Land," Holmes published two other lectures on the West in the same volume: "The Yellowstone National Park" and "The Grand Cañon of Arizona." Similarly, Holmes's predecessor John Stoddard published three lectures on the American West: "The Grand Cañon of the Colorado," "Yellowstone National

Park," and "Southern California." See John Stoddard, *John L. Stoddard's Lectures*, vol. 10 (Boston: Balch Brothers, 1898).

65. Christopher Pinney, "Notes from the Surface of the Image: Photography, Post-colonialism, and Vernacular Modernism," *Photography's Other Histories*, ed. Christopher Pinney and Nicolas Peterson (Durham: Duke University Press, 2003), 202.

66. See Erin Younger, "Changing Images: A Century of Photography on the Hopi Reservation," *Hopi Photographers, Hopi Images*, comp. Victor Masayesva Jr. and Erin Younger (Tucson: University of Arizona Press, 1983), 24.

67. Holmes, "Moki Land," 234.

68. Ibid., 232.

69. Ibid., 336.

70. Ibid., 330–32.

71. Depue began shooting with a 60 millimeter (mm) Demeny camera in 1897 and did not switch to 35mm until 1902: see Depue, "My First Fifty Years in Motion Pictures." These frame enlargements are from a 60mm film print (note the non-35mm sprocket holes).

72. "Publisher's Statement," in Holmes, *A Trip around the World through the Stereo-scope* (Meadville, Pa.: Keystone View Co., 1926), 5.

73. Tim Creswell, *Place: A Short Introduction* (Malden, Mass.: Blackwell, 2004), 11.

74. Ibid., 15.

75. Malcolm Andrews, *Landscape and Western Art* (New York: Oxford University Press, 1999), 15.

76. Unlike most early travelogues, this film has already been briefly discussed in print: see Musser, with Nelson, *High-Class Moving Pictures*, 261–62. The print I describe here is from the collection of the EYE Film Institute. The film's Dutch title is *De Hawaïaneilanden in vogelvlucht*, which translates as "A Bird's-Eye View of Hawaii."

77. Howe's program description of the film published in Musser, with Nelson, *High-Class Moving Pictures*, 261, describes a final section in which the active volcano of Kilauea is shown, but that segment is missing from the EYE Film Institute's print.

78. Musser, with Nelson, *High-Class Moving Pictures*, 261.

79. "History of Hawaii Consolidated Railroad," Laupahoehoe Train Museum web-site, available online at http://www.thetrainmuseum.com/history.html (accessed 25 September 2012).

80. Roland Barthes, "The Death of the Author," *Image, Music, Text*, trans. Stephen Heath (New York: Hill and Wang, 1977), 148.

81. Ibid.

2. "The Living Panorama of Nature"

Epigraphs: H. F. Hoffman, "What People Want," *Moving Picture World*, 9 July 1910, 77; Horace C. Baker, "The Moving Picture Industry," *Nickelodeon* 1, no. 5 (May 1909): 132.

1. "The Forte of the Scenic Film," *Nickelodeon* 3, no. 11 (1 June 1910): 275–76.

2. Ibid., 275.

3. See Bill Nichols, *Representing Reality: Issues and Concepts in Documentary* (Bloomington: Indiana University Press, 1992).

4. Bernadette Bensaude-Vincent and William R. Newman, "Introduction: The Artificial and the Natural: State of the Problem," *The Artificial and the Natural: An Evolving Polarity*, ed. Bernadette Bensaude-Vincent and William R. Newman (Cambridge: MIT Press, 2007), 3–4.

5. Charles Musser, "The Travel Genre in 1903–04: Moving towards Fictional Narrative," *Early Cinema: Space, Frame, Narrative*, ed. Thomas Elsaesser, with Adam Barker (London: British Film Institute, 1990), 123.

6. See Tom Gunning, "Attractions: How They Came into the World," *The Cinema of Attractions Reloaded*, ed. Wanda Strauven (Amsterdam: Amsterdam University Press, 2006), 37.

7. Stephen Bottomore, "'Every Phase of Present-Day Life': Biograph's Non-fiction Production," *Griffithiana* 66–70 (1999–2000): 149.

8. Tom Gunning similarly argues that early nonfiction is very different from documentary as it emerged in the 1920s. See Tom Gunning, "Before Documentary: Early Nonfiction Films and the 'View' Aesthetic," *Uncharted Territory: Essays on Early Nonfiction Film*, ed. Daan Hertogs and Nico de Klerk (Amsterdam: Stichting Nederlands Filmmuseum, 1997), 9–24. The term *documentaire* was used in France as early as 1906, but there too the word did not take on its established significance until the 1920s. See Georges Sadoul, *Dziga Vertov* (Paris: Éditions Champ Libre, 1971), 100.

9. *Moving Picture World* debuted in May 1907 (and continued publication until 1927), while the *Nickelodeon* began publication in January 1909. The *Nickelodeon* changed its name to *Motography* in April 1911 when it switched from weekly to monthly publication; it ceased publication in 1918. *Moving Picture News* ran from 1908 to 1912, when it was renamed *Motion Picture News*, which continued publication until 1930.

10. On early science films, see Oliver Gaycken, *Devices of Curiosity: Early Cinema and Popular Science* (Oxford: Oxford University Press, forthcoming). On early nature films, see Jennifer Peterson, "Glimpses of Animal Life: Nature Films and the Emergence of Classroom Cinema," *Learning with the Lights Off: Educational Film in the United States*, ed. Devin Orgeron, Marsha Orgeron, and Dan Streible (New York: Oxford University Press, 2012), 145–67.

11. Tom Gunning, "Systematizing the Electric Message: Narrative Form, Gender, and Modernity in *The Lonedale Operator*," *American Cinema's Transitional Era: Audiences, Institutions, Practices*, ed. Charlie Keil and Shelley Stamp (Berkeley: University of California Press, 2004), 16. See also the discussion of early cinema periodization in Charlie Keil, *Early American Cinema in Transition: Story, Style, and Filmmaking, 1907–1913* (Madison: University of Wisconsin Press, 2001).

12. André Gaudreault and Philippe Marion, "A Medium Is Always Born Twice . . .," *Early Popular Visual Culture* 3, no. 1 (May 2005): 4.

13. For more on intermediality and its complexity, see Andrew Shail, "Intermediality: Disciplinary Flux or Formalist Retrenchment?," *Early Popular Visual Culture* 8, no. 1 (February 2010): 3–15.

14. David Bordwell, Janet Staiger, and Kristin Thompson, *The Classical Hollywood Cinema: Film Style and Mode of Production to 1960* (New York: Columbia University Press, 1985).

15. For an indication of just how many scenics were released before 1915, see the filmography of early travelogue films released in the United States from 1910 to 1914, compiled from listings in the trade press, in my dissertation: Jennifer Lynn Peterson, "World Pictures: Travelogue Films and the Lure of the Exotic, 1890–1920" (PhD diss., University of Chicago, 1999), app. A, table 1, 290–326. This filmography lists over 1,000 travel films and related nonfiction subjects released in the United States in just these few years.

16. Gunning, "Systematizing the Electric Message," 17.

17. Pathéscope was used from 1911 to the mid-1920s; Edison's 22mm format was introduced in 1912: see Anke Mebold and Charles Tepperman, "Resurrecting the Lost History of 28mm Film in North America," *Film History* 15, no. 2 (2003): 137–51. Pathé also introduced 9.5mm film for the amateur market in Europe in 1922.

18. Anthony Slide, *Before Video: A History of the Non-theatrical Film* (New York: Greenwood, 1992), 35. See also Orgeron et al., *Learning with the Lights Off*.

19. For a sample of the voluminous writing on the Lumières, see Dai Vaughan, "Let There Be Lumière," in Elsaesser, with Barker, *Early Cinema*, 63–67.

20. Bottomore, "Every Phase of Present-Day Life," 149.

21. Ibid., 147.

22. Charles Musser, *The Emergence of Cinema: The American Screen to 1907* (Berkeley: University of California Press, 1990), 179, 259.

23. Charles Musser, with Carol Nelson, *High-Class Moving Pictures: Lyman H. Howe and the Forgotten Era of Traveling Exhibition, 1880–1920* (Princeton: Princeton University Press, 1991), 131–32.

24. This is not to deny the existence of fiction films before 1903–1904, for fiction films were produced from the start. The Lumière film *L'Arroseur arrosé* (1895), for example, is sometimes said to be the first "fiction" film. See André Gaudreault, "Film, Narrative, Narration: The Cinema of the Lumière Brothers," in Elsaesser, with Barker, *Early Cinema*, 68–75. It was the development of a more complex, multi-shot form of film *narrative*, however, that heralded the emergence of the story film in its more popular form in the early 1900s.

25. Charlie Keil and Shelley Stamp, *American Cinema's Transitional Era: Audiences, Institutions, Practices* (Berkeley: University of California Press, 2004), 1.

26. On nickelodeons, see also Russell Merritt, "Nickelodeon Theaters 1905–1914: Building an Audience for the Movies," *The American Film Industry*, ed. Tino Balio (Madison: University of Wisconsin Press, 1976), 59–79; Miriam Hansen, *Babel and Babylon: Spectatorship in American Silent Film* (Cambridge: Harvard University Press, 1991), chaps. 1–3.

27. Eileen Bowser, *The Transformation of Cinema: 1907–1915* (Berkeley: University of California Press, 1990), 122.

28. On the "variety format," see Brooks McNamara, "The Scenography of Popular Entertainment," *Drama Review* 18, no. 1 (March 1974): 59–79; Tom Gunning, *D. W. Griffith and the Origins of American Narrative Film: The Early Years at Biograph* (Urbana: University of Illinois Press, 1994), 86.

29. See Bowser, *The Transformation of Cinema*, esp. 13–20.

30. *Variety*, 24 September 1910; 9 May 1908; 28 August 1909.

31. For a discussion of reels and film length in this period, see Bowser, *The Transformation of Cinema*, chap. 12.

32. It is impossible to ascertain precisely how many travelogues were released in the United States between 1907 and 1915. Despite the apparent thoroughness of the lists of film releases published in the American trade press, there are many cases in which films were not listed. I have viewed numerous surviving travel films in archives that are not listed as releases anywhere in the American trade press. One conclusion to draw from this is that the lists in the trade press are not entirely reliable. (Their numerous misspellings and other errors would tend to confirm this hypothesis.) Nonetheless, app. A, table 1, in Peterson, "World Pictures," culled from these release lists, does contain what I believe to be the majority of the travel films released between 1910 and 1914, even if it is not complete. During those four years, approximately 1,200 travel films were listed as "released."

33. *Motography* 10, no. 6 (20 September 1913): 191.

34. Bowser, *The Transformation of Cinema*, 213.

35. Richard Koszarski, *An Evening's Entertainment: The Age of the Silent Feature Picture, 1915–1928* (Berkeley: University of California Press, 1990), 164.

36. Despite its name, Educational Pictures released mostly comedies in the 1920s. The connection between scenics and comedies in the silent era bears further investigation, for as we have seen, the comedy-scenic combination was perhaps the most common type of split-reel release.

37. For two accounts of early fairground cinema in Europe, see Vanessa Toulmin, "'Within the Reach of All': Traveling Cinematograph Shows on British Fairgrounds, 1896–1914," and Joseph Garncarz, "The Fairground Cinema: A European Institution," trans. Annemone Ligensa, both in *Travelling Cinema in Europe*, ed. Martin Loiperdinger, KINtop-Schriften vol. 10 (Frankfurt am Main: Stroemfeld Verlag, 2008).

38. Gregory Waller, "Tracking the Non-theatrical: The American Cinema in 1915," paper presented at the Chicago Film Seminar, 10 February 2011.

39. George Kleine, unpublished, undated lecture (ca. 1920s), George Kleine Papers, box 40, "Lectures" folder.

40. "Educational Lectures in the Keith and Proctor Theaters," *Moving Picture World*, 4 March 1911, 6–7.

41. Rick Altman, *Film/Genre* (London: British Film Institute, 1999), 50.

42. American Mutoscope and Biograph Company, "Picture Catalogue (November

1902), Museum of Modern Art, New York," *A Guide to Motion Picture Catalogs by American Producers and Distributors, 1894–1908*, ed. Charles Musser, microfilm (Frederick, Md.: University Publications of America, 1985). In his article on early film genres, Gunning finds a similar list in another Biograph catalogue from 1902: comedy views; sports and pastimes views; military views; railroad views; scenic views; views of notable persons; miscellaneous views; trick pictures; marine views; children's pictures; fire and patrol views; Pan American Exposition Views; vaudeville views; educational views; parade pictures: Tom Gunning, "'Those Drawn with a Very Fine Camel's Hair Brush': The Origins of Film Genres," *Iris* 20 (Fall 1995): 54. Apparently, Gunning's list is from a different Biograph catalogue dated 1902, and the slight variation between categories (the different order, the addition of the word "views" to many of the categories in one list) even in these two lists from the same company in the same year indicates the high level of slippage possible in early film classifications.

43. American Mutoscope and Biograph Company, "Picture Catalogue (November 1902), Museum of Modern Art, New York," 119.

44. Ibid., 130.

45. *Lifelong Learning: Visual Aids to Education* (Berkeley: University of California Extension, 1936). This catalogue is available for downloading from the Internet Archive at http://archive.org/details/lifelonglearning05richrich (accessed 30 September 2012).

46. Gunning, "Those Drawn with a Very Fine Camel's Hair Brush," 55.

47. *Nickelodeon* 4, no. 12 (15 December 1910): 343. A review of the film in *Variety* is a little more descriptive and reinforces my suspicion that it probably featured no landscapes whatsoever: "An interesting photographic reproduction of the various feats that Japanese firemen can accomplish on their long bamboo ladders. The interest largely develops through the comparisons that the audience will make with American fire-fighting methods. Picturing fair." The film's classification as scenic demonstrates how far the concept ranged beyond the quintessential pretty scenes of nature: see *Variety*, 7 January 1911, in *Variety Film Reviews*, 24 vols., vol. 1 (New York: Garland, 1983). Throughout this chapter, all quotes from *Variety* are from this volume of *Variety Film Reviews*, which does not use page numbers.

48. *Nickelodeon* 5, no. 7 (18 February 1911): 206; *Motography* 5, no. 6 (June 1911): 160.

49. *Nickelodeon* 4, no. 12 (15 December 1910); *Nickelodeon* 3, no. 8 (15 April 1910): 222; *Motography* 5, no. 5 (May 1911): 111; *Nickelodeon* 5, no. 2 (14 January 1911): 66; *Nickelodeon* 5, no. 1 (7 January 1911): 38; *Nickelodeon* 4, no. 5 (1 September 1910): 144; *Motography* 7, no. 3 (March 1912): 144.

50. *Nickelodeon* 5, no. 7 (18 February 1911): 205.

51. Charlie Keil, "Steel Engines and Cardboard Rockets: The Status of Fiction and Nonfiction in Early Cinema," *Persistence of Vision* 9 (1991): 38.

52. Anne Friedberg, *Window Shopping: Cinema and the Postmodern* (Berkeley: University of California Press, 1993), 96–100. The film is available for viewing or downloading at the Library of Congress's American Memory website. Search by title

at http://memory.loc.gov/ammem (accessed 30 September 2012). For a detailed analysis of another hybrid fiction–nonfiction film, see the discussion of *A Policeman's Tour of the World* (Pathé, 1906) in Philip Rosen, *Change Mummified: Cinema, Historicity, Theory* (Minneapolis: University of Minnesota Press, 2001), 201–24.

53. Charles Musser identifies this nonfiction footage as having come from the Edison films *S.S. "Coptic" Running against the Storm* (1898), *Pilot Leaving "Prinzessen Victoria Luise" at Sandy Hook* (1903), and *Skyscrapers of New York from the North River* (1903): see Musser, "The Travel Genre in 1903–04," 125.

54. *Variety*, 24 December 1910. *Charlie and Kitty in Brussels* was released in the United States on 14 December 1910.

55. *Variety*, 26 February 1910.

56. The film was retitled and rereleased in 1973 as *In the Land of the War Canoes*; a more recent restoration with the original title, *In the Land of the Head Hunters*, toured the United States in 2008: see the website at http://www.curtisfilm.rutgers.edu/index.php?option=com_frontpage&Itemid=1 (accessed 30 September 2012). For more on *In the Land of the Head Hunters* see Fatimah Tobing Rony, *The Third Eye: Race, Cinema, and Ethnographic Spectacle* (Durham: Duke University Press, 1996), 90–98; Brad Evans, "Commentary: Catherine Russell's Recovery of the Head-Hunters," *Visual Anthropology* 11 (Spring 1998): 221–42. The film is now on the National Film Registry under the title *In the Land of the War Canoes* and is available on DVD from Milestone Films.

57. Alison Griffiths, *Wondrous Difference: Cinema, Anthropology, and Turn-of-the-Century Visual Culture* (New York: Columbia University Press, 2002), 242.

58. Richard Abel has found that around 1910, Éclair's weekly travelogues were "usually shot by R. Moreau": Richard Abel, "Éclair: The Other French Film Company," *Griffithiana* 44–45 (May–September 1992): 7. However, production personnel for most of the films I analyze in this book are unknown.

59. Mesguich filmed actuality footage for the Lumière Company, but only in the early years: see Félix Mesguich, *Tours de Manivelle. Souvenirs d'un chasseur d'images* (Paris: Éditions Bernard Grasset, 1933). Holmes's cameraman, Oscar Depue, presented a brief autobiographical account of his film career at the SMPE (Society of Motion Picture Engineers) convention in Chicago in 1947. It was later published as Oscar B. Depue, "My First Fifty Years in Motion Pictures," *A Technological History of Motion Pictures and Television*, ed. Raymond Fielding (Berkeley: University of California Press, 1967), 60–64.

60. Burton Holmes, *The World Is Mine* (Culver City, Calif.: Murray and Gee, 1953), unnumbered plate after 180.

61. In particular, research on nonfiction production by the French companies Pathé, Eclipse, Éclair, and Gaumont is needed. In the United States, more sustained research on Selig's nonfiction production would undoubtedly yield new insights. Some of this kind of work has been undertaken, but much remains to be done. For an account of Éclair's educational Scientia series, see Thierry Lefebvre, "The Scientia Production (1911–1914): Scientific Popularization through Pictures," *Grif-*

fithiana 47 (May 1993): 137–52. For an overview of silent nonfiction in France, see Frédéric Delmeulle, "Production et distribution du documentaire en France (1909–1929)," *1895* 18 (Summer 1995): 200–215.

62. Review of the Eclipse film *Jersey of the British Isles*, "Recent Films Reviewed," *Nickelodeon* 5, no. 5 (4 February 1911): 138. This film is listed in ibid., 149, under the title *Scenes in Jersey Island*, and was released in the United States on 25 January 1911.

63. On Charles Urban and early nonfiction film, see Luke McKernan, "Putting the World before You: The Charles Urban Story," *Young and Innocent? The Cinema in Britain, 1896–1930*, ed. Andrew Higson (Exeter: University of Exeter Press, 2002), 65–77. See also Luke McKernan, "Something More Than a Mere Picture Show: Charles Urban and the Early Non-fiction Film in Great Britain and America, 1897–1925" (PhD diss., Birkbeck College, University of London, 2003).

64. See Peterson, "World Pictures," app. A, table 1.

65. Biograph appears to be an important exception; I have found no evidence that Biograph made any nonfiction films *after* the mid-1900s, and it certainly did not do so after 1910, a drastic turnaround from the early days when nonfiction dominated Biograph's production. Other possible exceptions to this rule — companies that may not have made any nonfiction at this time — are Comet and Republic, both of which were much smaller, independent companies. Further research in this area is needed to reveal which companies made no nonfiction and which companies made just a handful of nonfiction films and why.

66. *Moving Picture World*, 10 February 1912, 528.

67. *Nickelodeon* 3, no. 9 (1 May 1910): 242; *Nickelodeon* 3, no. 11 (1 June 1910): 302.

68. A description of this film was published in *Nickelodeon* 4, no. 3 (1 August 1910): 80: "This short educational subject was made on the beach at Catalina Island, off the coast of Southern California, and shows a party of tourists feeding the pet seals, famed to all tourists. These animals are very intelligent and absolutely fearless. Our picture shows Jupiter and Neptune, two of the largest of the herd, posing before the camera. — 170 feet — Released August 10." Eileen Bowser briefly refers to the establishment in 1910 of Essanay's western studio by Gilbert "Broncho Billy" Anderson: see Bowser, *The Transformation of Cinema*, 151. It is entirely possible that Broncho Billy was among the "party of tourists" mentioned in the film's description; however, the film is apparently no longer extant.

69. See the description in Herbert Reynolds, "Ancient Temples of Egypt," in John L. Fell, *Before Hollywood: Turn-of-the-Century American Film* (New York: Hudson Hills, 1987), 137. The George Eastman House holds a print of the film.

70. Review of Pathé's *Sports in Java*, *Variety*, 25 September 1909.

71. "The Educational Tendency," *Nickelodeon* 4, no. 11 (1 December 1910): 300. It is unclear whether the term "dictators" in the second line is meant as a joke or if the writer actually felt that Pathé was domineering. The term could also simply be a typographical error, substituting for the word "directors."

72. Richard Abel, *The Ciné Goes to Town: French Cinema, 1896–1914* (Berkeley: University of California Press, 1994), 96.

73. Musser, *The Emergence of Cinema*, 488. Musser cites information from Lawrence Karr, "Introduction," in Rita Horwitz, *An Index to Volume 1 of "The Moving Picture World and View Photographer"* (Washington, D.C.: American Film Institute, 1974).

74. Richard Abel, *The Red Rooster Scare: Making Cinema American, 1900–1910* (Berkeley: University of California Press, 1999), 87.

75. For a useful account of the MPPC see Scott Curtis, "A House Divided: The MPPC in Transition," in *American Cinema's Transitional Era*, ed. Charlie Keil and Shelley Stamp (Berkeley: University of California Press, 2004), 239–64.

76. *Moving Picture World*, 24 January 1914, 412. A print of the film is at the EYE Film Institute.

77. *Nickelodeon* 3, no. 10 (15 May 1910): 259.

78. *Motography* 6, no. 1 (July 1911): 43.

79. *Nickelodeon* 5, no. 12 (25 March 1911): 346.

80. General Film Company, *Catalogue of Educational Motion Pictures* (New York: General Film Company, 1912), 36–55, 58. For a more extended account of the General Film Company's reuse of educational films, see Jennifer Peterson, "'The Knowledge Which Comes in Pictures': Educational Films and Early Cinema Audiences," *The Blackwell Companion to Early Cinema, 1890–1914*, ed. André Gaudreault, Nicolas Dulac, and Santiago Hidalgo (Oxford: Blackwell, 2012), 277–97.

81. Advertisement for *How Wild Animals Live*, *Moving Picture World*, 8 November 1913, 645. A poster for this film is reproduced as plate 5.

82. *South: Ernest Shackleton and the Endurance Expedition* is available on DVD from Milestone Films.

83. *90 Degrees South* is available on DVD from Milestone Films.

84. *Simba: The King of the Beasts* and *Grass: A Nation's Battle for Life* are also available on DVD from Milestone Films. *Nanook of the North* is available on DVD from Criterion. For an analysis of *Grass*, see Hamid Naficy, "Lured by the East: Ethnographic and Expedition Films about Nomadic Tribes—The Case of *Grass* (1925)," *Virtual Voyages: Cinema and Travel*, ed. Jeffrey Ruoff (Durham: Duke University Press, 2006), 117–38. For an analysis of *Nanook*, see Rony, *The Third Eye*, 99–126.

85. "Bonehead Exhibitors," *Nickelodeon* 3 no. 6 (15 March 1910): 139.

86. "Picture Psychology," *Nickelodeon* 4, no. 9 (1 November 1910): 245–46; "Scientific and Educational Pictures," *Nickelodeon* 2, no. 6 (December 1909): 166. See also "Travel Pictures Again," *Motography* 7, no. 3 (September 1911): 105–6.

87. See, e.g., the dialogue among Sumiko Higashi, Robert Allen, and Ben Singer on class and Manhattan's nickelodeons in *Cinema Journal* 35, no. 3 (Spring 1996): 72–128. Higashi introduces the debate with "Dialogue: Manhattan's Nickelodeons"; Allen's essay is titled "Manhattan Myopia; or, Oh! Iowa!"; and Singer's essay is titled "New York, Just Like I Pictured It . . ." In addition to this debate, key works on early cinema audiences include Robert Allen, "Motion Picture Exhibition in Manhattan 1906–1912: Beyond the Nickelodeon," *Film before Griffith*, ed. John L. Fell (Berkeley: University of California Press, 1983), 162–75; Robert Allen,

Vaudeville and Film, 1895–1915: A Study in Media Interaction (New York: Arno, 1980); Hansen, *Babel and Babylon*; Merritt, "Nickelodeon Theaters 1905–1914."

88. Review of *O'er Crag and Torrent* (Gaumont, 1910), *Variety*, 9 April 1910.

89. *Variety*, 1 October 1910.

90. On color in silent-era cinema, see Joshua Yumibe, *Moving Color: Early Film, Mass Culture, Modernism* (New Brunswick: Rutgers University Press, 2012). See also Eirik Frisvold Hanssen, "Early Discourses on Colour and Cinema: Origins, Functions, Meanings" (PhD diss., Stockholm University, 2006); Daan Hertogs and Nico de Klerk, eds., *Disorderly Order: Colours in Silent Film* (Amsterdam: Stichting Nederlands Filmmuseum, 1996).

91. Joshua Yumibe, "On the Education of the Senses: Synaesthetic Perception from the 'Democratic Art' of Chromolithography to Modernism," *New Review of Film and Television Studies* 7, no. 3 (September 2009): 262.

92. J. A. Bell to George Kleine, 26 September 1910, George Kleine Papers, box 24, "Gaumont" folder.

93. J. R. Carter to George Kleine, 30 August 1910, George Kleine Papers, box 24, "Gaumont" folder.

94. *Moving Picture World*, 24 January 1914, 436–37.

95. For titles, see Peterson, "World Pictures," app. A, table 1; Bowser, *The Transformation of Cinema*, 104–5.

96. Bowser, *The Transformation of Cinema*.

97. *Ruins of Angkor, Cambodia* is in the collection of the EYE Film Institute Netherlands.

98. "Kleine Shows Scientific Pictures," *Nickelodeon* 3, no. 3 (1 February 1910): 81. For an account of a public education campaign involving this film, see Marina Dahlquist, "'Swat the Fly': Educational Films and Health Campaigns, 1909–1914," *Kinoöffentlichkeit (1895–1920): Entstehung—Etablierung—Differenzierung / Cinema's Public Sphere (1895–1920): Emergence, Settlement, Differentiation*, ed. Corinna Muller and Harro Segeberg (Munich: Schüren-Verlag, 2008), 220–25.

99. "Roosevelt and the Fly," *Nickelodeon* 3, no. 9 (1 May 1910): 223.

100. Ibid. On boxing films in early cinema, including an account of the rise and fall of the African American boxer Jack Johnson (who appeared in numerous early films including the *Jeffries-Johnson Fight* of 1910), see Dan Streible, *Fight Pictures: A History of Boxing and Early Cinema* (Berkeley: University of California Press, 2008).

101. C. Leyman to George Kleine, 17 May 1910, George Kleine Papers, box 24, "Gaumont" folder.

102. All sixteen shots of the six hundred-foot film *Life of a Wood Ant* are described in detail in George Kleine, *Catalogue of Educational Motion Pictures* (Chicago: George Kleine, 1910), 31–32. The same description appears in the *Urbanora Catalogue: Scientific and Educational Subjects* (London: Charles Urban Trading, 1908), 50–52. I discuss these two catalogues in chapter 3. *The Life of a Wood Ant* combined basic imagery of habitat and organisms (the wood ant's nest, the queen ant, winged males); fairground-style imagery that sounds like a copy of another early

nonfiction hit, *The Acrobatic Fly* (an ant lifting a half-sovereign, an ant holding a miniature globe); and the ever popular animal fight trope (ants versus spiders, ants versus caterpillars, ants versus toad). No wonder it sounded like a hit.

103. *Variety*, 30 April 1910.

104. *Variety*, 8 January 1910; 28 August 1909.

3. "The Five-Cent University"

Epigraphs: Oliver G. Pike, "Educational and Scientific Films," *Nickelodeon* 9, no. 10 (15 November 1910): 283; "Moral Teaching by Films," *Motography* 7, no. 1 (July 1911): 5.

1. "The Power of Moving Pictures: They Will Educate, through the Eye, Hundreds of Millions of Children," *New York Evening Journal*, 30 November 1912. This editorial apparently made an impression on George Kleine, who kept a clipping of it among his papers: George Kleine Papers, Library of Congress, box 27, "Historical–Publicity Clippings" folder.

2. "The Power of Moving Pictures."

3. For a related account of the campaign to promote educational films in 1910–13, with an emphasis on audiences, see Jennifer Peterson, "'The Knowledge Which Comes in Pictures': Educational Films and Early Cinema Audiences," *A Companion to Early Cinema*, ed. André Gaudreault, Nicolas Dulac, and Santiago Hidalgo (Malden, Mass.: Wiley-Blackwell, 2012), 277–97.

4. "Current Educational Releases," *Motography* 6, no. 4 (October 1911): 157; "Picture Psychology," *Nickelodeon* 4, no. 9 (1 November 1910): 245; "A Change of Heart toward Scenics," *Nickelodeon* 5, no. 11 (18 March 1911): 294.

5. "Educational Films Gaining Ground," *Nickelodeon* 3, no. 8 (15 April 1910): 196.

6. "Wage War on Shows," *New York Tribune*, 24 December 1908, 4, quoted in Charles Musser, with Carol Nelson, *High-Class Moving Pictures: Lyman H. Howe and the Forgotten Era of Traveling Exhibition, 1880–1920* (Princeton: Princeton University Press, 1991), 191.

7. On the film industry's early efforts to cultivate female audiences, see Shelley Stamp, *Movie-Struck Girls: Women and Motion Picture Culture after the Nickelodeon* (Princeton: Princeton University Press, 2000).

8. William Uricchio and Roberta E. Pearson, *Reframing Culture: The Case of the Vitagraph Quality Films* (Princeton: Princeton University Press, 1993); Rob King, "'Made for the Masses with an Appeal to the Classes': The Triangle Film Corporation and the Failure of Highbrow Film Culture," *Cinema Journal* 44, no. 2 (Winter 2005): 3–33. See also Scott Curtis, "The Taste of a Nation: Training the Senses and Sensibility of Cinema Audiences in Imperial Germany," *Film History* 6, no. 4 (1994): 445–69.

9. Uricchio and Pearson, *Reframing Culture*, 3.

10. King, "Made for the Masses with an Appeal to the Classes," 27.

11. Lee Grieveson, *Policing Cinema: Movies and Censorship in Early-Twentieth-Century America* (Berkeley: University of California Press, 2004).

12. "Prof. Starr's Valuable Contribution," *Nickelodeon* 1, no. 3 (March 1909): 64. Starr's screed was first published as part of a full-page advertisement for the Selig Polyscope Company in the *Chicago Sunday Tribune*, 7 February 1909, n.p.

13. Sidney M. Milkis, "Introduction: Progressivism Then and Now," *Progressivism and the New Democracy*, ed. Sidney M. Milkis and Jerome M. Mileur (Amherst: University of Massachusetts Press, 1999), 4.

14. Robert B. Westbrook, "Public Schooling and American Democracy," *Democracy, Education, and the Schools*, ed. Roger Soder (San Francisco: Jossey-Bass, 1996), 132.

15. Ibid. These enrollment statistics refer to children age fourteen to seventeen.

16. See Joel Spring, *American Education: An Introduction to Social and Political Aspects*, 4th ed. (New York: Longman, 1989), 11.

17. "Pictures in School," *Motography* 7, no. 3 (March 1912): 100–101.

18. *Moving Picture World*, 10 January 1912, 215.

19. *Moving Picture World*, 13 January 1912, 117.

20. Carl Holliday, "The Motion Picture Teacher," *World's Work* 26, no. 1 (May 1913): 49.

21. *Moving Picture World*, 13 January 1912, 117.

22. Gregory S. Jackson, "Cultivating Spiritual Sight: Jacob Riis's Virtual-Tour Narrative and the Visual Modernization of Protestant Homiletics," *Representations* 83 (Summer 2003): 159, n. 6.

23. J. A. Lindstrom, "'Almost Worse than the Restrictive Measures': Chicago Reformers and the Nickelodeons," *Cinema Journal* 39, no. 1 (Fall 1999): 95.

24. Kevin K. Gaines, *Uplifting the Race: Black Leadership, Politics, and Culture in the Twentieth Century* (Chapel Hill: University of North Carolina Press, 1996), 2.

25. Ibid., xv, 2.

26. See W. E. B. Du Bois, "The Talented Tenth" (1903), *The Negro Problem: A Series of Articles by Representative American Negroes of Today* (Miami: Mnemosyne, 1969), 31–75.

27. Emily Mieras, "Latter-Day Knights: College Women, Social Settlements, and Social Class in the Progressive-Era United States," *The Educational Work of Women's Organizations, 1890–1960*, ed. Anne Meis Knupfer and Christine Woyshner (New York: Palgrave Macmillan, 2008), 107.

28. National Kindergarten Association, *Annual Report 1909–1911*, 3, quoted in Barbara Beatty, "'Politics Are Quite Perplexing': Bessie Locke and the National Kindergarten Association Campaign, 1909–60," in Knupfer and Woyshner, *The Educational Work of Women's Organizations*, 199.

29. Grieveson, *Policing Cinema*, 91.

30. Jane Gaines, "From Elephants to Lux Soap: The Programming and 'Flow' of Early Motion Picture Exploitation," *Velvet Light Trap* 25 (Spring 1990): 35.

31. "The Lost Gallery," *Moving Picture World*, 29 July 1911, 186, quoted in Uricchio and Pearson, *Reframing Culture*, 46.

32. Musser, with Nelson, *High-Class Moving Pictures*, 55.

33. Ibid., 9.

34. Ibid., 55.

35. Charles Musser, *The Emergence of Cinema: The American Screen to 1907* (Berkeley: University of California Press, 1990), 222.

36. The "Complete Index to World Film since 1895" lists the length of *La fauvette et le coucou* as 125 meters: see www.citwf.com/film112264.htm (accessed 2 October 2012); advertisement for *How Wild Animals Live, Moving Picture World*, 1 November 1913, 513.

37. See Jennifer Peterson, "Glimpses of Animal Life: Nature Films and the Emergence of Classroom Cinema," *Learning with the Lights Off: Educational Film in the United States*, ed. Devin Orgeron, Marsha Orgeron, and Dan Streible (New York: Oxford University Press, 2012), 145–67.

38. Stephen Bush, review of *How Wild Animals Live, Moving Picture World*, 8 November 1913, 592.

39. H. F. Hoffman, "What People Want," *Moving Picture World*, 9 July 1910, 77.

40. Ibid., 78.

41. Uricchio and Pearson, *Reframing Culture*, 197.

42. Alonzo L. Hamby, "Progressivism: A Century of Change and Rebirth," *Progressivism and the New Democracy*, ed. Sidney M. Milkis and Jerome M. Mileur (Amherst: University of Massachusetts Press, 1999), 43.

43. Uricchio and Pearson, *Reframing Culture*, 21; Grieveson, *Policing Cinema*, esp. 24–26.

44. Lawrence Levine, *Highbrow/Lowbrow: The Emergence of Cultural Hierarchy in America* (Cambridge: Harvard University Press, 1988).

45. John Dewey, *Democracy and Education* (New York: Macmillan, 1916); Simon Patten, *The New Basis of Civilization* (New York: Macmillan, 1907).

46. See Alan Trachtenberg, *The Incorporation of America: Society in the Gilded Age* (New York: Hill and Wang, 1982), chap. 5.

47. Steven J. Ross, *Working-Class Hollywood: Silent Film and the Shaping of Class in America* (Princeton: Princeton University Press, 1998), 14.

48. Robert Allen, "Manhattan Myopia; or, Oh! Iowa!," *Cinema Journal* 35, no. 3 (Spring 1996): 91.

49. "Moving Pictures in Brussels' Schools," *Nickelodeon* 3, no. 2 (15 January 1910): 50.

50. "Travel Pictures Again," *Motography* 6, no. 3 (September 1911): 105.

51. Ibid.

52. "Educational Pictures," *Moving Picture News*, 2 December 1911, 5–6.

53. Louella Parsons, "In and Out of Focus," *New York Morning Telegraph*, 12 August 1923, sec. 5, 4, quoted in Rita Horwitz and Harriet Harrison, *The George Kleine Collection of Early Motion Pictures in the Library of Congress: A Catalog* (Washington, D.C.: Library of Congress, 1980), xiii.

54. Founded in 1847 as the Free Academy, the City University of New York continues to follow its tradition of educating working-class and immigrant students: see the City University of New York website at http://www1.cuny.edu/about/index.html (accessed 2 October 2012).

55. Autobiography of George Kleine for *Motion Picture News* directory, n.d., George Kleine Papers, box 26.

56. See "Kleine to Release Cines," *Motography* 7, no. 1 (January 1912): 34.

57. Kerry Segrave, *Foreign Films in America: A History* (Jefferson, N.C.: McFarland, 2004), 9.

58. Georges Méliès also imported "licensed" films from France in smaller numbers.

59. "Picture Theatre Inspection," *New York Daily Mirror*, 10 April 1909, 15, quoted in Uricchio and Pearson, *Reframing Culture*, 45.

60. See advertisements published in the New York *Clipper* on 1 May 1909, 320, and 17 April 1909, 268, quoted in Tom Gunning, *D. W. Griffith and the Origins of American Narrative Film: The Early Years at Biograph* (Urbana: University of Illinois Press, 1994), 146.

61. George Kleine to Charles Urban, 10 July 1909, George Kleine Papers, box 26.

62. Ibid.

63. For example, when one educator wrote to Kleine in 1911 suggesting a "plan of co-operation" that would assist him in presenting a series of lectures on geography using motion pictures, Kleine refused to help defray the professor's costs, explaining that "we decided long ago upon a policy of not participating in the business of our customers": Wallace A. Atwood to George Kleine, 3 February 1911, George Kleine to Wallace A. Atwood, 9 February 1911, George Kleine Papers, box 39, "Nontheatrical films — General 1911–Aug. 1921" folder.

64. R. D. Williams to George Kleine, 31 March 1921, George Kleine to R. D. Williams, 25 March 1921, George Kleine Papers, box 39, "Nontheatrical films — General 1911–Aug. 1921" folder.

65. Richard Abel, *The Red Rooster Scare: Making Cinema American, 1900–1910* (Berkeley: University of California Press, 1999), 96.

66. "Educational Motion Pictures Imported by George Kleine, 1909–1913," George Kleine Papers, box 26, "Historical file — clippings." See also "Co-operation in Visual Instruction," George Kleine Papers, box 18, "Educational Distribution to Universities 1921–28" folder.

67. Unnamed brief submitted 18 February 1913 to the Committee on Ways and Means, U.S. House of Representatives, George Kleine Papers, box 39, "Nontheatrical films — General, printed matter" folder.

68. George Kleine to Charles Urban, 27 April 1910, George Kleine Papers, box 26, "Historical file — General 1900–28" folder.

69. See, e.g., *Urbanora Catalogue: Scientific and Educational Subjects* (London: Charles Urban Trading, 1908), in the collection of the Margaret Herrick Library at the Academy of Motion Picture Arts and Sciences. Urban began publishing catalogues in 1903 and updated them almost annually until 1909. For a thorough account of Urban's career, including a discussion of some of his catalogues, see Luke McKernan, "'Something More Than a Mere Picture Show': Charles Urban and the Early Non-fiction Film in Great Britain and American, 1897–1925" (PhD diss., Birkbeck College, University of London, 2003).

70. Kleine wrote in a letter, "A vicious attack has been made upon me personally practically accusing me of stealing Mr. Urban's thunder. I have no doubt that he himself instigated the remarks made by 'Stroller' in the Kinematograph Journal": George Kleine to C. M. Rogers, 27 April 1910. George Kleine Papers, box 39, "Nontheatrical films — General 1909–10" folder. For more on "L'affaire Clegg," see Oliver Gaycken, "A Modern Cabinet of Curiosities: George Kleine and the Popular Science Film," chapter 4 of *Devices of Curiosity: Early Cinema and Popular Science* (Oxford: Oxford University Press, forthcoming).

71. George Kleine to C. M. Rogers, 27 April 1910, George Kleine Papers, box 39.

72. "Kleine's Big Educational Catalogue," *Nickelodeon* 3, no. 7 (1 April 1910): 180.

73. George Kleine, *Catalogue of Educational Motion Pictures* (Chicago: George Kleine, 1910), frontispiece, 4.

74. Ibid., 287–88.

75. Ibid., 288.

76. Gaycken, "A Modern Cabinet of Curiosities."

77. *Chicago Daily Journal*, 22 April 1910, clipping sent in a letter to George Kleine, George Kleine Papers, box 39, "Nontheatrical Films — General 1909–10" folder.

78. George Kleine to Mrs. B. R. Johnson, 19 March 1912, George Kleine Papers, box 39, "Nontheatrical Films — General 1911–August 1921" folder.

79. "A Scenic Poster," *Nickelodeon* 5, no. 9 (4 March 1911): 254.

80. Ibid.

81. "A Change of Heart toward Scenics."

82. Advertisement for *Tropical Java of the South Sea Islands*, George Kleine Papers, box 27, "Historical — Publicity — Advertisements" folder.

83. Advertisement for *O'er Crag and Torrent*, George Kleine Papers, box 27, "Historical — Publicity — Advertisements" folder.

84. Advertisements for *The Monastery in the Forest* and *The Mountain Lake*, George Kleine Papers, box 27, "Historical — Publicity — Advertisements" folder.

85. Frank Parker Hulette, "An Interview with Thomas A. Edison," *Moving Picture World*, 22 July 1911, 104.

86. John Nichols briefly discusses Edison's belief that film is a "window on the world" in the larger context of visual education in the 1920s and '30s in his excellent article, "Countering Censorship: Edgar Dale and the Film Appreciation Movement," *Cinema Journal* 46, no. 1 (Autumn 2006): 9.

87. Oliver Gaycken, "The Cinema of the Future: Visions of the Medium as Modern Educator, 1895–1910," *Learning with the Lights Off: Educational Film in the United States*, ed. Devin Orgeron, Marsha Orgeron, and Dan Streible (New York: Oxford University Press, 2012), 72.

88. Winthrop D. Lane, "Edison versus Euclid: Has He Invented a Moving Stairway to Learning," *Survey*, 6 September 1913, 682; Henry H. Goddard, "Pedagogy plus Science Needed," *Survey*, 6 September 1913, 688; Leonard Ayres, "Ladling Learning into Children," *Survey*, 6 September 1913, 686; John Dewey, "Cut-and-Try School Methods," *Survey*, 6 September 1913, 692.

89. See Orgeron et al., *Learning with the Lights Off*.

90. George Kleine to L. W. McChesney, 24 July 1917, George Kleine Papers, box 16, "Edison, Inc." folder. Kleine's sense of humor comes through in his extensive correspondence with McChesney. He concluded this particular letter, "Beware of losing your goat. I have detectives out now looking for various goats that have been lost by our associates, but I trust to find yours wellstabled [*sic*] and entirely at home when next I visit you. Cheer up! There is no Hell."

91. George Kleine to L. W. McChesney, 24 November 1917, George Kleine Papers, box 16, "Edison, Inc." folder. For more on *Conquest Pictures*, see Jennifer Horne, "Nostalgia and Non-fiction in Edison's 1917 *Conquest Program*," *Historical Journal of Film, Radio and Television* 22, no. 3 (2002): 315–31.

92. Despite the failure of Edison's *Conquest* series in 1917, Kleine made one final attempt to promote educational films in 1918, briefly establishing a deal to distribute Lincoln-Parker travelogues, but this attempt was a complete failure within a couple of months. In his papers, Kleine blames the irregularity of delivery and poor quality of the Lincoln-Parker films for this failure: George Kleine Papers, box 33, "Lincoln and Parker Co., 1917–19" folder.

93. "Mr. Edison Speaks Again," *Educational Screen*, February 1925, 69.

94. Curtis, "The Taste of a Nation," 452.

95. "Confidential Memorandum for Mr. Delacroix: Points to Be Covered in an Interview with the Cines Co[mpany]," George Kleine to Messrs. Sussfeld, Lorsch, and Company, New York, 28 June 1912, George Kleine Papers, box 7, "Cines 1912" folder, 2.

96. George Kleine, "Co-operation in Visual Instruction," n.p., George Kleine Papers, box 18, "Educational Distribution to Universities, 1921–28" folder.

97. George Kleine to Thomas Edison, 20 April 1921, George Kleine Papers, box 18, "Educational Films" folder.

98. George Kleine to William Selig, 3 January 1928, George Kleine Papers, box 52, "Selig" folder.

99. George Kleine to Thomas Edison, 20 April 1921, George Kleine Papers, box 18, "Educational Films" folder.

100. "Current Educational Releases."

101. John Dewey, *Art as Experience* (New York: Minton, Balch, 1934).

102. Unnamed, unpublished lecture, n.d., George Kleine Papers, box 40, "Lectures" folder.

4. "Atop of the World in Motion"

1. "Through Alaska and Siberia," *Moving Picture World*, 4 January 1913, 55. The film's survival status today is unknown. According to the *AFI Catalog*, the film was alternately titled *Beverly B. Dobbs Original Alaska-Siberia Motion Pictures*. One competing Alaska filmmaker claimed that Dobbs's film was a re-release of two-year-old footage that had previously been exhibited in nontheatrical venues: *American Film Institute Catalog of Motion Pictures Produced in the United States. Within Our*

Gates: Ethnicity in American Feature Films, 1911–1960 (Berkeley: University of California Press, 1997), 57.

2. Emilie Altenloh, *On the Sociology of the Cinema: The Cinema Business and the Social Strata of Its Audience* (1914), trans. Lance W. Garmer; excerpted in Richard W. McCormick and Alison Guenther-Pal, eds., *German Essays on Film* (New York: Continuum, 2004), 40.

3. In selecting this set of representative titles, I have drawn mostly from the filmography of more than 1,000 early travel films released in the United States from 1910 to 1914 that I compiled for my dissertation: see Jennifer Peterson, "World Pictures: Travelogue Films and the Lure of the Exotic, 1890–1920," PhD diss., University of Chicago, 1999, app. A, table 1, 290–326.

4. Japanese film, one of the first Asian cinemas to find an audience in the U.S. market after the success of Akira Kurosawa's *Rashomon* in 1950, was rarely exhibited in the United States before the Second World War. Mikio Naruse's *Kimiko* is considered the first Japanese sound film to be exhibited in the United States, in 1937, but its screening in New York was a commercial failure and ended after only one week: Kerry Segrave, *Foreign Films in America: A History* (Jefferson, N.C.: McFarland, 1994), 63; Kiyoaki Okubo, "*Kimiko* in New York," *Rouge* 10 (1997), available online at http://www.rouge.com.au/10/kimiko.html (accessed 1 October 2012). The Indian film industry, already producing about three hundred films per year by the mid-1950s, was still shut out of the American market at that time. "To ask a major company to distribute an Indian film would be insanity," one American film executive said in 1957, because the films were so "weird": "India Latest Foreign Land to Badly Understand U.S. Film Economics," *Variety*, 27 February 1957, 10, quoted in Segrave, *Foreign Films in America*, 102.

5. See Junko Ogihara, "Exhibition of Films for Japanese Americans in Los Angeles during the Silent Era," *Film History* 4 (1990): 81–87; Jan Olsson, "Hollywood's First Spectators: Notes on Ethnic Nickelodeon Audiences in Los Angeles," *Aztlán* 26, no. 1 (Spring 2001): 181–95. See also Jan Olsson, *Los Angeles before Hollywood: Journalism and American Film Culture, 1905–1915* (Stockholm: National Library of Sweden, 2008).

6. Edward Said, *Culture and Imperialism* (New York: Vintage, 1993), 159.

7. Christopher Pinney, "Introduction: 'How the Other Half . . . ,'" in *Photography's Other Histories*, ed. Christopher Pinney and Nicolas Peterson (Durham: Duke University Press, 2003), 6.

8. Comment by Ben Brewster, transcribed in Daan Hertogs and Nico de Klerk, *Nonfiction from the Teens: The 1994 Amsterdam Workshop* (Amsterdam: Stichting Nederlands Filmmuseum, 1994), 32.

9. Comment by Stephen Bottomore, transcribed in ibid., 33.

10. Tom Gunning, "Before Documentary: Early Nonfiction Films and the 'View' Aesthetic," *Uncharted Territory: Essays on Early Nonfiction Film*, ed. Daan Hertogs and Nico de Klerk (Amsterdam: Stichting Nederlands Filmmuseum, 1997), 14.

11. Walter Benjamin, "The Work of Art in the Age of Its Technological Reproduc-

ibility: Second Version," trans. Edmund Jephcott and Harry Zohn, *The Work of Art in the Age of Its Technological Reproducibility and Other Writings on Media*, ed. Michael W. Jennings, Brigid Doherty, and Thomas Y. Levin (Cambridge: Harvard University Press, 2008), 27.

12. George Kleine Papers, Manuscript Division, Library of Congress, Washington, D.C.

13. *Motography* 10, no. 13 (21 December 1913): 484.

14. There is some discrepancy about the length of the film's release print. *Motography* lists it at 315 feet, but Kleine's records indicate that it was only 88 feet long. The fiction film on the same reel is listed at 908 feet, making the split reel a standard 1,000-foot release: *Motography* 9, no. 2 (18 January 1913): 67; George Kleine Papers, Manuscript Division, Library of Congress. I suspect that Kleine's figure is the correct one, since his records should be a more reliable source, if only because he had money at stake in these figures. *Motography* seems to have made mistakes of this kind with some frequency (typos, listing the wrong manufacturer), perhaps in part because of the huge amount of information it recorded. Yet the print at the EYE Film Institute Netherlands is listed at an original length of 86 meters, or a little under 300 feet, which is closer to what *Motography* indicated. This may be evidence that the film was cut down for its American release, which is what I suspect to be the case. In any event, the existing print at EYE runs at about three minutes and is therefore nearly complete at the longer release length.

15. *Scenes along the Pescara River, Central Italy* (350 feet) was released on 8 April 1913: *Motography* 9, no. 8 (19 April 1913): 297. A print of the film is held at the EYE Film Institute Netherlands with the title *Aan de oevers van de Pascara*; the film's original title is *Il Pescare*.

16. Gunning, "Before Documentary," 14 (a shorter version of the essay, in German, was first published as "Vor dem Dokumentarfilm: Frühe non-fiction-Filme und die Ästhetik der 'Ansicht,'" *KINtop-Jahrbuch* 4 [1995]: 111–23).

17. Ibid., 15, 24.

18. Paolo Cherchi Usai, "Pornography," *The Encyclopedia of Early Cinema*, ed. Richard Abel (New York: Routledge, 2005), 524–25.

19. Of course, it is always possible that some of the intertitles have been lost over time. And certainly the intertitles on the U.S. print would have been different from the Dutch intertitles that exist on the EYE print.

20. I discuss this film in chapter 5: see figs. 5.9–5.12.

21. The film was released in Europe in August or November 1913, but I have not been able to determine whether it was released in the United States: see Paolo Cherchi Usai, "Société Française des Films et Cinématographes Éclair (1907–1919): A Checklist," *Griffithiana* (May–September 1992), 69, 67.

22. On the Gaumont river films, see Ivo Blom, "'Comme l'eau qui coule': Les films de rivières de Gaumont dans la collection Desmet," *1895* 18 (Summer 1995): 156–63.

23. This film is held by EYE under the title *Oogst van cocosnoten in Amerika*, which translates as *Harvesting Coconuts in America*. I suspect this print might actually be

The Story of a Cocoanut (Selig, 1912). The Selig film ran 150 feet and was released on 12 April 1912 on the same reel with an 850-foot Selig drama, *When the Heart Rules*.

24. Anne Friedberg, *Window Shopping: Cinema and the Postmodern* (Berkeley: University of California Press, 1993), 2. See also Giuliana Bruno, *Streetwalking on a Ruined Map: Cultural Theory and the City Films of Elvira Notari* (Princeton: Princeton University Press, 1993).

25. Review of *In Morocco* (production company unknown), *Variety*, 4 April 1908.

26. The term "tracking shot" came later, of course, but travelogues used this technique of the mobile camera very early on.

27. See Tom Gunning, "'An Unseen Energy Swallows Space': The Space in Early Film and Its Relation to American Avant-Garde Film," *Film before Griffith*, ed. John L. Fell (Berkeley: University of California Press, 1983), 355–66.

28. Although a print of this film exists at the Library of Congress, indicating that it was released in the United States, I have not been able to determine its U.S. release date. A print of this film is also at EYE under the title *Loetschberg*. The two prints have been edited somewhat differently.

29. *Variety*, 26 March 1910.

30. Tom Gunning, "Moving away from the Index: Cinema and the Impression of Reality," *differences* 18, no. 1 (2007): 38.

31. Gilles Deleuze's work on cinematic movement is obviously relevant here, although it follows a different path from that of film theorists of the 1920s, and I do not engage with this aspect of Deleuze in this book: Gilles Deleuze, *Cinema 1: The Movement-Image*, trans. Hugh Tomlinson and Barbara Habberjam (Minneapolis: University of Minnesota Press, 1986).

32. Gunning, "Moving away from the Index," 41.

33. Henri Bergson, *Creative Evolution* (1911), trans. Arthur Mitchell (New York: Modern Library, 1944), 332–33.

34. See Michel Georges-Michel, "Henri Bergson Talks to Us about Cinema," *Le Journal*, 20 February 1914; trans. Louis-Georges Schwartz, *Cinema Journal* 50, no. 3 (Spring 2011): 79–82.

35. Paula Amad, *Counter-archive: Film, the Everyday, and Albert Kahn's Archives de la Planète* (New York: Columbia University Press, 2010), 98–99.

36. Ibid., 103.

37. Hippolyte Adolphe Taine, *Voyage aux eaux des Pyrénées* (Paris: Librairie de L. Hachette et Cie, 1855).

38. Charles Packe, *A Guide to the Pyrenees*, 2d ed. (London: Longmans, Green, 1867), 1.

39. The print at EYE has been given the Dutch title *Een Autotocht in de Pyreneën*, which translates as *A Car Ride in the Pyrenees*. EYE dates its print at circa 1910. In the exhaustive filmography of Pathé by Henri Bousquet, only one film about the Pyrenees was released in the 1909–10 period, so I suspect this might be a film titled *Les Pyrénées pittoresques / The Picturesque Pyrenees*, released in France in October 1909 and in the United States on 2 May 1910: See Henri Bousquet, *Cata-*

logue Pathé des années 1907 à 1909 (Bures-sur-Vyette: Edition Henri Bousquet, 1993), 217; *Moving Picture World*, 5 July 1910, 751; *Nickelodeon* 3, no. 9 (1 May 1910): 238. However, neither the French nor the American reviews of *Les Pyrenees pittoresques* mention the auto-tour aspect of EYE's print, so I cannot be completely sure that this is a match.

40. W. J. T. Mitchell, "Imperial Landscape," *Landscape and Power*, ed. W. J. T. Mitchell (Chicago: University of Chicago Press, 1994), 23–24. See in the same volume David Bunn's cogent analysis of a popular eighteenth-century picturesque engraving that includes a European lead-in figure: "'Our Wattled Cot': Mercantile and Domestic Space in Thomas Pringle's African Landscapes," 129–36.

41. *L'Auvergne pittoresque* was released in the United States in fall 1913 with the title *The Auvergne Mountains, Central France*.

42. *Motography* 10, no. 12 (13 December 1913): 443–44.

43. Eric J. Hobsbawm, "Introduction: Inventing Traditions," *The Invention of Tradition*, ed. Eric Hobsbawm and Terence Ranger (Cambridge: Cambridge University Press, 1983), 2.

44. Dale L. Johnson, "On Oppressed Classes," *Dependence and Underdevelopment: Latin America's Political Economy*, ed. James D. Cockcroft, Andre Gunder Frank, and Dale L. Johnson (New York: Doubleday, 1972), 277, quoted in Cristóbal Kay, *Latin American Theories of Development and Underdevelopment* (New York: Routledge, 1989), 66. Chapter 3 of Kay's book provides a useful overview of the term "internal colonialism," including its various definitions, its use by Latin American studies, and critiques of the concept.

45. Michael Hechter, *Internal Colonialism: The Celtic Fringe in British National Development* (Berkeley: University of California Press, 1975).

46. Michael Hardt and Antonio Negri, *Empire* (Cambridge: Harvard University Press, 2000), xii.

47. David Spurr, *The Rhetoric of Empire: Colonial Discourse in Journalism, Travel Writing, and Imperial Administration* (Durham: Duke University Press, 1993).

48. Peter Dunwoodie, *Writing French Algeria* (Oxford: Clarendon, 1998), 51.

49. Ibid., 54.

50. The print at the British Film Institute is in black and white, however, while the print at EYE has color tinting.

51. John Barrell, *The Dark Side of the Landscape: The Rural Poor in English Painting, 1730–1840* (Cambridge: Cambridge University Press, 1980).

52. See Roland Barthes, "The Reality Effect," *The Rustle of Language*, trans. Richard Howard (New York: Hill and Wang, 1986), 141–48.

53. Robert J. C. Young, *Colonial Desire: Hybridity in Theory, Culture and Race* (London: Routledge, 1995), 13.

54. *Motography* 9, no. 5 (1 March 1913): 165. *Native Industries in Soudan, Egypt* was released in the United States on 28 February 1913. Its survival status today is unknown.

55. Spurr, *The Rhetoric of Empire*, 3.

56. For an extended analysis of these kinds of images of veiled women see Malek Al-loula, *The Colonial Harem*, trans. Myrna Godzich and Wlad Godzich (Minneapolis: University of Minnesota Press, 1986). See also Carole Naggar, "The Unveiled: Algerian Women, 1960," *Aperture* 119 (1990): 2–11. Naggar discusses photographs of unveiled Algerian women taken by the French army for identity cards during the war between France and Algeria as a kind of rape. The women's "angry look is the 'evil eye' that they cast to protect themselves and to curse their enemies": Naggar, "The Unveiled," 8. For Naggar, "These glaring gazes alone guarantee their real identities": Naggar, "The Unveiled," 8. It seems reductive to equate these women's "real identities" with their "glaring gazes," but what Naggar means, I think, is that these gazes are a protective mechanism to *prevent* strangers from knowing their real identities, a kind of substitute veil. Also relevant here are Frantz Fanon, "Algeria Unveiled," *A Dying Colonialism*, trans. Haakon Chevalier (New York: Grove, 1967); Winifred Woodhull, "Unveiling Algeria," *Genders* 10 (Spring 1991): 112–30.

57. Mark Vernet, "The Look at the Camera," trans. Dana Polan, *Cinema Journal* 28, no. 2 (Winter 1989): 55. Some earlier discussions about the look at the camera can be found in Paul Willemen, "Letter to John," *Screen* 21, no. 2 (Summer 1980): 53–66; Peter Lehman, "Looking at Ivy Looking at Us Looking at Her," *Wide Angle* 5, no. 3 (1983): 59–63.

58. Ibid., 56.

59. Lauren Rabinovitz, *For the Love of Pleasure: Women, Movies, and Pleasure in Turn-of-the-Century Chicago* (New Brunswick: Rutgers University Press, 1998), 46.

60. For more on Bergson and vitalism, see Inga Pollmann, "Cinematic Vitalism: Theories of Life and the Moving Image" (PhD diss., University of Chicago, 2011).

5. Scenic Films and the Cinematic Picturesque

1. *Picturesque Auvergne* (Lux Film, ca. 1912), *Picturesque Andalusia* (Pathé, ca. 1907), *Picturesque Japan* (Éclair, 1913), and *Picturesque Rocks of Baume-les-Messieurs* (Eclipse, 1913) are all in the collection of the EYE Film Institute Netherlands. *Picturesque Portugal* (Éclair, 1911), *Picturesque Venice* (Éclair, 1917), and *Picturesque Algeria* (Éclair, ca. 1919) are listed in Paolo Cherchi Usai, "Société Française des Films et Cinématographes Éclair (1907–1919): A Checklist," *Griffithiana* (May–September 1992). *Ceylon, Real-Life and Picturesque / Ceylan, vécu et pittoresque* (Pathé, 1905), *Picturesque Roumania* (Gaumont, 1912), *Picturesque Holland* (Pasquali, 1911), *Picturesque Colorado* (Rex Motion Picture Company, 1911), and *Picturesque India* (Vitagraph Company of America, 1912) are all in the collection of the BFI National Archive, London. The list could continue for pages, but you get the point.

2. Both Selig films are described in release flyers in the William Selig Papers, Academy of Motion Picture Arts and Sciences' Margaret Herrick Library, Beverly Hills, Calif.

3. The film itself apparently no longer exists.

4. Linda Nochlin, "The Imaginary Orient," *The Politics of Vision: Essays on Nineteenth-Century Art and Society* (New York: Harper and Row, 1989), 50.

5. Giorgio Bertellini, *Italy in Early American Cinema: Race, Landscape, and the Picturesque* (Bloomington: Indiana University Press, 2010).

6. Gary Harrison and Jill Heydt-Stevenson, "Variations on the Picturesque: Authority, Play, and Practice," *European Romantic Review* 13 (2002): 3–10.

7. Tom Gunning, "The Cinema of Attractions: Early Film, Its Spectator and the Avant-Garde," *Early Cinema: Space, Frame, Narrative*, ed. Thomas Elsaesser, with Adam Barker (London: British Film Institute, 1990), 58.

8. Tom Gunning, "An Aesthetic of Astonishment: Early Film and the (In)Credulous Spectator," *Viewing Positions: Ways of Seeing Film*, ed. Linda Williams (New Brunswick: Rutgers University Press, 1994), 121–22.

9. André Gaudreault and Philippe Marion, "The Mysterious Affair of Styles in the Age of Kine-attractography," *Early Popular Visual Culture* 8, no. 1 (February 2010): 21.

10. Hugo Munsterberg, *The Photoplay: A Psychological Study* (New York: D. Appleton, 1916), 233; Vachel Lindsay, *The Art of the Moving Picture* (New York: Macmillan, 1922 [1915]), 17. See also Laura Marcus, "'A New Form of True Beauty': Aesthetics and Early Film Criticism," chapter 3 of *The Tenth Muse: Writing about Cinema in the Modernist Period* (Oxford: Oxford University Press, 2007).

11. Joan Shelley Rubin provides a useful overview of the term's rising and falling cultural fortunes in the introduction to *The Making of Middlebrow Culture* (Chapel Hill: University of North Carolina Press, 1992). The classic essay on the middlebrow (first published in 1960, and thus relevant for a later era) is Dwight Macdonald's "Masscult and Midcult," in *Masscult and Midcult: Essays against the American Grain* (New York: New York Review of Books, 2011), 3–71.

12. Lawrence Levine has traced the emergence of terms such as "highbrow" and "lowbrow" in *Highbrow/Lowbrow: The Emergence of Cultural Hierarchy in America* (Cambridge: Harvard University Press, 1988), 221–23.

13. There has been (and continues to be) much writing on the picturesque: see, e.g., Christopher Hussey, *The Picturesque: Studies in a Point of View*, repr. ed. (London: Cass, 1967 [1927]); Walter John Hipple Jr., *The Beautiful, the Sublime, and the Picturesque in Eighteenth-Century British Aesthetic Theory* (Carbondale: Southern Illinois University Press, 1957); Martin Price, "The Picturesque Moment," *From Sensibility to Romanticism: Essays Presented to Frederick A. Pottle*, ed. Frederick W. Hilles and Harold Bloom (Oxford: Oxford University Press, 1965); Anne Bermingham, *Landscape and Ideology: The English Rustic Tradition, 1740–1860* (Berkeley: University of California Press, 1986); Sidney Robinson, *Inquiry into the Picturesque* (Chicago: University of Chicago Press, 1991); John Dixon Hunt, *Gardens and the Picturesque: Studies in the History of Landscape Architecture* (Cambridge: MIT Press, 1992); Kim Ian Michasiw, "Nine Revisionist Theses on the Picturesque," *Representations* 38 (Spring 1992): 76–100; Laurent Chatel, "'Getting the Picture' of the Picturesque: Some Thoughts on the Greatest British Aesthetic

Muddle of the Eighteenth and Nineteenth Centuries," *XVII–XVIII: Bulletin de la Société d'Études Anglo-Américaines du XVIIe et XVIIIIe Siècles* 51 (2000): 229–48; David Marshall, "The Problem of the Picturesque," *Eighteenth-Century Studies* 35, no. 3 (Spring 2002): 413–37; Harrison and Heydt-Stevenson, "Variations on the Picturesque." I discuss other examples more fully and cite them in the text. From Bermingham on, critics have tended to assail the picturesque for its reactionary politics. Michasiw astutely observes, "The intensity of these condemnations is somewhat surprising. Later eighteenth-century aesthetic fads and fashions tend not to rouse passions at this late date": Michasiw, "Nine Revisionist Theses on the Picturesque," 76. While this comment is certainly apt, Michasiw does not account for the way the picturesque persisted well beyond the confines of the eighteenth century. In fact, although the word is hardly used anymore, many of its visual strategies remain present in our culture today. I suspect the picturesque's unfashionable persistence is the source of many critics' impulse to condemn it.

14. William Gilpin, "On Picturesque Travel" (1792), reprinted in *The Picturesque: Literary Sources and Documents*, ed. Malcolm Andrews, 3 vols. (East Sussex: Helm Information, 1994), 2:22.

15. One of the most famous early accounts of picturesque travel is William Wordsworth's walking tour of the Wye Valley with his sister Dorothy in the summer of 1798, where they encountered the renowned Tintern Abbey. Wordsworth's own antagonistic relationship with the picturesque is well known, but it is interesting to note that he still went to the same places canonized by the typical picturesque tourist itinerary. The picturesque was certainly not the only rubric through which to experience natural landscapes at the turn of the nineteenth century, but it was the most popular, and therefore a force to contend with. For a useful discussion of the "man of taste," see Andrew Hemingway, *Landscape Imagery and Urban Culture in Early Nineteenth-Century Britain* (Cambridge: Cambridge University Press, 1992), chap. 4.

16. See William Gilpin, *Observations on the River Wye, and Several Parts of South Wales, etc. relative chiefly to Picturesque Beauty; made in the Summer of the Year 1770* (1782), and Thomas West, *A Guide to the Lakes in Cumberland, Westmoreland and Lancashire* (1778), both reprinted in Andrews, *The Picturesque*, 1:241–78, 281–314. Gilpin's text is reprinted in its entirety; West's is substantially extracted.

17. See William Gilpin, *Three Essays: On Picturesque Beauty; on Picturesque Travel; and on Sketching Landscape, to which is added a Poem, on Landscape Painting* (1792, 1794), Uvedale Price, *Essays on the Picturesque, as compared with the Sublime and the Beautiful* (1810), and Richard Payne Knight, *Analytical Inquiry into the Principles of Taste* (1805), all reprinted in Andrews, *The Picturesque*, 2:5–60, 72–141, 326–51. Gilpin's text is fully reproduced; Price's and Knight's are extensively extracted.

18. Michasiw, "Nine Revisionist Theses on the Picturesque," 84.

19. Malcolm Andrews, *The Search for the Picturesque: Landscape Aesthetics and Tourism in Britain, 1760–1800* (Aldershot: Scolar, 1989), 44. My discussion of the pictur-

esque is greatly indebted to Andrews's careful work, both in this text and in *The Picturesque*.

20. Burke's opposition to the French Revolution is emblematic here. For a good discussion of Burke's political views and influence, see Isaac Kramnick, *The Rage of Edmund Burke: Portrait of an Ambivalent Conservative* (New York: Basic Books, 1977). Kramnick writes, "Conservatism was born, the legend goes, with Edmund Burke": ibid., 4.

21. For more on this see W. J. T. Mitchell, "Eye and Ear: Edmund Burke and the Politics of Sensibility," *Iconology: Image, Text, Ideology* (Chicago: University of Chicago Press, 1986), chap. 5; Ann Bermingham, "System, Order, and Abstraction: The Politics of English Landscape Drawing around 1795," *Landscape and Power*, ed. W. J. T. Mitchell (Chicago: University of Chicago Press, 1994), 77–101.

22. Despite the fact that Burke's *Enquiry* was not held in high favor by many Romantics — William Blake, for example, felt "Contempt and Abhorrence" for it — it nonetheless had a great impact on the artistic practices of the nineteenth century, partly because it helped to generate the new picturesque aesthetics. The term "vogue of feeling" is from James T. Boulton, "Editor's Introduction," in Edmund Burke, *A Philosophical Enquiry into the Origin of Our Ideas of the Sublime and Beautiful*, ed. James T. Boulton (Notre Dame, Ind.: University of Notre Dame Press, 1968 [1757]), xciv; William Blake, *Works* (London: Nonesuch, 1948), 809, quoted in Boulton, "Editor's Introduction," lxxxii. See also Boulton, "Editor's Introduction," lxxxi–cxxvii, for a useful account of the *Enquiry*'s influence. Boulton demonstrates how influential Burke's writing was on Immanuel Kant, whose *Critique of Judgment* was published in 1790, but he also argues that Kant "points to the central weakness in Burke's empirical system: it depends purely on egoistic judgments, on the individual's appraisal of personal sensory experiences, and no universal laws can be laid down": Boulton, "Editor's Introduction," cxxvii.

23. Price, *Essays on the Picturesque*, 2:90, 85.

24. Burke, *Philosophical Enquiry into the Origin of Our Ideas of the Sublime and Beautiful*, 39, 57.

25. Ibid., 91, 114, 39.

26. Immanuel Kant, *Critique of Judgment*, trans. Werner S. Pluhar (Indianapolis: Hackett, 1987), 99. For one examination of the uses of the sublime in nineteenth- and twentieth-century America, see David Nye, *American Technological Sublime* (Cambridge: MIT Press, 1994).

27. Ibid., 49.

28. Gilpin, "On Picturesque Travel," 2:24.

29. For a good discussion of the Claude glass, see Malcolm Andrews, "Travelling 'Knick-Knacks,'" in Andrews, *The Search for the Picturesque*, esp. 67–73. See also Bertellini, *Italy in Early American Cinema*, 30–31.

30. Rosalind Krauss, *The Originality of the Avant-Garde and other Modernist Myths* (Cambridge: MIT Press, 1985), 163, 166.

31. Barbara Maria Stafford, *Voyage into Substance: Art, Science, Nature, and the Illustrated Travel Account, 1760–1840* (Cambridge: MIT Press, 1984), 3.

32. Price, *Essays on the Picturesque*, 2:85.

33. Ibid., 2:88.

34. John Ruskin, "On the Turnerian Picturesque," in *Modern Painters* vol. 4 (1856); reprinted in Andrews, *The Picturesque*, 3:352–54.

35. Ibid., 359, note 5. For a good discussion of Ruskin's attempts to modify the picturesque, see John Macarthur, "The Heartlessness of the Picturesque: Sympathy and Disgust in Ruskin's Aesthetics," *Assemblage*, no. 32 (April 1997): 126–41.

36. Gilpin, "On the Principles on Which the Author's Sketches Are Composed" (1804), reprinted in Andrews, *The Picturesque*, 2:287.

37. Gilpin, *Observations on the River Wye*, 245.

38. Ibid., 245.

39. William Marshall, *A Review of the Landscape* (1795), 255–56, quoted in Andrews, *The Search for the Picturesque*, 66.

40. These two films are in the EYE collection.

41. Nochlin, "The Imaginary Orient," 50.

42. Ann Bermingham has claimed that these were often derided by his contemporaries: "Unlike the tours, which were enormously popular, Gilpin's picturesque illustrations were generally disliked": Bermingham, "System, Order, and Abstraction," 87. While Gilpin's sketches are certainly not the work of a master artist, Bermingham's evidence for this dislike is rather scant, and, in fact, his tour books, of which his sketches were an essential feature, were enormously popular. One might hypothesize, then, that the disapproval was not unanimous, but limited to a specific realm of art "experts."

43. Bermingham, *Landscape and Ideology*, 84.

44. Andrews, *The Picturesque*, 1:22.

45. Chatel, "Getting the Picture," 237.

46. Edwin Lawrence Godkin, "Chromo-Civilization," *Nation*, 24 September 1874, 201–2.

47. Catharine Esther Beecher and Harriet Beecher Stowe, *The New Housekeeper's Manual*, rev. title (New York: J. B. Ford, 1873), 94, quoted in Peter Marzio, *The Democratic Art: Pictures for a 19th-Century America, Chromolithography 1840–1900* (Boston: David R. Godine, 1979).

48. G. W. Bitzer, *Billy Bitzer: His Story* (New York: Farrar, Straus and Giroux, 1973), 83–84. It is perhaps worth noting that Bitzer (or his editor) incorrectly attributes the original painting upon which the chromo was based to "Millay." I am grateful to Tom Gunning for bringing this Bitzer reference to my attention.

49. Joshua Yumibe, "On the Education of the Senses: Synaesthetic Perception from the 'Democratic Art' of Chromolithography to Modernism," *New Review of Film and Television Studies* 7, no. 3 (September 2009): 265–66.

50. Levine, *Highbrow/Lowbrow*, 160.

51. Sue Rainey, *Creating Picturesque America: Monument to the Natural and Cultural Landscape* (Nashville: Vanderbilt University Press, 1994), 292.

52. Review of *Wonders of Nature* (Kalem, 1909), by Rush, *Variety*, 28 August 1909.

53. William Combe, *The Tour of Dr. Syntax, in Search of the Picturesque* (London: Ackermann, 1813).

54. Mark Twain, *The Innocents Abroad* (New York: Signet Classic, 1966 [1869]), 37.

55. Review of *Motoring around the World* (production company unknown, 1908) by Rush, *Variety*, 18 July 1908.

56. Review of *Johnny's Pictures of the Polar Regions* (Pathé, 1910), U.S. release 15 April 1910, in *Nickelodeon* 3, no. 8 (15 April 1910): 217.

57. Review of *Johnny's Pictures* by Rush, *Variety* 23 April 1910. The polar regions were a popular film subject at this time, when the Cook and Peary expeditions were in the news. One month earlier, Pathé had released a straight-faced film on the polar regions, released in the United States under the title *The Polar Bear Hunt*. This film is reviewed in *Nickelodeon* 3, no. 7 (1 April 1910): 188. A print of it is at the EYE Film Institute Netherlands under the title *Een Berenjacht in de poolstrecken* (Bear Hunting in the Polar Regions).

58. Linda M. Austin, "Aesthetic Embarrassment: The Reversion to the Picturesque in Nineteenth-Century English Tourism," *English Literary History* 74 (2007): 629–53.

59. For a discussion of these cartoon parodies of the 1930s, see Hank Sartin, "Drawing on Hollywood: Warner Bros. Cartoons and Hollywood, 1930–1960" (PhD diss., University of Chicago, 1998), chap. 3.

60. I am grateful to the film historian and collector Joseph Eckhardt for making a copy of this print available to me.

61. The film's release is announced in *Nickelodeon*'s "Record of Current Films," 11 March 1911, with the title *The Thames from Richmond to Oxford*.

62. "Recent Films Reviewed," *Nickelodeon* 5, no. 12 (25 March 1911): 335.

63. *The Thames Illustrated* was still being reprinted as late as 1983.

64. For more on this and other Gaumont river films, see Ivo Blom, "'Comme l'eau qui coule': Les films de rivières de Gaumont dans la collection Desmet," *1895* 18 (Summer 1995): 156–63. Blom reports that *L'Orne* was released in the Netherlands on 13 December 1912 and shown at Jean Desmet's theater, the Cinéma Parisien in Rotterdam, the week of 16 December 1912. A print is in the EYE collection. I have not been able to find a U.S. release date for the film, although that does not mean it was never released in the United States. George Kleine imported other Gaumont river films around this time, such as *Gorges of the Bourne River, France* (U.S. release 28 January 1911) and *The Beautiful Gorges of Tarn* (U.S. release 11 March 1911).

65. Pathé released this film in the United States on 28 November 1913 with the title *The Capital of the Malay States* (333 feet). The film was classified as a scenic. A print is in the EYE collection.

66. Roland Barthes, "The *Blue Guide*," *Mythologies*, trans. Annette Lavers (1957; New York: Hill and Wang, 1972), 74.

6. "A Weird and Affecting Beauty"

1. James B. Crippen, "An Educational Innovation," *Nickelodeon* 5, no. 8 (25 February 1911): 215.
2. "Exporting the American Film," *Motography* 6, no. 2 (August 1911): 90.
3. Jean Epstein, *La Poésie d'aujourd'hui, un nouvel état d'intelligence* (Paris: La Sirène, 1921), 132. I am grateful to Christophe Wall-Romana for calling my attention to this quotation, and for providing this translation. The original reads: "Une idée qu'on croyait usée, vide et vieille, projetée contre une autre aussi finie, et du choc de ces décrépitudes naît une jeune étincelle."
4. Judith Thissen calls this the "founding myth of Hollywood's democratic nature" in "Jewish Immigrant Audiences in New York City, 1905–14," *American Movie Audiences: From the Turn of the Century to the Early Sound Era*, ed. Melvin Stokes and Richard Maltby (London: British Film Institute, 1999), 16. For an overview of revisionist debates about film audiences, see Melvin Stokes, "Introduction: Reconstructing American Cinema's Audiences," 2–5.
5. Mary Heaton Vorse, "Some Picture Show Audiences," *Outlook*, 24 June 1911, 442.
6. Ibid., 446–47.
7. Ibid., 441, 445, 447.
8. Kathy Peiss, *Cheap Amusements: Working Women and Leisure in Turn-of-the-Century New York* (Philadelphia: Temple University Press, 1986), 149. See also Lauren Rabinovitz, *For the Love of Pleasure: Women, Movies, and Culture in Turn-of-the-Century Chicago* (New Brunswick: Rutgers University Press, 1998).
9. Peiss, *Cheap Amusements*, 150.
10. Sabine Haenni, *The Immigrant Scene: Ethnic Amusements in New York, 1880–1920* (Minneapolis: University of Minnesota Press, 2008), 7.
11. Miriam Hansen, *Babel and Babylon: Spectatorship in American Silent Film* (Cambridge: Harvard University Press, 1991), 12.
12. Ibid., 12–13.
13. Ibid., 13.
14. Joseph Medill Patterson, "The Nickelodeons: The Poor Man's Elementary Course in the Drama," *Saturday Evening Post*, 23 November 1907, 11.
15. Barton W. Currie, "The Nickel Madness," *Harper's Weekly*, 14 August 1907, 1246.
16. Herbert A. Jump, "The Child's Leisure Hour," *Motography* 7, no. 3 (March 1912): 115. Of course, one wonders how this immigrant who claims not to speak English came to be quoted in English, a detail that casts doubt upon the veracity of the quotation.
17. W. T. Hewetson, "The Motion Picture Problem," address delivered to the Women's Club in Freeport, Ill., quoted in *Moving Picture World*, 20 January 1912, 216.
18. "The Forte of the Scenic Film," *Nickelodeon* 3, no. 11 (1 June 1910): 275.
19. Frederick Starr, "The World before Your Eyes," *Chicago Sunday Tribune*, 7 February 1909, sec. 7, reproduced under the headline "Prof. Starr's Valuable Contribution" in *Nickelodeon* 1, no. 3 (March 1909): 64.

20. Frederick Starr Papers, Regenstein Library Special Collections, University of Chicago, scrapbook no. 12, n.p.

21. Release flyer for *In Japan* (Selig, 1911), William Selig Papers, Academy of Motion Picture Arts and Sciences' Margaret Herrick Library, Beverly Hills, Calif.

22. Frederick Starr Papers. See also Nancy L. Evans, "Frederick Starr: Missionary for Anthropology" (master's thesis, Department of Anthropology, Indiana University, Bloomington, 1987).

23. Jonathan Culler, "The Semiotics of Tourism," *Framing the Sign: Criticism and Its Institutions* (Norman: University of Oklahoma Press, 1988), 155.

24. Ibid., 165. See also Guy Debord, *Society of the Spectacle*, trans. Donald Nicholson-Smith (New York: Zone Books, 1995).

25. Review of *One Thousand Miles through the Rockies* (Edison, 1912), *Moving Picture World*, 6 April 6, 1912, 31.

26. "The Only Filipino Amusement," *Motography* 7, no. 2 (February 1912): 88.

27. "South Africa's Picture Shows," ibid., 78.

28. "Russia's Picture Shows," ibid., 72. Indeed, I have found some evidence that such exhibitions of travelogues to potential immigrants did take place: see Jennifer Peterson, "Travelogues and Immigrants," *Domitor 2008: Proceedings of the Domitor Conference on Early Cinema* (Perpignan: Presses Universitaires de Perpignan, 2010), 269–80.

29. "Growing Importance of Motion Picture Shows," *Nickelodeon* 1, no. 2 (February 1909): 53.

30. Hiroshi Komatsu, "From Natural Colour to the Pure Motion Picture Drama: The Meaning of Tenkatsu Company in the 1910s of Japanese Film History," *Film History* 7, no. 1 (Spring 1995): 70–73.

31. Siegfried Kracauer, "Photography" (1927), *The Mass Ornament: Weimar Essays*, trans. and ed. Thomas Y. Levin (Cambridge: Harvard University Press, 1995), 57–58.

32. Ibid., 59.

33. Miriam Hansen, *Cinema and Experience: Siegfried Kracauer, Walter Benjamin, and Theodor W. Adorno* (Berkeley: University of California Press, 2012), 30.

34. Ibid., 37.

35. Ibid. Hansen is quoting here from Kracauer, "Photography," 62–63.

36. A print of this film is in the collection of the EYE Film Institute Netherlands. Although this book focuses primarily on travelogues that were exhibited in the United States, I have not been able to find evidence that this film was shown in the United States. However, the film is filled with images of European tourists; thus, I intend for it to stand here as one example of the many travelogue films that explicitly document modern experience.

37. Mark Twain, "Marienbad—A Health Factory," first published as "An Austrian Health Factory," *Chicago Daily Tribune*, 7 February 1892, and reprinted in *The Complete Essays of Mark Twain*, ed. Charles Neider (New York: Da Capo, 2000), 100.

38. Henri Lefebvre, *Critique of Everyday Life*, trans. John Moore (London: Verso, 1992), 40.

39. Thomas Mann, *The Magic Mountain*, trans. John E. Woods (New York: Vintage, 1996 [1924]), 481.

40. Ibid., 310–11.

41. Ibid., 311–12.

42. Ibid., 312.

43. Janelle Blankenship, "Arno Holz vs. Thomas Mann: Modernist Media Fantasies," *Modernist Cultures* 1, no. 2 (October 2005): 98.

44. Lauren Rabinovitz, "'Bells and Whistles': The Sound of Meaning in Train Travel Film Rides," *The Sounds of Early Cinema*, ed. Richard Abel and Rick Altman (Bloomington: Indiana University Press, 2001), 168.

45. Rick Altman, *Silent Film Sound* (New York: Columbia University Press, 2004), 182.

46. On the lecturer in early film, see the special volume of *Iris* (22 [Autumn 1996]). See also Tom Gunning, "The Scene of Speaking: Two Decades of Discovering the Film Lecturer," *Iris* 27 (Spring 1999): 67–79; Richard Crangle, "'Next Slide Please': The Lantern Lecture in Britain, 1890–1910," in Abel and Altman, *The Sounds of Early Cinema*, 39–47; Altman, *Silent Film Sound*, chap. 8.

47. George W. Beynon, *Musical Presentation of Motion Pictures* (New York: G. Schirmer, 1921), 90.

48. Erno Rapee, *Encyclopaedia of Music for Pictures* (New York: Belwin, 1925), 9–10.

49. Beynon, *Musical Presentation of Motion Pictures*, 92–93.

50. Ibid., 91.

51. Ibid., 92.

52. Ibid., 94.

53. Altman, *Silent Film Sound*, 195.

54. Ibid., 196.

55. E. B. Lockwood, "Travelogues and Topicals," *Motography* 7, no. 6 (June 1912): 257.

56. "Bonehead Exhibitors," *Nickelodeon* 3, no. 6 (15 March 1910): 139–40.

57. "Rainey African Pictures Making Good," *Moving Picture World*, 11 May 1912, 533. For a description of these films, see "The Paul Rainey African Pictures," *Moving Picture World*, 20 April 1912, 214–15.

58. Benyon, *Musical Presentation of Motion Pictures*, 138.

59. Slightly different prints of this film are at EYE and the Library of Congress. The print at EYE is titled *Loetschberg*; the print at the Library of Congress is titled *From Spiez to Loetschberg, Switzerland*, and the original French title is *Chemin de fer du Loetschberg*. I have not been able to find the film's U.S. release date.

60. See Raymond Fielding, "Hale's Tours: Ultrarealism in the Pre-1910 Motion Picture," *Film before Griffith*, ed. John L. Fell (Berkeley: University of California Press, 1983), 116–30.

61. David B. Clarke and Marcus A. Doel, "Engineering Space and Time: Moving Pictures and Motionless Trips," *Journal of Historical Geography* 31 (2005): 42.

62. Alison Byerly, "'A Prodigious Map beneath His Feet': Virtual Travel and the Panoramic Perspective," *Nineteenth-Century Contexts* 29, nos. 2–3 (June–September 2007): 157.

63. Gaston Bachelard, *The Poetics of Reverie: Childhood, Language, and the Cosmos*, trans. Daniel Russell (Boston: Beacon, 1969), 5, 15.

64. Ibid., 10.

65. Ibid., 1, 6, 8.

66. Jules Romains, "The Crowd at the Cinematograph" (1911), *French Film Theory and Criticism*, vol. 1, ed. Richard Abel (Princeton: Princeton University Press, 1988), 53.

67. Louis Delluc, "Beauty in the Cinema" (1917), in Abel, *French Film Theory and Criticism*, 1:137.

68. This argument follows what Robert Ray has called the lost tradition of Impressionist-Surrealist film criticism: see Robert Ray, "Impressionism, Surrealism, and Film Theory: Path Dependence, or How a Tradition in Film Theory Gets Lost," *The Oxford Guide to Film Studies*, ed. John Hill and Pamela Church Gibson (Oxford: Oxford University Press, 1998), 67–76.

7. "The Nation's First Playground"

1. *Variety*, 29 January 1910, 13.

2. These films are all in the Paper Print Collection at the Library of Congress, Washington, D.C. Descriptions and frame enlargements for the Edison films *Royal Gorge, Colorado* and *Upper Falls of the Yellowstone* are in Charles Musser, *Edison Motion Pictures, 1890–1900: An Annotated Filmography* (Washington, D.C.: Smithsonian Institution Press, 1997), 319, 356–57.

3. Reviews and descriptions of these films were published in *Moving Picture World*, 24 February 1912, 716; 12 October 1912, 142; 10 February 1912, 510.

4. For a history of tourism in the West that thoroughly traces the uses of this slogan, see Marguerite S. Shaffer, *See America First: Tourism and National Identity, 1880–1940* (Washington, D.C.: Smithsonian Institution Press, 2001).

5. Mark David Spence, *Dispossessing the Wilderness: Indian Removal and the Making of the National Parks* (New York: Oxford University Press, 1999).

6. Musser, *Edison Motion Pictures*, 316.

7. This chapter is a revised and expanded version of an essay I published several years ago. See Jennifer Peterson, "'The Nation's First Playground': Travel Films and the American West, 1895–1920," *Virtual Voyages: Cinema and Travel*, ed. Jeffrey Ruoff (Durham: Duke University Press, 2006), 79–98. In that version, my analysis focused more exclusively on the subjectification of American Indians in early travelogue films. While such ideological readings are not incorrect, I now feel that my earlier film interpretations were both too obvious and too closed, denying the potential of these films as living texts with multiple possibilities for reception and interpretation. This chapter unpacks the imperial ideology of early travelogues of the American West in such a way that resistant readings become possible. As I argue, the American Indians in these films were not just victims. They could also function to disrupt nationalistic ideologies.

8. *Edison Kinetogram*, 15 December 1911, 4, Academy of Motion Picture Arts and Sciences' Margaret Herrick Library, Beverly Hills, Calif.

9. *Motography* 12, no. 14 (3 October 1914): 458.

10. Bill Brown, *The Material Unconscious: American Amusement, Stephen Crane, and the Economies of Play* (Cambridge: Harvard University Press, 1996).

11. For more on travelogues and their promotion of the West for settlement, see Jennifer Peterson, "Travelogues and Immigrants," *Domitor 2008: Proceedings of the Domitor Conference on Early Cinema* (Perpignan: Presses Universitaires de Perpignan, 2010), 269–80.

12. *Motography* 7, no. 4 (April 1912): 169.

13. Earl Pomeroy, *In Search of the Golden West: The Tourist in Western America* (New York: Alfred A. Knopf, 1957), 34.

14. Quoted in Anne Farrar Hyde, *An American Vision: Far Western Landscape and National Culture, 1880–1920* (New York: New York University Press, 1990), 208.

15. Edward Buscombe, "Painting the Legend: Frederic Remington and the Western," *Cinema Journal* 23, no. 4 (Summer 1984): 25.

16. Some of the classic studies on the myth of the American West are Richard Slotkin, *Gunfighter Nation: The Myth of the Frontier in Twentieth-Century America*, 2d ed. (Norman: University of Oklahoma Press, 1998); Roderick Nash, *Wilderness and the American Mind*, rev. ed. (New Haven: Yale University Press, 1973); William H. Goetzmann, *Exploration and Empire: The Explorer and the Scientist in the Winning of the American West* (New York: W. W. Norton, 1966); Henry Nash Smith, *Virgin Land: The American West as Symbol and Myth*, rev. ed. (Cambridge: Harvard University Press, 1970).

17. On nineteenth-century photography, see Rebecca Solnit, *River of Shadows: Eadweard Muybridge and the Technological Wild West* (New York: Viking, 2003); Joel Snyder, "Territorial Photography," *Landscape and Power*, ed. W. J. T. Mitchell (Chicago: University of Chicago Press, 1994), 175–201; Rosalind Krauss, *The Originality of the Avant-Garde and Other Modernist Myths* (Cambridge: MIT Press, 1983).

18. The term "scenic nationalism" is also used in Alfred Runte, *National Parks: The American Experience*, 2d rev. ed. (Lincoln: University of Nebraska Press, 1987).

19. Hyde, *An American Vision*, 208.

20. For a discussion of landscape in the fictional Western film genre, see Jean-Louis Leutrat and Suzanne Liandrat-Guigues, "John Ford and Monument Valley," *Back in the Saddle Again: New Essays on the Western*, ed. Edward Buscombe and Roberta E. Pearson (London: British Film Institute, 1998), 160–69.

21. "Exporting the American Film," *Motography* 6, no. 2 (August 1911): 90.

22. Robert Warshow, *The Immediate Experience: Movies, Comics, Theatre and Other Aspects of Popular Culture* (New York: Atheneum, 1970).

23. Frederick Jackson Turner, *The Frontier in American History*, repr. ed. (New York: Dover, 1996 [1920]).

24. Slotkin, *Gunfighter Nation*, 10.

25. Lynne Kirby, *Parallel Tracks: The Railroad and Silent Cinema* (Durham: Duke University Press, 1997).

26. Richard J. Orsi, *Sunset Limited: The Southern Pacific Railroad and the Development of the American West* (Berkeley: University of California Press, 2005), 134–36, 163.

27. Ibid., 136–48, 156–65, 163.

28. "Railroad Motion Picture Shows," *Motography* 6, no. 1 (July 1911): 30.

29. "Southern Pacific Plans Pictures," *Nickelodeon* 3, no. 5 (1 March 1910): 126.

30. "Montana in Films," *Motography* 5, no. 6 (June 1911): 140; "Pictures Aid 'Back to Land' Movement," *Motography* 8, no. 13 (21 December 1912): 489; "Government Takes Scenic Films," *Nickelodeon* 5, no. 7 (18 February 1911): 184.

31. *Moving Picture World*, 12 October 1912, 142.

32. Even then, according to Marguerite Shaffer, automobile touring "remained a relatively exclusive pastime into the 1920s and beyond. In 1921 an estimated 20,000 Americans out of a population of 100 million Americans, approximately .02% of the total population, made transcontinental tours": Marguerite S. Shaffer, "Seeing America First: The Search for Identity in the Tourist Landscape," *Seeing and Being Seen: Tourism in the American West*, ed. David M. Worel and Patrick T. Long (Lawrence: University Press of Kansas, 2001), 190. Tourism in the 1910s was not yet the mass pastime it would become after the Second World War: see John A. Jakle, *The Tourist: Travel in Twentieth-Century North America* (Lincoln: University of Nebraska Press, 1985).

33. Emily Post, *By Motor to the Golden Gate* (New York: D. Appleton, 1916), 12.

34. Ibid., 7.

35. Ibid., 242–43.

36. For a history of auto touring in the United States, see Warren James Belasco, *Americans on the Road: From Autocamp to Motel, 1910–1945* (Baltimore: Johns Hopkins University Press, 1979). After the Second World War, General Motors started a new radio and television ad campaign with the jingle "See the USA in your Chevrolet": see Shaffer, *See America First*, 311.

37. "Filming Auto Tour," *Motography* 10, no. 9 (1 November 1913): 320.

38. *Moving Picture World*, 2 February 1918, 680. Earle had filmed the national parks for Pathé at least once before, in 1913: see *Motography* 10, no. 6 (20 September 1913): 195.

39. "Pictures Aid 'Back to Land' Movement," 490.

40. The U.S. government first set aside Yosemite as a scenic park in 1864. Next came Yellowstone, the first land to be officially called a national park, in 1872. Sequoia National Park followed in 1890; Mount Rainier National Park, in 1899; Crater Lake National Park, in 1902; the Grand Canyon, in 1908; and Glacier National Park, in 1910. The U.S. National Park Service was finally instituted in 1916: see Runte, *National Parks*. The National Park Service has published many books and histories about itself; one volume from the 1910s that I have found useful is Robert Sterling Yard, *The National Parks Portfolio*, 2d ed. (Washington, D.C.: U.S. Department of the Interior, National Park Service, 1917).

41. Prints of these six films are held at the Library of Congress, which dates them at 1903, but they are listed in Biograph's catalogue for 1902, indicating that they were

shot in 1902 or earlier. Three of the films also have slightly different titles in the Biograph catalogue. *Cascade Near Wawona Cal.* is listed as *A Wonderful Waterfall*, but the film's description—"showing the splendid cascade near Wawona, California, which attracts tourists from far and near"—clearly indicates that it is the same film. Similarly, *Glacier Point* is titled *Picturesque Yosemite* in the Biograph catalogue, and *Tourists Arriving at Wawona Hotel* is titled *In the Yellowstone*: see American Mutoscope and Biograph Company, "Picture Catalogue (November 1902), Museum of Modern Art, New York," *A Guide to Motion Picture Catalogs by American Producers and Distributors, 1894–1908*, ed. Charles Musser, microfilm (Frederick, Md.: University Publications of America, 1985), 142–43.

42. Prints of these three films are held at the Library of Congress. For descriptions and frame enlargements see Musser, *Edison Motion Pictures*, 317–20. These films were shot on 19–25 July 1899 by James White (producer) and Frederick Blechynden (camera). *Tourists Going Round Yellowstone Park* and *Coaches Arriving at Mammoth Hot Springs* can be viewed online at the Library of Congress's American Memory site. Search by title at http://memory.loc.gov/ammem/index.html (accessed 10 October 2012). *Coaches Going to Cinnabar from Yellowstone Park* is not available online, but a different film from this series, *Lower Falls, Grand Canyon, Yellowstone Park* (1899), can be viewed online, also at the LoC's American Memory site.

43. *Lower Falls, Grand Canyon, Yellowstone* is available for viewing at the LoC's American Memory site.

44. Brian J. Hudson, "Waterfalls, Tourism, and Landscape," *Geography* 91, no. 1 (Spring 2006): 4.

45. The EYE Film Institute Netherlands holds a print of this film, which bears the Dutch title *Het aardsche paradijs* (Paradise on Earth). No information is known about its manufacturer or release date, though the Kodak edge marks on the nitrate print date it at 1919. Curiously, the head title on the film print reads, "Paradise on Earth: A Trip through Wyoming (N. America)," but the film was clearly made at Yosemite in California, not at Yellowstone in Wyoming. It remains unclear whether the print was mistitled for Dutch release or if the title was carelessly put on the film at a later date.

46. An excerpt of *Seeing Yosemite with David A. Curry* was released as part of the DVD box set *Treasures from the American Film Archives, Volume 5: The American West* (2011). I provide the DVD commentary for the film, which also can be accessed online, with commentary, at http://www.filmpreservation.org/dvds-and-books/clips/seeing-yosemite-with-david-a-curry-1916 (accessed 10 October 2012). The complete print is at the National Archives and Records Administration (NARA) in College Park, Md.

47. William Cronon, "The Trouble with Wilderness, or, Getting Back to the Wrong Nature," *Uncommon Ground: Toward Reinventing Nature*, ed. William Cronon (New York: W. W. Norton, 1995), 80.

48. The print of *Our National Parks—Yellowstone Park: The Geysers* at EYE bears the

title *Yellowstone National Park*. The film was released by Pathé in the United States on 3 March 1918, on a split reel with another travel film, *Buxton (Derbyshire, England)*.

49. On lead-in figures in landscape painting, see W. J. T. Mitchell, "Imperial Landscape," *Landscape and Power*, ed. W. J. T. Mitchell (Chicago: University of Chicago Press, 1994), 23–24.

50. *Selig Polyscope Company Catalogue*, 1907, 134, in Musser, *A Guide to Motion Picture Catalogs by American Producers and Distributors*. On Yellowstone National Park as a "wonderland," see Shaffer, *See America First*, 49–52.

51. American Mutoscope and Biograph Company, *Picture Catalogue*, 143.

52. For reproductions of many of the covers of these "Wonderland" guides, see http://www.sharinghistory.com/RR4.htm (accessed 10 October 2012).

53. R. W. Hepburn, *"Wonder" and Other Essays* (Edinburgh: Edinburgh University Press, 1984), 132.

54. Ibid., 132.

55. Olin D. Wheeler, *Wonderland '96: Picturing the Country, the Cities, the Resorts, the Game Found along the Northern Pacific Railroad* (1896), 75, quoted in Musser, *Edison Motion Pictures*, 320.

56. Alison Griffiths, *Wondrous Difference: Cinema, Anthropology, and Turn-of-the-Century Visual Culture* (New York: Columbia University Press, 2002), 52–53.

57. Roslyn Poignant, "The Making of Professional 'Savages': From P. T. Barnum (1883) to the *Sunday Times* (1998)," *Photography's Other Histories*, ed. Christopher Pinney and Nicolas Peterson (Durham: Duke University Press, 2003), 55–84.

58. On the "vanishing American" trope, see Brian Dippie, *The Vanishing American: White Attitudes and U.S. Indian Policy* (Lawrence: University Press of Kansas, 1982).

59. *Moving Picture World*, February 1912, 510.

60. Fatimah Tobing Rony, *The Third Eye: Race, Cinema, and Ethnographic Spectacle* (Durham: Duke University Press, 1996), 91.

61. As noted earlier, I strongly suspect that *Glacier National Park* (Pathé, 1917) is the release title of a film at EYE that bears the title *Het Nationaal park in Amerika (The National Park in America)*. Film descriptions and reviews support this hypothesis. See review in *Moving Picture World*, 9 June 1917, 1603, and description in *Moving Picture World*, 2 June 1917, 1464. However, because travelogues tend to show the same locations when documenting national parks, it is difficult to absolutely verify if this is the correct identification. Despite having edge codes that indicate the print is from 1917, I still have some hesitation about this identification because the EYE print contains animated segments, and animation is not mentioned in the reviews of the Pathé film. *Our National Parks — Glacier* was released by Pathé in the United States on 3 June 1917, on a split reel with a film titled *Odd Small Birds*. For simplicity's sake, I use the shorter title *Glacier National Park* here.

62. On anthropometric photography, see Griffiths, *Wondrous Difference*, 93–100.

63. Spence, *Dispossessing the Wilderness*, 3.

64. Quoted in ibid., 80.

65. For a history of Glacier National Park, see C. W. Buchholtz, *Man in Glacier* (West Glacier, Mont.: Glacier Natural History Association, 1976).

66. This film is at the Library of Congress. Its release date is unknown, but I believe it was produced in the late 1920s. The film's main title reads, "The Great Northern Railway presents *Twelve Minutes in Glacier National Park*, Photographed in Natural Colors by the Technicolor Process. Produced by Colorart Pictures, Inc., Boston, Mass."

67. "The Native American on the other side of the coin was a composite of several plains Indians who sat for [James Earle] Fraser in his Westport, Conn. studio. Shortly after the Buffalo nickel was released Fraser wrote: 'The three Indians were Iron Tail, a Sioux; Big Tree, a Kiowa; and Two Moons, a Cheyenne. . . . The three had [the] combined features of the hardy, virile types of Great Plains Indian.' Many other men eventually claimed to have modeled for the coin": Tom La-Marre, "Designing the Buffalo Nickel," *Coins*, November 1994, 70.

68. Hyde, *An American Vision*, 284.

69. "Pathe Pictures Indians on Tented Roof," *Motography* 9, no. 7 (5 April 1913): 247.

70. The same stunt was restaged in 1921, only the hotel roof and, presumably, some of the participants had changed: see "Indians on Hotel Roof," *New York Times*, 30 April 1921, n.p.

71. Descriptions of these films are in *Motography* 6, no. 6 (December 1911): 267; 8, no. 4 (17 August 1912): 201.

72. An excerpt of *Picturesque Colorado* is in the DVD box set *Treasures from the American Film Archives, Volume 5: The American West* (2011). I provide the DVD commentary for the film. The complete print is at NARA. An incomplete print with German intertitles is at the British Film Institute National Archive, London.

73. The excerpted version available on DVD unfortunately omits this imagery.

74. Griffiths, *Wondrous Difference*, 194. *Picturesque Colorado* is also mentioned (but not analyzed) in Giorgio Bertellini, *Italy in Early American Cinema: Race, Landscape, and the Picturesque* (Bloomington: Indiana University Press, 2010), 112–13.

75. Griffiths, *Wondrous Difference*, 194.

76. "Millions to See Colorado Scenes by Picture Films," *Denver Post*, 1 September 1911, 2.

77. Ibid.

78. "One Hundred Thousand Cheer Greater Colorado's Royal Industrial Parade," *Denver Post*, 18 July 1911, 1. Swanson can be seen with a cameraman and other figures riding in a car emblazoned with American flags and a sign advertising his film concern, the Wm. H. Swanson Film Co. The photo was printed in the *Denver Post*, 18 July 1911, 5. Unfortunately this image exists only on microfilm today, and it is too poor quality for book reproduction.

79. In his article on film exchanges, Max Alvarez explains that, along with George Kleine, Swanson's film exchange was among the most important Chicago-based distributors in the country. Both opened in 1898. Swanson opened several new ex-

changes across the country in 1907; he was also running an exchange in Denver in 1911: see Max Alvarez, "The Origins of the Film Exchange," *Film History* 17, no. 4 (2005): 431, 435.

80. "One Hundred Thousand Cheer Greater Colorado's Royal Industrial Parade," 1–5.

81. "Motion Pictures of Colo[rado] Scenes Now On Screens," *Denver Post*, 7 September 1911, 6.

82. "Review of *Picturesque Colorado*," *Moving Picture News*, 2 September 1911, 29.

83. Ja[mes] S. McQuade, "Review of *Picturesque Colorado*," *Moving Picture World*, 23 September 1911, 870–71.

84. *The City of Denver, "The Queen of the Plains," Edison Kinetogram*, 1 February 1912, 9, Academy of Motion Picture Arts and Sciences' Margaret Herrick Library, Beverly Hills, Calif.

85. This film is at EYE with the title *Los Angelos*. It was released in the United States by Imp on 25 May 1912. In the United States, the film had the alternative title *Views of Los Angeles, Cal.*

86. *Moving Picture World*, 18 May 1912, 664.

87. The Lubin Company released two films in April 1912: *The Alligator Farm* and *California Ostrich and Pigeon Farm*. A review of *Ostrich Farm near Pasadena, Cal.* (Nestor, 1912) states, "This farm has been pictured several times. This is an instructive and amusing item, however": John Stoddard, "Southern California," *John L. Stoddard's Lectures*, 10:26–27; *Moving Picture World*, 13 January 1912, 127; 13 April 1913.

88. Harry Ellington Brook, *Los Angeles, California, the City and County*, 23d ed. (Los Angeles: Los Angeles Chamber of Commerce, 1910), 45.

89. Ibid., 75.

90. "Doings in Los Angeles," *Moving Picture World*, 29 June 1912, 1219.

91. William Selig Papers, Academy of Motion Picture Arts and Sciences' Margaret Herrick Library, Beverly Hills, Calif.

Epilogue

1. See Devin Orgeron, Marsha Orgeron, and Dan Streible, eds., *Learning with the Lights Off: Educational Film in the United States* (New York: Oxford University Press, 2012).

2. "Superb Human Interest Film," *Motography* 12, no. 7 (15 August 1914): 225.

3. "'Quicksands' Is Scenically Beautiful," *Motography* 9, no. 13 (28 June 1913): 457.

4. Eileen Bowser, *The Transformation of Cinema: 1907–1915* (Berkeley: University of California Press, 1990), 162. Bowser discusses camera movement in fiction film at greater length on pages 249–50.

5. See Richard M. Barsam, *Nonfiction Film: A Critical History*, rev. ed. (Bloomington: Indiana University Press, 1992), chap. 3; Kevin Brownlow, *The War, The West, and the Wilderness* (New York: Alfred A. Knopf, 1979), 400–567. See also Fatimah Tobing Rony, *The Third Eye: Race, Cinema, and Ethnographic Spectacle* (Durham:

Duke University Press, 1996), chap. 5. For a good discussion of *Nanook*, see Rony, *The Third Eye*, chap. 4.

6. For discussions of Cooper and Schoedsack, see Rony, *The Third Eye*, chap. 6; Cynthia Erb, *Tracking King Kong: A Hollywood Icon in World Culture* (Detroit: Wayne State University Press, 1998).

7. For a discussion of the use of nonfiction in contemporary media, see Thomas Elsaesser, "Archives and Archaeologies: The Place of Non-fiction Film in Contemporary Media," *Films That Work: Industrial Film and the Productivity of Media*, ed. Vinzenz Hediger and Patrick Vonderau (Amsterdam: Amsterdam University Press, 2009), 30–31. On *From the Pole to the Equator*, see Catherine Russell, *Experimental Ethnography: The Work of Film in the Age of Video* (Durham: Duke University Press, 1999), 58–62.

8. For an analysis of *Motion Painting No. 1*, see James Tobias, "For Love of Music: Oskar Fischinger's Modal, Musical Diagram," chapter 3 of *Sync: Stylistics of Hieroglyphic Time* (Philadelphia: Temple University Press, 2010), 76–108.

9. William Moritz, *Optical Poetry: The Life and Work of Oskar Fischinger* (Bloomington: Indiana University Press, 2004), 207.

10. More information about the *Oskar Fischinger: Ten Films* DVD is available online at http://www.centerforvisualmusic.org/DVD.htm (accessed 10 October 2012).

11. Moritz, *Optical Poetry*, 207.

12. Jean-Jacques Rousseau, *Reveries of the Solitary Walker* (1782), trans. Peter France (London: Penguin, 1979), 108–9.

FILMOGRAPHY

This selected filmography includes only extant films that I have analyzed in the text. Most of these are 35mm archival prints that I viewed in film archives. Films are listed alphabetically, using their English-language release titles (when I have been able to verify them) or using an English translation of a foreign release title or archival print title. To promote access, I list archival locations for each title. Some films are more readily accessible, and for these I list DVD or Internet availability.

I have left out of this filmography: (1) films I refer to in the text that are no longer extant (to the best of my knowledge); (2) films I refer to in the text that *are* or *might be* extant in film archives but that I have not been able to view myself; and (3) the hundreds of other archival films that I watched while researching this book that I do not analyze in the text.

For a listing of *all known* travel subjects released during the period covered by this book, extant or not, culled from the lists of film releases published in the motion picture trade press, see Jennifer Peterson, "World Pictures: Travelogue Films and the Lure of the Exotic, 1890–1920" (PhD diss., University of Chicago, 1999), app. A, table 1.

Information given (when known):
- Film title: English-language release title (or English translation of title in original language or English translation title of archival print)
- Date of production
- Film production company, director, or other crew
- Country of production
- U.S. release date or other release date
- Alternative titles (alternative release title, foreign-language release title, or title of archival print)
- Access information: archival collection, DVD release, Internet access

Film archives and abbreviations:
- Academy Film Archive, Los Angeles (AMPAS)
- BFI National Archive, London (BFI)

- Center for Visual Music, Los Angeles (CVM)
- EYE Film Institute Netherlands, Amsterdam (EYE)
- Library of Congress, Washington, D.C. (LoC)
- National Archives and Records Administration, College Park, Md. (NARA)

Short Films

The Acrobatic Fly (1910)
> Percy Smith, dir. Charles Urban Trading Company (U.K.). EYE. The BFI has a slightly different version in its collection, which is available for viewing online at http://www.youtube.com/watch?v=8hlocZhNcoM.

The Auvergne Mountains, Central France (1912)
> Lux Film (France). U.S. release: Fall 1913. Alternative titles: *L'Auvergne pittoresque* (original release), *Het Schilderachtige Auvergne* (EYE), *Picturesque Auvergne*. EYE.

The Beautiful Gorges of Tarn (1911)
> Gaumont (France). U.S. release: 11 March 1911. Alternative titles: *Les gorges du Tarn* (original release), *Uitstapje door het dal van de Tarn* (EYE). EYE.

A Car Ride in the Pyrenees (ca. 1910)
> Pathé (France). Alternative title: *Een Autotocht in de Pyreneën* (EYE). EYE.

Ceylon, Real-Life and Picturesque (1905)
> Pathé (France). Alternative title: *Ceylan, vécu et pittoresque* (original release). BFI.

Coaches Arriving at Mammoth Hot Springs (1899)
> James White, prod. Edison Manufacturing Company (U.S.). LoC. Available online at http://memory.loc.gov.

Coaches Going to Cinnabar from Yellowstone Park (1899)
> James White, dir. Edison Manufacturing Company (U.S.). LoC.

Cork Production in France (1913)
> Cines (Italy). Alternative title: *Industria del sughero in Francia* (original release). Available on the DVD *Exotic Europe: Journeys into Early Cinema*, co-released in 2000 by the Bundesarchiv-Filmarchiv Berlin; the Nederlands Filmmuseum, Amsterdam; and the Cinema Museum, London.

The Country Doctor (1909)
> D. W. Griffith, dir. Biograph (U.S.). U.S. release: 8 July 1909. Available online at http://archive.org/details/TheCountryDoctor.

The European Rest Cure (1904)
> Edwin S. Porter, dir. Edison Manufacturing Company (U.S.). U.S. release: 1 September 1904. Available online at http://archive.org/details/EuropeanRest Cure1904EdwinS.PorterUsa.

The Fly Pest (1910)
Percy Smith, dir. Charles Urban Trading Company (U.K.). EYE.

From Spiez to Loetschberg, Switzerland (1913)
Eclipse (France). Alternative titles: *Chemin de fer du Loetschberg* (original release), *Loetschberg* (EYE). EYE, LoC.

Glacier National Park (1917) [title unverified]
Pathé (France). Alternative titles: *Our National Parks—Glacier* (alternative U.S. title), *Het Nationaal park in Amerika* (EYE). EYE.

Gorges of the Bourne River, France (1911)
Gaumont (France). U.S. release: 28 January 1911. Alternative title: *Les gorges de la Bourne* (original release). EYE.

Harvesting Coconuts in America (1912)
Selig Polyscope (U.S.). Alternative titles: *The Story of a Cocoanut* (original release), *Oogst van cocosnoten in Amerika* (EYE). EYE.

Hawaii, the Paradise of the Pacific (1916)
Lyman Howe, dir. (U.S.). Alternative title: *De Hawaïaneilanden in vogelvlucht* (EYE). EYE.

Hungarian Folklore (1913)
Pathé (France). U.S. release: 12 February 1913. Alternative titles: *A Peasant Marriage in Hungary* (U.S. release), *Hongaarse folklore* (EYE). EYE; available on the DVD *Exotic Europe: Journeys into Early Cinema*, co-released in 2000 by the Bundesarchiv-Filmarchiv Berlin; the Nederlands Filmmuseum, Amsterdam; and the Cinema Museum, London.

Indian and Ceylonese Types (1913)
Éclair (France). French release: 7 November 1913. Alternative titles: *Types des Indes et de Ceylan* (original release), *Indische en Ceylon Typen* (EYE). EYE.

In Egypt (ca. 1920)
Pathé (France). Alternative title: *En Egypte* (EYE). EYE.

Kuala Lumpur: Capital of the Malay States (1912)
Pathé (France). U.S. release: 28 November 1913. Alternative titles: *Kuala-Lampour, Asie Méridionale, capitale des Etats Fédéres Malais* (original release), *Kuala-Lumpour, Hoofdstad der Gefedereerde Maleische Staten* (EYE). EYE.

Life and Times in the Bohemian Baths of Marienbad, Karlsbad, Franzensbad (1911)
Bavaria-Film-Straubing (Germany). Alternative title: *Leben und Treiben in den böhmischen Bädern Marienbad, Karlsbad, Franzensbad*. EYE.

Lower Falls, Grand Canyon, Yellowstone Park (1899)
James White, prod. Edison Manufacturing Company (U.S.). LoC. Available online at http://memory.loc.gov.

Making Getas in Japan (1911)
>Pathé (France). Alternative title: *Au Japon, fabrication de getas* (original release).
>EYE.

Moroccan Shoemakers (ca. 1915)
>Pathé (France). Alternative title: *Marokkaansche schoenlappers* (EYE). EYE.

The Oasis of El-Kantara (1913)
>Éclair (France). French release: 5 September 1913. Alternative titles: *L'Oasis d'El-Kantara* (original release), *De Oase van el-Cantora* (EYE). EYE.

On the Banks of the Yerres (1912)
>Gaumont (France). Alternative titles: *Les bords de l'Yerres* (original release), *Aan de oevers van de Yerres* (EYE). EYE.

The Orne (1912)
>Gaumont (France). Netherlands release: 13 December 1912. Alternative titles: *L'Orne* (original release), *Aan de oevers van de Orne* (EYE).

Our National Parks—Yellowstone Park: The Geysers (1918)
>Pathé (France). Alternative title: *Het Nationale Park van Yellowstone, USA* (EYE). EYE.

Paradise on Earth (ca. 1919)
>Production company unknown. Alternative title: *Het aardsche paradijs* (EYE). EYE.

Parks in Japan (ca. 1915)
>Production company unknown. Alternative title: *Parken in Japan* (EYE). EYE.

Picturesque Andalusia (ca. 1907)
>Pathé (France). Alternative title: *Schilderachtig Andalusië* (EYE). EYE.

Picturesque Auvergne (1912)
>Lux Film (France). U.S. release: Fall 1913. Alternative titles: *L'Auvergne pittoresque* (original release), *The Auvergne Mountains, Central France* (U.S. release), *Het Schilderachtige Auvergne* (EYE). EYE.

Picturesque Colorado (1911)
>Rex Motion Picture Company (U.S.). U.S. release: 7 September 1911. BFI. Excerpt available on the DVD *Treasures from the American Film Archives, Volume 5: The American West*, released in 2011 by the National Film Preservation Foundation.

Picturesque Holland (1911)
>Pasquali (Italy). BFI.

Picturesque India (1912)
>Vitagraph Company of America (U.S.). BFI.

Picturesque Japan (1913)
Éclair (France). French release: 5 September 1913. Alternative titles: *Le Japon pittoresque* (original release), *Het Schilderachtige Japan* (EYE). EYE.

Picturesque Rocks of Baume-les-Messieurs (1913)
Eclipse (France). Alternative titles: *Les roches et grottes de Baume* (original release), *De Schilderachtige rotsen van Baume-les-Messieurs* (EYE). EYE.

Picturesque Roumania (1912)
Gaumont (France). BFI.

The Polar Bear Hunt (1910)
Pathé (France). U.S. release: 28 March 1910. Alternative titles: *Capture d'oursons blancs dans les glaces de l'ocean* (original release), *Een Berenjacht in de poolstreken* (EYE). EYE.

Rocks and Waves (ca. 1911)
Gaumont (France). Alternative title: *Rotsen en golven* (EYE). EYE.

Rough Sea at Dover (1895)
Birt Acres, dir. (U.K.). Available on the DVD *The Movies Begin*, released in 2002 by Kino Video.

Ruins of Angkor, Cambodia (1912)
Méliès (France). Alternative titles: *Les Ruines d'Angkor, Cambodge. Indo-Chine Française* (original release), *Angkor Vat* (EYE). EYE.

Santa Lucia (ca. 1910)
Ambrosio (Italy). EYE.

Scenes along the Pescara River, Central Italy (1913)
Cines (Italy). U.S. release: 8 April 1913. Alternative titles: *Il Pescare* (original release), *Aan de oevers van de Pascara* (EYE). EYE.

Seeing Los Angeles (1912)
Imp (U.S.). French release: 8 February 1912. Alternative titles: *Views of Los Angeles, Cal.* (alternative U.S. title), *Une promenade dans Los Angeles* (French release), *Los Angelos* (EYE). EYE.

Seeing Yosemite with David A. Curry (1916)
Arthur C. Pillsbury, dir. (U.S.). NARA. Available on the DVD *Treasures from the American Film Archives, Volume 5: The American West*, released in 2011 by the National Film Preservation Foundation.

South America (ca. 1920)
Production company unknown. Alternative title: *Zuid-Amerika* (EYE). EYE.

South Tyrolean Folkloristic Dress (ca. 1920)
Pathé. Alternative title: *Zuid-Tiroler klederdrachten* (EYE). EYE.

Stockholm (ca. 1912)
Production company unknown. EYE.

Swiss Trip [Rivers and Landscapes] (1934)
Oskar Fischinger, dir. AMPAS, CVM.

The Thames from Oxford to Richmond (1911)
Eclipse (France). U.S. release: 15 March 1911. Alternative title: *The Thames from Oxford to London*. Private collection.

The Touaregs in Their Own Country (1908)
Pathé (France). Alternative titles: *Chez les Touaregs* (original release), *Bij de Tuaregs* (EYE). EYE.

Tourists Going round Yellowstone Park (1899)
James White, prod. Edison Manufacturing Company (U.S.). LoC. Available online at http://memory.loc.gov.

Uncle Tom's Cabin (1903)
Edwin S. Porter, dir. Edison Manufacturing Company (U.S.). Available on the DVD *Edison: The Invention of the Movies, 1891–1918*, released in 2005 by Kino Video.

Under Basque Skies (1913)
Eclipse (France). Alternative titles: *On the Coast of the Bay of Biscay, France* (U.S. release), *Onder den Baskischen hemel* (EYE). EYE, LoC. Available online at http://memory.loc.gov.

The Velino River and Falls (Central Italy) (1913)
Cines (Italy). U.S. release: 14 January 1913. Alternative title: *Velino River* (EYE). EYE.

Venice and Its Monuments (1914)
Éclair (France). French release: 2 April 1914. Alternative titles: *Venise et ses monuments* (original release), *De Wonderen van Venetië* (EYE). EYE.

A Visit to Peek Frean and Co.'s Biscuit Works (1906)
Cricks and Martin (U.K.). BFI; available on the DVD *The Movies Begin* (Kino Video). The complete thirty-six-minute version is available online (to registered schools and libraries in the United Kingdom) at http://www.screenonline.org.uk/film/id/711535/index.html.

Walking from Munich to Berlin (1927)
Oskar Fischinger, dir. (Germany). Alternative title: *Munchen-Berlin Wanderung* (original release). Available on the DVD *Oskar Fischinger: Ten Films*, released in 2006 by the Center for Visual Music.

Workers Leaving the Lumière Factory (1895)
Louis Lumière, camera (France). Access: readily available online.

Feature Films

In addition to these early film shorts, which reside mostly in archives and are thus difficult to access (except as noted), I mention several feature films in the text that are more readily available today on DVD (some from the silent era and some more recent films that reuse and reinterpret archival footage). Even though I do not analyze these films at any great length (with the exception of *Letter from an Unknown Woman*), I list them here because they are easier to access (many of these are available on DVD). I hope they will inspire the reader to further viewing of and thinking about the early history of nonfiction film.

Among the Cannibal Isles of the South Pacific (Martin and Osa Johnson, 1918)
Decasia (Bill Morrison, 2001)
Film Ist (Gustav Deutsch, 2000–2009)
From the Pole to the Equator (Yervant Gianikian, 1987)
Grass: A Nation's Battle for Life (Merian C. Cooper and Ernest B. Schoesdack, 1925)
In the Land of the Head Hunters (Edward S. Curtis, 1914). Alternative title: *In the Land of the War Canoes*
Letter from an Unknown Woman (Max Ophüls, 1948)
Lyrical Nitrate (Peter Delpeut, 1991)
Mother Dao, the Turtlelike (Vincent Monnikendam, 1996)
Nanook of the North (Robert Flaherty, 1922)
90 Degrees South: With Scott to the Antarctic (Herbert G. Ponting, 1933)
Simba: The King of the Beasts (Martin and Osa Johnson, 1928)
South (Frank Hurley, 1919)

BIBLIOGRAPHY

Abel, Richard. *The Ciné Goes to Town: French Cinema, 1896–1914*. Berkeley: University of California Press, 1994.

———. "Éclair: The Other French Film Company." *Griffithiana* 44–45 (May–September 1992): 4–24.

———. *The Red Rooster Scare: Making Cinema American, 1900–1910*. Berkeley: University of California Press, 1999.

Abel, Richard, and Rick Altman, eds. *The Sounds of Early Cinema*. Bloomington: Indiana University Press, 2001.

Allen, Robert. "Manhattan Myopia; or, Oh! Iowa!" *Cinema Journal* 35, no. 3 (Spring 1996): 75–103.

———. "Motion Picture Exhibition in Manhattan 1906–1912: Beyond the Nickelodeon." *Film before Griffith*, ed. John L. Fell, 162–75. Berkeley: University of California Press, 1983.

———. *Vaudeville and Film, 1895–1915: A Study in Media Interaction*. New York: Arno, 1980.

Allen, Robert C., and Douglas Gomery. *Film History: Theory and Practice*. New York: McGraw-Hill, 1985.

Alloula, Malek. *The Colonial Harem*, trans. Myrna Godzich and Wlad Godzich. Minneapolis: University of Minnesota Press, 1986.

Altenloh, Emilie. *On the Sociology of the Cinema: The Cinema Business and the Social Strata of Its Audience* (1914), trans. Lance W. Garmer. *German Essays on Film*, ed. Richard W. McCormick and Alison Guenther-Pal, 29–47. New York: Continuum, 2004.

Altman, Rick. *Film/Genre*. London: British Film Institute, 1999.

———. "From Lecturer's Prop to Industrial Product: The Early History of Travel Films." *Virtual Voyages: Cinema and Travel*, ed. Jeffrey Ruoff, 61–76. Durham: Duke University Press, 2006.

———. *Silent Film Sound*. New York: Columbia University Press, 2004.

Alvarez, Max. "The Origins of the Film Exchange." *Film History* 17, no. 4 (2005): 431–65.

Amad, Paula. *Counter-archive: Film, the Everyday, and Albert Kahn's Archives de la Planète*. New York: Columbia University Press, 2010.

American Mutoscope and Biograph Company. "Picture Catalogue (November 1902), Museum of Modern Art, New York." *A Guide to Motion Picture Catalogs by American Producers and Distributors, 1894–1908*, ed. Charles Musser, microfilm. Frederick, Md.: University Publications of America, 1985.

Ames, Eric. *Carl Hagenbeck's Empire of Entertainments*. Seattle: University of Washington Press, 2008.

———. "From the Exotic to the Everyday: The Ethnographic Exhibition in Germany." *The Nineteenth-Century Visual Culture Reader*, ed. Vanessa R. Schwartz and Jeannene M. Przyblyski, 313–27. New York: Routledge, 2004.

Andrew, Dudley. "Praying Mantis: Enchantment and Violence in French Cinema of the Exotic." *Visions of the East: Orientalism in Film*, ed. Matthew Bernstein and Gaylyn Studlar, 232–52. New Brunswick: Rutgers University Press, 1997.

Andrews, Malcolm. *Landscape and Western Art*. New York: Oxford University Press, 1999.

———, ed. *The Picturesque: Literary Sources and Documents*, 3 vols. East Sussex: Helm Information, 1994.

———. *The Search for the Picturesque: Landscape Aesthetics and Tourism in Britain, 1760–1800*. Aldershot: Scolar, 1989.

Askari, Kaveh. "From 'The Horse in Motion' to 'Man in Motion': Alexander Black's Detective Lectures." *Early Popular Visual Culture* 3, no. 1 (May 2005): 59–76.

Auerbach, Jeffrey A. *The Great Exhibition of 1851: A Nation on Display*. New Haven: Yale University Press, 1999.

Austin, Linda M. "Aesthetic Embarrassment: The Reversion to the Picturesque in Nineteenth-Century English Tourism." *English Literary History* 74 (2007): 629–53.

Bachelard, Gaston. *The Poetics of Reverie: Childhood, Language, and the Cosmos*, trans. Daniel Russell. Boston: Beacon, 1969.

Barber, X. Theodore. "The Roots of Travel Cinema: John L. Stoddard, E. Burton Holmes and the Nineteenth-Century Illustrated Travel Lecture." *Film History* 5, no. 1 (1993): 68–84.

Barrell, John. *The Dark Side of the Landscape: The Rural Poor in English Painting, 1730–1840*. Cambridge: Cambridge University Press, 1980.

Barsam, Richard M. *Nonfiction Film: A Critical History*, rev. ed. Bloomington: Indiana University Press, 1992.

Barthes, Roland. "The *Blue Guide*," trans. Annette Lavers. *Mythologies*, 74–77. New York: Hill and Wang, 1972.

———. "The Death of the Author." *Image, Music, Text*, trans. Stephen Heath, 142–48. New York: Hill and Wang, 1977.

———. "The Reality Effect." *The Rustle of Language*, trans. Richard Howard, 141–48. New York: Hill and Wang, 1986.

Beatty, Barbara. "'Politics Are Quite Perplexing': Bessie Locke and the National Kindergarten Association Campaign, 1909–60." *The Educational Work of Women's*

Organizations, 1890–1960, ed. Anne Meis Knupfer and Christine Woyshner, 195–213. New York: Palgrave Macmillan, 2008.

Behdad, Ali. *Belated Travelers: Orientalism in the Age of Colonial Dissolution*. Durham: Duke University Press, 1994.

Belasco, Warren James. *Americans on the Road: From Autocamp to Motel, 1910–1945*. Baltimore: Johns Hopkins University Press, 1979.

Benjamin, Walter. *The Arcades Project*, trans. Howard Eiland and Kevin McLaughlin. Cambridge: Harvard University Press, 1999.

———. "Surrealism," trans. Edmund Jephcott. *Reflections*, 177–92. New York: Schocken Books, 1986.

———. "The Work of Art in the Age of Its Technological Reproducibility: Second Version," trans. Edmund Jephcott and Harry Zohn. *The Work of Art in the Age of Its Technological Reproducibility and Other Writings on Media*, ed. Michael W. Jennings, Brigid Doherty, and Thomas Y. Levin, 19–55. Cambridge: Harvard University Press, 2008.

Bensaude-Vincent, Bernadette, and William R. Newman. "Introduction: The Artificial and the Natural: State of the Problem." *The Artificial and the Natural: An Evolving Polarity*, ed. Bernadette Bensaude-Vincent and William R. Newman, 1–20. Cambridge: MIT Press, 2007.

Beynon, George W. *Musical Presentation of Motion Pictures*. New York: G. Schirmer, 1921.

Bergson, Henri. *Creative Evolution* (1911), trans. Arthur Mitchell. New York: Modern Library, 1944.

Bermingham, Ann. *Landscape and Ideology: The English Rustic Tradition, 1740–1860*. Berkeley: University of California Press, 1986.

———. "System, Order, and Abstraction: The Politics of English Landscape Drawing around 1795." *Landscape and Power*, ed. W. J. T. Mitchell, 77–101. Chicago: University of Chicago Press, 1994.

Bertellini, Giorgio. *Italy in Early American Cinema: Race, Landscape, and the Picturesque*. Bloomington: Indiana University Press, 2010.

Bhabha, Homi K. *The Location of Culture*. London: Routledge, 1994.

Bitzer, G. W. *Billy Bitzer: His Story*. New York: Farrar, Straus and Giroux, 1973.

Blankenship, Janelle. "Arno Holz vs. Thomas Mann: Modernist Media Fantasies." *Modernist Cultures* 1, no. 2 (October 2005): 72–109.

Blom, Ivo. "'Comme l'eau qui coule': Les films de rivières de Gaumont dans la collection Desmet." *1895* 18 (Summer 1995): 156–63.

———. *Jean Desmet and the Early Dutch Film Trade*. Amsterdam: Amsterdam University Press, 2003.

Bordwell, David, Janet Staiger, and Kristin Thompson. *The Classical Hollywood Cinema: Film Style and Mode of Production to 1960*. New York: Columbia University Press, 1985.

Bottomore, Stephen. "'Every Phase of Present-Day Life': Biograph's Non-fiction Production." *Griffithiana* 66–70 (1999–2000): 147–211.

Bourdieu, Pierre. *Distinction: A Social Critique of the Judgment of Taste*, trans. Richard Nice. Cambridge: Harvard University Press, 1984.

Bousquet, Henri. *Catalogue Pathé des années 1907 à 1909*. Bures-sur-Vyette: Édition Henri Bousquet, 1993.

Bowser, Eileen. *The Transformation of Cinema: 1907–1915*. Berkeley: University of California Press, 1990.

Brendon, Piers. *Thomas Cook: 150 Years of Popular Tourism*. London: Secker and War-burg, 1991.

Breton, André. "As in a Wood." *The Shadow and Its Shadow: Surrealist Writings on the Cinema*, ed. and trans. Paul Hammond, 72–77. San Francisco: City Lights, 2000.

Brook, Harry Ellington. *Los Angeles, California, the City and County*, 23d ed. Los Angeles: Los Angeles Chamber of Commerce, 1910.

Brown, Bill. *The Material Unconscious: American Amusement, Stephen Crane, and the Economies of Play*. Cambridge: Harvard University Press, 1996.

Brownlow, Kevin. *The War, the West, and the Wilderness*. New York: Alfred A. Knopf, 1979.

Bruno, Giuliana. *An Atlas of Emotion: Journeys in Art, Architecture, and Film*. London: Verso, 2002.

———. *Streetwalking on a Ruined Map: Cultural Theory and the City Films of Elvira Notari*. Princeton: Princeton University Press, 1993.

Buchholtz, C. W. *Man in Glacier*. West Glacier, Mont.: Glacier Natural History Asso-ciation, 1976.

Buck-Morss, Susan. *The Dialectics of Seeing: Walter Benjamin and the Arcades Project*. Cambridge: MIT Press, 1991.

Bunn, David. "'Our Wattled Cot': Mercantile and Domestic Space in Thomas Pringle's African Landscapes." *Landscape and Power*, ed. W. J. T. Mitchell, 129–36. Chicago: University of Chicago Press, 1994.

Burke, Edmund. *A Philosophical Enquiry into the Origin of Our Ideas of the Sublime and Beautiful* (1757), ed. James T. Boulton. Notre Dame, Ind.: University of Notre Dame Press, 1968.

Buscombe, Edward. "Painting the Legend: Frederic Remington and the Western." *Cinema Journal* 23, no. 4 (Summer 1984): 12–27.

Buttner, Nils. *Landscape Painting: A History*. New York: Abbeville, 2006.

Buzard, James. *The Beaten Track: European Tourism, Literature, and the Ways to "Cul-ture," 1800–1918*. New York: Oxford University Press, 1993.

Byerly, Alison. "'A Prodigious Map beneath His Feet': Virtual Travel and the Pano-ramic Perspective." *Nineteenth-Century Contexts* 29, nos. 2–3 (June–September 2007): 151–68.

Caldwell, Genoa. *Burton Holmes Travelogues: The Greatest Traveler of His Time, 1892–1952*. New York: Taschen, 2006.

Chatel, Laurent. "'Getting the Picture' of the Picturesque: Some Thoughts on the Greatest British Aesthetic Muddle of the Eighteenth and Nineteenth Centuries."

XVII–XVIII: Bulletin de la Société d'Études Anglo-Américaines du XVIIe et XVIIIIe Siècles 51 (2000): 229–48.

Cherchi Usai, Paolo. "Pornography." *The Encyclopedia of Early Cinema*, ed. Richard Abel, 524–25. New York: Routledge, 2005.

———. "Société Française des Films et Cinématographes Éclair (1907–1919): A Checklist." *Griffithiana* (May–September 1992): 28–88.

Clarke, David B., and Marcus A. Doel. "Engineering Space and Time: Moving Pictures and Motionless Trips." *Journal of Historical Geography* 31 (2005): 41–60.

Clifford, James. "On Ethnographic Surrealism." *The Predicament of Culture: Twentieth-Century Ethnography, Literature, and Art*, 117–51. Cambridge: Harvard University Press, 1988.

Combe, William. *The Tour of Dr. Syntax, in Search of the Picturesque*. London: Ackermann, 1813.

Crafton, Donald. "Pie and Chase: Gag, Spectacle and Narrative in Slapstick Comedy." *Classical Hollywood Comedy*, ed. Kristine Brunovska Karnick and Henry Jenkins, 106–10. New York: Routledge, 1995.

Crangle, Richard. "'Next Slide Please': The Lantern Lecture in Britain, 1890–1910." *The Sounds of Early Cinema*, ed. Richard Abel and Rick Altman, 39–47. Bloomington: Indiana University Press, 2001.

Creswell, Tim. *Place: A Short Introduction*. Malden, Mass.: Blackwell, 2004.

Cronon, William. "The Trouble with Wilderness, or, Getting back to the Wrong Nature." *Uncommon Ground: Toward Reinventing Nature*, ed. William Cronon, 69–90. New York: W. W. Norton, 1995.

Culler, Jonathan. "The Semiotics of Tourism." *Framing the Sign: Criticism and Its Institutions*, 153–67. Norman: University of Oklahoma Press, 1988.

Curtis, Scott. "A House Divided: The MPPC in Transition." *American Cinema's Transitional Era: Audiences, Institutions, Practices*, ed. Charlie Keil and Shelley Stamp, 239–64. Berkeley: University of California Press, 2004.

———. "The Taste of a Nation: Training the Senses and Sensibility of Cinema Audiences in Imperial Germany." *Film History* 6, no. 4 (1994): 445–69.

Dahlquist, Marina. "'Swat the Fly': Educational Films and Health Campaigns, 1909–1914." *Kinoöffentlichkeit (1895–1920): Entstehung—Etablierung—Differenzierung / Cinema's Public Sphere (1895–1920): Emergence, Settlement, Differentiation*, ed. Corinna Muller and Harro Segeberg, 220–25. Munich: Schüren-Verlag, 2008.

Debord, Guy. *Society of the Spectacle*, trans. Donald Nicholson-Smith. New York: Zone Books, 1995.

Deleuze, Gilles. *Cinema 1: The Movement-Image*, trans. Hugh Tomlinson and Barbara Habberjam. Minneapolis: University of Minnesota Press, 1986.

Deleuze, Gilles, and Félix Guattari. *Kafka: Toward a Minor Literature*, trans. Dana Polan. Minneapolis: University of Minnesota Press, 1986.

———. *A Thousand Plateaus: Capitalism and Schizophrenia*, trans. Brian Massumi. Minneapolis: University of Minnesota Press, 1987.

Delluc, Louis. "Beauty in the Cinema" (1917). *French Film Theory and Criticism*, vol. 1, ed. Richard Abel, 137–39. Princeton: Princeton University Press, 1988.

Delmeulle, Frédéric. "Production et distribution du documentaire en France (1909–1929)." *1895* 18 (Summer 1995): 200–215.

Depue, Oscar B. "My First Fifty Years in Motion Pictures." *A Technological History of Motion Pictures and Television*, ed. Raymond Fielding, 60–64. Berkeley: University of California Press, 1979.

Dewey, John. *Art as Experience*. New York: Minton, Balch, 1934.

———. *Democracy and Education*. New York: Macmillan, 1916.

Dippie, Brian W. *The Vanishing American: White Attitudes and U.S. Indian Policy*. Lawrence: University Press of Kansas, 1982.

Du Bois, W. E. B. "The Talented Tenth" (1903). *The Negro Problem: A Series of Articles by Representative American Negroes of Today*, 31–75. Miami: Mnemosyne, 1969.

Dunwoodie, Peter. *Writing French Algeria*. Oxford: Clarendon, 1998.

Elsaesser, Thomas. "Archives and Archaeologies: The Place of Non-fiction Film in Contemporary Media." *Films That Work: Industrial Film and the Productivity of Media*, ed. Vinzenz Hediger and Patrick Vonderau, 30–31. Amsterdam: Amsterdam University Press, 2009.

———. "The New Film History as Media Archaeology." *Cinémas* 14, nos. 2–3 (2004): 75–117.

Elsaesser, Thomas, with Adam Barker, eds. *Early Cinema: Space, Frame, Narrative*. London: British Film Institute, 1990.

Epstein, Jean. *La poésie d'aujourd'hui, un nouvel état d'intelligence*. Paris: La Sirène, 1921.

Erb, Cynthia. *Tracking King Kong: A Hollywood Icon in World Culture*. Detroit: Wayne State University Press, 1998.

Evans, Brad. "Commentary: Catherine Russell's Recovery of the *Head-Hunters*." *Visual Anthropology* 11 (Spring 1998): 221–42.

Evans, Nancy L. "Frederick Starr: Missionary for Anthropology." Master's thesis, Department of Anthropology, Indiana University, Bloomington, 1987.

Fanon, Frantz. "Algeria Unveiled." *A Dying Colonialism*, trans. Haakon Chevalier, 35–67. New York: Grove, 1967.

Fell, John L., ed. *Film before Griffith*. Berkeley: University of California Press, 1983.

Fielding, Raymond. "Hale's Tours: Ultrarealism in the Pre-1910 Motion Picture." *Film before Griffith*, ed. John L. Fell, 116–30. Berkeley: University of California Press, 1983.

Friedberg, Anne. *Window Shopping: Cinema and the Postmodern*. Berkeley: University of California Press, 1993.

Fussell, Paul. *Abroad: British Literary Travelling between the Wars*. New York: Oxford University Press, 1980.

Gaines, Jane. "From Elephants to Lux Soap: The Programming and 'Flow' of Early Motion Picture Exploitation." *Velvet Light Trap* 25 (Spring 1990): 29–43.

Gaines, Kevin K. *Uplifting the Race: Black Leadership, Politics, and Culture in the Twentieth Century*. Chapel Hill: University of North Carolina Press, 1996.

Garncarz, Joseph. "The Fairground Cinema: A European Institution," trans. Annemone Ligensa. *Travelling Cinema in Europe*, ed. Martin Loiperdinger, 78–90. Frankfurt: Stroemfeld Verlag, 2008.

Gaudreault, André. "Film, Narrative, Narration: The Cinema of the Lumière Brothers." *Early Cinema: Space, Frame, Narrative*, ed. Thomas Elsaesser, with Adam Barker, 68–75. London: British Film Institute, 1990.

Gaudreault, André, and Philippe Marion. "A Medium Is Always Born Twice . . ." *Early Popular Visual Culture* 3, no. 1 (May 2005): 3–15.

———. "The Mysterious Affair of Styles in the Age of Kine-attractography." *Early Popular Visual Culture* 8, no. 1 (February 2010): 17–30.

Gaycken, Oliver. "The Cinema of the Future: Visions of the Medium as Modern Educator, 1895–1910." *Learning with the Lights Off: Educational Film in the United States*, ed. Devin Orgeron, Marsha Orgeron, and Dan Streible, 67–89. New York: Oxford University Press, 2012.

———. *Devices of Curiosity: Early Cinema and Popular Science*. Oxford: Oxford University Press, forthcoming.

General Film Company. *Catalogue of Educational Motion Pictures*. New York: General Film Company, 1912.

Georges-Michel, Michel. "Henri Bergson Talks to Us about Cinema." *Le Journal*, 20 February 1914. Trans. Louis-Georges Schwartz. *Cinema Journal* 50, no. 3 (Spring 2011): 79–82.

Gilpin, William. *Observations on the River Wye, and Several Parts of South Wales, etc. relative chiefly to Picturesque Beauty; made in the Summer of the Year 1770* (1782). Reprinted in *The Picturesque: Literary Sources and Documents*, 3 vols., ed. Malcolm Andrews, 1:241–78. East Sussex: Helm Information, 1994.

———. "On the Principles on Which the Author's Sketches Are Composed" (1804). Reprinted in *The Picturesque: Literary Sources and Documents*, 3 vols., ed. Malcolm Andrews, 2:287–95. East Sussex: Helm Information, 1994.

———. *Three Essays: On Picturesque Beauty; on Picturesque Travel; and on Sketching Landscape, to which is added a Poem, on Landscape Painting* (1792, 1794). Reprinted in *The Picturesque: Literary Sources and Documents*, 3 vols., ed. Malcolm Andrews, 2:5–60. East Sussex: Helm Information, 1994.

Goetzmann, William H. *Exploration and Empire: The Explorer and the Scientist in the Winning of the American West*. New York: W. W. Norton, 1966.

Grieveson, Lee. *Policing Cinema: Movies and Censorship in Early-Twentieth-Century America*. Berkeley: University of California Press, 2004.

Griffiths, Alison. "Time Traveling IMAX Style: Tales from the Giant Screen." *Virtual Voyages: Cinema and Travel*, ed. Jeffrey Ruoff, 238–58. Durham: Duke University Press, 2006.

———. *Wondrous Difference: Cinema, Anthropology, and Turn-of-the-Century Visual Culture*. New York: Columbia University Press, 2002.

Gunning, Tom. "An Aesthetic of Astonishment: Early Film and the (In)Credulous Spectator." *Viewing Positions: Ways of Seeing Film*, ed. Linda Williams, 114–33. New Brunswick: Rutgers University Press, 1994.

———. "Attractions: How They Came into the World." *The Cinema of Attractions Reloaded*, ed. Wanda Strauven, 31–40. Amsterdam: Amsterdam University Press, 2006.

———. "Before Documentary: Early Nonfiction Films and the 'View' Aesthetic." *Uncharted Territory: Essays on Early Nonfiction Film*, ed. Daan Hertogs and Nico de Klerk, 9–24. Amsterdam: Stichting Nederlands Filmmuseum, 1997.

———. "The Cinema of Attractions: Early Film, Its Spectator and the Avant-Garde." *Early Cinema: Space, Frame, Narrative*, ed. Thomas Elsaesser, with Adam Barker, 56–62. London: British Film Institute, 1990.

———. *D. W. Griffith and the Origins of American Narrative Film: The Early Years at Biograph*. Urbana: University of Illinois Press, 1994.

———. "Early Cinema as Global Cinema: The Encyclopedic Ambition." *Early Cinema and the "National,"* ed. Richard Abel, Giorgio Bertellini, and Rob King, 11–21. New Barnet, Herts.: John Libbey, 2008.

———. "Moving away from the Index: Cinema and the Impression of Reality." *differences* 18, no. 1 (2007): 29–52.

———. "The Scene of Speaking: Two Decades of Discovering the Film Lecturer." *Iris* 27 (Spring 1999): 67–79.

———. "Systematizing the Electric Message: Narrative Form, Gender, and Modernity in *The Lonedale Operator*." *American Cinema's Transitional Era: Audiences, Institutions, Practices*, ed. Charlie Keil and Shelley Stamp, 15–50. Berkeley: University of California Press, 2004.

———. "'Those Drawn with a Very Fine Camel's Hair Brush': The Origins of Film Genres." *Iris* 20 (Fall 1995): 49–61.

———. "Towards a Minor Cinema: Fonoroff, Herwitz, Ahwesh, Lapore, Klahr and Solomon." *Motion Picture* 3, nos. 1–2 (Winter 1989–90): 2–5.

———. "'An Unseen Energy Swallows Space': The Space in Early Film and Its Relation to American Avant-Garde Film." *Film before Griffith*, ed. John L. Fell, 355–66. Berkeley: University of California Press, 1983.

———. "'The Whole World within Reach': Travel Images without Borders." *Virtual Voyages: Cinema and Travel*, ed. Jeffrey Ruoff, 25–41. Durham: Duke University Press, 2006.

Haenni, Sabine. *The Immigrant Scene: Ethnic Amusements in New York, 1880–1920*. Minneapolis: University of Minnesota Press, 2008.

Hall, C. Michael, and Stephen J. Page. *The Geography of Tourism and Recreation: Environment, Place, and Space*, 3d ed. London: Routledge, 2006.

Hamby, Alonzo L. "Progressivism: A Century of Change and Rebirth." *Progressivism and the New Democracy*, ed. Sidney M. Milkis and Jerome M. Mileur, 40–80. Amherst: University of Massachusetts Press, 1999.

Hansen, Miriam. *Babel and Babylon: Spectatorship in American Silent Film*. Cambridge: Harvard University Press, 1991.

———. *Cinema and Experience: Siegfried Kracauer, Walter Benjamin, and Theodor W. Adorno*. Berkeley: University of California Press, 2012.

———. "The Mass Production of the Senses: Classical Cinema as Vernacular Modernism." *Modernism/Modernity* 6, no. 2 (1999): 59–77.

Hanssen, Eirik Frisvold. "Early Discourses on Colour and Cinema: Origins, Functions, Meanings." PhD diss., Stockholm University, 2006.

Hardt, Michael, and Antonio Negri. *Empire*. Cambridge: Harvard University Press, 2000.

Harrison, Gary, and Jill Heydt-Stevenson. "Variations on the Picturesque: Authority, Play, and Practice." *European Romantic Review* 13 (2002): 3–10.

Hechter, Michael. *Internal Colonialism: The Celtic Fringe in British National Development*. Berkeley: University of California Press, 1975.

Hediger, Vinzenz, and Patrick Vonderau, eds. *Films That Work: Industrial Film and the Productivity of Media*. Amsterdam: Amsterdam University Press, 2009.

———. "Record, Rhetoric, Rationalization: Industrial Organization and Film." *Films That Work: Industrial Film and the Productivity of Media*, ed. Vinzenz Hediger and Patrick Vonderau, 35–49. Amsterdam: Amsterdam University Press, 2009.

Hemingway, Andrew. *Landscape Imagery and Urban Culture in Early Nineteenth-Century Britain*. Cambridge: Cambridge University Press, 1992.

Hepburn, R. W. *"Wonder" and Other Essays*. Edinburgh: Edinburgh University Press, 1984.

Hertogs, Daan, and Nico de Klerk, eds. *Disorderly Order: Colours in Silent Film*. Amsterdam: Stichting Nederlands Filmmuseum, 1996.

———. *Nonfiction from the Teens: The 1994 Amsterdam Workshop*. Amsterdam: Stichting Nederlands Filmmuseum, 1994.

———. *Uncharted Territory: Essays on Early Nonfiction Film*. Amsterdam: Stichting Nederlands Filmmuseum, 1997.

Higashi, Sumiko. "Dialogue: Manhattan's Nickelodeons." *Cinema Journal* 35, no. 3 (Spring 1996): 72–74.

Hipple, Walter John, Jr. *The Beautiful, the Sublime, and the Picturesque in Eighteenth-Century British Aesthetic Theory*. Carbondale: Southern Illinois University Press, 1957.

Hobsbawm, Eric J. *The Age of Empire: 1875–1914*. London: Weidenfeld and Nicolson, 1987.

———. "Introduction: Inventing Traditions." *The Invention of Tradition*, ed. Eric J. Hobsbawm and Terence Ranger, 1–14. Cambridge: Cambridge University Press, 1983.

Holmes, Burton, ed. *The Burton Holmes Lectures*. 10 vols. New York: McClure, 1908.

———. "Moki Land." *Burton Holmes Travelogues*, 6:227–336. New York: McClure, 1908.

———. "The Stereoscope as a Title Deed to the World." *A Trip around the World through the Stereoscope*, ed. Burton Holmes, 9–10. Meadville, Penn.: Keystone View Company, 1926.

———. *A Trip around the World through the Stereoscope*. Meadville, Penn.: Keystone View Company, 1926.

———. *The World Is Mine*. Culver City, Calif.: Murray and Gee, 1953.

Horne, Jennifer. "Nostalgia and Non-fiction in Edison's 1917 *Conquest Program*." *Historical Journal of Film, Radio and Television* 22, no. 3 (2002): 315–31.

Horowitz, Rita. *An Index to Volume 1 of "The Moving Picture World and View Photographer."* Washington, D.C.: American Film Institute, 1974.

Horwitz, Rita, and Harriet Harrison. *The George Kleine Collection of Early Motion Pictures in the Library of Congress: A Catalog.* Washington, D.C.: Library of Congress, 1980.

Hudson, Brian J. "Waterfalls, Tourism, and Landscape." *Geography* 91, no. 1 (Spring 2006): 3–12.

Hulme, Peter, and Tim Youngs, eds. *The Cambridge Companion to Travel Writing.* Cambridge: Cambridge University Press, 2002.

Hunt, John Dixon. *Gardens and the Picturesque: Studies in the History of Landscape Architecture.* Cambridge: MIT Press, 1992.

Hussey, Christopher. *The Picturesque: Studies in a Point of View* (1927), repr. ed. London: Cass, 1967.

Hyde, Anne Farrar. *An American Vision: Far Western Landscape and National Culture, 1880–1920.* New York: New York University Press, 1990.

Jackson, Gregory S. "Cultivating Spiritual Sight: Jacob Riis's Virtual-Tour Narrative and the Visual Modernization of Protestant Homiletics." *Representations* 83 (Summer 2003): 126–66.

Jakle, John A. *The Tourist: Travel in Twentieth-Century North America.* Lincoln: University of Nebraska Press, 1985.

Jauss, Hans Robert. "Modernity and Literary Tradition." *Critical Inquiry* 31, no. 2 (Winter 2005): 329–64.

Kant, Immanuel. *Critique of Judgment*, trans. Werner S. Pluhar. Indianapolis: Hackett, 1987.

Kaplan, Caren. *Questions of Travel: Postmodern Discourses of Displacement.* Durham: Duke University Press, 1996.

Kaplan, E. Ann. *Looking for the Other: Feminism, Film, and the Imperial Gaze.* New York: Routledge, 1997.

Kay, Cristóbal. *Latin American Theories of Development and Underdevelopment.* New York: Routledge, 1989.

Keil, Charlie. *Early American Cinema in Transition: Story, Style, and Filmmaking, 1907–1913.* Madison: University of Wisconsin Press, 2001.

———. "Steel Engines and Cardboard Rockets: The Status of Fiction and Nonfiction in Early Cinema." *Persistence of Vision* 9 (1991): 37–45.

Keil, Charlie, and Shelley Stamp, eds. *American Cinema's Transitional Era: Audiences, Institutions, Practices.* Berkeley: University of California Press, 2004.

King, Rob. "'Made for the Masses with an Appeal to the Classes': The Triangle Film Corporation and the Failure of Highbrow Film Culture." *Cinema Journal* 44, no. 2 (Winter 2005): 3–33.

Kirby, Lynne. *Parallel Tracks: The Railroad and Silent Cinema*. Durham: Duke University Press, 1997.

Kleine, George. *Catalogue of Educational Motion Pictures*. Chicago: George Kleine, 1910.

Kleinman, Sharon S., and Daniel G. McDonald. "Silent Film and the Socialization of American Immigrants: Lessons from an Old New Medium." *Journal of American and Comparative Cultures* 23, no. 3 (Fall 2000): 79–87.

Knight, Richard Payne. *Analytical Inquiry into the Principles of Taste* (1805). Reprinted in *The Picturesque: Literary Sources and Documents*, 3 vols., ed. Malcolm Andrews, 2:326–51. East Sussex: Helm Information, 1994.

Knupfer, Anne Meis, and Christine Woyshner, eds. *The Educational Work of Women's Organizations, 1890–1960*. New York: Palgrave Macmillan, 2008.

Koch, Howard. "Script to Screen with Max Ophüls." *Letter from an Unknown Woman*, ed. Virginia Wright Wexman and Karen Hollinger, 197–203. New Brunswick: Rutgers University Press, 1986.

Komatsu, Hiroshi. "From Natural Colour to the Pure Motion Picture Drama: The Meaning of Tenkatsu Company in the 1910s of Japanese Film History." *Film History* 7, no. 1 (Spring 1995): 70–73.

Koszarski, Richard. *An Evening's Entertainment: The Age of the Silent Feature Picture, 1915–1928*. Berkeley: University of California Press, 1990.

Kracauer, Siegfried. "Photography" (1927). *The Mass Ornament: Weimar Essays*, trans. and ed. Thomas Y. Levin, 47–63. Cambridge: Harvard University Press, 1995.

Kramnick, Isaac. *The Rage of Edmund Burke: Portrait of an Ambivalent Conservative*. New York: Basic Books, 1977.

Krauss, Rosalind. *The Originality of the Avant-Garde and Other Modernist Myths*. Cambridge: MIT Press, 1985.

Lagny, Michèle. "Film History: Or History Expropriated." *Film History* 6 (1994): 26–44.

Lears, T. J. Jackson. *No Place of Grace: Antimodernism and the Transformation of American Culture, 1880–1920*. Chicago: University of Chicago Press, 1994.

Lefebvre, Henri. *Critique of Everyday Life*, trans. John Moore. London: Verso, 1992.

Lefebvre, Martin. "Between Setting and Landscape in the Cinema." *Landscape and Film*, ed. Martin Lefebvre, 19–59. New York: Routledge, 2006.

———, ed. *Landscape and Film*. New York: Routledge, 2006.

Lefebvre, Thierry. "The Scientia Production (1911–1914): Scientific Popularization through Pictures." *Griffithiana* 47 (May 1993): 137–52.

Lehman, Peter. "Looking at Ivy Looking at Us Looking at Her." *Wide Angle* 5 no. 3 (1983): 59–63.

Leutrat, Jean-Louis, and Suzanne Liandrat-Guigues. "John Ford and Monument Valley." *Back in the Saddle Again: New Essays on the Western*, ed. Edward Buscombe and Roberta E. Pearson, 160–69. London: British Film Institute, 1998.

Levine, Lawrence. *Highbrow/Lowbrow: The Emergence of Cultural Hierarchy in America*. Cambridge: Harvard University Press, 1988.

Lifelong Learning: Visual Aids to Education. Berkeley: University of California Extension, 1936.

Lindsay, Vachel. *The Art of the Moving Picture* (1915). New York: Macmillan, 1922.

Lindstrom, J. A. "'Almost Worse Than the Restrictive Measures': Chicago Reformers and the Nickelodeons." *Cinema Journal* 39, no. 1 (Fall 1999): 90–112.

Loiperdinger, Martin, ed. *Travelling Cinema in Europe.* KINtop-Schriften vol. 10. Frankfurt: Stroemfeld Verlag, 2008.

Macarthur, John. "The Heartlessness of the Picturesque: Sympathy and Disgust in Ruskin's Aesthetics." *Assemblage* 32 (April 1997): 126–41.

MacCannell, Dean. *The Tourist: A New Theory of the Leisure Class.* New York: Schocken Books, 1989.

Macdonald, Dwight. "Masscult and Midcult." *Masscult and Midcult: Essays against the American Grain,* 3–71. New York: New York Review of Books, 2011.

MacDonald, Scott. *The Garden in the Machine: A Field Guide to Independent Films about Place.* Berkeley: University of California Press, 2001.

Mackenzie, John M. "Empires of Travel: British Guide Books and Cultural Imperialism in the 19th and 20th Centuries." *Histories of Tourism: Representation, Identity, and Conflict,* ed. John K. Walton, 19–38. Buffalo, N.Y.: Channel View Publications, 2005.

Mann, Thomas. *The Magic Mountain* (1924), trans. John E. Woods. New York: Vintage, 1996.

Marcus, Laura. "'A New Form of True Beauty': Aesthetics and Early Film Criticism." *The Tenth Muse: Writing about Cinema in the Modernist Period,* 179–233. Oxford: Oxford University Press, 2007.

Marshall, David. "The Problem of the Picturesque." *Eighteenth-Century Studies* 35, no. 3 (Spring 2002): 413–37.

Marzio, Peter. *The Democratic Art: Pictures for a 19th-Century America, Chromolithography 1840–1900.* Boston: David R. Godine, 1979.

Massey, Doreen. *Space, Place, and Gender.* Minneapolis: University of Minnesota Press, 1994.

Mebold, Anke, and Charles Tepperman. "Resurrecting the Lost History of 28 mm Film in North America." *Film History* 15, no. 2 (2003): 137–51.

McKernan, Luke. "Putting the World before You: The Charles Urban Story." *Young and Innocent? The Cinema in Britain, 1896–1930,* ed. Andrew Higson, 65–77. Exeter: University of Exeter Press, 2002.

———. "Something More Than a Mere Picture Show: Charles Urban and the Early Non-fiction Film in Great Britain and America, 1897–1925." PhD diss., Birkbeck College, University of London, 2003.

McNamara, Brooks. "The Scenography of Popular Entertainment." *Drama Review* 18, no. 1 (March 1974): 59–79.

Merritt, Russell. "Nickelodeon Theaters 1905–1914: Building an Audience for the Movies." *The American Film Industry,* ed. Tino Balio, 59–79. Madison: University of Wisconsin Press, 1976.

Mesguich, Félix. *Tours de Manivelle. Souvenirs d'un chasseur d'images.* Paris: Éditions Bernard Grasset, 1933.

Michasiw, Kim Ian. "Nine Revisionist Theses on the Picturesque." *Representations* 38 (Spring 1992): 76–100.

Mieras, Emily. "Latter-Day Knights: College Women, Social Settlements, and Social Class in the Progressive-Era United States." *The Educational Work of Women's Organizations, 1890–1960,* ed. Anne Meis Knupfer and Christine Woyshner, 101–19. New York: Palgrave Macmillan, 2008.

Milkis, Sidney M. "Introduction: Progressivism Then and Now." *Progressivism and the New Democracy,* ed. Sidney M. Milkis and Jerome M. Mileur, 1–39. Amherst: University of Massachusetts, Press, 1999.

Mitchell, W. J. T. "Eye and Ear: Edmund Burke and the Politics of Sensibility." *Iconology: Image, Text, Ideology,* 116–49. Chicago: University of Chicago Press, 1986.

———. "Imperial Landscape." *Landscape and Power,* ed. W. J. T. Mitchell, 5–34. Chicago: University of Chicago Press, 1994.

———, ed. *Landscape and Power.* Chicago: University of Chicago Press, 1994.

Moch, Leslie Page. "Moving Europeans: Historical Migration Practices in Western Europe." *The Cambridge Survey of World Migration,* ed. Robin Cohen, 126–30. Cambridge: Cambridge University Press, 1995.

Moritz, William. *Optical Poetry: The Life and Work of Oskar Fischinger.* Bloomington: Indiana University Press, 2004.

Munsterberg, Hugo. *The Photoplay: A Psychological Study.* New York: D. Appleton, 1916.

Musser, Charles, ed. *Edison Motion Pictures, 1890–1900: An Annotated Filmography.* Washington, D.C.: Smithsonian Institution Press, 1997.

———. *The Emergence of Cinema: The American Screen to 1907.* Berkeley: University of California Press, 1990.

———. *A Guide to Motion Picture Catalogs by American Producers and Distributors, 1894–1908,* microfilm. Frederick, Md.: University Publications of America, 1985.

———. "The Travel Genre in 1903–04: Moving towards Fictional Narrative." *Early Cinema: Space, Frame, Narrative,* ed. Thomas Elsaesser, with Adam Barker, 123–32. London: British Film Institute, 1990.

Musser, Charles, with Carol Nelson. *High-Class Moving Pictures: Lyman H. Howe and the Forgotten Era of Traveling Exhibition, 1880–1920.* Princeton: Princeton University Press, 1991.

Naficy, Hamid. "Lured by the East: Ethnographic and Expedition Films about Nomadic Tribes—The Case of *Grass* (1925)." *Virtual Voyages: Cinema and Travel,* ed. Jeffrey Ruoff, 117–38. Durham: Duke University Press, 2006.

Naggar, Carole. "The Unveiled: Algerian Women, 1960." *Aperture* 119 (1990): 2–11.

Nash, Roderick. *Wilderness and the American Mind,* rev. ed. New Haven: Yale University Press, 1973.

Neider, Charles, ed. *The Complete Essays of Mark Twain.* New York: Da Capo, 2000.

Nichols, Bill. *Representing Reality: Issues and Concepts in Documentary.* Bloomington: Indiana University Press, 1992.

Nichols, John. "Countering Censorship: Edgar Dale and the Film Appreciation Movement." *Cinema Journal* 46, no. 1 (Autumn 2006): 3–22.

Nochlin, Linda. "The Imaginary Orient." *The Politics of Vision: Essays on Nineteenth-Century Art and Society*, 33–59. New York: Harper and Row, 1989.

Nye, David. *American Technological Sublime*. Cambridge: MIT Press, 1994.

Ogihara, Junko. "Exhibition of Films for Japanese Americans in Los Angeles during the Silent Era." *Film History* 4 (1990): 81–87.

Okubo, Kiyoaki. "*Kimiko* in New York." *Rouge* 10 (1997). Available at www.rouge.com.au/10/kimiko.html.

Olsson, Jan. "Hollywood's First Spectators: Notes on Ethnic Nickelodeon Audiences in Los Angeles." *Aztlán* 26, no. 1 (Spring 2001): 181–95.

———. *Los Angeles before Hollywood: Journalism and American Film Culture, 1905–1915*. Stockholm: National Library of Sweden, 2008.

Orgeron, Devin, Marsha Orgeron, and Dan Streible, eds. *Learning with the Lights Off: Educational Film in the United States*. New York: Oxford University Press, 2012.

Orsi, Richard J. *Sunset Limited: The Southern Pacific Railroad and the Development of the American West*. Berkeley: University of California Press, 2005.

Packe, Charles. *A Guide to the Pyrenees*, 2d ed. London: Longmans, Green, 1867.

Parr, Adrian, ed. *The Deleuze Dictionary*. New York: Columbia University Press, 2005.

Patten, Simon. *The New Basis of Civilization*. New York: Macmillan, 1907.

Peiss, Kathy. *Cheap Amusements: Working Women and Leisure in Turn-of-the-Century New York*. Philadelphia: Temple University Press, 1986.

Peterson, Jennifer. "Glimpses of Animal Life: Nature Films and the Emergence of Classroom Cinema." *Learning with the Lights Off: Educational Film in the United States*, ed. Devin Orgeron, Marsha Orgeron, and Dan Streible, 145–67. New York: Oxford University Press, 2012.

———. "'The Knowledge Which Comes in Pictures': Educational Films and Early Cinema Audiences." *A Companion to Early Cinema*, ed. André Gaudreault, Nicolas Dulac, and Santiago Hidalgo, 277–97. Malden, Mass.: Wiley-Blackwell, 2012.

———. "'The Nation's First Playground': Travel Films and the American West, 1895–1920." *Virtual Voyages: Cinema and Travel*, ed. Jeffrey Ruoff, 79–98. Durham: Duke University Press, 2006.

———. "Travelogues and Immigrants." *Domitor 2008: Proceedings of the Domitor Conference on Early Cinema*, 269–80. Perpignan: Presses Universitaires de Perpignan, 2010.

———. "World Pictures: Travelogue Films and the Lure of the Exotic, 1890–1920." PhD diss., University of Chicago, 1999.

Pinney, Christopher, and Nicolas Peterson. *Photography's Other Histories*. Durham: Duke University Press, 2003.

Poignant, Roslyn. "The Making of Professional 'Savages': From P. T. Barnum (1883) to the *Sunday Times* (1998)." *Photography's Other Histories*, ed. Christopher Pinney and Nicolas Peterson, 55–84. Durham: Duke University Press, 2003.

Pollmann, Inga. "Cinematic Vitalism: Theories of Life and the Moving Image." PhD diss., University of Chicago, 2011.

Pomeroy, Earl. *In Search of the Golden West: The Tourist in Western America*. New York: Alfred A. Knopf, 1957.

Post, Emily. *By Motor to the Golden Gate*. New York: D. Appleton, 1916.

Pratt, Mary Louise. *Imperial Eyes: Travel Writing and Transculturation*. London: Routledge, 1992.

Price, Martin. "The Picturesque Moment." *From Sensibility to Romanticism: Essays Presented to Frederick A. Pottle*, ed. Frederick W. Hilles and Harold Bloom, 259–92. Oxford: Oxford University Press, 1965.

Price, Uvedale. *Essays on the Picturesque, as compared with the Sublime and the Beautiful* (1810). Reprinted in *The Picturesque: Literary Sources and Documents*, 3 vols., ed. Malcolm Andrews, 2:72–142. East Sussex: Helm Information, 1994.

Rabinovitz, Lauren. "'Bells and Whistles': The Sound of Meaning in Train Travel Film Rides." *The Sounds of Early Cinema*, ed. Richard Abel and Rick Altman, 167–80. Bloomington: Indiana University Press, 2001.

———. *For the Love of Pleasure: Women, Movies, and Pleasure in Turn-of-the-Century Chicago*. New Brunswick: Rutgers University Press, 1998.

Rainey, Sue. *Creating Picturesque America: Monument to the Natural and Cultural Landscape*. Nashville: Vanderbilt University Press, 1994.

Rapee, Erno. *Encyclopaedia of Music for Pictures*. New York: Belwin, 1925.

Ray, Robert. "Impressionism, Surrealism, and Film Theory: Path Dependence, or How a Tradition in Film Theory Gets Lost." *The Oxford Guide to Film Studies*, ed. John Hill and Pamela Church Gibson, 67–76. Oxford: Oxford University Press, 1998.

Reynolds, Herbert. "Ancient Temples of Egypt." In John L. Fell, *Before Hollywood: Turn-of-the-Century American Film*, 137. New York: Hudson Hills, 1987.

Roan, Jeanette. *Envisioning Asia: On Location, Travel, and the Cinematic Geography of U.S. Orientalism*. Ann Arbor: University of Michigan Press, 2010.

———. "Exotic Explorations: Travels to Asia and the Pacific in Early Cinema." *Re/collecting Early Asian America*, ed. Josephine Lee, Imogene L. Lim, and Yuko Matsukawa, 187–99. Philadelphia: Temple University Press, 2002.

Robinson, Sidney. *Inquiry into the Picturesque*. Chicago: University of Chicago Press, 1991.

Romains, Jules. "The Crowd at the Cinematograph" (1911). *French Film Theory and Criticism*, vol. 1, ed. Richard Abel, 53–54. Princeton: Princeton University Press, 1988.

Rony, Fatimah Tobing. *The Third Eye: Race, Cinema, and Ethnographic Spectacle*. Durham: Duke University Press, 1996.

Rose, Bernice B., ed. *Picasso, Braque, and Early Film in Cubism*. Exhibition catalogue. New York: Pace Wildenstein, 2007.

Rosen, Philip. *Change Mummified: Cinema, Historicity, Theory*. Minneapolis: University of Minnesota Press, 2001.

Ross, Steven J. *Working-Class Hollywood: Silent Film and the Shaping of Class in America*. Princeton: Princeton University Press, 1998.

Rousseau, Jean-Jacques. *Reveries of the Solitary Walker* (1782), trans. Peter France. London: Penguin, 1979.

Rubin, Joan Shelley. *The Making of Middlebrow Culture*. Chapel Hill: University of North Carolina Press, 1992.

Runte, Alfred. *National Parks: The American Experience*, 2d rev. ed. Lincoln: University of Nebraska Press, 1987.

Ruoff, Jeffrey. "Show and Tell: The 16 mm Travel Lecture Film." *Virtual Voyages: Cinema and Travel*, ed. Jeffrey Ruoff, 217–37. Durham: Duke University Press, 2006.

———, ed. *Virtual Voyages: Cinema and Travel*. Durham: Duke University Press, 2006.

Ruskin, John. "Of the Turnerian Picturesque." *Modern Painters*, vol. 4. (1856). Reprinted in *The Picturesque: Literary Sources and Documents*, 3 vols., ed. Malcolm Andrews, 3:348–59. East Sussex: Helm Information, 1994.

Russell, Catherine. *Experimental Ethnography: The World of Film in the Age of Video*. Durham: Duke University Press, 1999.

Sadoul, Georges. *Dziga Vertov*. Paris: Éditions Champ Libre, 1971.

Said, Edward. *Culture and Imperialism*. New York: Vintage, 1993.

———. *Orientalism*. New York: Vintage, 1979.

Salzani, Carlo. "The Atrophy of Experience: Walter Benjamin and Boredom." *Essays on Boredom and Modernity*, ed. Barbara Dalle Pezze and Carlo Salzani, 127–55. Amsterdam: Rodopi, 2009.

Sandberg, Mark. *Living Pictures, Missing Persons: Mannequins, Museums, and Modernity*. Princeton: Princeton University Press, 2002.

Sartin, Hank. "Drawing on Hollywood: Warner Bros. Cartoons and Hollywood, 1930–1960." PhD diss., University of Chicago, 1998.

Schwartz, Vanessa R. *Spectacular Realities: Early Mass Culture in Fin-de-Siècle Paris*. Berkeley: University of California Press, 1998.

Sears, John. *Sacred Places: American Tourist Attractions in the Nineteenth Century*. New York: Oxford University Press, 1989.

Segrave, Kerry. *Foreign Films in America: A History*. Jefferson, N.C.: McFarland, 2004.

Shaffer, Marguerite S. *See America First: Tourism and National Identity, 1880–1940*. Washington, D.C.: Smithsonian Institution Press, 2001.

———. "Seeing America First: The Search for Identity in the Tourist Landscape." *Seeing and Being Seen: Tourism in the American West*, ed. David M. Worel and Patrick T. Long, 165–93. Lawrence: University Press of Kansas, 2001.

Shail, Andrew. "Intermediality: Disciplinary Flux or Formalist Retrenchment?" *Early Popular Visual Culture* 8, no. 1 (February 2010): 3–15.

Sibley, David. *Geographies of Exclusion*. London: Routledge, 1995.

Singer, Ben. *Melodrama and Modernity: Early Sensational Cinema and Its Contexts*. New York: Columbia University Press, 2001.

———. "New York, Just like I Pictured It . . ." *Cinema Journal* 35, no. 3 (Spring 1996): 104–28.

Sitney, P. Adams. "Landscape in the Cinema: The Rhythms of the World and the Camera." *Landscape, Natural Beauty, and the Arts*, ed. Salim Kemal and Ivan Gaskell, 103–26. Cambridge: Cambridge University Press, 1993.

Slide, Anthony. *Before Video: A History of the Non-theatrical Film*. New York: Greenwood, 1992.

Slotkin, Richard. *Gunfighter Nation: The Myth of the Frontier in Twentieth-Century America*, 2d ed. Norman: University of Oklahoma Press, 1998.

Smith, Henry Nash. *Virgin Land: The American West as Symbol and Myth*, rev. ed. Cambridge: Harvard University Press, 1970.

Snyder, Joel. "Territorial Photography." *Landscape and Power*, ed. W. J. T. Mitchell, 175–201. Chicago: University of Chicago Press, 1994.

Solanas, Fernando, and Octavio Getino. "Towards a Third Cinema." *New Latin American Cinema*, vol. 1, ed. Michael T. Martin, 33–58. Detroit: Wayne State University Press, 1997.

Solnit, Rebecca. *River of Shadows: Eadweard Muybridge and the Technological Wild West*. New York: Viking, 2003.

———. *Wanderlust: A History of Walking*. New York: Penguin, 2000.

Spence, Mark David. *Dispossessing the Wilderness: Indian Removal and the Making of the National Parks*. New York: Oxford University Press, 1999.

Spring, Joel. *American Education: An Introduction to Social and Political Aspects*, 4th ed. New York: Longman, 1989.

Spurr, David. *The Rhetoric of Empire: Colonial Discourse in Journalism, Travel Writing, and Imperial Administration*. Durham: Duke University Press, 1993.

Stafford, Barbara Maria. *Artful Science: Enlightenment, Entertainment, and the Eclipse of Visual Education*. Cambridge: MIT Press, 1994.

———. *Voyage into Substance: Art, Science, Nature, and the Illustrated Travel Account, 1760–1840*. Cambridge: MIT Press, 1984.

Stamp, Shelley. *Movie-Struck Girls: Women and Motion Picture Culture after the Nickelodeon*. Princeton: Princeton University Press, 2000.

Stoddard, John L. *John L. Stoddard's Lectures*, vol. 10. Boston: Balch Brothers, 1898.

Stowe, William W. *Going Abroad: European Travel in Nineteenth-Century American Culture*. Princeton: Princeton University Press, 1994.

Streible, Dan. *Fight Pictures: A History of Boxing and Early Cinema*. Berkeley: University of California Press, 2008.

Taine, Hippolyte Adolphe. *Voyage aux eaux des Pyrénées*. Paris: Librairie de L. Hachette et Cie, 1855.

Thissen, Judith. "Jewish Immigrant Audiences in New York City, 1905–14." *American Movie Audiences: From the Turn of the Century to the Early Sound Era*, ed. Melvin Stokes and Richard Maltby, 15–28. London: British Film Institute, 1999.

Tobias, James. "For Love of Music: Oskar Fischinger's Modal, Musical Diagram."

Sync: Stylistics of Hieroglyphic Time, 76–108. Philadelphia: Temple University Press, 2010.

Toulet, Emmanuelle. "Cinema at the Universal Exposition, Paris, 1900." *Persistence of Vision* 9 (1993): 10–36.

Toulmin, Vanessa. "'Within the Reach of All': Traveling Cinematograph Shows on British Fairgrounds, 1896–1914." *Travelling Cinema in Europe*, ed. Martin Loiperdinger, 18–33. Frankfurt: Stroemfeld Verlag, 2008.

Trachtenberg, Alan. *The Incorporation of America: Society in the Gilded Age*. New York: Hill and Wang, 1982.

Turner, Frederick Jackson. *The Frontier in American History* (1920), repr. ed. New York: Dover, 1996.

Twain, Mark. *The Innocents Abroad* (1869). New York: Signet Classic, 1966.

Urbanora Catalogue: Scientific and Educational Subjects. London: Charles Urban Trading, 1908.

Uricchio, William, and Roberta E. Pearson. *Reframing Culture: The Case of the Vitagraph Quality Films*. Princeton: Princeton University Press, 1993.

Variety Film Reviews, 1907–1920, 24 vols. New York: Garland, 1983.

Vaughan, Dai. "Let There Be Lumière." *Early Cinema: Space, Frame, Narrative*, ed. Thomas Elsaesser, with Adam Barker, 63–67. London: British Film Institute, 1990.

Vernet, Mark. "The Look at the Camera," trans. Dana Polan. *Cinema Journal* 28, no. 2 (Winter 1989): 48–63.

Waller, Gregory. "Tracking the Non-theatrical: The American Cinema in 1915." Paper presented at the Chicago Film Seminar, February 10, 2011.

Warshow, Robert. *The Immediate Experience: Movies, Comics, Theatre and Other Aspects of Popular Culture*. New York: Atheneum, 1970.

West, Thomas. *A Guide to the Lakes in Cumberland, Westmoreland and Lancashire*, 2d ed. (1780). Reprinted in *The Picturesque: Literary Sources and Documents*, 3 vols., ed. Malcolm Andrews, 1:281–314. East Sussex: Helm Information, 1994.

Westbrook, Robert B. "Public Schooling and American Democracy." *Democracy, Education, and the Schools*, ed. Roger Soder, 125–150. San Francisco: Jossey-Bass, 1996.

Whissel, Kristin. *Picturing American Modernity: Traffic, Technology, and the Silent Cinema*. Durham: Duke University Press, 2008.

White, Trumbull. "Burton Holmes, the Man and His Work." *A Trip around the World through the Stereoscope*, ed. Burton Holmes, 11–30. Meadville, Penn.: Keystone View Company, 1926.

Willemen, Paul. "Letter to John." *Screen* 21, no. 2 (Summer 1980): 53–66.

Woodhull, Winifred. "Unveiling Algeria." *Genders* 10 (Spring 1991): 112–30.

Yard, Robert Sterling. *The National Parks Portfolio*, 2d ed. Washington, D.C.: U.S. Department of the Interior, National Park Service, 1917.

Young, Robert J. C. *Colonial Desire: Hybridity in Theory, Culture and Race*. London: Routledge, 1995.

Younger, Erin. "Changing Images: A Century of Photography on the Hopi Reservation (1880–1980)." *Hopi Photographers, Hopi Images,* comp. Victor Masayesva Jr. and Erin Younger, 14–39. Tucson: University of Arizona Press, 1983.

Yumibe, Joshua. *Moving Color: Early Film, Mass Culture, Modernism.* New Brunswick: Rutgers University Press, 2012.

———. "On the Education of the Senses: Synaesthetic Perception from the 'Democratic Art' of Chromolithography to Modernism." *New Review of Film and Television Studies* 7, no. 3 (September 2009), 257–74.

Archives and Special Collections

British Film Institute National Archive, London

EYE Film Institute Netherlands, Amsterdam

Frederick Starr Papers, Regenstein Library Special Collections, University of Chicago

George Eastman House, Rochester, N.Y.

George Kleine Collection, Motion Picture, Broadcast, and Recorded Sound Division, Library of Congress, Washington, D.C.

George Kleine Papers, Manuscript Division, Library of Congress, Washington, D.C.

UCLA Film and Television Archive, University of California, Los Angeles

William Selig Papers, Academy of Motion Picture Arts and Sciences' Margaret Herrick Library, Beverly Hills, Calif.

Newspapers, Periodicals, and Motion Picture Trade Publications

I have drawn heavily from period newspapers, periodicals, and especially the early motion picture trade press. Film reviews published in *Variety, Moving Picture World, Moving Picture News,* and the *Nickelodeon* (which changed its name to *Motography* in 1911) were mostly anonymous in this period, and I have given these citations in the notes. I have listed selected articles below in which an author's name or at least a title was given.

Ayres, Leonard. "Ladling Learning into Children." *Survey,* 6 September 1913, 686.

Baker, Horace C. "The Moving Picture Industry." *Nickelodeon* 1, no. 5 (May 1909): 132.

"Bonehead Exhibitors." *Nickelodeon* 3, no. 6 (15 March 1910): 139–40.

Bush, Stephen. "Review of *How Wild Animals Live.*" *Moving Picture World,* 8 November 1913, 592.

"A Change of Heart toward Scenics." *Nickelodeon* 5, no. 11 (18 March 1911): 294.

Crippen, James B. "An Educational Innovation." *Nickelodeon* 5, no. 8 (25 February 1911): 215.

"Current Educational Releases." *Motography* 6, no. 4 (October 1911): 156–57.

Currie, Barton W. "The Nickel Madness." *Harper's Weekly,* 14 August 1907, 1246.

Dewey, John. "Cut-and-Try School Methods." *Survey,* 6 September 1913, 692.

"Doings in Los Angeles." *Moving Picture World,* 29 June 1912, 1219.

"Educational Films Gaining Ground." *Nickelodeon* 3, no. 8 (15 April 1910): 196.

"Educational Lectures." *Moving Picture News*, 11 March 1911, 9.

"Educational Lectures in the Keith & Proctor Theaters." *Moving Picture News*, 4 March 1911, 6–7.

"Educational Pictures." *Moving Picture News*, 2 December 1911, 5–6.

"The Educational Tendency." *Nickelodeon* 9, no. 11 (1 December 1910): 300.

"Exporting the American Film." *Motography* 6, no. 2 (August 1911): 90.

"Filming Auto Tour." *Motography* 10, no. 9 (1 November 1913): 320.

"The Forte of the Scenic Film." *Nickelodeon* 3, no. 11 (1 June 1910): 275–76.

Goddard, Henry H. "Pedagogy plus Science Needed." *Survey*, 6 September 1913, 688.

Godkin, Edwin Lawrence. "Chromo-Civilization." *Nation*, 24 September 1874, 201–2.

"Government Takes Scenic Films." *Nickelodeon* 5, no. 7 (18 February 1911): 184.

"Growing Importance of Motion Picture Shows." *Nickelodeon* 1, no. 2 (February 1909): 53.

Hewetson, W. T. "The Motion Picture Problem." Address delivered to the Women's Club in Freeport, Ill., quoted in *Moving Picture World*, 20 January 1912, 216.

Hoffman, H. F. "What People Want." *Moving Picture World*, 9 July 1910, 77–78.

Holliday, Carl. "The Motion Picture Teacher." *World's Work* 26, no. 1 (May 1913): 49.

Hulette, Frank Parker. "An Interview with Thomas A. Edison." *Moving Picture World*, 22 July 1911, 104.

"Indians on Hotel Roof." *New York Times*, 30 April 1921, n.p.

Jump, Herbert A. "The Child's Leisure Hour." *Motography* 7, no. 3 (March 1912): 115.

"Kleine's Big Educational Catalogue." *Nickelodeon* 3, no. 7 (1 April 1910): 180.

"Kleine Shows Scientific Pictures." *Nickelodeon* 3, no. 3 (1 February 1910): 81.

"Kleine to Release Cines," *Motography* 7, no. 1 (January 1912): 34.

LaMarre, Tom. "Designing the Buffalo Nickel." *Coins*, November 1994, 66–74.

Lane, Winthrop D. "Edison versus Euclid: Has He Invented a Moving Stairway to Learning." *Survey*, 6 September 1913, 682.

Lockwood, E. B. "Travelogues and Topicals." *Motography* 7, no. 6 (June 1912): 257.

"The Lost Gallery." *Moving Picture World*, 29 July 1911, 186.

McQuade, Ja[mes] S. "Review of *Picturesque Colorado*." *Moving Picture World*, 23 September 1911, 870–71.

"Millions to See Colorado Scenes by Picture Films." *Denver Post*, 1 September 1911, 2.

"Miss Steiner Shows Moving Pictures of Northern Ice Fields." *Moving Picture News*, 4 May 1912, 22.

"Montana in Films." *Motography* 5, no. 6 (June 1911): 140.

"Moral Teaching by Films." *Motography* 6, no. 1 (July 1911): 5.

"Motion Pictures of Colo[rado] Scenes Now on Screens." *Denver Post*, 7 September 1911, 6.

"Moving Pictures in Brussels' Schools." *Nickelodeon* 3, no. 2 (15 January 1910): 50.

"Mr. Edison Speaks Again." *Educational Screen*, February 1925, 69.

"One Hundred Thousand Cheer Greater Colorado's Royal Industrial Parade." *Denver Post*, 18 July 1911, 1.

"The Only Filipino Amusement." *Motography* 7, no. 2 (February 1912): 88.

"Pathe Pictures Indians on Tented Roof." *Motography* 9, no. 7 (5 April 1913): 247.

Patterson, Joseph Medill. "The Nickelodeons: The Poor Man's Elementary Course in the Drama." *Saturday Evening Post*, 23 November 1907, 11.

"The Paul Rainey African Pictures." *Moving Picture World*, 20 April 1912, 214–15.

"Picture Psychology." *Nickelodeon* 4, no. 9 (1 November 1910): 245–46.

"Pictures Aid 'Back to Land' Movement." *Motography* 8, no. 13 (21 December 1912): 489.

"Pictures in School." *Motography* 7, no. 3 (March 1912): 100–101.

Pike, Oliver G. "Educational and Scientific Films." *Nickelodeon* 9, no. 10 (15 November 1910): 283–84.

"The Power of Moving Pictures: They Will Educate, through the Eye, Hundreds of Millions of Children." *New York Evening Journal*, 30 November 1912.

"Prof[essor] Starr's Valuable Contribution." *Nickelodeon* 1, no. 3 (March 1909): 64.

"'Quicksands' Is Scenically Beautiful." *Motography* 9, no. 13 (28 June 1913): 457.

"Railroad Motion Picture Shows." *Motography* 6, no. 1 (July 1911): 30.

"Rainey African Pictures Making Good." *Moving Picture World*, 11 May 1912, 533.

"Roosevelt and the Fly." *Nickelodeon* 3, no. 9 (1 May 1910): 223.

"Russia's Picture Shows." *Motography* 7, no. 2 (February 1912): 72.

"A Scenic Poster." *Nickelodeon* 5, no. 9 (4 March 1911): 254.

"Scientific and Educational Pictures," *Nickelodeon* 2, no. 6 (December 1909): 165–66.

"South Africa's Picture Shows." *Motography* 7, no. 2 (February 1912): 78.

"Southern Pacific Plans Pictures." *Nickelodeon* 3, no. 5 (1 March 1910): 126.

Starr, Frederick. "The World before Your Eyes." *Chicago Sunday Tribune*, 7 February 1909, sec. 7.

"Superb Human Interest Film." *Motography* 12, no. 7 (15 August 1914): 225–26.

"Through Alaska and Siberia." *Moving Picture World*, 4 January 1913, 55.

"Travel Pictures Again." *Motography* 6, no. 3 (September 1911): 105–6.

Vorse, Mary Heaton. "Some Picture Show Audiences." *Outlook*, 24 June 1911, 441–47.

INDEX

Note: Page numbers followed by "f" indicate figures.

consumerism and commodification: the American West and, 237, 238, 240, 244, 250, 259; education as commodity, 125; European foreignness and, 121; global distribution and, 218; industrial films and, 148; instructive entertainment and, 281n34; landscapes and, 12, 13, 28; leisure travel and, 10; mass culture and, 103, 182, 211; modernity thesis and, 5; parody and, 196; the picturesque and, 175, 176, 179, 187; private/public divide and, 39; recreational tourism and, 236; spectatorship and, 150; travelogue films as commodity, 3, 7; Veblen's "conspicuous consumption," 42; visual culture of travel and, 8, 26

Cook, Frederick, 195, 310n57

Cook, Thomas, 11

Cook's Tours, 11

Cooper, Merian C., 93, 272

Cork Production in France (Cines, 1913), 157

Cory, Kate, 45

cosmopolitanism, 53, 214, 219

Country Doctor, The (Griffith; Biograph, 1909), 181

Crafton, Donald, 281n34

Crazy Cruise (Avery/Clampett, 1942), 196

Crippen, James B., 207

Cronon, William, 248

Cross Country Detours (Avery, 1940), 196

Culler, Jonathan, 10, 216–17

cult films, 281n43

culture: Arnoldian paradigm, 112–13, 182; "flood of images" and, 220–21; middlebrow, 182; from reformer vs. audience perspective, 212; uplift and, 113; visual culture of travel and, 8, 26–30

current events films. *See* topical (current events) films

Curtis, Edward S., 45, 259; *In the Land of the Head Hunters*, 87

Curtis, Scott, 133

Customs of the Buddhists in India (Pathé, 1910), 92

Daumier, Honoré, 167

Debord, Guy, 217

Decasia (Morrison, 2001), 272

decay and the picturesque, 187–88

Deleuze, Gilles, 14, 15, 16, 303n31

Delluc, Louis, 152, 232–33

Denver Post, 260, 319n78

Depue, Oscar B., 15, 38, 45, 87, 286n71, 291n59

desire, x, xi, xii

Desmet, Jean, 17

Desmet Collection, EYE Film Institute, Netherlands, 17

Dewey, John, 113, 131, 135

difference, exoticism, and the Other: Bhabha on ambivalence and, 33; construction of the exotic, 154, 163; desire-fear dynamic, 33; everyday, tension with, 28; foreignness, 121; Holmes's "Moki Land" and, 45; near exotic, 157; the picturesque and, 176–77, 191; in postcolonial and literary studies, 30–34; spaces signifying past and nature, 156; spatiality, place, and, 34–35; typology and, 166; World's Fair live displays and, 27. *See also* American Indians; empire and colonialism

dioramas, 27

disappearance, trope of, 157

discomfort before the camera, 164–65, 167, 169

disruption. *See* resistance and disruption

distribution: European films, domination of, 90; global, 217–20; Kleine and, 118; MPPC and licensed vs. independent circuits, 90–91; split reels, 76–77, 76f

Dobbs, Beverly B., 137, 300n1

documentary, 65, 84, 93, 287n8

Doel, Marcus, 230

Domitor, 68

Doré, Gustave, 154

Dr. Charcot's Trip Toward the South Pole (Eclipse, 1911), 207–8

dreamworld, 6–7, 279n10. *See also* poetic reverie

Du Bois, W. E. B., 106–7

Dulac, Germaine, 152

Dumas, Alexandre, 42

Dunwoodie, Peter, 161

resistance and disruption: by American Indians, 251–59, 260; dreamworld and, 6; Holmes as figure of, 25; Hopi refusal to be represented, 48; Kracauer's "flood of images" and, 220–21; minor cinema and, 16; the picturesque and, 179–80, 184, 202; popular ethnography and "imperial gaze" critiques vs., 31–32; power of the returned gaze, 9, 32, 169–74. *See also* ambivalence and contradiction

reverie, 208, 224–25, 230–33. *See also* dreamworld

Reveries of the Solitary Walker (Rousseau), 275

Rex Motion Picture Company, 261

Richter, Hans, 272

Riis, Jacob, 105–6

Roan, Jeanette, 25, 41–42, 43

Rocks and Waves (Gaumont, ca. 1911), 148

Romains, Jules, 232–33

Rony, Fatimah Tobing, 31–32, 259

Roosevelt in Africa (Kearton; Pathé, 1910), 98

Ross, Steven J., 113–14

Rough Sea at Dover (Acres, 1895), 148

Rousseau, Jean-Jacques, 275

Rowlandson, Thomas, 194

Rubin, Joan Shelley, 182

ruins, 187–88, 214

Ruins of Angkor, Cambodia (Méliès, 1912), 96, 151

Ruoff, Jeffrey, xiv–xv, 42

Ruskin, John, 188–89

Russell, Catherine, 32

Ruttman, Walter, 272

Sabot Making (Unique, 1908), 75

Said, Edward, 30, 33, 140

Salmon Fishing in Canada (Solax, 1911), 83

Salzani, Carlo, 279n10

Sandberg, Mark, 27

Sandmore District, The (Urban, 1913), 73–75, 74f

Sans Soleil (Marker, 1983), xv

Santa Lucia (Ambrosio, ca. 1910), 19

Saturday Evening Post, 212

scenery. *See* picturesque, the

Scenes along the Pescara River, Central Italy (Cines, 1913), 143, 144f

"Scenes and Incidents en Route from Cairo to Khartoum" (Howe, 1903), 71

Scenes in Korea (Selig, 1912), 175

Scenes in the Celestial Empire (Eclipse, 1910), 75

scenic backgrounds, 271

scenic nationalism, 238–39, 315n18

"scenics," as term, 54. *See also* travelogue films

Schoedsack, Ernest B., 93, 272

Schwartz, Vanessa, 28

science vs. entertainment, 28

Scott, Robert Falcon, 92

Sea of Clouds, A (Gaumont, 1910), 127

Seeing Los Angeles (Imp, 1912), 19, 264–66, 265f

Seeing Spokane (Selig, 1912), 266

Seeing Yosemite with David A. Curry (Pillsbury; NARA, 1916), 248, 248f, 317n46

segments, 57, 142, 146

Selig, "Colonel" William, 127

Selig Polyscope Company, 88, 91, 249

Sembène, Ousmane, 14

semiotic analysis of travel, 216–17

Sevres Porcelain (Gaumont, 1909), 75

Shackleton, Ernest, 92–93

Shaffer, Marguerite, 316n32

Shakespeare, William, 113

shots: camera tilts, 151; child-at-the-end and woman-at-the-end shots, 19; clusters of, 146; landscape shots in travelogue formula, 18–20; long, 143, 197; pans, 150–51; perceptual point-of-view shots, 25; standalone quality of, 17–18, 142; subversion of concluding shot, 170; sunset shots, 19; tracking, 20, 151–52, 303n26

Simba: The King of the Beasts (Johnson and Johnson, 1928), 93, 272

Singer, Ben, 5, 278n5

"single-reel" era, 68

16mm film, 69

Slotkin, Richard, 241

Solanas, Fernando, 14

"Some Picture Show Audiences" (Vorse), 210

Song of the Soul (Celio, 1914), 270–71

sound, 69, 226–30, 270

South America (unknown, ca. 1920), 171–72, 172f, 191

Southern Pacific Railroad, 242

South: Sir Ernest Shackleton's Glorious Epic of the Antarctic (Hurley, 1920), 93, 272

South Tyrolean Folkloristic Dress (Pathé, ca. 1920), 167

spectacle as landscape mode, 280n34

spectatorship and audience: attention called to looking, 4; cinematic motion and, 153; composition of audiences, 209–12; exhibitions and museums and, 27; filmed tourists as lead-in figures, 156–57; global, 217–20; *Hawaii, Paradise of the Pacific* (Howe, 1916) and, 60–61; Holmes and, 25, 35; *The Magic Mountain* (Mann) and, 224–26; mass audience concept, 115–16; and migration, displacement of, 12; modern alienation and, 220–26; passive, 131; poetic reverie, 208, 230–33; public experience of, 31; public sphere theory and alternative use value, 211–12; recognition within the spectator, 224; returned gaze and, 9, 172–73; silence and, 228–29; sound and, 226–30; "tourist viewpoint," 8–9; vicarious travel and, 212–17; voyeurism, attention called to, 173. *See also* gaze

Spence, Mark David, 236

split reels, 76–77, 76f

sports films, 83

Spurr, David, 161, 167

Stafford, Barbara, 28, 187

staging, 87, 191

Staiger, Janet, 68–69

stand-alone shots, 17–18

Starr, Frederick, 104, 124, 213–15, 225, 296n12

stereographs, 28–30, 29f

Stockholm (unknown, ca. 1912), 170–71, 170f

Stoddard, John L., 24, 36, 38, 264, 285n64

Stowe, Harriet Beecher, 193

string-of-pearls editing structure, 149, 199

style. *See* form and style of travel film

sublime, the, 184–86

subversiveness. *See* resistance and disruption

surrealism, xvi–xvii, 279n10

Swanson, William H., 260–61, 319nn78–79

Swiss Trip [Rivers and Landscapes] (Fischinger, 1934), 275

Taine, Hippolyte Adolphe, 154

Tamai, Noboru, 219

Taos Indians at Home — New Mexico, The (Selig, 1912), 259

technology, 55–56, 80. *See also* camera; railroads

territorialization and deterritorialization, 16, 44

Thames from Oxford to Richmond, The (Eclipse, 1911), 197–99, 198f

Thames Illustrated, The (Leyland), 199, 200f

theaters. *See* nickelodeon theaters

theatricality, 30, 48

Third Cinema, 14–15

Thissen, Judith, 311n4

Thomas, Lowell, 24

Thompson, Kristin, 68–69

Through Snow to Sunshine (Lubin, n.d.), 85

tilts, camera, 151

time: "aged native" trope, 57, 157; condensed by fragmenting space, 197; inconsistent relationship of travelogues to, 55; the picturesque and pastness, 177f, 188; spaces signifying past, 156. *See also* nostalgia

topical (current events) films: as genre, 72, 81, 84, 92; popularity of, 98; shelf life of, 92

"to travel is to possess the world" motto (Holmes), 35

Touaregs in Their Own Country, The (Pathé, 1908): concluding shot, 19

Toulet, Emmanuelle, 27

tourism: the American West and, 236, 242, 244; filmed tourists as lead-in figures, 156–57, 201; history of access to, 11,